D1565234

Lord God, forgive white Europe

Léopold Sédar
Senghor

Léopold Sédar Senghor
An Intellectual Biography by Jacques Louis Hymans

for the University Press, Edinburgh

EDINBURGH UNIVERSITY PRESS
22 George Square, Edinburgh

ISBN 0 85224 119 4

North America
Aldine·Atherton Inc.
529 South Wabash Avenue, Chicago

Library of Congress
Catalog Card Number 71–106478

Printed in Great Britain by
Western Printing Services Ltd, Bristol

Author's Note

This book is the result of my fascination with the complex intellectual personality of Léopold Sédar Senghor, an African man of letters and a powerful political force in his country and on his continent. It was built upon a series of personal interviews, an exchange of letters and extensive research which took place during the 1960s. Following two years of study at the *Université d'Aix-Marseille* on a Fulbright award, I continued my work at the *Fondation Nationale des Sciences Politiques* and at the Sorbonne in Paris on a grant from the Newhouse Foundation of San Francisco. The academic year that I spent teaching the history of ideas at Stanford University was invaluable to the writing of this work, which was presented at the Sorbonne in partial fulfilment of the requirements for the degree of *Docteur en Etudes Politiques*.

In the first place I want to convey my appreciation to President Senghor for the many precious hours that he was willing to spend with me during my stay in Senegal. He also replied to many written questions during the course of my research and granted 'his white shadow' a long interview in November 1964, after reading the initial manuscript. His reaction to the study, included in a letter to me, appears in Appendix 11. President Georges Pompidou of France was kind enough to write a letter in answer to certain questions I had posed (Appendix 111). Gaston Defferre, former Minister of Overseas France, introduced me to his associates of the *Loi-Cadre* period, notably Monsieur Espinasse. Governor-General Robert Delavignette patiently recounted his memories of the 1940s. Bernard Lecompte, responsible for much of the research that went into the making of the Senegalese Development Plan, allowed me to consult his dossiers; his frank discussions as well as those of his assistant, Guy Belloncle, clarified many obscure points. Dr L. P. Aujoulat, former French Minister, kindly allowed me to consult his invaluable personal archives on the *Indépendants d'Outre-Mer* parliamentary group.

During my stay in Senegal, government officials were most generous with their hospitality and their time. I wish to thank Gabriel d'Arboussier, former Senegalese Ambassador to Paris and Ambassador in Bonn; Lamine-Guèye, the late President of the

Senegalese National Assembly; Jean Collin, Minister of Finance; and André Guillabert, Vice-President of the National Assembly, who, together, gave me an invaluable introduction to the political life of their country. In addition, the brilliant Senegalese opposition leader, recently Minister, Abdoulaye Ly, devoted countless hours of his time at the beginning of my research and added an important dimension to my understanding of Senghor.

For a more personal view of Senghor's childhood and adolescence, I am greatly indebted to the President's family and friends : Charles Senghor, Hyacinthe Lat Senghor, Madame Jean Collin (*née* Senghor), Alioune Diop (Director of *Présence Africaine*), and Birago Diop (Senegalese Ambassador in Tunisia) generously recounted their memories of the years when Senghor was still a student or *professeur*. Jean Larché, director of the overseas French newspaper chain *Breteuil*, helped me to understand the basis for certain political decisions made by Senghor. Similarly, Edouard Basse, Senegalese Ambassador to Rome, a *Serer* and a Catholic as is Senghor, originally drew my attention to the Catholic influence on Senghor's thought. The late El Hadj Seydou Nourou Tall, venerable leader of the Senegalese Muslim Marabouts, gave me an important insight into his own role in the political life of Senegal and his effect on party policy.

My special gratitude must be given to Mademoiselle Paulette Nardal, one of the first French-speaking black women to advocate cultural nationalism, who graciously replied to my questions, despite her illness. The French-speaking African students, amongst whom I lived for three years at the *Maison Française des Pays et États d'Outre-Mer* (FOM) of the *Cité Internationale de l'Université de Paris*, also gave me their generous help, particularly the Senegalese scholar Pathé Diagne, who has a deep understanding and love of his country.

Both Professor Georges Balandier and Professor Alfred Grosser of the *Université de Paris* guided me with their expert knowledge of the history of decolonization and helped illuminate the form and content that this work should take. Marcel Ombolo-Mvogo, a Camerounese student, read and corrected the original French manuscript. Dr Peter Duignan of the Hoover Institution of Stanford University encouraged me to publish in English by extending a grant for translation.

I also wish to express my appreciation of the invaluable advice of Mademoiselle Jeannine Bourdin, research associate at the *Fondation Nationale des Sciences Politiques* of the *Université de Paris*. Mlle Bourdin not only read the clumsy first draft, but she brought to my notice an enormous amount of material on the intellectual life of the French inter-war years on which she is a specialist. The final draft of the book was expertly typed by Diane Litchfield, secretary to the history department at San Francisco State College.

I am also grateful for the perceptive observations of many students in my African history classes at Northwestern University, Lovanium University in the Congo (Kinshasa), and at San Francisco State College.

My final thanks I have reserved for my editor and for my wife. Walter Cairns, editor of the Edinburgh University Press, made the publication of this work memorable both by his skill and by his hospitality. Myrna Kelley Hymans has wittily and effectively played the role of 'loyal opposition' through the dreary last stages of cutting and shaping. Had it not been for her, this book would have appeared in print earlier but more imperfectly.

It seems inevitable that I have overlooked or failed to mention other, necessary contributors to this effort. But I hope that they will know that my appreciation extends to all who have participated in some way to the analysis, interpretation, and production of this book. They, more than anyone, will know that the omissions and errors in form and content are mine, and I ask the reader to excuse any shortcomings he may observe.

Although I consulted the earlier, separate publications of Senghor's speeches and articles, for the convenience of the reader I have referred in the notes to the more recent, collected edition entitled *Liberté I : Négritude et Humanisme* (Paris, Seuil 1964), which covers the period from 1937 to 1964. For anything outside this period, I have referred to original sources or publications.

The notes also contain references to English translations wherever possible. In an attempt to be faithful to Senghor's thought, however, I have frequently used my own translations in preference to those published, even to the extent of violating Senghor's poetic style.

One final remark : the French word *noir* can be translated as either 'negro' or 'black' and, therefore, in most cases the two have been used interchangeably in this English text, despite the present American distinction between them. The frequent use of these terms, rather than the term 'African', results from the fact that the intellectual movement called *négritude* was the product of black men from the New World as well as from Africa.

J. L. H.

Contents

Introduction

Among African leaders today, Léopold Sédar Senghor stands unique. He is the living symbol of the possible synthesis of what appears irreconcilable: he is as African as he is European, as much a poet as a politician, as influenced by rationalism as by irrationalism, as much a revolutionary as a traditionalist. His life might be summarized as an effort to restore to Africa an equilibrium destroyed by the clash with Europe. It has been an effort to create a new balance, a *Weltanschauung*, a philosophy of life, an ethic and a political policy from what Georges Balandier has called the ambiguity of modern Africa : that Janus-like quality in which what is old is no longer viable, yet what is new is not entirely adequate. He has laboured persistently to create a new Africa 'in accord with traditional civilization and the requirements of the twentieth century'.[1]

Senghor has called himself 'the itinerant',[2] a perpetual wanderer not only between Africa and France, but also between the worlds of traditional, colonial, and nationalist Africa. His individual drama holds lessons for many African and other 'Third World' intellectuals who live in the precarious state of *asynchronie*[3] and may illuminate for the Westerner the tragic predicament facing such men. This book attempts to retrace Senghor's intellectual wanderings between two civilizations and three historical eras.[4]

Forty-two years ago young Léopold left Africa as an alienated, 'civilized' black Frenchman.[5] Only then did he begin his quest for Africa, for his African heritage, for himself. He found Africa in Paris, in the books he read, in the courses he took, among his West Indian friends. The tension caused by his longing for Africa while remaining in France was resolved by a poetic outburst. In recreating the distant continent by verse, Senghor helped blaze the trail that led to the phenomenon of *négritude*.[6] The new black consciousness gave him the philosophic means of reconciling admiration of Europe and love of Africa.

Négritude was the product of a twentieth-century triangular trade : a trade in ideas between black America, Europe, and Africa. It developed out of an encounter in Paris between black men whose ancestors had been dispersed as the product of another, historic triangular trade. Senghor wove the intellectual contributions of three continents into a far-reaching philosophy.

To explain the meaning that Senghor has given to this philosophy, it is necessary to understand the basic personal characteristics of its author. He is a Catholic intellectual, stirred by an ardent faith; he is the African political leader most possessed with French culture.

The cultural, political, and socio-economic aspects of Senghor's philosophy are manifested in his theories of *négritude*, Franco-African Federation and the 'African Road to Socialism'. Each lies squarely in the middle of the road. *Négritude* holds to the centre between nationalism and cultural assimilation promoted by France. Franco-African Federation lies between independence and colonial domination; in fact, Senghor hoped it would be a 'Third Force' between the two blocs that divide the world. The 'African Road to Socialism' is half-way between capitalism and communism, holding a central position between individualism and collectivism.

Senghor would say of his theories that they are 'above and beyond' two opposing currents, that they tend to resolve contradiction. It is not by chance that the thought of a man such as Senghor searches to reconcile, to 'bridge the gap'. Senghor is a half-caste in the figurative sense of the term, a half-caste who advocates cross-breeding, whether it be cultural, political, economic, or biological. By his glorification of cross-breeding, he has hoped to resolve his interior conflict and the exterior divisions that produced it.

In retracing the steps that Senghor followed to discover *négritude*, it becomes increasingly evident that his radically African philosophy was paradoxically the outgrowth of a Western intellectual tradition. Although the emotional response of Senghor seemed to be African, the intellectual response was Western. European nationalist, federalist, and socialist philosophies weighed heavily in the development of the new African ideologies, and the role played by Senghor was that of putting Barrès, Proudhon, Hitler and Marx into the service of black men.

The paradox of European sources for African consciousness was but one of the many in Senghor's thought. His constant advocacy of Africa's rehabilitation did not lead him to become an African nationalist. The man most closely identified with the 'Return to Africa' was, in fact, the man least willing to cut his ties with France. Throughout the years of militancy for *négritude*, Senghor remained favourable to Franco-African federation. A symptom of this paradox is the fact that, until 1960, Senghor's political career took place in France more than in Africa. As one of the leading African *Députés* in the French National Assembly, Senghor spent most of his time working for civil rights rather than national liberation. And the implicit irony is that the resolutely anti-nationalist politician became the first president of the new nation of Senegal.[7]

Senghor was the first leader on his continent to formulate a theory of African socialism. Incredibly, this socialism echoed many of the same themes espoused by the national socialists of the 1930s. Senghor's 'African Road' shared the national socialists' aversion to both capitalism and communism. As did national socialism, African socialism attempted to transform the class struggle from an internal affair to one which pitted 'proletarian nations' against 'affluent nations'. By Senghor's own admission, the same Romantic anti-rationalism that fathered racism among the fascists of the 1930s underlay his early reaction against the West.

But, as is typical in Senghor's thought, his socialist theory did not solidify like lava, but remained matter in the process of fusion.[8] The fascist neo-socialism from which it developed was blended with Marxian and Teilhardian elements until the original sources were no longer evident. This characteristic ambivalence makes it very difficult to label Senghor's social and economic thought. The Marxists see in it a fascism or a camouflaged capitalism. It should, perhaps, be called an anti-capitalist capitalism, an anti-communist communism, in much the same way that Jean Paul Sartre termed Senghor's *négritude* an anti-racist racism.

Paradox, ambiguity, *asynchronie*, alienation – all these qualities characterize not only the thought, but also the life, of the poet-President of Senegal. They are his burden as well as the burden of all modern Africans and black men the world over. They are caused by the inescapable cultural, political, social and economic conditions which determine the nature of life in the African world. However, Senghor is not resigned to forever remaining divided between the West and Africa. One constant in his thought appears to surmount the contradictions it contains : universal reconciliation is his only goal and Africa's only salvation.

> African night my black night, mystical-lucid black-brilliant
> . . .
> Night delivering me from arguments and sophistries of salons,
>   from pirouetting pretexts, from calculated hatred and
>   humane butchery
>
> Night dissolving all my contradictions, all contradictions in
>   the primal unity of your blackness

Léopold Sédar Senghor *For Kôras and Balafong*

Léopold Sédar Senghor

Léopold Senghor as a member of the French Parliament
Photo, Service Info-Senegal

Part 1. The Early Years 1906—29

1. The 'Childhood Kingdom'[1]

When Léopold Sédar Senghor was born in Joal on 9 October 1906, the acculturation, the alienation, and the *asynchronie*[2] characteristic of underdeveloped colonial areas had begun to affect the interior of Senegal. French penetration, several centuries old at Saint-Louis-du-Sénégal, accelerated notably after the military campaigns of the second half of the nineteenth century. Establishment of French schools, missionary action, development of the ground-nut trade, and direct colonial administration followed the 'pacification of the natives' living in outlying areas. The construction of the railroad between Dakar and the Niger River, undertaken in the early years of the twentieth century, finally tipped the scales against the traditional way of life. Senghor cries out poetically:

> White hands which pulled the triggers
> that destroyed the empires
> White hands which cut down the tangled forest
> that dominated Africa, in the centre of Africa
> They cut down the black forest to make
> railroad ties[3]

These same 'white hands' placed the

> …long narrow rails
> Inflexible will imposed on the listless sands.[4]

Rails crossing Senegal symbolized that intrusion of the white man, and his technical civilization, which was both destruction and progress: destruction of the 'Garden of Eden' which existed before colonization, progress into the modern world of machines. Henceforth return to the past was impossible.

> Now dies the Africa of the Empires –
> it is the agony of a pitiful princess[5]

In less poetic terms: the famous 'ground-nut railroad' doubled Senegalese exports around 1901, and Governor-General Roume, noting this progress, used the dictum of Colonel Thys (Belgian constructor of the Congolese railway) that 'Civilization follows the locomotive'. The advent of the railroad propelled the Africans into a world of economic progress and a period of acute social change.[6]

Senghor's first seven years were the only happy ones of his life, until he re-discovered traditional Africa in books (in Paris) and formulated his theory of cultural cross-breeding.

> The Paradise of my African Childhood,
> which kept me innocent of Europe[7]

The child was unconscious of the great transformations occurring around him. That did not prevent them from weighing heavily on his destiny.

At the moment of his baptism this situation was already present. The *Serer*, the major ethnic group of the Joal region where Senghor was born, were in the process of abandoning their traditional faith in favour of the Catholicism of the French colonizer. Thus it was natural that Catholic experiences were among the first memories of the future Senegalese president:

> Joal!
> I remember.
>
> I remember the funeral festivals
> steaming with the blood of slaughtered herds
> The noise of quarrels, rhapsodies of the *griots*
> *I remember pagan voices rhyming the Tantum Ergo*
> and the processions and the palms and the arches
> of triumph[8]

His name symbolized this underlying struggle, the *asynchronie* existing between traditional and modern civilizations, for his Catholic name of Léopold was followed by a *Serer* middle name: Sédar.

Officially he had two dozen brothers and sisters, and probably there were more: 'In this climate, the rigours of Christian monogamy have been tempered by a few concessions to the changing seasons and the hot blood'. The Catholicism of the *Serer* was as southerly as it was ardent.[9]

From the turn of the century world of the *Serer* came Senghor's first experience with cultural fusion. Two opposed worlds, one French, one Senegalese, found themselves coexisting side-by-side. It was not difficult for a man born in such circumstances to be attracted to the dialectic: the clash of these opposing cultures required synthesis. If the life or thought of men born in this state of *asynchronie* does not represent a compromise, there is left the choice of either the Western world or the traditional world. Senghor could not choose between them.

Other experiences of his youth left their imprint on the thought of the political leader. Senghor's childhood was spent in Djilor, twenty-three kilometres from Joal. There, in a white stucco house, a sign of prosperity in the midst of the round mud huts, he lived with his family. His father, Basile Diogoye Senghor, a relatively prosperous trader in a poor region, owned several hundred head of cattle, possessed numerous grain storage bins, and controlled a certain amount of near-by land.

The elder Senghor's fortune was derived from commercial operations based on the ground-nut, the cultivation of which took on a growing importance in Senegal with the development of French colonization and the introduction of a money economy. He himself was the son of a Mandingo trader who died defending one of his caravans against robbers.[10] During the dry season, when the peasants needed grain or money, they knew they could borrow from Basile Senghor.[11] Senghor remembered the nights that his father spent counting the pile of 'gold pieces', which 'clung to his fingers'.[12] By clever transactions with European trading firms, the Senghor fortune grew.

His father was even visited by the king of the Sine-Saloum region, a visit which enormously impressed the young son:

The sanctuary's poetesses nourished me
The king's *griots* sang to me the true legend of my race,
accompanied by the great *kôras*[13]

What month? What year?
Koumba Ndofène[14] reigned at Dyakhaw, proud vassal
And governed the administrator of Sine-Saloum
The noise of his ancestors and of the *dyoung-dyoungs*[15]
preceded him.
The royal pilgrim crossed his provinces listening in the
woods to the murmured complaint

He called my father 'Tokor'. They exchanged objects
carried by greyhounds with golden bells
Peaceful cousins, they exchanged presents on the banks
of the Saloum[16]
Precious skins, bars of salt, gold from Bouré,
gold from Boundou
And high counsel like horses of the river[17]

These events witnessed at an early age left Senghor with the memory of a glorious Africa:

And my father stretched out on peaceful mats, but tall,
but strong, but handsome
Man of the Kingdom of Sine, while all around on the
kôras, heroic voices, *griots* make their impassioned
fingers dance
Whilst from afar ascends, swelling with strong and
hot odours, the classic murmur of a hundred herds[18]

In the *Serer* region social organization remained matrilineal. Young Léopold's mother was born in Djilas, where several families of the *Fulani* ethnic group lived. Her brother, like many *Fulani*, tended cattle. The *Serer* considered these *Fulani* to be their inferiors. Senghor, however, felt himself a member of his mother's family and sought out his uncle's company. The young boy was charmed by his uncle's stories of animal life and supernatural phenomena.

Toko' Waly my uncle, do you remember the nights
of old when my head grew heavy on the
patience of your back?
Or, holding me by the hand, your hand guided me
through darkness and signs?

You, Toko' Waly, you listen to the inaudible
And you explain to me the signs that the Ancestors
say in the oceanic serenity of the constellations[19]

Senghor comments on the importance of this 'childhood universe':

I…lived in this kingdom, saw with my eyes, with my ears
heard, the fabulous beings beyond things: the *Kouss*
(genies which recall the first inhabitants of black
Africa, the Pygmies, who were exterminated or driven away
by the larger black men) living in the trees; crocodiles,
guardians of the fountains; *Lamantins*, who sing in the
river; the Dead of the village and the Ancestors who spoke
to me, initiating me into the alternating truths of night
and noon.[20]

Now I was returning from Fa'oye, and horror was at its
zenith
And it was the hour in which one sees Spirits, when
light is transparent
And it was necessary to keep clear of the paths so
as to avoid their fraternal and mortal hand.
The soul of a village was beating on the horizon. Was
it that of the living or of the Dead?[21]

And it is the hour of primary fears, which surge up from
ancestors' entrails.
Away inane dark faces with evil breath and snout!
By the power of the palm tree and water, by the power of
the Speaker of most hidden things, away![22]
...Childhood Nights, among the *tanns*, among the woods
Nights palpitating with presences...[23]

These 'distant escapades to the enchanted domain of the Spirits'[24]
left their mark. His African heritage will never entirely leave him,
and these indelible childhood impressions are the vital basis for
Senghor's thought.

Intimacy with the world of spirits prepared Senghor to appreciate
Maurice Barrès, the Surrealists, and the Catholic mystic poets Péguy
and Claudel. All through his life he has eagerly sought to regain the
mystical experiences of his childhood.[25]

But Senghor's 'escapades' were important for yet another reason.
Disdain for the *Fulani* probably mixed with jealousy prodded Senghor's father to object to his son's spending so much time with his
uncle:

'I lived, previously, with herders and peasants. My father beat me
often in the evening, reproaching me for my vagabond life; and in
order to punish and "train" me, he finally sent me to the white
man's school, to the great despair of my mother, who protested
that at seven years of age it was too soon.'[26]

The classic tension in a matrilineal society between father and maternal uncle caused Senghor's removal to the missionary school and
his first uprooting. The theme of opposites complicating Senghor's
life is exposed by this conflict. In addition to the cultural cross-
breeding of Catholic and pagan in *Serer* society, there was the biological cross-breeding – the mixture of *Fulani, Mandingo*, and *Serer*
blood.[27] His father, a Catholic involved in trading and commerce,
belonged to the modern world, while his 'pagan' uncle, a cattle
herder, was part of the traditional world. This circumstance reinforced the ethnic conflict. Senghor has remained torn between bourgeois and peasant tendencies.[28] His father gave him pride in his
family and in his *Mandingo* name. From his uncle Toko' Waly came
the compensating influence of peasant and 'commoner' instincts.[29]
Even after obtaining high university honours, he still considered
himself to be a simple peasant.[30]

His love of the hinterland made him the spokesman of the peasants against the city bourgeoisie after he was elected *Député* to the
French National Assembly in the 1940s. Certain Africans who

opposed him used Senghor's ethnic multiplicity against him.[31] He answered these accusations by affirming that he was a true African, not just the member of one ethnic group.

These conflicts between father and uncle, Catholic and pagan, bourgeois and peasant, *Serer* and *Fulani*, shaped Senghor's life in many ways. The immediate effect, however, was his departure for the Catholic Mission School at Joal.[32] For the child it was the end of seven years of pastoral life, the memories of which, bathed in a magical aura, have continued to nourish his literary and philosophical works.

2. Schooling and Acculturation

In 1914, at the age of eight, Senghor was sent by his father to the boarding school run by the Fathers of the Holy Spirit at Ngasobil, six kilometres north of Joal. With about seventy other youngsters, he was exposed to European civilization, while that civilization began to tear itself apart on the battlefields of World War 1.

A new life began for the young Senegalese. Father Le Douaron, an excellent Latinist, patiently urged his students to conjugate their verbs. To start with, the children generally expressed themselves in their native tongues. Senghor still remembers the canticles that were taught for catechism. The Latin words, twisted to resemble *Serer* expressions, were strung together in African rhythms.[1]

The missionaries taught Senghor and his friends to abandon and scorn the culture of their ancestors by imposing a nineteenth-century teaching programme which was, by its content, largely foreign to African tradition.[2] The Fathers sincerely believed they were acting for the good of their pupils by exposing them to 'culture' and the modern way of life, but the effect was a complete destruction of the primary equilibrium of the child. Following this period Senghor's life 'became a perpetual effort tending towards a perfect, a divine equilibrium...';[3] and, writing about this condition, he complained:

Be blessed, my Fathers, be blessed!
You who permitted contempt and mockery, polite offence, discreet allusions
And prohibitions and segregations.
And then you tore from this overloving heart the ties which linked it to the pulse of the world[4]
And this other exile harder for my heart, the tearing away of self from self
From the mother tongue, from the ancestor's skull, from the tom-tom of my soul...[5]
My God! My God! but why deprive me of my pagan senses which cry out?
I can't sing your plain-chant without swinging it or dancing it.[6]
I will sleep long in the Joalian peace

Until the Angel of Dawn delivers me to your light
To your brutal and so cruel reality, O Civilization![7]

One young African has summarized the period's spirit in violent
terms: 'Refusing political assimilation to those colonized, French
colonialism sought to achieve the cultural assimilation of men, thus
violating their conscience, their reason, and their sentiments'.[8]
Schoolbooks were identical to those used in France. French history became the history of these young Africans; their kings became
savages.[9] Senghor has written that, in the years which followed World
War I, 'I was boarding at the Fathers' school... To him who would
have asked us who were our favourite poets we should doubtless
have replied: Pierre Corneille and in preference to Corneille, Victor
Hugo'. And he continues: 'When on Sundays we played at soldiers
on the forest paths, we were neither Joffre, nor Foch, but Olivier and
Roland, Ruy Blas, the great Campeador of Castille, and Napoleon
Bonaparte and his old guard'.[10] The Fathers succeeded marvellously.
The tales of the *Serer griots* faded away and were forgotten.

At Ngasobil pupils were not allowed to see their parents for several
months at a time. The use of native tongues was strictly prohibited.[11]
After the initial shock, Senghor began to study seriously. He hoped
to become an *évolué* (native who has become Westernized) – a difficult
and disappointing task. His first effort to regain his equilibrium thus
was centred on becoming assimilated: if he was not allowed to be an
African, then he had to become a black-skinned Frenchman. For a
while he succeeded in repressing the conflicts which inevitably arose.

Since he was a good student, the lessons Senghor learned at
Ngasobil left a more profound impression on him than on his classmates, and his integration into French culture was much more thorough than was the case for others. From this time on, his mother
called him *Toubab* (the white man), as many African mothers called
their sons when they returned from school.[12] But for Senghor that
nickname seemed especially significant.

From childhood Senghor was almost entirely uprooted. A Catholic, he had not been exposed to Koranic instruction or initiation
rites as were his Muslim schoolmates. The Senegalese writer Birago
Diop, who obtained his *baccalaureat* a year after Senghor, felt much
less alienation.[13]

Years later Senghor confessed that he only realized he was an
African when he was in France.[14] There, in the 1920s he read the
following lines from Maurice Barrès's *Les Déracinés*, describing a
case similar to his own:

'...singled out at the age of eight years for his precocious intelligence and studiousness, he obtained a scholarship... Taken out of his natural milieu at such a youthful age and spending even his vacations at the *lycée*, orphaned and unable to obtain emotional satisfaction outside of his teachers' esteem, he is a pedagogical product, a son of reason, foreign to our traditional, local, or family customs, completely abstract, and truly suspended in a void.'[15]

Senghor was not aware that this was happening to him at first. The Fathers at Ngasobil had helped young Senghor find momentary equilibrium:

'In fact, my inner feelings were quite early torn between the call of the ancestors and the attraction of Europe, between the requirements of African culture and those of modern life...I have always attempted to resolve these conflicts by a *"conciliatory agreement"*... thanks to *confession and direction of conscience* in my youth, thanks later to the *spirit of method* taught by my French masters.'[16]

Many Africans have undoubtedly felt the same disorder and need for equilibrium, but usually the conflicts arose later in their lives or under different circumstances, as in the case of Birago Diop. These early experiences at Ngasobil were shared by his brother Charles Diène Senghor; Isaac Forster, who later became Chief Justice of the Senegalese Supreme Court and Justice at The Hague International Court of Justice; and Joseph Faye, who, at the end of the Paris Colonial Exhibition of 1931, was ordained Father in the Order of the Holy Spirit at Notre Dame Cathedral by the late Cardinal Verdier.[17]

Senghor was a successful student because he was endowed with a superb memory and a lively intelligence. He worked hard and was not by nature gregarious. His brother has accurately described him as a 'bookworm'. The Missionary Fathers, perceiving his qualities, directed his footsteps towards a religious vocation. A pious child, he served Mass and was choirboy at church. When he was thirteen, Léopold felt he had the calling and entered the category of pupils preparing for priesthood. According to his brother Charles, the lot of the Seminarists was better than that of the other pupils: they did not have to perform menial tasks.[18]

In 1922, at the age of sixteen, Léopold left Ngasobil to enter the Libermann Seminary at Dakar. He has had much difficulty in ridding himself of a certain legacy inherited from these 'conservative and Royalist' Fathers.[19] (One of his companions remembers Senghor as a monarchist during his Paris *Lycée* years.[20]) But Ngasobil taught him other, more positive lessons: he has said that he owes to the Fathers his reasonableness, his mastery of self, and the fact that he does not 'waste words'.[21] His assimilation of Western civilization was well under way.

3. Acquiring Western Intellectual Discipline

In Dakar, the colonial capital of French West Africa, Senghor plunged into Catholic theology and philosophy. The Libermann Seminary introduced Senghor to the writings of Saint Thomas Aquinas. Senghor was steeped in the Scholastic Method during these years; the *sic et non* is fundamental to all of his writings. Dialectics, the art of examining opinions or ideas logically, often by the method of question and answer, became basic to Senghor's thought. His later attraction to the Marxist method might thus stem from his early attraction to scholasticism. The dialectic process also seems characteristic of certain traditional African philosophers. Senghor began a 1937 lecture by declaring: 'I even contemplated proceeding dialectically, by question and answer, following the method of Socrates and of our wise man Kotye Barma'.[1]

Answering a question about his personal Pantheon, Senghor began by naming Aristotle, whose 'Golden Mean' was adopted by St Thomas Aquinas. St Thomas kept to the middle of the road, avoiding adherence to either the Nominalist or the Realist side. Senghor's penchant for these middle positions is well known.[2] The future President's conception of political responsibility (subordination of the political to the spiritual) also finds its source in his prolonged study of St Thomas during the years from 1922 to 1926. This conception also grew out of his later study of Jacques Maritain's Neo-Thomism. Senghor's attraction to Maritain in 1932 was undoubtedly due to his love of St Thomas. The desire to bring about a synthesis of Arab, Greek, and Christian thought, which characterized the Thomistic approach, also played a role in Senghor's syncretism. Thus, both Aquinas and Senghor attempted to synthesize pagan and Christian thought into a new philosophy.[3]

Senghor later criticized the education typical of French colonial schools, which ironically give him his own philosophical grounding:
'Culture consisted in the study of composition and elocution; also in the application of discursive intelligence to the anlaysis of concepts. It is what I would call a scholastic-rhetoric concept of culture...More than a scholastic concept it is a formal rhetoric concept of culture. It loathes what is concrete and practical, perhaps what is African; what there is of a bourgeois or of a utilitarian

nature in the spirit of "Engineering Schools" affects it but little. Without doubt, this training tends to advocate encyclopaedic knowledge and to prefer the lawyer to the agricultural engineer.'[4] This description seems to apply to Senghor himself, for he later reminisced: 'Oh! I know, when I wore out my breeches on the benches of the Secondary School...I had but contempt, I, a student of Greek, for technicians and other "scientific eggheads". I called myself a humanist'.[5]

His stay with the Fathers of the Holy Spirit influenced even his literary style. He willingly gives an evangelical turn to what he says. Senghor's poetry has a tone which is that of prayer or of a Gregorian Chant. A critic has noted:

'This deacon's voice, with its apostrophes, its repetitions and its flux, keeps the imprint of the Old Testament and especially of the Psalms – tending, when it thunders, to echo the Prophets. In his *Chants pour Naëtt* it resembles the Song of Songs.'[6]

This style even crops up in his political speeches:

'...I have concluded: Socialism, Federation, Religion: I have tried to show you that the three ideas were interdependent. That the three acts of the trilogy form but one sole drama, that of the human condition, ours. It is necessary, if we want to extract the "substantial marrow" from it, to make it, for our spirit, a living food....'[7]

And the critic Aimé Patri wrote that the essential difference between the black poet Aimé Césaire and Senghor lay in 'the Christian education which left, in Senghor's mind, profound traces which he has never concealed...'.[8]

Senghor believed firmly in his calling, but his difficult character, his stubbornness, and his African pride made him protest vigorously against the racialism of the Father Superior, who one day called Léopold's parents 'savages' or 'primitives'.[9] The priest who so offended Senghor only expressed the 'supreme self-confidence' of the European *vis-à-vis* the African.[10] This feeling of European superiority was very common in the colonies. Much later Senghor still spoke of that attitude with disgust: 'The "civilizing mission", the "white man's burden", everyone had spoken to us about them since our childhood: teachers and professors, missionaries and colonial officials...'.[11]

Senghor's reaction to the Father Superior's careless slur on his parents took place in 1926 during Senghor's third year at the Seminary. A few days later, Father Lalouse, director of the Seminary, summoned the young African and told him of a vision he had had: Senghor did not have the priestly vocation. For Senghor this was a brutal shock.[12] He has always regretted not being able to enter the orders. Noting this unfulfilled dream, his political adversaries have called him a 'priest who failed to make the grade'.[13] When one of his former Seminary companions was consecrated Bishop of Ziguinchor in Senegal, the statesman that Senghor had meanwhile become, wistfully declared: 'I could have stood there'.[14]

Obliged to leave the Seminary, the adolescent Senghor entered the public Secondary School of Dakar, which later became the *Lycée Van Vollenhoven*. A brilliant pupil, Senghor obtained first prizes in many subjects, notably in Greek. That subject was taught by *Professeur* Prat, who had none of the racial prejudice common in the European community. He encouraged Senghor to continue his studies. In 1928, Senghor obtained his high school degree with honours.[15] Placing his faith in Senghor's intelligence, Monsieur Prat exerted much effort to persuade the Government General of French West Africa to grant Senghor a scholarship which would permit him to pursue his literary studies in France. At that time, most of the students who received financial aid were obliged to study veterinary medicine, for political as well as practical reasons.[16] The Government General 'generously' awarded him half a scholarship. With additional funds from an uncle, Senghor left for Paris to complete his education.[17] Senghor's friend James Benoît asserted that Monsieur Prat threatened to resign if the scholarship were not granted, and only after this courageous stand did the Government General change its attitude. Without Prat's act of faith, Senghor might not have gone to France.[18]

An additional reason for administrative hostility might have been the political activities of Senghor's distant cousin Lamine. Lamine Senghor, a former Senegalese rifleman who had been wounded in World War I, was living in Paris and studying at the Sorbonne. In 1927 he helped organize a *Comité de Défense de la Race Nègre*. As Secretary of the *Comité*, he participated with Mme Sun-Yat-Sen and Nehru in the February 1927 Brussels congress, which founded the 'League against Imperialism and Colonial Oppression'.[19]

By the time he graduated, Léopold Senghor had acquired a certain renown among the Senegalese students. Abdoulaye Ly, future *Docteur ès Lettres* in History, remembered that on entering the public Secondary School in Dakar the year that Senghor left for France, he had heard of a black pupil who had 'beaten all the white kids by winning all the prizes'.[20]

At the end of the summer of 1928, young Léopold took the steamer *Médie II* for France.[21] A provisional balance sheet of these twenty-two years in Africa would show an unconscious but progressive and profound alienation: a break with an ancestral culture, but an entry into 'Civilization'. From his stays at Ngasobil and Dakar he has retained a striking appetite for work, a deep and lively religious faith, and a very developed sense of order. Of his native *Sine*, of the hallucinating *griot* rhythms, of the antique beauty of Joal, there remained only dreams: 'The peasants of *Sine* nourished my childhood dreams, and so did the games and the songs and the dances of *Sine*. These dreams have peopled my nights throughout my life'.[22]

With the trip to Paris began Senghor's second uprooting. A physical *déracinement* followed the cultural one. Awareness of this double alienation is important for an understanding and interpretation of the *négritude* phenomenon. Upon his arrival in France in 1928, the future Senegalese leader was not very happy: 'A cold drizzle fell the morning I arrived in Paris. And all was grey, even the famous monuments. What a disappointment!'[23] Despite this first impression of the Paris he had strongly idealized in Senegal, the young man was soon under the spell of the city.

He boarded at the *Lycée Louis-le-Grand*, where the most brilliant French students have always prepared for the stiff entrance exams to France's most exclusive institutes of higher education. From November 1928 his closest friend was Georges Pompidou,[24] who later became Director of the Rothschild Bank, Prime Minister under De Gaulle, and then President of France in 1969. Pompidou also befriended the other 'exotic' member of the class, Pham Duy Khiem from Indochina. Senghor's other classmates were Robert Brasillach, future novelist and Nazi collaborator; Thierry Maulnier, later to be elected to the *Académie Française;* the brilliant author Henri Queffelec; well-known writers Paul Guth and Robert Merle; and Robert Verdier who, like Pompidou and Senghor, later embarked on a political career. Their master was Albert Bayet, 'apostle of anti-clerical morality'. Along with Thierry Maulnier and Henri Queffelec, who regularly attended Mass, Senghor remained faithful to his religious convictions. During these years he had little time for girls.[25]

He maintained his royalist sympathies inherited from the Fathers of Ngasobil and the *College Libermann*: 'I proclaimed myself a "monarchist", making no attempt to hide my sympathy for the Pretender "inheritor of forty kings, who in a thousand years, made France"'.[26] In espousing the monarchist cause he joined his classmate Thierry Maulnier.

Maulnier has described these years at the *Lycée Louis-le-Grand* which were for him and his fellow students 'the discovery in common of Paris, of friendship, of literature, of the theatre, of politics, and of a certain number of means by which the young citizen can escape censures and regulations'. And he adds: 'a bit of time was also devoted to studies'.[27]

Senghor's companions, especially his friend Georges Pompidou, told him about their favourite authors. Pompidou transmitted to Senghor his love of Proust, Gide, and above all, Baudelaire. Senghor has described Pompidou's influence: 'I can still hear him reciting Baudelaire's poems, with a grave voice, a bit muffled and monotonal. It was true diction, that of African *griots*. It was not by chance that I later wrote my Master's thesis on "Exoticism in Baudelaire".'[28]

The French University completed his 'Frenchification':

'And with docility we accepted the values of the West; its discursive reason and its techniques...Our ambition was to become photographic negatives of the colonizers: "black-skinned Frenchmen". It went even further, for we would have blushed, if we could have blushed, about our black skin, our frizzled hair, our flat noses, above all for the values of our traditional civilization... Our people..., secretly, caused us shame.'[29]

His first poems, later thrown away, were copies of the Symbolists and the Parnassians.[30] It is tempting to believe that the 1932 description of certain French West Indian poets by another black student in Paris applies to the young Senghor of the 1920s. Etienne Léro, young Surrealist poet from Martinique, wrote:

'Some members of a mulatto society, intellectual and physical bastards, were literarily [*sic*] nourished with white decadence... There, the poet ... is recruited from the class which has the privilege of comfort and instruction... The West Indian, stuffed full of white morality, white culture, white education, white prejudices, displays in his volumes a bloated image of himself. To be a good carbon copy of a pale man takes the place of social as well as of poetic standing for him. To his taste he is never decent enough, eager enough. He does not fail to say "You're acting like a nigger" indignantly when you give way to natural exuberance in his presence. Thus he does not want to "be like a nigger" in his verses. He makes it a point of honour that a white man can read his entire book without suspecting his pigmentation...He will maintain that it's his right to show of himself only what he esteems good to show, for raised by the Reverend Fathers, or indirectly imbued with their imported religion, he is an awful Jesuit...His inferiority complex pushes him along beaten paths: "I'm a Negro", he will tell you, "it is not at all becoming for me to be extravagant".'[31]

The hypothesis that this description could be applied to Senghor is all the more plausible because these lines were directed against those

French West Indians who were also attracted by the Parnassians and the Symbolists.[32] Thus it is probable that Senghor, who was considered as an *assimilé* by all those who knew him during this period, actually had become one.

At the end of the first years in Paris, Senghor had acquired the Frenchman's thinking habits.[33] A short and brutal reaction between 1930 and 1932 scarcely helped him to divorce himself from French attitudes concerning 'Anglo-Saxons':

'My intention is not to go to war with England. It would be contrary to the principle that I am defending here. Although I feel very little inclination for English civilization – it's an affair of situation and of culture – I have esteem for the English people.'[34]

It is striking to see how much Senghor has adopted typical French prejudices in this area. In 1947 he wrote on the unhappy state of English-speaking Africans as compared with French-speaking Africans: '...English capitalism is stricter, and the English people less revolutionary, in any case less sensible about ethnic differences and, naturally, less universalist'.[35] It is very interesting to compare this quotation with one from the French Catholic writer François Mauriac: 'It appears to me that English culture is more than our own a prison for Arabs and for Negroes. It compromises them more since it is less humane. It doesn't have that universal character of French genius'.[36]

Senghor has admitted: 'I am a Frenchman culturally and a man of good will. I only fear the idea of a French absence'.[37] It is therefore natural for Africans of the younger generation to accuse Senghor of remaining too French.[38] But this 'Frenchification' was not all negative, despite the comments of 'revolutionary' Africans. Senghor has explained the preponderant influence of these years in France:

'This grimy *Lycée Louis-le-Grand* appears to me thirty years afterwards as a halo of light in my life. Here, between 1928 and 1931, I received the essentials of my intellectual and moral training. "A question of methodology," Sartre would say. Yes, all that I learned in France was a method for thinking and living – I will even say: the method which today enables me to analyse and overcome problems.'[39]

Senghor wrote: 'The only thing I learned in Europe...that I learned in preparing for the *Ecole Normale Supérieure*...was intellectual discipline, or rather the spirit of methodical analysis. Facing a problem, the natural reaction of the African is indignation: we are the sons of emotion. The European's reaction is an expression of will, the will to resolve the difficulty: he *has* to solve it'.[40]

In becoming a black Frenchman he assimilated the critical habits of his acquired culture. Frenchmen's criticism of French society never failed to surprise the young Senghor. In the Colonies he had never heard a Frenchman criticize France. The period of assimilation thus ended by his acquiring the very French habit of finding fault with France. From that time on, if he remained loyal to France, it was not an absolute loyalty, but a critical one: he had so assimilated French culture that he could criticize it from within.[41] Henceforth, his thoughts were a very complex tapestry combining both admiration of, and infidelity to, Western civilization. France was simultaneously venerated and disparaged.

The period of his 'Frenchification' ended abruptly by what Senghor himself has termed an 'anti-white racist crisis'.[42] In 1930, after having passed the written entrance examination to the crack *Ecole Normale Supérieure*, he surprisingly failed the orals.[43] In addition, he had a romantic disappointment, perhaps due to the blackness of his skin.[44] He discarded his Catholic faith because he was profoundly struck by 'the divorce existing between the doctrine and the life of European Christians, between Christ's word and Christian acts'.[45] These events explain the lines he wrote several years later:

'Was it necessary to submit to the temptation of despair, as I did after those three years of preparation for the *Ecole Normale Supérieure*, at the end of which Europe had taught me to doubt her because she did not offer me a universal recipe, but rather only a simple problem-solving method? Europe thus also had its "shadows" and its "sunny spots", exactly like our black Africa.'[46]

To the self-discipline, to the critical spirit imparted by his European teachers, can be added a much more difficult lesson: that of difference. Senghor had wished to re-establish his equilibrium by becoming an *évolué*, an *assimilé*; he suddenly realized that he had erred. The French theory of cultural assimilation was based on the belief that there existed but one type of man, one universal civilization, of which the West provided the most perfect example. According to those who held this idea, in order to be completely civilized, it was necessary to become 'completely European, preferably French'.[47] After many months in France, Senghor saw the impossibility of such a transformation:

'Whatever friendship our classmates afforded us...it didn't take a long time for us to feel different from them. We hadn't the same reactions to reality, to life. Their preoccupation with a career, their feeling for money and their taste for good food were, for me, perpetually surprising. More deeply, we didn't react in the same way to our teacher's lessons, nor to works of art. Rather than to the lessons of order, clarity, or high morality that the classics im-

parted to us, I was sensitive, first, to their style, their language, to the sensual qualities of images and rhythms. We Negroes felt quite different from our white companions. Thus arose our habit of meeting together on Sundays.'[48]
On certain Sundays he was invited by his legal guardian in Paris, Blaise Diagne, the first Negro *Député* of the four communes of Senegal (those which were considered as parts of metropolitan France) in the French parliament. Here he had a chance to meet with politicians, but he considered himself a 'humanist' and was scarcely attracted by the men he met.

His education in the West thus played the role of initiator, stimulant, and finally, of reagent.[49] 'The herald of the black soul went to white schools...on coming into contact with white culture *négritude* passed from dormant existence to the conscious state of reflection... It thus commences in exile.'[50] Senghor 'discovered Africa in France',[51] because the critical spirit imparted to him brought on a '*désintoxication*'.[52] After their long detour through Western Humanities[53] the black intellectuals reacted against assimilation and discovered their 'own characteristics': a taste for haunting rhythms, a 'reason, but not in rational form', and the legacy of common suffering due to skin colour.

The French, who appeared from afar to be a race of noblemen, now revealed to Senghor their failings: rampant individualism, the struggle for daily bread, the slavery of the factory, 'miserable drunkards sleeping along the banks of the most noble of rivers'.[54] In a moment of despair, in a moment when he withdrew inside himself away from his teachers, from the people with whom he broke spiritual bread,[55] he re-discovered the 'Childhood Kingdom': Africa and its message, his 'pagan sap which mounts and which prances and which dances'.[56]

And I am reborn to the land which was my mother[57]

Senghor conscientiously sought to develop a scholarly foundation for this emotional return to Africa. He plunged into the works of anthropologists, seeking substance for the Africa of his dreams. This intellectual search partially paralleled that of Gandhi. During his first stay in England, the future Mahatma read the British theosophical books which revealed to him the spiritual heritage of India. It was in an English translation that Gandhi first read the *Bhagavad-Gita*. In a similar foreign setting Senghor re-discovered Africa in the works of anthropologists such as the French scholar Delafosse and the German Africanist Frobenius.[58]

The Anglo-Polish sociologist Malinowsky noted the conditions shaping the character of the African intellectual's search for Africa. If he had the opportunity to go to a European university it did not take him long to discover that equality of rights and rewards was refused him on all levels: judicial, scientific, social and political. Malinowsky thought that, since Europeans refused to share material and moral benefits with African intellectuals, these Africans naturally returned to their own native traditional system of values, sentiments, and beliefs; they thus turned with the passion of an ethnographer to tribal history and native law, as well as to the artistic and spiritual accomplishments of their race.[59]

The irrational crisis which preceded the return to Africa was as characteristic of black men from the New World as it was of Senghor. The French West Indian Frantz Fanon wrote: 'I had rationalized the world and the world had rejected me because of race prejudice. Since on the level of reason no agreement was possible, I pushed myself towards irrationality...I am built with irrationality; I wade in the irrational. Irrational up to my neck'.[60]

Senghor's reaction was less intense. His African childhood memories rose out of the past to give birth to a positive intellectual phenomenon.

Night which melts all my contradictions,
All contradictions in the primal unity of your *négritude*
Receive the infant, still infant, that twelve years of
wandering have not aged.[61]

Part 2. The Discovery of Négritude 1929–48

4. What is Négritude?

The phenomenon of *négritude* was at the origin of nationalism in French-speaking Africa. The discovery, the exaltation, and the development of *négritude* has been described by Senghor as a 'powerful leaven' in the birth of a national sentiment of the peoples of sub-Saharan Africa.[1]

Senghor has defined *négritude* as 'Negro-African cultural values', but this definition does not take into account the richness of this complex phenomenon which changes according to the period considered or according to the 'militant' espousing it. It is impossible to define the term scientifically or philosophically.[2] *Négritude* is the product of an irrational current of thought[3] and neither lends itself to definition, nor permits precise demarcation. It is a preoccupation that must be lived and felt to be apprehended.

There are many *négritudes*: the aggressive *négritude* clamouring for recognition of African values; the conciliatory *négritude* advocating cultural miscegenation or cross-breeding; and an inventive *négritude* tending towards a new humanism. These three major currents have been present from 1931 onwards; but according to the period and the 'militant', one of these aspects has taken precedence over the others.

The historical approach is perhaps the best way to capture the meaning of *négritude*. The Senegalese historian Cheikh Anta Diop wrote that *négritude* has 'a whole history of its own'. Senghor, following Diop, has stressed that the content of the phenomenon 'has been enriched with the passing of time, and has been renewed as circumstances have altered'. He stated that 'like life, the concept of *négritude* has become historical and dialectical. It has evolved'.[4] Senghor affirmed recently that the French West Indian poet Aimé Césaire invented the term sometime between 1932 and 1934. By recognizing his friend's contribution he hoped 'to render unto Césaire what is Césaire's'.[5]

If it was Césaire who invented the term, it was Senghor who was most responsible for developing the philosophy. They were, however, but two of the black men and women who launched the movement. It would indeed be difficult to understand *négritude* without including the contributions of writers and poets such as Paulette

Nardal, Etienne Léro, Alioune Diop, and Jacques Rabemananjara. Our interest in these other figures, however, is limited to their relationship with Senghor and his thought. A large part of this study deals with influences on Senghor's thought and describes how each reinforces and complements another. These influences awakened Senghor to a new racial consciousness.

During the years 1934 to 1948 Senghor wove the influences of the previous period into an intellectual scheme composed of four complementary themes: 'Primacy of Culture', 'Cultural Cross-breeding', 'Assimilate, don't be Assimilated', and 'The Contribution of the Negro'. By 1948 Senghor advanced his theories by publishing an anthology of new black poetry. 'Black Orpheus', which was Jean-Paul Sartre's preface to Senghor's book, made it apparent that *négritude* could no longer be ignored and that a revolutionary intellectual movement was well under way.

5. The Provincial Heritage

While they were classmates at the *Lycée Louis-le-Grand*, Senghor's 'best friend' Georges Pompidou introduced him to Maurice Barrès's concept of provincial renaissance. Barrès proved a revelation to Senghor – a 'thunderclap', as he has said – and, on reading the *Déracinés* in 1929, Senghor began to understand his own uprooted state. 'Barrès', he wrote, 'helped me in my search for authenticity and *négritude*.'[1] After reading Barrès, Senghor felt the need to root himself in his native *Serer* soil; he remembered the Dead that he had left behind him. Barrès wrote that there was nothing more important in the forming of a people's soul than the voice of the Ancestors and the lessons of the provincial soil. The native soil was vital to Barrès's thought for the living were 'the extension of the Dead'.[2] This belief was in the tradition of the African griots that young Léopold had listened to during the years in Joal.[3] Poetically Senghor repeats over and over this relationship of death to life.

But in my head, open to the winds and pillage of the North,
I do not raze the footprints of my fathers or my father's
fathers[4]

...the procession of the village Dead on the horizon of the
tanns...
the same sky provoked by hidden presences
the same sky feared by those who have debts to the Dead.
Here are my Dead who advance towards me...[5]

I see two sister cities beyond the *bolong*, the purple
of the living, the blue of the Dead.
In the evening I dream of a lost country, where Kings and
the Dead were my familiars[6]
Let me think of my Dead!
Yesterday was the feast of the Dead, the solemn birthday
of the sun
And no memory in any cemetery.
O Dead, who have always refused to die, who knew how to
resist death.
Even in Sine, even in Seine, and in my fragile veins, my
irrepressible blood[7]

Let me breathe the odour of our Dead, that I may
gather and repeat their living voice…[8]

Senghor has described the African feeling towards death as a 'familiarity'. In Africa 'there is no irrepressible opposition between life and death, and buried ancestors continue to participate in the life of the living'.[9] Here was yet another African belief that paralleled Barrès's thinking: the possibility of the co-existence of things which seem as opposed as are life and death.

I do not remember what time it was, I always confuse
childhood and Eden
As I mix Death and Life – a bridge of sweetness links them.

I do not remember what time it was, I always confuse present
and past
As I mix Death and Life – a bridge of sweetness links them[10]

Senghor's penchant for joining opposites, thus 'bridging the gap', seems to be rooted in his desire to unite that which appears distinct.[11]

After reading Barrès, Senghor consciously developed the African traditions learned during those distant nights spent with his uncle. His dreams of the *Serer* countryside, the residue of his 'Childhood-Eden' took on a growing importance. Due in part to his experience with Barrès, Senghor's poetry has been termed 'a poetry of *enracinement*'.[12] Senghor's detailed descriptions of the *Serer* landscape, its customs and people, conformed to Barrès's dictum that men should gain spiritual strength from their native province. Barrès opposed the idea that what was learned from one's provincial ancestors was 'contemptible' and should be replaced by 'cosmopolitan academic teaching'. Barrès believed that such an attitude produced colourless and incapable 'vagrants'. Only the 'voice' of race and the instinct which came from the earth of one's native province could form the complete man.

To those people who believed that the genius of the provinces was extinct, Barrès replied that the provinces could 'still furnish the great interior light to warm and enliven France'.[13]

Barrès's ideas were strongly influenced by those of the Provençal poet Frederic Mistral. He quoted a letter of Mistral's to underscore this relationship: 'Convinced for a long time that the destruction of the provinces and all that gave life to their personality could but weaken the old free races who have mixed their sap in the Gallo-Frankish trunk, I have with a few others devoted my poet's life to reactivating, to rejuvenating the roots by which the province holds to the soil and the special links which make us love this soil. All this is to say that our *particularisme* (regionalism) is less dangerous for France than the uniformity produced by the hateful unitarist level-ling...'. Mistral went on to advocate an emancipation of provincial forces and a regional reawakening.[14] Directly influenced by Barrès and indirectly by the poet Mistral, Senghor thus conceived of a return to his own native sources.

Barrès also spoke of 'remaking one's soul to produce a total one'. This idea inspired Senghor's search for his black soul.[15] He did not want to remain suspended in a void like the person in Barrès's *Déracinés*.[16] He had to return to his native origins. 'Wash me bare', he cried out in a poem, 'of all my contagions of a civilized man.'[17]

It is interesting to note that Charles Maurras, the right-wing monarchist who was influential among French intellectuals in the 1920s and 1930s, paralleled these ideas of Barrès. Although con-sidered a Fascist, Maurras inspired the black writer Jean Price-Mars, who quoted Maurras: 'I have received everything from my native soil'.[18]

Senghor's experience with Barrès was not unlike that of Lucien, a character in Jean-Paul Sartre's *Enfance d'un Chef*. Like Senghor, Lucien first was influenced by Surrealism, and after reading Barrès, '...he had to study the soil and subsoil of Ferolles, he had to decipher the meaning of the rolling hills...now...words, phrases, resounded within him: "renew with tradition"... "the soil and the dead"'.[19]

Barrès is often considered to have been opposed to André Gide. To Senghor, however, their approaches were complementary. Barrès saw in submission to traditional order an achievement of one's individuality; Gide conceived individualism as something to be sur-passed. The early advocates of *négritude* often quoted Gide: 'It is by pursuing one's uniqueness that one arrives at universality'.[20] Gide inspired Senghor to assume his human condition 'with all its par-ticularity, its heritage, that is to say, its *négritude*' in order to go from that particular to the general: human brotherhood.[21] He encouraged Senghor to 'accept his difference' or better yet 'to cultivate it'.[22] By the example of his acceptance of his own homosexuality, Gide helped Senghor to accept his own *négritude* – the condition and trials of being black. 'We know', stated Senghor, 'that in fully accepting past reali-ties, we will be able to surpass them in our struggle to build our present and our future'.[23] Thus, taking the insult tossed at him in the form of the word 'nigger', he made it a 'decoration, a challenge'.[24] He glorified the black colour: 'black woman dressed in your colour which is life...'.[25] Like Gide's homosexuality, Senghor's blackness was a burden, but no longer a negative and shameful one.

There was a striking parallel between the lives of Gide and Senghor. Having read Goethe, Gide, as Senghor after him, accentuated the distance between his multiple origins. He emphasized the conflict between the Cevenol Protestantism of the Gide family and the Normandy Catholicism of his mother's family. A critic wrote that 'Gide saw himself and willed himself the fruit of the cross-breeding of two races, of two religions, of two traditions – a double and ambiguous fruit, inclined or rather condemned to an interior dialogue, to battles and divisions'. It was Gide who wrote: 'Born in Paris, of a father from Uzès and of a Normandy mother, where do you wish me to root myself, Monsieur Barrès? I have thus made the decision to travel'. Gide opposed the Barrèsian thesis of rooting oneself exclusively in one's native soil and among one's dead ancestors. Gide created within himself a conflict which produced originality.[26] Senghor much later followed the same course. As a member of a race scattered all over the world in the Negro 'diaspora', Senghor modified Barrès's ideas with those of Gide. The *Serer* region was but part of the homeland of black men, who lived not only in Africa, but also in Europe and the Americas. The natural expression of the search for cultural identity was in *négritude*, or *Pan-Negroism*, rather than *Africanitude* or Pan-Africanism limited to the African continent. This search was not Senghor's alone. He was only one of a group of black intellectuals in Paris, mostly French West Indians, who sought an understanding of their uniqueness.[27]

They drew inspiration from many nationalists besides Barrès. The French nationalist historian Jules Michelet had written 'The essential is not to climb, but in climbing to remain onself'. The West Indian Césaire often quoted this line.[28] Dostoevsky also reinforced this theme: 'As soon as a people ceases to believe it is the unique possessor of the truth, as soon as it does not believe it is the only chosen one, the only one capable of resuscitating and saving the world by its truth, it ceases immediately to be a great people and is only a subject for ethnographers...'.[29] In Senghor's mind this statement of Dostoevsky was reduced to: 'Any race who does not believe it has an exceptional message to deliver to the world is ready to be stored in a museum'.[30] Through Dostoevsky the great Pan-Slav movement of the nineteenth century directly weighed in the formulation of *négritude*.

Senghor's ideas on provincial patriotism bear a close resemblance to those of the nineteenth-century romantic nationalist Mazzini. Mazzini's thought was profoundly idealistic and religious, and like Senghor, he preached human brotherhood. He deplored national antagonisms, but nonetheless advocated rebirth for Italy. Michelet,

Mazzini, and Senghor after them, believed that the national home-land, the nation-state, was the forerunner of the universal home-land.[31]

Senghor set out to discover the 'exceptional message' mentioned by Dostoevsky; once he discovered it he devoted his life to spreading it, hoping in this way to stress the contribution of black men to universal civilization. In doing so he reconciled Barrès's idea of 'rooting himself' with Gide's contrary notion of 'wandering'. It is characteristic of Senghor that his theories are derived from diametrically opposed influences which he synthesized into a new philosophical assertion.

This search for a provincial heritage was not limited to the Blacks. Among their white companions there were many who felt a similar need to re-establish links with their rural past. All, black and white, were part of what has been termed the 'Parisian intellectual generation of the 1930s'.

Senghor participated in an intellectual movement spearheaded by a group of young French writers of the 1930s who attempted to revitalize French political thought.[2] Their ideas were widely discussed because they published a number of *revues* which developed similar themes.

One of the first journals founded by these men was *Réaction*, which advocated neo-traditionalism. Senghor's classmate Thierry Maulnier and the French Catholic writer Georges Bernanos both worked for the publication. *Réaction* took a middle path between capitalism and communism, rejecting bourgeois values but at the same time referring to Christian order, the lessons of the past, and natural social frameworks. It proclaimed fidelity to the cause of monarchism. The great idols of *Réaction* were, among others, Barrès and Maurras.[3] Senghor, who was both a Monarchist and a Barrèsian, adopted ideas characteristic of a large number of his intellectual generation.

The attempt to renew French political thinking also gave birth to Emmanuel Mounier's liberal Catholic philosophy of 'Personalism' and to his journal, *Esprit*, founded in 1932. From that time on, the Catholic intellectuals of *Esprit*, Daniel-Rops, Mounier, Denis de Rougement, André Philip, and especially Jacques Maritain, exerted a highly important influence on Senghor's thought.[4]

Mounier founded his *revue* partly because of his 'perceiving, beneath the growing economic crisis, a total crisis of civilization'.[5] The economic crises which followed World War I, above all the Great Crash of 1929, contributed to the increasing scepticism concerning the value of industrial civilization. The intellectual crisis of the 1930s had causes which preceded the Crash, and certain signs of this intellectual ferment can be found prior to 1929. However, it is clear that the economic crises brought to a head the intellectual crisis, proving that it was no longer possible to wait to renew French thinking and values.[6]

A growing doubt thus gripped the entire intellectual generation in Paris. The black community in Paris showed the same misgivings. The first article of the November 1931 issue of their *Revue du Monde Noir* pessimistically stated:

'...the world is at grips with the most acute and most anguishing

crisis that it has ever known, a crisis spreading to all continents...
Germany is on the eve of a new bankruptcy, Hungary is at grips
with grave difficulties... Austria does not know to which lender
she must turn, Romania struggles in a thousand torments, Yugo-
slavia, hardly rid of dictatorship, is in crisis, Russia seeks its way,
Spain is still in revolution, Portugal goes from one pronuncia-
mento to another, England is in a full industrial and financial
crisis, Holland is worried about its money, the Scandinavian
countries are terrified by the decreasing value of their crowns,
Poland seeks its equilibrium: that takes care of Europe. Elsewhere? China succumbs under the scourge of climatic calamities,
Japan prepares for war, the USA have ten million unemployed,
and South America is bankrupt: that takes care of the world.'[7]
This preoccupation with the apparent disintegration of the old order
found confirmation in such books as Albert Demangeon's *Déclin de
l'Europe*, Oswald Spengler's *Decline of the West*, as well as *Décadence
de la Liberté* by Daniel Halévy, and *Décadence de la Nation Française* by
Robert Aron and Arnaud Dandieu.[8] Senghor could not help but be
influenced by the morbid interest that Europeans took in their own
downfall. He read *Le Crépuscule de l'Occident* by A. Labriola which
could easily be added to the above list.[9] The whole feeling of this
period is well expressed by Paul Valéry in his famous pessimistic
dictum: 'We other civilizations, we now know that we too are
mortal'. Africa's rehabilitation could only profit from such a state
of affairs.

The major themes developed by this generation were what Jean
Touchard calls the 'anti' themes: anti-politics, anti-rationalism, anti-
mechanization, anti-materialism, anti-capitalism, anti-bourgeoisie,
anti-individualism, and last, but not least, anti-Americanism.[10] Each
has appeared in Senghor's thought. His reflections on the subject of
culture and his theory of *négritude* as well as his socio-economic thinking, his 'African Road to Socialism', developed on the basis of these
eight negative themes.[11]

The attitude expressed in the intellectual milieu of Paris sprang
from the counter-industrial revolution of the nineteenth and early
twentieth centuries. Despising the rationalist and industrial civilization that was developing around them, artists and writers of the
'belle époque' such as Gauguin and Rimbaud tried to escape to a
more natural life in Tahiti and Ethiopia. The symbolist poet Rimbaud 'shrieked his horror at Western civilization and beliefs' and
'proclaimed himself a black savage and a pagan in order to show
plainly his innocence':

'If I had antecedents in but a single point of French history! But no, nothing…I have never been Christian; I am of the race that sang while being tortured; I don't understand laws; I have no morality, I am a brute;…yes, I've my eyes closed to your light. I am a beast a black savage…Cries, drums, dance, dance, dance, dance!'[12]

7. A Taste for Things Black

It is easy to understand why Rimbaud's lines were a revelation to Senghor: he found in them his own condition once again perfectly described. It was not mere chance that placed Rimbaud's words under Senghor's eyes.[1] The climate created by the crises in the West helped the diffusion of Rimbaud's thought, but it was thanks to an encounter that Senghor became attracted to the works of the symbolist poet. 'There is no...meeting of ideas which is not first a meeting of men.'[2] Paris provided the necessary crossroads.

The Latin Quarter was the place where the black students from the New World and from Africa had, for the first time, the opportunity to form groups, to exchange ideas, to realize the similarity of their problems.[3] Their rejection of the colonial mentality is underlined in an 'Appeal to the Students of French Colonies' which was published in 1928 in *La Dépêche Africaine*, a newspaper read by West Indians in Paris: 'You who have to exile yourselves to come here to France to seek the intellectual nourishment which is systematically refused you...Comrades from Algeria, Tunisia, Indochina, the West Indies, Senegal – stand up for the defence of your interests!'[4] It was therefore with French West Indian friends, above all Aimé Césaire whom he met in 1929, that Senghor developed the new attitude towards Africa which had begun with his reading of Barrès.

At the same time the Parisians were showing increased interest in Negro arts. This phenomenon of the 1930s has been termed the 'Negro Revolution' in French culture. The year 1931 saw the inauguration of the Colonial Exhibition in Paris. This exhibition had brought to Paris African artisans and musicians who attracted a large and interested audience. The Parisian enthusiasm encouraged the young *déraciné* in his idealization of his native land. The African villages constructed in the Parc de Vincennes brought back his memories of Joal and Djilor. Josephine Baker, the American Negro singer, was playing to full houses, and the *Biguine* dance from Martinique became popular in the new Negro dance-halls of Montparnasse.

Negroes also held positions of influence. Blaise Diagne, Negro *Député* to the French National Assembly from Senegal, was a member of the French Government. By the end of 1931 His Eminence

Cardinal Verdier had ordained a Negro missionary into the Order of the Holy Spirit at Notre-Dame Cathedral. The new priest was Senghor's former companion at Ngasobil, Joseph Faye.[5]

From the 1920s on the success of books by Blaise Cendrars,[6] Paul Morand,[7] and René Maran underlined the triumph of a certain kind of literature devoted to the Negro world. A novel by René Maran, a French West Indian and former Administrator of French Colonies, had already obtained the coveted Goncourt Prize in 1921. The novel, *Batouala*, was a first effort to see Africans from a black point of view, and it included a severe criticism of 'Civilization':

> 'After all, if they (black men) starve by thousands, like flies, it is because their country is being developed. Only those who do not adapt themselves to Civilization disappear. Civilization, Civilization! pride of Europeans, and their charnel-house of the innocent, Rabindranath Tagore, the Hindu poet, one day in Tokyo, said what you were! You build your kingdom on cadavers. Whatever you wish, whatever you do, you wallow in lies. On seeing you, tears flow and pain develops. You are a force which takes precedence over right. You are not a torch, but a holocaust. Whatever you touch, you consume....'[8]

André Gide, following the example of René Maran, published his *Travels to the Congo* in 1927 and the following year his *Return from Tchad*. These accounts also emphasized the despoliation of Africa and criticized the West.[9]

European culture met competition from the fresh approach of the black artist. Jazz had in a few years made classical music appear faded. African art, 'discovered' by Derain, Vlaminck, and Picasso, had become the rage of enlightened collectors as well as followers of fashion. Those who worshipped African statues were iconoclasts in their attitudes towards Western art.[10]

In this atmosphere of Negrophilia, a small group of West Indians began a monthly review devoted to exploring black consciousness and towards the end of the Colonial Exhibition, in November 1931, the first of six issues appeared. The *Revue du Monde Noir* was published in English and French and was edited by Mademoiselle Paulette Nardal, a West Indian student of English. Through Paulette Nardal, Senghor met Etienne Léro, a West Indian Surrealist poet and connoisseur of Rimbaud.[11] She also introduced him to René Maran.[12] The *Revue du Monde Noir* proved to be an intellectual mine for Senghor. It acquainted him with American Negro poetry and with anthropology, two of the most important influences on his cultural thought. It may also have formed the basis of his political thought.

The list of contributors to the *Revue* is a directory of the men whose ideas, absorbed and reworked by Senghor, gave birth to his theory of *négritude*. The list includes Etienne Léro, Jules Monnerot and René Ménil, black Surrealist poets attracted by communism who in June 1932 published a call for militancy in their Manifesto *Légitime Défense*.[13] American Negro writers Claude MacKay, Alain Locke, Langston Hughes; the novelist René Maran; and anthropologists such as Price-Mars, Delafosse, and Frobenius were important to the *Revue*.[14] The French West Indian poets Léon Damas and Gilbert Gratiant were also attached to the group.[15] Even future Governor-General Félix Eboué[16] sent articles to the *Revue* as did the future President of the French Senate, Gaston Monnerville,[17] and the future President of Nigeria, Azikiwe.[18] A number of these men met at Paulette Nardal's literary salon where René Maran played the role of mentor.[19] The contributors gathered there to deepen their understanding of mutual problems as well as to maintain their friendship.[20] The *Revue du Monde Noir* broke with the tradition of Negro reviews which were termed 'tributaries to Latin culture'. The *Revue* studied the conditions facing black men and expressed 'faith in the future of the race, and the necessity of creating a sentiment of solidarity among the different black groups spread out all over the world'.[21] In addition its editors hoped to 'promote within the white race a mutual, complete, affectionate, and unprejudiced appreciation of the intelligentsia of all coloured races'.[22]

The *Revue* thus pursued the goal of equality. Senghor has said that certain Negroes wanted to be accepted in French society and therefore exalted Negro values for that purpose. It is even possible that such an attitude was his for a certain time. He wrote: 'I have known young Africans who lengthily, methodically, studied African civilization in European books...in order to use it'. And Senghor continued: 'I want to be still more precise. I have known Negro intellectuals who only advocated Negro values to gain admittance into the white world'.[23] Senghor's critics maintain that he made such an attempt.[24] Senghor does state that he was never 'so fraternal with Europeans in general, with Frenchmen in particular...as from the moment in which [he] discovered the value of *négritude*, in which [he] felt proud to be a Negro'.[25]

8. A Forum for New Negro Ideologies

Paulette Nardal complained bitterly in 1963 that a complete 'silence was maintained for a long period' about her activities in the 1930s. She wrote that her sister Jane Nardal was the first 'promoter of this movement of ideas, so broadly exploited later'. It was Senghor and Césaire who 'took up the ideas tossed out by us and expressed them with more flash and brio'. She noted that 'we were but women, real pioneers – let's say that we blazed the trail for them'.[1]

The ideas developed in the *Revue* thus merit serious study, for in them lay the roots of the cultural nationalism which so strongly influenced French African thinking in the period of decolonization. The major themes of the *Revue*, themes which Senghor later elaborated in his cultural theories, included:

1. The need for a Negro literature and a rehabiliation of Negro values.
2. The unique contribution of the Negro world to Western Civilization.
3. Negro humanism and the need for cultural cross-breeding.

In November 1931, with the publication of its first issue, the *Revue* spelled out its primary objectives:

'Our aim is to give the intelligentsia of the black race and their adherents an official organ in which to publish their artistic, literary and scientific works; to study and to popularize by means of the press, books, lectures, courses, all that concerns *Negro Civilization* and the natural riches of Africa, thrice sacred to the black race. The objectives of the *Revue du Monde Noir* will be: to create among the Negroes of the entire world, regardless of nationality, an intellectual and moral tie, which will permit them to know each other better, to love one another, to defend more effectively their collective interests and to glorify their race. By this means, the Negro race will contribute, along with thinking minds of other races and with all those who have received the light of truth, beauty and goodness, to the material, the moral and the intellectual improvement of humanity.'[2]

The non-political nature of the *Revue* is evident. The major thrust was to be cultural, partly as a reaction to the French policy of assimilation, and partly because the experience of American Negroes with cultural integration provided a precedent.[3] The transplantation of the American Negro emphasis on culture to Paris occurred largely because most of the French Negro writers of the 1930s were West Indians and were naturally much more conscious of what was transpiring in the American 'Colossus to the North' than were their African brothers.

Senghor's decision to devote his efforts to artistic creation was influenced by an idea which appeared in the December 1931 issue of the *Revue du Monde Noir*:

'It is undeniable', wrote Marc Logé in 1927, 'that Negro poets endowed American literature with works of rare power and original sensitivity. It is a fact that merits consideration, for *nothing would contribute as much to raising the stature of the Negro race than a demonstration of their continuing intellectual progress through the creation of works of art of unquestioned value....*'[4]

The theme of 'Primacy of Culture', which was characteristic of Senghor's *négritude* until 1956, grew out of the desire to promote the black race through poetry, music, and the other arts.[5] It played a no less important role in the subordination of politics which characterized Senghor's approach when he became a *Député* to the French National Assembly after World War II.[6] The Senghor of the 1950s reiterates this theme of the early 1930s:

'Experience has proved that cultural liberation is an essential condition of political liberation. If white America has conceded the claims of the Negroes it has been because writers and artists, by showing the true aspect of the race, have restored its dignity; if Europe is beginning to reckon with Africa, it is because Africa's traditional sculpture, music, dancing, literature and philosophy are now being forced upon an astonished world.'[7]

Paulette Nardal's article on the 'Awakening of Race Consciousness', published in the April 1932 issue of the *Revue du Monde Noir*, described the process which led to this black cultural renaissance. She began by stating that 'there is certainly something new' in the Paris West Indian's attitude towards racial questions, and went on to say that even a few months previously, these black students did not proclaim their 'pride in being descendants of African Blacks', but 'now this almost disdainful indifference seems to transform itself to an astonished interest...to a real enthusiasm'. If this race-consciousness was awakened in certain French West Indians, 'it was necessary for them to put a certain distance between them and their little homeland. The uprooting that they felt in the colonial motherland, where the Negro has not always enjoyed the esteem which has been shown him since the opening of the Colonial Exhibition, had made them aware of their black soul despite their Latin upbringing. Yet, that state was not exhibited outwardly'.[8]

This was an accurate description of Léopold Senghor in 1932. Reading these lines must have troubled him. The attitude of the group of intellectuals who contributed to the *Revue*, encouraged him to express openly his 'Blackness'. For both Senghor and these intellectuals 'the sentiment of uprooting...lay at the starting point of their evolution'.[9]

According to Paulette Nardal the precedent for finding 'Blackness' was in the experience of those American Negroes who had already begun to study Africa and the history of the Negro race. It was therefore important to understand the repercussions this experience had on 'Aframerican' literature: 'First an indispensable period of absorption, during which the imported African Negro had to learn a new language and to adapt himself to a hostile milieu. This is the period of the absorption of the Negro element by the white element. From the literary point of view, the Negroes could produce only docile imitations of the works of their white models...Starting in 1880, the Negroes accede to real culture...the Aframericans, having rid themselves of their inferiority complex, calmly express their individual black-skinned being, without fear and without shame'.[10] The apparent success of the 'Aframerican' experience emboldened the French-speaking Negroes to produce a black literature in French. The Gidian idea of 'cultivating one's difference' thus was strongly reinforced. The young black intellectuals used as their motto an African proverb translated by Paul Morand in 1930: 'The Zebra cannot get rid of his stripes'. This proverb, quoted by a contributor to the *Revue du Monde Noir*, seems to sum up admirably the new spirit of these Negroes.[11]

In 1932 the *Revue du Monde Noir* published an article which stimulated Senghor and his companions to poetical rather than political activity. The article, 'Ethnic poetry: the poetical retort of Negroes', greatly influenced Senghor. It attacked the position of Albert Sarraut, former French Colonial Minister, who had published *Grandeurs et Servitudes Coloniales*. Sarraut held that 'colonized peoples, educated by our mechanized methods will one day turn on us and use our own weapons against us'. It was this 'cry of alarm' which provoked the article's reply:

'It is rather curious to note that M. Sarraut, having come to colonization by way of exotic art, as he himself asserts, does not understand a phenomenon which might have guided his prophecy in a better direction. In fact, what he calls "the backlash of colonization" is already present, not in armed revolt, but in an intellectual storm whose lightning flashes have profoundly affected us.'[12]

It was the article's contention that, in comparison with colonial insurrection, the penetration of Negro art and literature into the white world 'is a much wider and deeper offensive that affects people the world over'. American Negroes, instead of utilizing Western commercial and industrial processes against the white race, 'devoted themselves to the pleasures of poetry, dance or the theatre'. The *Revue* concluded on a prophetic note: 'Everywhere coloured people show a marked devotion to poetry, the new form of the future war that civilized man has not foreseen'.[13]

The development of black literature required a changed attitude towards Africa. Until this time French-speaking Blacks had looked down upon their African origin. As Paulette Nardal indicates, French assimilation of colonials was at fault:

'The attitude of French West Indians towards matters concerning their own race, so different from that of American Negroes, can be easily explained by the liberalism which characterized France's policy *vis-à-vis* coloured peoples. Sieburg's book *Is God French?* contains among other things, a very judicious observation on the French genius for assimilation. According to the German writer, the absence of colour prejudice among the French comes from their certitude that they can make the Negro a real Frenchman in a relatively short period of time. Besides that, it was natural that French West Indians, the product of the crossing of two races, Negro and white, endowed with Latin culture, and ignorant of the history of the Negro race, should turn to the culture which honoured them most. The situation facing American Negroes was quite different.'[14]

The American Negroes suffering from 'systematic disdain' had to 'seek motives for pride in the history of the black race'. Paulette Nardal invited the Negro students in Paris to do the same thing. She explained that certain Negro women living in Paris and influenced by 'Aframericans', had already 'turned to the history of their race and of their respective lands'. They began to deplore the absence of African subjects and ethnic studies in the curriculum of schools in the French West Indies. Regaining confidence in the value of kindred 'and in the possibility of the Negro race becoming the equal of the Aryan race', they began serious study. Paulette Nardal expressed her hope 'that those students who are preparing their *Licence* (equivalent of B.A.) in history or geography will avail themselves of the riches which the history of the Negro race and the African continent offers them...'.[15] She cited the novel published by René Maran in

1932, *Le Livre de la Brousse*, as 'a true and magnificent rehabilitation of African civilization'.[16]

The *Revue du Monde Noir* emphasized the contribution of African civilization to European civilization. In the March 1932 issue, the Senegalese student, art critic and future politician, Baye-Salzmann[17] concluded that the West 'without limiting itself, can find in African aesthetics an original source of inspiration and an important factor contributing to renewal'.[18] The article was entitled 'Black Art, its Inspiration, its Contribution to the West'.[19] Baye-Salzmann compiled an inventory of French artists who were inspired by African art: the painters Picasso, Derain, Matisse, Segonzac, Vlaminck, Modigliani; the writers, Valdemer-George, Paul Guillaume, Thomas Munro, André Breton, André Salmon; the poets Apollinaire, Cocteau, Blaise Cendrars, and Paul Eluard. All of these artists 'were not afraid to praise in their works the virtues of Negro aesthetics, which nourished, renewed and deepened their inspiration'.[20]

The value of African civilization and its potential contributions to the West were underscored in an article published by a Frenchman and reprinted in the *Revue*: 'Rather than drawing the Negro world behind us in the wake of our errors, it would be better to try to understand it more thoroughly than in the past, to develop its own qualities and, in the orbit of human civilization, to leave it its own place, its own contribution, by which the common heritage will grow'. French policy should not be *assimilation*, but rather an effort to allow Negroes to awaken themselves in friendship with France so that they might enrich the Latin tradition by a 'human contribution of undeniable value'.[21]

Baye-Salzmann maintained that a contribution was possible because of basic differences between Western and African civilization, as expressed in their art: 'Black art is contrary to Western art which draws upon nature for its inspiration, a nature which is concrete and sensible. Black art is an emotional interpretation of a symbolic concept, which at times reflects a psychological state and at times social traditions thousands of years old'.[22] Baye-Salzmann proceeded to develop a thesis-antithesis theory describing the relationship between black men and white men. 'While Western man...refusing the absolute dissolving of self in God...takes creative intelligence as a means of delivering himself from instinct and its torments, the black man on the other hand takes intuitive sensitivity as an objective and asks of it the religious and poetic expression of the problem of the great beyond....'[23] He termed the black man's art a 'deaf Dionysism' which 'comes directly from pure mystic passion'.[24] It is not surprising that years later Sartre used Nietzsche's Dionysism to explain *négri-*

tude.[25] Senghor's reflections on black art gained greatly from his friendship with Baye-Salzmann, who inspired Senghor's famous distinction between 'Dionysiac' Africa and 'Apollonian' Europe.[26] Another member of the *Revue du Monde Noir*'s staff instrumental in the development of Senghor's philosophy was Louis Th. Achille, Paulette Nardal's cousin.[27] His ideas helped shape Senghor's thought on the subject of 'Negro rationality' and its contrast to 'Hellenic rationality'. In November 1931, Achille described the distinction between the European reliance on the mind versus the African's trust in instinct:

'... there is less an aesthetic *sense* (the exercise of which requires an indispensable and primary contribution by the *intelligence* ...) than an artistic *instinct* (requiring from the *body*, as much as of the soul, an urgent and frequent satisfaction)... Art is thus no longer a luxury, a superfluous activity which can be easily done without, because of human preoccupation with primary needs; it is a highly necessary activity, such as drinking and eating, and almost as sensual... That is why Negroes... are above all dancers... no instrument is interposed between the creating artist and the created object. One and the other are inextricably intermingled. Aesthetic emotion, thus constantly maintained at the ready, bestows upon the individual a continuing happiness... From that state doubtless comes the "broad Negro laugh" which is present from his birth to his death, and stretches from Africa to America.'[28]

Senghor's famous *cogito ergo sum*, 'I feel the other; I dance the other; therefore I am!', continued the emphasis begun by Louis Achille.[29]

That the Negro 'possesses to a very remarkable degree the gifts of emotivity and originality in artistic conception, and excels in creating that which addresses itself to the heart and senses of all men, regardless of race' is another statement of belief contributed by the *Revue* to the development of a Negro humanism.[30] Because of this belief the staff of the *Revue* directed their creative efforts towards the world at large. Having passed through a 'period of revolt' against Western culture these young Negroes, especially Paulette Nardal and her sisters, felt 'more mature' and 'became less severe, less intransigent, since all is relative'. Paulette Nardal described their 1932 position as 'middle of the road':

'Should one see in the tendencies that are expressed here an implicit declaration of war against Latin culture and the white world in general? Such an interpretation would be misleading and we would be at fault if we did not clarify it. We are fully aware of what we owe to white culture and we have no intention of abandoning it to encourage any return to obscurantism. Without white culture we would not have realized our situation. But we intend to leave behind the limits of that culture and, with the aid of men of science of the white race and all friends of Negroes, bring once again to our kindred the pride of belonging to a race whose civilization is perhaps the oldest in the world.'[31]

Jane Nardal, who wrote under the pseudonym Yadhé, was about to publish an article entitled 'For a Negro Humanism' when the *Revue* ceased publication because funds became scarce.[32] Senghor often saw the Nardal sisters, and many of his ideas on Negro humanism came out of discussions with Jane.

The theme of Negro humanism was complemented by the theme of 'solidarity of all races', from which Senghor seems to have derived his theory of 'cultural cross-breeding'. The idea of the 'solidarity of all races' is the particular contribution of Louis Finot, the French Jew who greatly helped the staff of the *Revue*:

'There can no longer be particularism...solidarity of peoples must make way for solidarity of races. Let us smile at the ignorant who speak of the 'French race' – a superior nation certainly, and we are proud of it; but a nation which is the product of an extreme mixing of races, an example of what results from the peaceful fusion of the characteristics of the different races who formed it and who modify it each day.'[33]

The review noted that an 'intelligently understood' mixing of races was 'necessary to human evolution'.[34] Cross-breeding was essential, according to Philippe de Zara, for the '*assimilation* of such a varied and large ethnic group cannot be seriously considered; it would lead to a perpetual carnival'. It appeared to De Zara that French civilization could assume 'a sort of superior spiritual direction which would have as principal mission the awakening of Negro qualities, the utilization of Negro resources without the destruction of the source of their energy'.[35] Thus France would impregnate Negro civilizations while these civilizations, in turn, would bring their fruits to European civilization.

The moderate position of the *Revue du Monde Noir* was later labelled 'rose-water' by the French West Indian Surrealist and communist Etienne Léro, who had often contributed to it.[36] The apolitical stand taken by the *Revue* resulted in Senghor's 'Culture first' which strongly opposed Léro's 'Politics first'.[37] Paulette Nardal wrote in defence that it was essential not to make the mistake of considering her friends and herself as the militants of any political party: 'We only felt the need of bringing back the Negro into the human community and of getting him to rid himself of his complexes...Our preoccupations were of a racial, literary, and artistic order'.[38]

One possible reason for Léro's vehement denunciation may have been the *Revue*'s respect for religion. Paulette Nardal wrote that Christian charity had played an important role in the 'transcending of hate' by her friends and herself. Later the Reverend Father Ducaillon 'opened wide the doors of the review *Le Cerf*' to them and Paulette Nardal worked with the Dominicans. The progressive attitude of *Le Cerf* at that time encouraged the relationship between Catholic and black intellectuals.[39]

By April 1932 when it ceased publication the *Revue du Monde Noir* had introduced the themes that the *négritude* movement later developed. Since the initial impulse towards a black Renaissance came from French West Indians, Senghor was led to see the Negro problem as a whole, with the African problem subordinated to the general question of a racial awakening. This way of thinking slowed the development of French-speaking Africa's continental nationalism and was characteristic until recently.

Because of its themes *négritude* càn be classified as a 'Pan' movement. The parallel with 'Pan-Slavism' in the nineteenth century is striking. The succinct analysis of the latter movement by Karl Marx in 1855 helps point out their similarities:

'The first form of Pan-Slavism was a literary form. Dobrowsky, a Bohemian, the founder of scientific philology of Slavic dialects, and Kolar, a Slovak poet from the Hungarian Carpathian mountains, were the inventors. Dobrowsky had the enthusiasm of the learned man making discoveries. For Kolar political ideas rapidly took over. But at that moment Pan-Slavism was still content with elegies and the greatness of the past. The shame and misfortune of foreign oppression constituted the principal theme of its poetry. "My God! Isn't there on earth a single man who will render justice to the Slav?"' [40]

The first form of nationalism in French-speaking Africa was also literary. Senghor, as was Dobrowsky, is a philologist and has studied African languages.[41] He, too, quickly opposed those who turned from literary to political protest. The themes of Pan-Slavism (studying the greatness of the past, laments over slavery, etc.) are echoed in the *Revue du Monde Noir* and the *négritude* movement. Senghor later wrote: 'The new African literature is a didactic literature, and in a sense it is more scientific than literary'. He concluded: 'In reflection, this literature is following the right path, for philological and ethnographical studies are at the origin of every renaissance'.[42]

The similarity continues. Karl Marx noted:

'But the period of lamentation was not long in disappearing, and with it the demand for "simple justice for the Slavs". Historical

research, embracing the political, literary, and the linguistic evolution of the Slavic race (began)...The glorious epoch of Bohemian
and Serbian history were depicted in glowing colours, contrasting
with the present situation of these nationalities, one of inferiority
and suffering.' [43]

Marx concluded with an ironic description of a Pan-Slav congress
which foreshadowed certain problems of Pan-African congresses:

'The difference among Slavic tongues is so great that with a few
exceptions these Slavs do not understand each other. This was
demonstrated in amusing fashion at the Slav Congress of 1848 in
Prague: after several fruitless attempts to find a tongue compre-
hensible to all, it was necessary, in the last resort, to use the
language that all hated the most: German.' [44]

Marx finally criticized the Pan-Slav party for being 'limited to a frac-
tion of the cultivated classes who have no influence on the people'. [45]
The criticism of *négritude* by Abdoulaye Ly, for example, repeats this
same charge. [46]

9. The Mark of Surrealism

Surrealism grew out of nineteenth-century Romanticism which had opposed Reason. Freudian and Bergsonian theories on the unconscious and the instinctual had given new importance to intuition, dreams, and the irrational. Influenced by them the Surrealists, as the anthropologist Lévy-Bruhl, tried to recapture a 'primitive mentality'.

The West Indian intellectuals served as intermediaries between Senghor and Surrealist writers, who were *avant-garde* in the interwar period. As early as 1928 Jane Nardal wrote of their influence in *La Dépêche Africaine*, the journal which preceded the *Revue* as an organ for the expression of French West Indian opinion. She was strongly attracted to the Surrealist poetry of Philippe Soupault, who had written of black men in a novel *Le Nègre* in 1927. She wrote of his 'violent alcohols' which replaced the 'grenadine syrups' of preceding poets and writers.[1] The West Indian Etienne Léro understood Jane Nardal's thinking and, after studying Rimbaud, he also turned to the Surrealists for inspiration.

Between 1928 and June 1932 (the month Léro published the manifesto *Légitime Défense*) the economic crisis in the West gave substance to Surrealist criticisms of capitalist society. The disenchantment with the rational world had developed rapidly after 1914. In Senghor's words World War 1 'had marked for the most lucid Europeans, by its absurdity, as by its ruination – moral and material – a certain bankruptcy of Civilization'.[2] These men escaped into nonrational ideologies and labelled the nineteenth century 'absurd'.[3]

In June 1932 the black Surrealist Etienne Léro decided to publish a journal which would take up where the *Revue du Monde Noir* left off. In doing so he broke with the group to which Senghor belonged because he considered their position too moderate.[4] Together with two other West Indians he published a manifesto, *Légitime Défense*, the title for which came from a short book published by the French Surrealist André Breton in 1926. By the very act of issuing a manifesto as much as by the message contained within it, Léro showed himself to be a child of the times; for, as Jean Touchard noted in his 'Esprit des Années 1930', it was a 'time of Manifestoes'.[5] Publishing these protests was a Surrealist habit.

Léro's manifesto criticized non-Surrealist West Indian writing: 'A stranger vainly searches in this literature for an original or profound accent, the sensual imagination of the black man, the echo of the grudges or the aspirations of an oppressed people'.[6] Léro drew upon Surrealists for revolutionary inspiration. He also adapted their techniques and style.

From the Surrealist movement Léro borrowed automatic writing, a taste for the supernatural, and the use of dreams, hallucinations, and other visions. 'He was above all, defined by his reaction to Western civilization.'[7] He wrote that he was 'suffocated by this capitalist, Christian and bourgeois world' and that he declared war on that 'abominable system of constraint and restrictions, of extermination of love and limitation of dreams, generally known under the name of Western civilization'.[8] Léro here appropriated the ideas of many members of his intellectual generation. He too refused rationalism and its repercussions: capitalism and machinism. He too exalted intuition, but he expressed his hatred with much more violence than his white companions, for *he* really felt himself outside the civilization he criticized. After all, he was black. It is nevertheless a fact that white Surrealists were at the root of the rejection of the white world. Before Léro, these European revolutionaries hoped with 'all their force that revolutions, wars and colonial insurrections would come to annihilate Western civilization...'.[9] Léro joined a movement begun by Rimbaud and Lautréamont, and followed by the Surrealists André Breton, Apollinaire, Jarry, Reverdy, Philippe Soupault (who later became a friend of Senghor), Paul Eluard, Tristan Tzara, Aragon, and Salvador Dali.[10]

One of the first 'militants of *négritude*', Léon Damas, affirmed that it was to Léro and no one else that French colonial poetry owed its new blood and its chance for success. According to Damas, Léro was the first to break with the tradition of romantic verbalism, the theory of art for art's sake, the easy impassiveness of the Parnassians and the troubled desires of the Symbolists.[11] It would seem, especially if one has read the *Revue du Monde Noir*, that this interpretation is somewhat unbalanced: both Léon Damas, and his admirer Lilyane Kesteloot, appear to have underestimated the role of the *Revue* and overestimated the uniqueness of Léro.

It is nevertheless true that Léro's contribution was his attempt to bring about the mutual interpenetration of literature and politics.[12] In doing so, he moved away from the ideology of the *Revue du Monde Noir*. The *négritude* movement did not follow him in his political concern and rejected the Marxism to which he was 'addicted'.[13] *Négritude* did, however, inherit Surrealism from *Légitime Défense*.

Several years later Jean-Paul Sartre summarized Léro's role: 'Léro was the forerunner; he conceived the use of Surrealism as a "miraculous weapon"...'.[14] It is possible that Senghor intended paying homage to Léro when he entitled the important *Post-face* to his poems *Ethiopiques*: 'As the Lamentins go to drink at the Source'.[15] One of the first to make that pilgrimage was Léro, born in 1910 in Lamentin in the French West Indies.[16]

It was Césaire, more than Senghor, who was influenced by Léro's Surrealist message. Senghor himself wrote: 'When Jules Monnerot, Etienne Léro, and René Ménil tossed their manifesto *Légitime Défense* at the French West Indian bourgeoisie, Aimé Césaire, then a student at the Lycée Louis-le-Grand preparing to enter the *Ecole Normale Supérieure*, was the first to listen to and understand it'.[17]

For Senghor the Surrealist lesson reinforced the idea of using his dreams poetically and eventually led him back to the 'Childhood Kingdom' which he dreamt about. The Surrealist influence on Senghor, however, was less important than that of Barrès and the 'Spiritual thinkers' – Bergson, Claudel, Péguy, and Jacques Maritain. Surrealists had a limited influence on Senghor primarily because of his inability to accept their atheism.[18]

The Surrealists nevertheless resembled the 'Spiritual thinkers' on several points. Breton invited his contemporaries to seek out the final reality which abolishes all contradictions between logical thought and dreams, between the conscious and the unconscious, between the individual and the world which surrounds him. As a model he chose the wise men of the Orient who live in constant communication with the essence of things. The African sages whom Senghor had known in his childhood were no different.[19] It is for the Surrealists contribution to this rehabilitation of non-Western thought that Senghor has called them 'sharpshooters...infiltrated behind the enemy lines', who 'attacked the strongholds of logic with the miraculous weapons of Africa and Asia'.[20]

The renouncement of Western civilization, which led Léro to Surrealism and Marxism, did not have the same effect on Senghor. Throughout the 1930s Senghor remained a follower of Charles Péguy, an early twentieth-century Catholic liberal. He discovered in Péguy's writing 'a rhythm of the tom-tom which could not help but appeal to Negro sensitivity'.[1]

The French historian of ideas Jean Touchard has written that 'the two principal intercessors' of a large part of the French intellectual generation of the 1930s were Péguy and the utopian socialist Proudhon.[2] Senghor was drawn to their thinking and both men figure prominently in his personal Pantheon.

The 'perfect Thomist' Péguy wrote that Catholicism, if it is to be universal, must listen to the pagan and the Jew. It was his belief that by integrating non-Catholic thought, Catholics could renew their faith. The pagan Victor Hugo as well as the Jew Henri Bergson were necessary to Péguy's religion.[3] Péguy's search for renewal outside traditional Christianity encouraged Senghor to fuse African thought with Catholicism.

Péguy's thought often resembles that of the famous philosopher of the *élan vital*, Bergson. Péguy joined Bergson in affirming that the intelligence and the conscious are constantly mistaken, that they deceive, and that the final reality is an unknown force. Senghor also admired Bergson's thought which helped him rid himself of the narrow rationalism that had characterized his intellectual approach until the beginning of the 1930s.[4] 'Criticism of Rationalism became radical' wrote Senghor; French thinkers advocated 'the rehabilitation of intuitive reason and of the *collective soul*, of archetypal-images, which surged up from the abysmal depths of the heart, from the obscure regions of the groin and of the womb, finally the rehabilitation of primordial rhythms, in accordance with the very heart-beats of the cosmos'.[5] This new irrationalism in the West appealed to Senghor for it resembled the lessons of his uncle Toko' Waly.[6] Senghor has noted that the West 'adopted the vocabulary of ethnologists who had begun to decipher darkest Africa. Philosophers spoke, as did Africanists, of vital forces while scientists exposed the discontinuity and the indeterminate in the very heart of matter'.[7] The

French anthropologist Claude Lévi-Strauss stated much later that 'Bergson's philosophy irresistibly evokes that of the Sioux Indians'.[8]

In many ways Senghor's philosophy parallels Bergson's. According to Sartre, Bergson's philosophy is paradoxical in that it offers 'an anti-intellectual doctrine entirely built by the most reasoning and critical intelligence'. It is possible to see in the philosophical approach of the two thinkers 'the supreme defence of a persecuted man: an attack in order to defend onself, a conquering of the irrationalism of the adversary, that is to say an act which renders it harmless and absorbs it into constructive reason'. The irrationalism of Bergson (and Senghor) is 'perfectly harmless and can only serve universal reconciliation'.[9]

After re-discovering his Catholic faith in 1931, one year after he had lost it, Senghor tried to obtain the 'universal reconciliation' that Bergson pursued. This was also the preoccupation of Paul Claudel, the French Catholic poet. Claudel had rejected rationalism and positivism and wished to marry the natural and supernatural. He was most lyrical in those moments when 'he unites all that is divided, mixes all that is distant, as if he were a God beyond good and evil, the soul and the world – but also epochs greatly separated in time, places as distant as possible from one another, the most incomparable accents and styles'.[10] In his play *The Satin Slipper* written in 1929 he praised the God who is the conciliator rather than the divider; he accepted both the visible and the invisible with a 'catholic heart'.[11]

'I am a lighthouse between the two worlds; those that the abyss separates have only to regard me to find themselves brought together.'[12]

Claudel's *Satin Slipper* appealed to Senghor in yet another way. In this play all the Continents are represented; their differences complementing one another.

'The call of Africa. The earth wouldn't be what it is if it didn't have this fiery spot on its stomach, this gnawing cancer, this ray which devours its liver, this tripod stirred by the ocean's breath, this fuming cave, this furnace....'[13]

Two ideas observed in Senghor's philosophy developed out of his reading of Claudel. The idea of *con-naissance* (literally, 'to be born with') represents Claudel's reliance on intuitive knowledge or empathy for *understanding* things outside oneself. The other contribution of Claudel was his 'great chain of being'. Through this concept Claudel, and Senghor after him, expressed the belief that man, his ancestors and descendants, were links between God and nature. They provided the bond between the pebble in the road and the sky.[14] These two notions were also part of traditional African philosophy that Senghor had absorbed at the feet of his uncle Toko' Waly.

Senghor has placed Claudel next to Bergson and Péguy in the list of those who helped him to understand African folklore. Claudel was very close to the African *griot* and sage, because for him, as for them, 'sign and meaning are but two facets of a same Divine Essence', and this is 'one of the "canons" of Negro poetry'.[15] The French writer Jean Guéhenno has affirmed that 'Claudel's poems recall African *Dogon* cosmogonies'.[16] Senghor frankly confesses his debt to Claudel: '...I have read a lot, from the troubadours to Paul Claudel. And imitated a lot'.[17]

These various influences on Senghor's thought reinforced one another because they were mutually compatible and often parallel to one another. Claudel's and Bergson's approaches are surprisingly compatible: although a philosopher, Bergson was attracted by poetry. The poet Claudel on the other hand avidly studied philosophy. As for Péguy, an admirer of Bergson, Barrès and St Thomas Aquinas, he lived to unite within himself the most opposed instincts. The reconciliation of opposites, for which these thinkers were striving, made Senghor their disciple for the same reason that he had been drawn to Gide and Goethe.[18]

The influence of Claudel and Bergson on Senghor prevented him from being attracted to Surrealism and militant Marxism in contrast to Etienne Léro and the group behind *Légitime Défense*. The Surrealists whom Léro admired sent a famous letter of insults to Claudel. The Communists of the 1930s were fiercely anti-Bergsonian and ridiculed the 'sentimentalism' of the Jewish thinker. At the end of the 1920s the Marxist philosopher Georges Politzer published his *Bergsonisme, une Mystification Philosophique*. This party-line opposition to Bergson's thought strongly influenced Communist criticism of Senghor's *négritude* in the 1940s and 1950s.[19] Senghor's spirituality thus opposed the Marxists' materialism and the Surrealists' atheism. His attraction to the 'Spiritualist Thinkers' was preconditioned by his education with the Fathers of the Holy Spirit at Ngasobil, as well as by the legacy of his basic African religiosity.[20]

Senghor could not accept orthodox Marxism and therefore sought a religious foundation for building a new world. Péguy's *théologale* theory that civic values are based on religious values was his starting point. Péguy believed that the exclusive domain of the *théologale* was temporal. The earth is the place where we must found a human city that God can be proud of.[21]

This theory was seriously developed by the French Catholic intellectual Jacques Maritain, whom Senghor started reading in 1932.[22]

Maritain also tried to reconcile what seemed at first sight to be impossibly opposite. He showed Senghor a means for synthesizing Bergsonian (and African) irrationalism and Greek rationalism, intuitive and rational tendencies. Maritain advocated a mystical knowledge which, by faith and contemplation, transcended the rational.[23]

Maritain's neo-Thomism traced a 'third road' towards a new society which refused the philosophy of a discredited capitalism and which avoided the new gods of Marxism and Fascism. Senghor followed Maritain in opposing the 'Politics first' advocated by Charles Maurras and numerous members of their generation. Both Maritain and Senghor believed in the 'Primacy of the Spiritual'.[24] Péguy's rejection of politics was renewed here. Senghor also adopted Maritain's 'catholic' rejection of Maurras' *Nationalisme Intégral* after reading Maritain's *Humanisme Intégral* which was written to counter Maurras' ideas.[25]

Maritain advocated a society of believers reconstructed along communal lines. Senghor used this idea to rehabilitate African collectivism in his own philosophy. Although Senghor had recognized earlier the pre-eminence of the spiritual in African life, it was Maritain's 'Primacy of the Spiritual' that gave philosophic support to Senghor's position. Baye-Salzmann already had written in the *Revue du Monde Noir* that the essential characteristic of Negro life was religious fervour.[26] African religiosity, which had made its mark on Senghor indelibly, and the rationalism of his French education were thus reconciled by Maritain.

The influence of spiritual thought thus contributed to Senghor's repudiation of atheistic materialism. According to Senghor, a rejection of religion would lead to a denial of his African-ness. In the books he had read about Africa he had rediscovered that the African cannot separate the natural and the supernatural. The famous French Africanist Delafosse had written: 'No institution exists in black Africa, whether in the social or political domains, even in economic matters, that has not religion as its cornerstone'.[27] The sacred penetrates everything; it is the vital force which is the supreme value for the black man. The African is religious above all: for him life and religion are inseparable.[28] As the Christian Socialist Georges Le Brun Keiris has noted, 'The first dimension of Africa is metaphysical'.[29] Senghor therefore turned to Maritain and ignored Marx.

In 1930 Senghor lost his Catholic faith because he was 'profoundly struck by the gap existing between the doctrine and the life of Christians'.[30] Liberal Catholics such as Jacques Maritain and Emmanuel Mounier, who hoped to detach religion from its alliance with the 'established disorder', convinced Senghor of the goodwill of certain

Christians, however, and he returned to the Church one year after his crisis. But if he renewed his faith, he nevertheless maintained a critical loyalty towards Rome. This critical loyalty was the position of many French intellectuals. Senghor's anti-materialism was basic to his return to the Church. From this time on, Senghor, following Mounier, chose the left, but not the extreme left.[31]

The reaction of American Negroes to Western culture was similar to that of the French-speaking Blacks. American efforts at integration paralleled French attempts at assimilation, and neither quite made it. It was impossible for either the black American or the black Frenchman to suppress his African-ness. For example, the blending of African tradition and contemporary Western religion is characteristic of American Negro Spirituals with which Senghor became familiar during the 'Negro Revolution' of the twenties and thirties in Paris. With the group behind the *Revue du Monde Noir*, Senghor discovered that 'animism continues to well up in his soul', coming from 'the far reaches of time as a lively spring below the shadow of Eastern religions'.[1] In American Negro music he re-discovered the forgotten lesson of Joal where 'pagan voices' rhymed the Catholic Tantum Ergo.[2]

A passage written by W.E.B.Du Bois in 1903 [3] could easily have come from Senghor's hand:

'It is a peculiar sensation, this double consciousness, this sense of always looking at one's self through the eyes of others, of measuring one's soul by the tape of a world that looks on in amused contempt and pity. One ever feels his two-ness – an American, a Negro: two souls, two thoughts, two unreconciled strivings; two warring ideals in one dark body, whose dogged strength alone keeps it from being torn asunder.' [4]

The Negro American influence on Senghor reinforced his consciousness of dualism, previously encountered in Gide and Goethe. Senghor himself has written about the American Negro author, Countee Cullen:

'Cullen was from a bourgeois and very religious family...Remember too that he was a French teacher, having a solid classical culture, translating from time to time Greek tragedies. And here he is, torn between two traditions: the European, rather the American, and the African.' [5]

To fight cultural alienation American Negro writers in 1925 began a movement which they called the 'Negro Renaissance'. This 'Renaissance' was designed to rehabilitate the Negro's past as well as to re-establish pride in a dark skin. An Anthology-Manifesto of 1925 called *The New Negro* declared that the American Negro must 're-build his past to build his future'.[6] Alain Locke, a black Professor of Philosophy at Howard University, contributed to *The New Negro*. During the 1930s Locke was also a frequent visitor to Paulette Nardal's salon.[7] Senghor met with him there and at René Maran's house.

The *Néo-Nègre* or *Nègre-Nouveau* movement begun by Senghor, Césaire, and Léon Damas in 1934 borrowed its name from its American Negro predecessor. In fact, the word *négritude* only appeared in 1939.[8] *Néo-Nègre* or *Nègre-Nouveau* was used in place of *négritude* until that term gained popularity after Sartre had analysed it in 1948. However Senghor continued to use *Néo-Nègres* interchangeably with *Militants de la Négritude* after that time.[9]

Barrès had led the way, but it was the Negro poet and novelist from Jamaica, Claude MacKay, who finally swept away Senghor's complexes about African civilization. MacKay, a member of the New Negro movement in the 1920s, wrote in his novel *Banjo*: 'To plunge to the roots of our race and to build on our own foundations is not returning to a state of savagery', and concluded: 'it is culture itself'.[10] MacKay had helped the French West Indians behind the *Revue du Monde Noir* turn to African history and anthropology.[11] In America for many years the New Negroes had studied the history and characteristics of their race in order to rehabilitate it in the eyes of the world. For this reason Senghor has written that 'Claude MacKay can be considered...as the veritable inventor of *négritude*...not of the word...but of the values of *négritude*'.[12]

The ideas of American Negroes reinforced Barrès's influence, which itself was inspired by Mistral's return to Provençal culture. The Negro re-awakening thus extended the ideas of a provincial re-awakening advocated by Barrès and Mistral.

Senghor found many reasons for turning to American Negro writing for inspiration:

'It has been said and repeated that, as long as the Latin elements dominated, "the Frenchman did not have an epic spirit". This meant that for him intoxication was light; intelligence always controlled imagination and instinct. The American Negro has an epic spirit...As in the Spirituals [there is] no dogma, but rather an absorbed mysticism, a communion with the heroic, with the divine.'[13]

American Negro literature had an accent which 'pierced him right to his intestines'. Senghor found that Negro culture whether in the Americas or in Africa had a common heritage: 'In its diversity, it remained one, characterized in literary and artistic works by the constant, almost obsessive, use of rhythmic images to translate the vital forces which animate the world'.[14] American Negro literature in which nature is 'animated by a human presence' proved to Senghor that this literature had preserved 'the most profound, the eternal trait of the Negro soul'. In 1939 he used this belief to affirm that the Negro quality 'has resisted all attempts at economic slavery and "moral liberation" '.[15]

This discovery helped greatly in the elaboration of his cultural theories. He used this literature to demonstrate the differences between the Negro soul and the white soul.[16] For Senghor it is soul which 'explains Negro religion and society'.[17] The mystical belief that soul was the mainspring of civilizations is an expression of Senghor's 'spiritual determinism' which rejected economic determinism. For Senghor society and religion are determined by the innate qualities of a people rather than by their mode of production.

Césaire also studied the writings of the New Negroes and wrote his *Diplôme d'Etudes Supérieures* on 'The Theme of the South in American Negro Literature'.[18] Paulette Nardal who advocated the study of Negro topics by Parisian black students had been listened to.

The experience of American Negroes served as a model for Blacks from French Colonies. The Senegalese historian Abdoulaye Ly, who frequently saw Senghor during the latter's stay in Paris, has affirmed that, from 1931 on, Senghor only saw the African personality through a transposition of what he knew about American Negroes. In 1947 Senghor's adversaries accused him of confusing American Negroes and Africans: 'Thus Monsieur Senghor...use your energies in more constructive and more disinterested domains. [In doing so] perhaps and doubtlessly you will attain one day the height of those giant American Negroes whom you bear so much affection'.[19] Certain of Senghor's writings seem to justify this criticism: 'What the Negro contributes is the faculty of perceiving the supernatural in the natural, the transcendental sense and the active abandon which accompanies it, the abandon of love. It is as living an element in his ethnic personality as animism. *The study of the American Negro furnishes proof* of it'.[20] Because he was so captivated by American Negroes, he followed them along the path which led towards the rejection of cultural *assimilation* but which simultaneously advocated political integration. He hardly departed from this path until 1958.[21]

A begrudging admiration for Western civilization is very important in American Negro literature and rapidly became one of the themes of the *Revue du Monde Noir*,[22] but it was reworked and elaborated above all by Senghor.[23] In his poem, 'America', Claude

MacKay expressed a black man's awe of material power despite the hardship which it caused him:

> Although she feeds me bread of bitterness,
> And sinks into my throat her tiger's tooth,
> Stealing my breath of life, I will confess
> I love this cultured hell that tests my youth!
> Her vigour flows like tides into my blood,
> Giving me strength against her hate.
> Her greatness sweeps my being like a flood
> Yet as a rebel fronts a king in state,
> I stand within her walls with not a shred
> Of terror, malice, not a word of jeer... [24]

In 1937 Senghor described this Negro spirit of forgiving: 'To those who destroyed his civilization, to the slave trader, to the lyncher, Afro-American poets only respond by peaceful words...This "humanity" of the Negro soul, this incapacity of hating permanently helped resolve the racial problem in Latin America, even in North America'.[25] This fundamental Christian 'turning the other cheek' was characteristic not only of the religious poets such as MacKay, but of 'the "radical" poets too, that is to say the communist poets, who suddenly show their religious sentiment which gushes high from the depths their *négritude*'.[26] Senghor has affirmed that he is incapable of permanently hating anyone; his associates claim that he pardons too much and too quickly.[27]

The lack of rancour, the 'reaction against the reaction' which characterized Senghor's attitude (he was incapable of hating France) developed at the moment of the *Front Populaire* in liaison with his theme of begrudging admiration of France.[28] But from the beginning of the 1930s there appeared positive elements which allowed the construction of a solid theory. Mysticism, the division between two civilizations, the necessity of racial rehabilitation, the absence of hate, the search for cultural uniqueness, the marriage between African traditionalism and modern religion – all these themes of American Negro literature of the 1920s and 1930s re-appeared in Senghor's thought as they did in the *Revue du Monde Noir*.

The Negroes of the United States also awakened Senghor and Paulette Nardal to the unique role of the 'Aframerican' in a cold industrial world: 'The Negro in a milieu tyrannized by mechanization and standardization has preserved his profound sensitivity, his fantasy, his *élan vital* which make him the true and only poetry in American life'.[29] In 1939 Senghor quoted Paul Morand who had written that the Negroes 'break the mechanical rhythm of America, and one

should be grateful to them; one had forgotten that men could live
without bank accounts and bathtubs'.[30] The mysticism and spiritualism of Negroes joined the anti-materialism and anti-mechanism that
Senghor shared with French intellectuals. These attitudes dominated
Senghor's cultural, political and socio-economic thought.[31]

The distrust of mechanization and standardization characteristic
of the 1920s is closely linked to Langston Hughes's and Claude
MacKay's anti-capitalism. It is but one step from anti-materialism to
anti-capitalism. MacKay:

Darkly I gaze into the days ahead
And see her might and granite wonders there,
Beneath the touch of Time's unerring hand,
Like priceless treasures sinking in the sand

Hughes:

I am building a road,
......
Building a road so that old rich whites can ride
in their big cars
......
Rich folks ride.[32]

The Afro-American poets, affirms Senghor, 'have a completely romantic idea of Africa: it is a refuge from the ugliness and inhumanity
of the American world; it is a bath of primitive life cleaning away the
sophistication of white culture'. Senghor describes the Africa of
Hughes: 'Africa is a land of innocence, a sort of earthly paradise before original sin'.[33] This idealization of Africa was absorbed by
Senghor in the 1930s; he envisioned Africa in the same way as those
Negroes who had never set foot on the Dark Continent. When he
wrote of Africa, it was a distant, abstract, strongly idealized continent. This romantic image has remained so fundamental to him
that he confesses he cannot write poems about Africa while he is
there.[34] For the African Senghor, as for the West Indian Etienne
Léro, translations of Afro-American poetry read in the communist
review *Nouvel Age* of October 1931, and in the *Revue du Monde Noir*
starting in November 1931, convey 'the African love of life, the
African joy of love, the African dream of death'.[35] The winds from
black America[36] carried Africa to France.

Senghor was also attracted by the racial rehabilitation contained in
American Negro poets' 'particular cult of the Negro woman, made of
respect and love, of desire and adoration; for the Negro woman is
the perfect symbol of the race – the woman being more sensitive to

the mysterious currents of life and the cosmos, more humanly permeable to joy and pain...For the black woman is a symbol. This is why, as in Africa, poets try to convey all aspects of her physical beauty, and below that surface, her spiritual riches'.[37] This Afro-American attitude inspired Senghor to write his famous 'Black Woman':

> Naked woman, black woman, dressed in your colour which is life, in your form which is beauty![38]

The Afro-American writers were conscious of their difference but refused the notion of inferiority.[39] In his 'I, Too' published by the *Revue du Monde Noir* in January 1932 and quoted by Senghor, Langston Hughes expressed black pride:

> I too sing America
> I am the black brother
>   ......
> Tomorrow
> I will sit at the table
>   when company comes.
> No one then
>   will dare tell me
> 'Go eat in the kitchen'
> Besides
> They will see how handsome I am.[40]

Afro-Americans gave Senghor reasons for pride in his black people. The *Revue du Monde Noir* had published Marc Logé's praise of Negro literature.[41] In 1931 the *Revue* proudly affirmed:

> '...in music American Negroes have acquired since the War a place which one can call pre-eminent; for they have impressed the entire world with their vibrating or melancholy rhythms.'[42]

The fact that American Negroes exerted such a strong influence on Senghor seems to carry out the predictions of the 'Theses on the Negro Question' which had been adopted in 1922 by the Fourth Congress of the Communist International. The communists held that American Negroes were the *avant-garde* of the black race, that they were the leaders, and that the Communist International, by establishing its influence over them, could indirectly influence all Negro peoples. 'History', according to the 'Theses', 'has devolved on American Negroes an important role in the liberation of the entire African race'. It continued: 'For 250 years, they have worked under the American proprietor's whip: they cut the forests, constructed the roads, planted the cotton, placed the railroad ties and sustained the southern aristocracy..."Free" Negro muscles, blood and tears helped establish American Capitalism...American Negroes, and above all, North American Negroes [are] at the *avant-garde* of the African struggle against oppression...The Negro movement should be organized in America, as the centre of Negro culture and the centre of the crystallization of Negro protests'.[43]

Having initiated a move to the study of anthropology, American Negroes were once again the precursors of a theme developed in the *Revue du Monde Noir*. Senghor later paid tribute to the pioneering efforts of Afro-Americans:

'However great their inferiority complex, precisely because they suffered from it, Negro intellectuals were interested in everything that touched on the racial question; it is marvellous how educated American Negroes are aware, often much more than we Africans, of the most recent work of Africanists. They were thus brought to revise their ideas on the question and to establish a new scale of values. This is the origin of the New Negro movement.'[1]

However, American Negroes were not the only group preoccupied with anthropology. In 1928, the Haitian, Price-Mars, published an essay which exerted an enormous influence on other Parisian Blacks behind the *Revue du Monde Noir*. This essay, *Ainsi Parla l'Oncle* (Thus Spake the Uncle), was a revelation to Senghor. 'And I swallowed it "in one gulp" like water from the well, at night, after a long trip across the desert.'[2] Price-Mars invited Haitians (and the Parisian Negroes who read his book[3]) to repudiate 'nothing of their ancestral heritage'[4] and never to forget that they were first of all Africans.[5] He criticized the Negroes who had uncritically accepted the expression: 'our ancestors, the Gauls'[6] which frequently appeared in the French textbooks used in Haiti and in the colonies, and which children were expected to memorize. His ambition was 'to raise the status of their folklore in the eyes of Haitians'. He condemned the 'scarcely hidden embarrassment, or even shame' that Haitians felt when their distant past was mentioned. This situation was the result of 'those who for four centuries have been the artisans of black servitude because they had at their disposal force and science'. The white man had 'magnified his adventure by making up the story that Negroes were humanity's rubbish, devoid of history, morality, or religion, whom it was necessary to fill with new moral values by any means whatsoever'. The Haitian intellectuals who swallowed this rationalization 'strove' to achieve what they considered a 'superior destiny' by modelling their thoughts and their feelings on those of France, and by 'identifying themselves with France'. But, continued

Price-Mars, 'by an implacable logic, the more we try to believe our-selves "coloured Frenchmen", the more we forget to be Haitians. We are men, born in certain historical conditions, who have stored up in their soul, as have all other human groups, a complex of psy-chological elements which gives to the Haitian community its spe-cific physiognomy'. Price-Mars went so far as to rehabilitate the word *nègre*, 'formerly a neutral term' which had acquired 'a pejorative sense'. The idea of using the term *négritude* may well be traced to this statement.

Certain Haitians, according to Price-Mars, would rather be mis-taken for 'Eskimos, Samoyeds, or Toungouzes than remember their Guinean or Sudanese origin'. Price-Mars attacked their litera-ture, labelling it 'a collective Bovaryism', because it showed a desire to imitate and 'to adopt a borrowed soul' in the manner of *Madame Bovary*. Attacking a Haitian writer of the nineteenth century, Price-Mars noted that he included nothing in his literature 'which might recall, even distantly', that it was written by a Haitian pen. This criti-cism continued: 'M. Delorme has sacrificed to one of the most stupid among the banal prejudices which throttle Haitian activity; namely, that our society, in the past as well as in the present, offers no in-terest to the art of the novelist'.[7] These lines are at the source of Etienne Léro's criticism of the French West Indian bourgeoisie. They also influenced the writers of the *Revue du Monde Noir*, and, in consequence, Senghor himself.

But Price-Mars also believed that a study of Negro folklore would serve humanity in general: '…the problems which influence the be-haviour of a group of men' could not be a matter of indifference to the rest of humanity. Price-Mars saw value in ethnographic research: it 'is not useless to gather the facts of our social life, to note the do-ings, the attitudes of our people, however humble it may be, to compare them to those of other peoples, to scrutinize their origins and situate them in the general life of man on the planet'. He begged his compatriots to accept their ancestral patrimony in total: 'Look at it from all sides, weigh it, examine it intelligently and circumspectly, and you will see, as in a broken mirror, that it reflects the whole of humanity'. Gide's dictum, 'cultivate your difference', found a black echo in Price-Mars's thought.

Price-Mars began by describing the African marriage ceremony and other religious practices. In his opinion this type of study should have the effect of 'compiling the immortal acts from which the race could regain the intimate sense of its genius and the cer-tainty of its indestructible vitality'.[8]

Price-Mars's essay posed a critical question about the 'collective soul of the people': 'Who has ever contested the existence of Swiss, Belgian, or Canadian literature in French? What has ever hindered the English language from expressing the state of American Negroes …and why therefore would language be an obstacle to Haitians bringing to the world a notion of art, an expression of their spirit, which might be at one and the same time very human and very Haitian?'[9] This question was discussed by the French West Indians of Paris from 1928 onwards. The search for their own culture characteristics as a means for enriching universal culture attracted the attention of all Parisian Negro writers of the 1930s.

But Price-Mars's book had another meaning for Senghor. Its title, *Ainsi Parla l'Oncle*, stressed Price-Mars's desire to transcribe the stories, legends, and 'wisdom of Uncle Bouqui who rocked the cradle of our childhood'. A photograph of the white bearded uncle was included in the book.[10] In reading the lines devoted to Uncle Bouqui Senghor probably thought of his own Uncle Toko' Waly who spent long evenings initiating the young *Serer* to his ancestors' wisdom.

According to Price-Mars, folklore, voodoo religion, and native languages should serve as the basis for Haitian literature. The *Revue du Monde Noir* took up his plea. In his article on Price-Mars, Guy Zuccarelli noted in 1932:

'A people that has lived gloriously can hope for a re-awakening. No matter how profound her sleep has been, all she needs to do is bestir herself, to consider seriously her existence and the splendid part she can play upon this planet… As long as the Haitian intelligentsia owes its education to foreigners, her people will necessarily undergo the mental slavery imposed by certain processes of thinking. To me, this slavery is, and ought to be for you, more hateful than that which would be imposed by a blind and brutally overwhelming force… Why not use our talents to enrich the human heritage?'[11]

In his desire to rehabilitate his race and culture, Price-Mars's interest spread beyond Haiti. He wanted to put the spotlight on pre-colonial Africa and based his studies on the work of the French Africanist Delafosse and on Félix Dubois who, in 1898, had written *Tombouctou la Mystérieuse* which dealt with pre-colonial African empires.[12]

Price-Mars wished to be a modern *griot*, recalling the splendour and the widespread influence of these empires. He emphasized the distinctive contribution of Negro culture to world civilization. He laboured to popularize the originality of Africa, a fact too long left obscure.[13] Deeply impressed by Price-Mars, Senghor returned to the 'school of *griots* and sorcerers'. 'To the rhythms of the tom-tom', he wrote, 'we abandoned ourselves to Voodoo trances and lamented our suffering by the voice of the jazz trumpet, at first furious, then nostalgic'.[14]

Ainsi Parla l'Oncle was only a first step towards anthropology. Senghor deepened his understanding of the subject by reading Delafosse. Several long excerpts from the French Africanist's writings were published by the *Revue du Monde Noir* in December 1931. These passages showed Senghor a way of rehabilitating the Negro past. They had a profound effect on the 'black-skinned Frenchman'.[15] Professor Delafosse, a former Colonial Governor in West Africa, wrote:

'The Negroes of Africa present a spectacle, unmatched the world over, of a race forced to rely wholly upon itself for development, having received nothing from the outside world. They have been the object of as many, if not more, thrusts in the direction of retrogression than in the direction of progress. Would we have done better than they if we found ourselves in the same circumstances? When peoples placed in such conditions have been able, depending only on their own resources, to organize states; to establish and maintain study centres such as, for example, Timbuktu; to produce statesmen like the *Mansa* Gongo-Moussa or the *Askia* Mohammed, conquerors like Usman dan Fodio or El Hadj Omar, scientists and writers who, without the aid of dictionaries or of recourse to any translation, have succeeded in mastering Arabic to the point of reading it fluently and writing it correctly; in forming expressions whose elasticity, wealth and accuracy have astounded all who study them, expressions which might, by the simple and natural working of their morphological laws, without foreign interpolations, furnish the necessary instrument to those who use them; in inventing...as did a hundred years ago the Vais of the *Côte des Graines*, and more recently the Bamoum of Cameroun, a system of writing which is likely to endure – it must be admitted that these peoples do not deserve to be treated as inferiors from the intellectual point of view.'

The *Revue du Monde Noir* reviewed Delafosse's effort to discover African accomplishments:

'Professor M. Delafosse, to whom we must always refer whenever the intellectual and artistic manifestations of the so-called savages of Africa are in question, says: "It is impossible to ignore that the Negroes of Africa are remarkably gifted for the arts. Their innate musical talent, the instruments which they have known how to create, or which they play with surprising skill, their chants and their poetic impromptus, the fineness of the jewellery and the pottery which they fashion, and of certain of their wood and ivory carvings, the design and colouring of their mats, cloths, the sureness of their gift for decoration – these are the indisputable proofs of artistic faculties which will give in the future greater and better results than they have been able to produce up to now".'

The review concluded: 'It can no longer be questioned that, since the war, Negroes have acquired a very important place in all artistic circles, particularly in music. They have impressed the whole world with their tunes, their peculiar rhythms, lively or sad as the case may be'.[16]

In 1939, Senghor called Delafosse 'the greatest of French Africanists – I mean the most attentive'.[17] Delafosse invited Senghor and the other black men to create works of art that could equal the heritage that ethnographers had discovered in Africa. Delafosse also rejected racism: 'We suppose', Delafosse wrote disapprovingly in 1927, 'that our race is the prototype of civilization... We are willing to accord the Negro race a pseudo-equality with our own, providing that it is placed on our children's level... that is, in kinder but no less absolute terms, to proclaim again that inferiority of coloured races, upheld, with more tenacity if not with more logic and in any case with less hypocrisy, by Gobineau and his disciples'.[18] Delafosse supported those Negroes seeking justification for their battle to upgrade the race.

Delafosse was but one of several men who took an interest in understanding what he termed the Negro soul. Lucien Lévy-Bruhl in his *Mentalité Primitive* had underlined the difference between the 'primitive' and the European mentalities. The concept of a unique Negro soul gave Senghor an argument with which he could refute the French policy of cultural assimilation. The French ethnocentric definition of civilization would have to be stretched if black men were to find a place in it.

The German anthropologist Frobenius also developed an idea of a Negro soul. In March 1932 the *Revue du Monde Noir* published a passage from one of Frobenius' books which alerted Senghor to this Africanist's work. Senghor was attracted by Frobenius's anti-rationalism:

'By an audacious act, Leo Frobenius, from the very beginning, broke with the old school of vigorous rationalism... In his work there dominates the spirit of organic life which requires a special mode of observation: intuition.'[19]

The power of this attraction was explained by Senghor:

'In this adventurous search for the Holy Grail – *Négritude*, we made allies of all those in whom we found an affinity... We let ourselves be seduced by Leo Frobenius's brilliant thesis according

to which the Negro soul and the German soul were sisters. Were
not they daughters of Ethiopian civilization which signified "sur-
rendering to a childlike spirit", gifted with emotion, a sense of
reality, while Hamitic civilization, to which Western rationalism
was related, meant desire to dominate, gifted with invention and a
sense for facts? Leo Frobenius had enlisted us in a new *Sturm und
Drang*....' [20]

Senghor read Frobenius' *Histoire de la Civilisation Africaine* in 1936
when the translation appeared. By its very title the book refuted
the 'colonialist' notion that Africans had neither history nor civilization.

The ideas of Frobenius are the development of certain attitudes
found in nineteenth-century European thought. Henri Heine had
stressed in the middle of the nineteenth century that the earth belonged to the Russians and the French, that the sea belonged to the
British, but that the Germans held unchallenged sovereignty over
the cloudy realm of dreams. Mme de Stael had also discussed the
contrast between the soul of Germany and the intelligence of France
in her *De l'Allemagne* and had believed in the complementary nature
of the two countries. Mme de Stael wrote: 'Intellectual Germany is
hardly known in France...It can be true that a literature does not
conform to our rules of what is in good taste, yet it can contain new
ideas which can enrich us *if we modify them in our own fashion*...The
sterility which menaces our literature makes one believe that the
French spirit itself needs *to be renewed by a more vigorous sap*...Why
don't Frenchmen render justice to German letters?' [21] This appeal
strangely resembles Senghor's plea for the recognition of African
culture and its potential contribution to Western culture.

The need for combining elements of both cultures was brought
home to Senghor by a comment made during World War II by a
Sengalese rifleman Dargui N'Diaye who remarked: 'They have more
intelligence than we; we have more soul than they'. [22] It was, however, Frobenius who proposed a means for synthesis in his 'conciliating agreement' between Hamitic and Ethiopian civilizations.
This accord foreshadowed Senghor's theory of cultural cross-
breeding, which would assimilate European civilization into a new
African humanism.

Frobenius's romantic, sweeping, and prophetic style easily attracted Senghor. Frobenius had written: '...Negro slave trade was
never a calm matter; it needed justification: thus the Negro was
made a half-beast, a piece of merchandise... The idea of the "barbarous Negro" is a European invention...'. [23] However, Frobenius
was not satisfied with affirming this fact and he actively sought to

discover proof of refined civilizations among Africans. At the end of his search he stated:

'The Western Sudan also has a marvellous native civilization. It is a fact that explorers encountered in Equatorial Africa nothing but ancient civilizations, vigorous and fresh, wherever the preponderance of Arabs, of Hamitic blood, or of European civilization had not removed the bloom from the once beautiful wings of the black moth. Everywhere!...I do not know of any Northern people who can be compared to these primitives in unity of civilization.' [24]

This affirmation invalidated the colonial rationalization that the cultural vacuum of pre-colonial Africa had to be filled by European civilization. The political and cultural dependence of Africa had been justified on this basis. It was believed that African Negroes had not 'invented anything, created anything, written anything or sculpted, or painted, or sung. Dancers, perhaps. And even there one could doubt...'. [25]

The black intellectuals replied to these prejudices in poetry:

Those who invented neither gunpowder nor compass
Those who never knew how to master steam or electricity
Those who explored neither sea nor sky
......
Eia for those who never invented anything [26]
And the voice states that for centuries Europe has stuffed us
    with lies and bloated us with disease,
for it is not true that man's work is finished
That we have nothing to do for the world
......
And no race possesses the monopoly of beauty, intelligence,
    strength
And there is room for all at the rendezvous of conquest...[27]

In his search for arguments against the notion of racial inferiority, Senghor curiously turned to Gobineau's *Essay on the Inequality of Human Races*. The fact that Gobineau's *Essay* was used by the Nazis in their racial theories did not deter Senghor. Senghor adopted Gobineau's phrase 'emotion is Negro, while reason is Hellenic'.[28] Gobineau, quoted by Senghor, had written that '...the Negro is the human being most energetically involved by artistic emotion'. He also stated that artistic genius only developed when Whites cross-bred with Negroes.[29] Senghor also found support in the German Count von Keyserling who wrote of the 'stormy vitality' and the 'great emotional warmth of Negro blood'.[30]

Senghor found another aspect of the Negro soul in reading the works of Lucien Lévy-Bruhl. Senghor contrasted Negro reason 'which is intuitive through participation' and analytical European reason. This analysis drew heavily upon Lévy-Bruhl's *La Mentalité Primitive*: 'The primitive mentality is governed by the *law of participation*, and as such, is indifferent to the logical law of contradiction...For the primitive mentality...the visible and invisible world are but one'.[31] Lévy-Bruhl thus recalls the childhood universe Senghor lived in with his uncle Toko' Waly.[32]

Another Africanist, Robert Delavignette, also helped Senghor rehabilitate his civilization. Senghor wrote that Delavignette, a French Colonial official, 'greatly helped him in discovering the virtues of intellectual cross-breeding'.[33] Delavignette's *Soudan-Paris-Bourgogne*, published in 1935, was highly regarded by the Africans in Paris. It was even placed by Ousmane Socé Diop (future Senegalese Ambassador to the United States) in the library of his African intellectual in the novel *Mirages de Paris* published in 1937.[34] Senghor dedicated a 1944 essay to Delavignette, 'this Imperial Humanist'[35] who became his friend. Robert Delavignette advanced the belief that it was possible 'to taste the sweetness of being different yet together'.[36] In 1935 Delavignette proposed that the work of Africanists be used to create a 'new Humanism'.[37] The new order proposed by Delavignette was a two-way affair:

'Use the Sudan to remake society in France. Africa, the Saviour of Europe! Yes, if she leads you to reform France...The 20,000 Sudanese students of my time will soon be 200,000. They will put themselves to the study of their Sudan. They will restore it by its own values while at the same time renewing it by associating it with France.'[38]

According to Delavignette, Africa would contribute its humanism to Europe while Europe would help Africa modernize itself. This idea has been central to Senghor's thinking since the 1930s. Initially Senghor had believed that the civilizations of Africa and Europe were incompatible. He later substituted 'complementary' for 'incompatible' in his theories.

Delavignette wrote of a 'new West', 'a new World' which would be the result of the mixing of civilizations.[39] His idea was similar to Paul Valéry's reflections on the mixture of cultures. Senghor has quoted Valéry's 1937 declaration: 'Because of the different bloods which went into its making...the French nation makes one think of a tree which has been grafted several times. The quality and the taste of its fruit result from a happy alliance of differing saps and juices...'.[40]

Senghor also attributed an important role in African rehabilitation to the French colonial official, Georges Hardy: 'Monsieur Georges Hardy renewed the classical expression *Africa Portentosa*. This is the place to say that M. Hardy was at the source of the *Néo-Nègre* movement. He was important because of his writings but, above all, because of his activities while Director of the Department of Education for French West Africa. He presided at the birth of the William Ponty Teachers' College, giving it an African spirit. In this way he prepared the teachers to undertake respectful and scientific research on African values'.[41] The anthropological work of Hardy and many other French Africanists thus contributed to the deepening of Senghor's knowledge of his native land.

The return to African values by the future militants of *négritude* was aided significantly by the study of European works devoted to exotic civilizations. Elaborating a 'theory' out of what was at first but a vague refusal of Western civilization, the black students in Paris proceeded by stages. They first noted the weaknesses of modern Europe. They proceeded to establish the positive value of 'primitive' civilization. Consequently they turned to the study of anthropological writing. According to Césaire, '*Négritude* was at first the discovery of Africa by Africans'.[42] Senghor added another element: '... following ethnologists we rediscovered *négritude*, that is to say the cultural values of African Negro civilization : the quality of emotion and of empathy, the quality of rhythm and form, the quality of imagery and myth, communal spirit and democracy'.[43]

The black intellectuals felt it necessary to 'draw up the inventory of the values of Negro culture, to show its historical and living character'. They insisted on the idea of a living culture, for numerous ethnologists had tended to present 'African societies as static, closed, and definitely arrested in their development'.[44] Despite their criticism of certain ethnologists, Senghor and Césaire appreciated the contribution of ethnology through which 'Europe had discovered that we had art, music, language, and thought – in short a culture – and that we were not merely superior apes'.[45] Senghor continued this testimonial in a very striking text written many years later:

'...a few... African students had awakened along with other young people from the French West Indies, as stripped, nude and black as they. They had for years repeated "our ancestors the Gauls" and had declined the Latin word *rosa* sitting beside their rosy-eared classmates. And now they were criticized, and they were told that they had no patrimony, that they would only be able to build, like children on the beach, sand castles and imitation houses. But suddenly the West's foundations were shaken, vigorous thinkers battled Reason...Since the end of the nineteenth century...

orientalists and ethnologists...had stored in museums and lib-
raries (the proof of Negro culture). They were our masters who
saved us from despair by revealing to us our own riches. But no,
our real masters, we went to seek them out in the heart of Africa...
We marched, equipped with the miraculous weapons of double
vision, piercing blind walls, discovering, re-creating the marvels
of the Childhood Kingdom. We were reborn to *négritude*.'[46]
Senghor has remained thankful to these Africanists. As a young
Député at the French National Assembly in 1947, Senghor tried to
convince his colleagues that Negroes were not inferior: 'After run-
ning out of arguments our adversaries use the words "primitive" or
"barbarous". They attempt to dredge up old notions that ethnologists and linguists destroyed long ago'.[47]

The Africanists also helped to destroy certain prejudices that these
Parisian Negroes had about their own civilization. Frobenius and
Delafosse refuted notions about black men that Senghor had come to
believe, thus ridding him of his *own* opinion of Africa, an opinion derived from the contrast between African poverty and French grandeur. It could even be said that the contribution of anthropologists
was as important in destroying the black man's own prejudices
(which were not always the result of European disdain or criticism)
as they were in countering European criticism of African civilization.

After his initial encounter with the writings of anthropologists,
Senghor enrolled at the *Institut d'Ethnologie* and at the *Ecole Pratique
des Hautes Etudes* of the University of Paris where he took formal
course work in anthropology. One of his professors was the famous
French Africanist Marcel Griaule. Much later Senghor spoke of his
teacher: '...the ardent figure of Marcel Griaule. Was it not you, old
Sorbonne, maternal Sorbonne, who created for him, on the saintly
hill, a chair of Negro-African ethnology? As for me, I rejoiced in
that decision as if it were a revolution in the French *esprit*...Faithful
to your mission, you invited *négritude* to the universal banquet'.[48]
Senghor had written of Griaule: 'He doesn't fail to destroy misconceptions, and solid ones at that: the stagnation of African Negroes,
their incapacity to build cities, etc.'; and he quoted from Griaule's
book which tried to sweep away some of the misconceptions about
pre-colonial Africa: 'Brutes do not build towns; savages could not
live together in groups of several thousand, as did these people, with
their police, their public services, their army, and their doors open
to their friends'.[49]

During this same period Senghor read the works of the German
anthropologist Diedrich Westermann, notably his *Noirs et Blancs en
Afrique* which was translated into French in 1937.[50] He also read the

books of the American anthropologist Melville Herskovits. He devoured with 'intellectual gluttony' all that did justice to African civilization.[51] He remained grateful to Paris for those fruitful years of study:

'In opening me to others, France the mother country opened me to self-knowledge. Even if Paris is not the greatest museum of Negro African art, nowhere else has Negro art been understood, commented on, exalted, absorbed to such an extent. Really...in revealing to me the values of my ancestral civilization, Paris obliged me to receive them and to make them bear fruit within me. Not only me, but an entire generation of Negro students, French West Indians and, as me, Africans.'[52]

Senghor has paid tribute to those professors who encouraged him to leave behind his study of Latin and to forget his 'ancestors the Gauls'. These same professors 'inspired him to return to (his) African experiences, to study them and to organize them', enlightened by their spirit, equipped with their analytical instruments.[53] Well before the publication of Claude Lévi-Strauss' *Pensée Sauvage*, Senghor had discovered that the long-separated paths of 'concrete "savage" thought and abstract cultivated thought could be brought together'.[54] His European humanistic background and his basic African background found a meeting place in anthropology.

Since the 'enormous iniquities' that were committed against Africans were the result of an ignorance of their history and thought,[55] the Parisian black intellectuals had to search everywhere to recover that history and that thought.[56] It was thus natural for the militants of *négritude* to turn to the Africanists who had long since begun this work of rehabilitation.

These same anthropologists were influenced by anti-Western thought of the 1920s and 1930s. Deceived and bitter, a number of European intellectuals had for more than fifty years taken upon themselves to 'deny the diverse ideals of their own culture'.[57] Participating in this intellectual abandonment of the West, many Africanists felt the need to discover other worlds. The same influences which directly affected Senghor's disillusionment with Western ideals were also transmitted to him indirectly through Africanists. Since they were affected by the intellectual climate of the 1920s and 1930s, these anthropological writings had a concentrated effect on Senghor.

However, the mission of the militants of *négritude* did not stop with the rehabilitation of African civilizations. It was necessary to produce literary works, astonish the world, and offer an 'unheard of message'.

Senghor's 'return to the source' occurred between 1929 and 1933, the period when Nazi racism grew and appeared to be victorious. For many reasons, *négritude* was influenced by certain attitudes predominant in the Nazi ideology. The primary reason for this influence lay in a common ancestry – both *négritude* and Nazism were part of an anti-rational intellectual tradition.

The 'mission' of the militants of *négritude* strongly resembled the messianic character of the German movement, particularly in its early stages. Senghor noted this messianism and qualified it as 'racism':

> 'Our distrust of European values quickly turned into disdain – why hide it – into racism. We thought – and we said – that we Negroes were the salt of the earth, that we were the bearers of an unheard of message – and that no other race could offer it but us. Unconsciously, by osmosis and reaction at the same time, we spoke like Hitler and the Colonialists, we advocated the virtues of the blood.'[1]

Négritude also relied on ethnology to support a racial doctrine of superiority. Senghor explained this strange liaison of social science and racism:

> 'Relying on the work of anthropologists, prehistorians, ethnologists – paradoxically white – we proclaimed ourselves, along with Aimé Césaire, the "Eldest sons of the Earth". Did we not dominate the world, up to and including the neolithic period, fertilize the civilizations of the Nile and of the Euphrates before they became the innocent victims of white barbarians, nomads melting out of their Eurasian plateaux? I confess it, our pride turned quickly into racism. Even Nazism was accepted to reinforce our refusal to co-operate... We then had the sincerity of youth and passion.'[2]

Although he abandoned racism by 1935, racial pride has remained characteristic of Senghor: 'In the hours of grave difficulties, in the hours of discouragement and doubt, we only have to think of Pharaonic Egypt to convince ourselves that Africa played a primordial role in the elaboration of civilization'.[3] And again: 'Africa, cradle of the Negro, indeed of *Homo Sapiens*'.[4]

Senghor has stressed that Egypt was inhabited by Negroes at the moment of its greatest splendour: '...a third were Mediterranean whites and about a third were Negroid, a third were half-bloods'. But he does not confine himself to Africa: 'Similarly...India was built on a Dravidian foundation, basically black, over which an Aryan superstructure was laid'. He notes that in these two civilizations, 'Negroes brought the sense of rhythm, the sense of colour, the sense of joy, they brought the artistic sense', while the 'whites brought the methodical spirit, the spirit of organization'.[5] He has written that 'one can write page after page, dismissing the notion of race, but that does not prevent it from being a reality'.[6]

Senghor absorbed some of Hitler's *blut und boden* (blood and soil) which complemented Barrès's ideas on the importance of race: 'To the platitude of their reason we opposed the trunks of our forests; to the smiling wisdom of their "pale rosy-eared God" we opposed the bush-fire of our head, above all the incoercible *élan* of our blood in our breasts', 'the tornadoes of blood'.[7] In 1936 Senghor wrote: 'Let the protecting spirits ensure that my blood does not fade like that of an *assimilé*, like that of a civilized man'.[8]

Senghor's anti-Western reaction lasted only a short while. During this period, 1930–1, he became disillusioned with France. Through bad luck he flunked the entrance exam to the *Ecole Normale Superieure*.[9] He even left the Church. His reaction was so strong that he became bitter.

In 1930 he 'hypnotized himself' to such a degree that when he saw white women, he found them ugly:[10] 'All that belonged to white Europe was insipid to us: its reason, its art, its women'.[11] During this period Senghor conceived his poem, *Femme Noire*. 'We were racists, we were delirious under the sign of *négritude*. No dialogue was then possible with Europe'.[12] Césaire took up this theme: 'Because we hate you and your reason, we claim the precocious insanity, the flaming folly of tenacious cannibalism'.[13] Senghor and Césaire waged war on civilization: 'Yes, I attacked Descartes with a machete and upheld, with a barbarian passion, intuitive reason against discursive reason'.[14]

Eventually, both Césaire and Senghor returned to a more moderate position. By 1939 Césaire had written the following plea: '... my heart, preserve me from all hate...'.[15] Senghor altered his previous intransigent rejection of reason: 'In Paris, by contact with artists, writers, intellectuals, and philosophers, we learned to distrust *intellectualism* – I don't mean intellect – and Rationalism – I don't mean reason'.[16]

An ambiguous racism has nevertheless continued to play a role in Senghor's thinking. It underlies his exaggeration of the difference between Whites and Negroes. Certain ideas coloured by this tendency seem bizarre. He told his 1937 Dakar audience: 'It is necessary not to misjudge and to force one's genius, even, above all, in the domain of soul and spirit. Do you believe that we can ever beat Europeans in mathematics, except in a few isolated cases, exceptions which would confirm that we as a race are not capable of abstraction?'[17] He continued by saying: 'Race is a reality, I do not mean racial purity'.[18]

It is difficult to separate racism from racial preoccupation in *négritude*. Césaire has tried to distinguish between them. He repudiates *négritude* 'when it is racist and not racial, for *négritude* is fully racial...'. He pleads that there is in *négritude* 'something racial and... Narcissistic at one and the same time, but nothing racist'. To support this idea, Césaire, as Senghor, notes that *négritude* was born in France and in the French language: 'And...how could we be racist when Michelet helped us to understand ourselves?'[19] Senghor developed this point:

'What then is this *négritude* which frightens the delicate, which has been depicted as a new racism? It was first expressed, sung and danced, in French...This sole fact should reassure you. How could we be racists, we who had been for centuries the innocent victims, the black sacrificial offerings to racism? Jean-Paul Sartre is not entirely right when, in *Black Orpheus*, he defines *négritude* as "an anti-racist racism"; he is certainly accurate when he presents it as a "certain affective attitude towards the world".'[20]

According to Senghor, racism 'was traitor to' African Negro humanism and led to a dead end by instituting war between races and continents.[21]

These contradictory interpretations of the *négritude* phenomenon should not be surprising. At different times and with different spokesmen the meaning of *négritude* changes. *Négritude* moved from the influence of racist-Fascist ideas to an opposite pole, that of the left-wing *Front-Populaire*, which appeared in 1936. The year 1936 also marks a turning point in Senghor's life. The invasion of Ethiopia by Italian Fascists shocked him into an awareness of the dangers of irrationalism and racism.

In his 'reaction to the reaction', Senghor recovered his faith and saw racial pride as a means through which the black man could contribute to universal civilization. This position was modelled on that of the *Revue du Monde Noir*. Despite this subsequent moderate stand, the racist influence has continued to play a part in Senghor's thinking. It is only with great difficulty that the militants of *négritude* have suppressed a tendency to racism.

One of the last important influences on Senghor during the 1930s was the anti-racist *Front Populaire*. This movement fraternally grouped together several French worker associations. Jean-Paul Sartre discussed the effect of the *Front Populaire* in his analysis of *négritude*: French Negro poetry 'which at first appears to be racial is, in the last analysis, a song of all and for all'.[1] *Négritude*, which at first was racist, took up the cause of all oppressed men: colonials and workers, Blacks and Whites.

Although the language of the poets of *négritude* was Marxian, they continued to distinguish themselves from the communists. Upon arriving in Europe, Senghor and other Negro students were subjected to French communist propaganda. A few French Negroes – from the West Indies for the most part – had succumbed. They, in turn, 'tried to seduce' Senghor and Césaire.[2] The 'seducers' were none other than the group behind *Légitime Défense*: Etienne Léro, René Ménil, and Jules Monnerot. The 'fraternity' they advocated was 'proletarian solidarity' for which Senghor substituted Catholic brotherly love.

Although Senghor joined the anti-Communist 'Socialist Students' group during his racist crisis of 1930–1,[3] he remained apolitical. Along with his friend Georges Pompidou, he had been attracted by the articles written by Léon Blum, which he read each morning in the Socialist organ, *Le Populaire*.[4] Georges Pompidou wrote: 'I was myself an admirer of Jean Jaurès and of Léon Blum and it is possible that I influenced [Senghor]...'.[5] Senghor later stated that Georges Pompidou converted him to socialism.[6] However, it seems more likely that it was Léon Blum's literary criticism which attracted these two young connoisseurs of poetry rather than the 'crooked road' of politics. A reason for Senghor's later membership in the French Socialist Party may lie in his early admiration of Léon Blum during the 1930s. His friends of that period considered him, 'above all a literary man',[7] and this judgement seems valid.

The socialists' concern with the development of Fascism, the invasion of Ethiopia by the Italians, and the persecution of Jews in Germany encouraged Senghor to seek friends among leftists. But even though his inclinations were left-wing, he was not a militant for any party. His militancy was saved for *négritude*.

At the time of the *Front Populaire* the African Senghor was teaching French students their own language at the *Lycée Descartes* in Tours.[8] It seems ironic that one who so vigorously opposed Descartes began his teaching career in a school bearing the famous rationalist's name.

Although Senghor failed the examination for the *Ecole Normale Supérieure*, he had nevertheless obtained his *Licence* at the Sorbonne in 1931. In 1932 he wrote his *Diplôme d'Etudes Supérieures* on 'Exoticism in Baudelaire's Poetry'. During the summer of 1933 he travelled to Greece and Turkey.[9] Upon his return from Greece, he prepared for the *Agrégation*, an extremely difficult French competition which selects teachers for the crack *Lycées*. After successfully completing the written and oral exams for the coveted degree in French Grammar in 1935, he began a year of compulsory military service. Senghor was required to serve in the French army because he had become naturalized in order to participate in the *Agrégation* competition. Naturalization was necessary since he had been born outside the four Senegalese communes which were considered part of metropolitan France.[10] At the end of his military training, he obtained his teaching post at Tours, where the spirit of the *Front Populaire* reigned supreme.

His colleagues invited him to join a group which met regularly to discuss social problems. This group was permeated by the new social spirit of the time.[11] Senghor helped them organize a 'Worker's College' at the CGT union headquarters. He taught French and French literature to the 'sons of the people'. The idea for a 'Worker's College' had been inspired by the CGT union which, during that period, was not yet communist-dominated. Senghor voted communist in 1936,[12] probably because of friendships with certain communists rather than because of any Marxist conviction.[13]

He continued to devote himself to union activity. From 1936 to 1938 he was treasurer of the local secondary teachers' union, and several times he was a delegate to the national congress of this union. In 1938, while teaching in Paris, his colleagues elected him secretary of the union chapter at the *Lycée Marcellin-Berthelot*, where he taught from 1938 to 1940. He proudly admitted that as secretary he had transmitted the order for the general strike against the Paul Reynaud government.[14]

During these years Senghor associated with disciples of the young left-wing Catholic philosopher Emmanuel Mounier and his review, *Esprit*. Albert Magne, who ironically later became Director of the right-wing review *Carrefour*, organized discussions. Senghor became a member of the *Comité de Vigilance des Intellectuels anti-Fascistes*.[15] These biographic details show Senghor's perfect integration into French life, a situation which is all to the credit of his colleagues at Tours and Paris, who accepted him without making any distinction on the basis of colour.

A poem written by Senghor in 1936 already showed the influence of the *Front Populaire*:

> There we were all together...
>   ......
> ...and others and still others, I did not know their faces,
>   but I knew them by the fever in their eyes
> For the last assault on the Boards of Directors that
>   govern the governors of colonies.
>   ......
> And victory; on the hillside where the air is pure and the
>   pot-bellied bankers have built their villas in pink and
>   white
> Far from the outskirts, far from the misery of native quarters
>   ......
> The catholic Marseillaise.
> For there we are all together, different colours – some
>   are the colour of roast coffee and others banana and
>   golden, others like the earth of rice paddies.
> Different features and dress, customs and language, but in
>   the depths of their eyes the same song of suffering
>   beneath the long feverish lashes.
> The Kaffir the Kabyle the Somali, Moor Fan Fon Bambara
>   and Bobo and Mandingo
> The nomad the miner the hireling, the peasant and worker
>   the grantee and rifleman
> *And all the white workers in the brotherly struggle*
> *See – the Asturian miner the Liverpool docker the Jew*
>   *driven out of Germany, and Dupont and Dupuis and all*
>   *the guys from Saint Denis.*[16]

He applied this lesson of brotherhood to Africa in the same poem:

> ...From now on, there is neither slave nor *guelwar*
>   nor *griot's griot*
> Only the lithe and virile comradeship in battle, and
>   let the captive's son be my equal, and let the Moor
>   and the Targui hereditary enemies, be my companions.[17]

Using the rhetoric of the *Front Populaire*, Senghor scorned 'the merchants and bankers' who 'had banished him from the country', those 'gold barons, lords of the suburbs where the forest of chimneys grows', those Capitalists who 'bought their nobility'.[18] These social preoccupations led Senghor back to Péguy's concern with the lot of the peasant. A poem Senghor wrote in 1939 at the home of Georges Pompidou's parents-in-law[19] makes this point: 'I've chosen my toiling black people, my peasant people, the peasant race throughout the world'.[20]

Césaire, even more than Senghor, used his race to express 'the struggle of the world proletariat...against the dictatorship of police and bankers'.[21] In Césaire's work this theme of proletarian solidarity grew, while in Senghor's it progressively disappeared, giving way to the vaguer and more general theme of brotherly love: 'I have wished all men to be brothers' he wrote in his poem 'Chaka':[22] 'I have dreamed of a sunlit world of fraternity with my blue-eyed brothers'.[23]

Senghor's human solidarity seemed to have been inspired more by the Vatican's 'Black International' than by Moscow's 'Red International'. 'Bless you my Fathers, bless you!...Blessed be you who didn't permit hate to grovel in this man's heart.'[24]

> And I forget
> White hands that fired the shots which brought the
>   empires crumbling down
> Hands that flogged the slaves, that flogged You
> Chalk-white hands that slapped You, the
>   powdered painted hands that slapped me
> Confident hands that delivered me to solitude to hatred
>   ......
> They cut down the forests of Africa to save Civilization,
>   for there was a shortage of human raw-material.
> Lord, I know I will not bring out my store of hatred
>   against the diplomats who bare their long teeth
> And tomorrow will barter black flesh.
> My heart, Lord, melted like snow on roofs of Paris
> Under the sun of Your gentleness.
> It is gentle to my enemies, to my brothers with white
>   hands without snow.[25]

Although Césaire lacked this religious outlook, he voiced the same prayer: 'My heart, preserve me from all hate. Do not make me that spiteful man for whom I have only hate; you know my tyrannical love...You know that it is not through hate of other races that I devote myself to this race alone'.[26] Césaire had originally used the expression 'my *catholic* love',[27] according to Senghor, who described Césaire as being 'filled with a "tyrannical love" for all men, his brothers, "a catholic love", as he had at first written'.[28] This later substitution of 'tyrannical' for 'catholic' symbolizes the fact that 'universal love' gave way to 'proletarian solidarity' in Césaire's thought. Césaire became a member of the Communist Party in 1945 at the same time that his friend Senghor joined the moderate socialists of the SFIO.[29]

Senghor's religiosity was linked to the theme of brotherhood and reached its climax in a poem 'Prayer for Peace' which was written in 1945 and dedicated to Claude and Georges Pompidou. This poem could be thought of as the continuation of poetry written during the *Front Populaire* period. It, too, relates *Front Populaire* social thought and the Christian ethic:

> At the feet of my Africa, which has been crucified for
>   four hundred years yet is still breathing
> Let me say to Thee, Lord, her prayer of peace and pardon.
> Lord God, forgive white Europe.
>   ......
> Lord, forgive them who turned the *Askia* into insurrectionists,
>   my princes into warrant officers
> My household servants into 'boys', my peasants into wage-
>   earners, my people into a people of proletarians.
> For Thou must forgive those who have hunted my children
>   like wild elephants,
> And broken them in with whips, have made them the black
>   hands of those whose hands were white.
>   ......
> And lo, the serpent of hatred raises its head in my heart,
>   that serpent I believed was dead...
> Kill it Lord, for I must continue on my way, and I
>   want to pray, especially for France.
>   ......
> Bless this people who brought me Thy Good Tidings, Lord,
>   and opened my heavy eyelids to the light of faith,
> Who opened my heart to the understanding of the world,
>   showing me the rainbow of fresh faces that are my brothers!
> I greet you brothers: you Mohammed Ben Abdallah, you
>   Razafymahatratra, and you Pham-Manh-Tuong, you from
>   the pacific seas and you from the enchanted forests
> I greet you all with a catholic heart.
>   ......

O bless this people...
And with them all the peoples of Europe, all the peoples
   of Asia, all the peoples of Africa, all the peoples of
   America

   ......

And grant to them warm hands that they may clasp the
   earth in a girdle of brotherly hands
BENEATH THE RAINBOW OF THY PEACE.[30]

Echoing Senghor's poetry of the *Front Populaire* period, the Senegalese national anthem proclaims: 'The Bantu is my brother, and the
Arab, and the white man'.[31]

By 1934 it was clear to Senghor that he must take positive steps to end his cultural alienation and that of his black companions. He transformed his ideas into theories. In fact, the reaction against the West continued, but at the same time an affirmation of African values gave Senghor the foundation on which to build a new ideology. The themes of the previous five years developed and became richer.

Senghor has given one key to the understanding of his desire for positive action in a letter addressed to a young literary critic:

'It is exactly because the Eden-Africa-Childhood is absent that I am torn between Europe and Africa, between politics and poetry, between my white brother and myself, that I challenge otherness and rupture, which is, however, my earthly destiny – Europeans would say, my human dignity. As for me, I think that, to realize myself as a man, it is essential for me to overcome Negation, to bridge the chasm, to fill in the vacuum....'[1]

In response to this need to overcome negation of European values and bridge the chasm between the West and Africa, Senghor formulated his theory of cultural cross-breeding, a theory that he has never stopped developing and defining.[2]

In November 1933, upon his return from Greece and Turkey, Senghor and other students organized an 'Association of West African Students'. One of its objectives was to help its members both financially and socially. 'But...above all', stated a French West Indian student journal of May 1934, 'it has a precise cultural purpose. It could be given the motto "assimilate European culture while remaining close to your people".'[3] The Association organized monthly talks, followed by discussion. 'Thanks to these frequent exchanges of ideas, West African students could elaborate, little by little, a common ideology, born of the accord between their native civilizations and the requirements of the modern world.'[4]

Like Paulette Nardal and the group behind the *Revue du Monde Noir*, the Association did not want to be accused of anti-European or anti-French sentiments: 'It would be too easy, not to say simplistic'. Those who were active in the Association 'knew, more than anyone, how to appreciate the riches of French culture. They thought that French culture, if it were properly understood, should help them develop a critical spirit and originality, rather than mechanical and aerated imitation'.[5] The group thus adopted Senghor's 'critical loyalty' to France. The Association intended to put into practice the ideas Senghor had absorbed from the *Revue du Monde Noir* two years previously, namely, the study of African civilization, the creation of a new literature, and the development of a new African humanism.

The officers of the Association were: Senghor, *President*; Soulèye Diagne, Senegalese law student, *Secretary*; Ousmane Socé Diop, future Senegalese Ambassador to the United States and United Nations, *Assistant Secretary*; and Aristide Issembé, future Ambassador of Gabon, *Treasurer*. During 1934 the Association sponsored talks on 'The West African Woman and Us' by P. P. Corrêa (a law student) and on 'The Creation of Modern West African Literature' by Ousmane Socé Diop.[6]

Ousmane Socé Diop expressed the new cultural themes in his novel *Karim*, written soon after the Association was founded: 'Fundamentally, they (African students) all hesitated to make a definite break with the old Senegal in order to espouse European customs... Their heart spoke in favour of the practical modernism of the West. But over and above their speeches, year by year a cross-bred civilization was building'.[7] In a novel published in 1937, Diop advocated this idea of cross-breeding: 'the half-breed will be the man of the future...all is cross-bred...There is no civilization on earth which is not the product of cross-breeding'. And the author concluded by evoking the intellectual cross-breeding characteristic of Africans who had absorbed European culture.[8]

This idea is central to Senghor's philosophy and has appeared since 1934. The theme of cross-breeding enabled Senghor to unite all the diverse influences of which he himself was the product. The forgotten childhood tensions seemed to justify his new ideas: 'I think of those youthful years, of that age of change in which I had not yet been born, torn as I was between my Christian conscience and my *Serer* blood. But was I *Serer*, I who had a *Mandingo* name – while that of my mother was *Fulani* in origin?'[9] The conflict between *Fulani* maternal uncle and *Serer* father, which had been the main reason for his being sent to school in 1914, took on a new significance for him.[10] The theory helped Senghor recover his internal equilibrium which had been destroyed by the years of mission schooling. But he recognized that cross-breeding was something 'fragile, unstable, always in the process of accomplishment'.[11]

Senghor formulated his theory of cross-breeding on the basis of ideas first introduced in the *Revue du Monde Noir*. In 1932 an article which appeared in the review stated: 'The future of humanity lies in

incorporating into a new man all superior physical and mental qualities of mankind. The perfect man is the composite of the best in all
the races of humanity'.[12] In another article, an African student advocated this cross-breeding by arguing 'in favour of an actual synthesis
between the different races'.[13]

The *Revue* saw racial conflict as the alternative to racial collaboration:

'Nation fights Nation, and it seems inevitable that the struggle of
race against race will follow, unless we develop a greater interest
in each other, a fuller understanding, a more friendly feeling, and
heartier co-operation to bring about the brotherhood of man....'[14]

Other intellectual influences on Senghor extended the theory.
Claudel's lesson as well as his vocabulary supported Senghor's new
cultural ecumenical spirit: 'Now', wrote Senghor, 'I no longer am
ashamed of my difference. I find my joy and my assurance in embracing in a *catholic* view all these complementary worlds'.[15]

The contribution of Gobineau was his theme of racial contrast.
Frobenius provided his 'conciliating agreement'. Intellectual cross-
breeding came from Delavignette. A recent speech by Senghor
showed the reasons for his syncretic approach:

'Such is my situation, our situation, which obliges us to refuse
nothing of our history, to conciliate all: to graft the Latin sprig on
the African wild-stock. On this sole condition we can be ourselves,
products of education and heredity; on this condition alone, we
will fulfil ourselves because we will be advancing along with history. We do not believe in dogmatisms nor in dichotomies or in
sectarianism. Peoples accomplish their human mission only by
leaving behind the limitations of their immediate environment in
order to enrich themselves with values at first foreign to their
native territory.'[16]

This 1962 statement is completely faithful to the 1934 ideas and
could have been written by the young Senghor. These ideas and their
expression have remained constant, and in his writing, whether it be in
1939 or 1970, it is easy to find whole phrases repeated. Political and
economic theories later developed by Senghor have employed and am-
plified the concept of cross-breeding outside of the cultural sphere.[17]

A reason for the theory of cross-breeding lay in the colonial situation: 'Whether we like it or not, we are half French because of our
cultural training...',[18] and Senghor refused to deny his other half.
He has 'always' thought that 'true civilization was in cultural, even
biological, cross-breeding'.[19] Senghor went on to stress the Arab-
Berber influence on Senegalese culture. Cultural cross-breeding
meant not only the mixture of French and African elements but the

mixture of different African cultures – those of North Africa and those of Africa south of the Sahara. Thus with the aid of French *and* Arab-Berber contributions, Negro African culture would be transformed.

The growth of the reign of Nazi terror seems to have played an important role in the development of the theory of cultural cross-breeding:

> 'The myth of the Aryan, supported by technology and formidable mechanization, directly menaced the myth of *négritude*. We had to seek out allies...At the end of our studies and our reflections, every great civilization seemed to us to be a symbiosis of two or several complementary civilizations: as a cross-breeding, always of cultures, often of races. This is what led us to modesty and positive co-operation.'[20]

Although at one time Senghor had hated reason and had advocated the cult of blood,[21] he soon recognized inherent dangers in racial isolation: 'The contribution of foreign elements is quite as necessary. Civilizations, as races, perish of too great a purity'. In 1937, he cited France in support of cultural cross-breeding: 'The example of French civilization in this respect is very striking. The "few materials" which compose it frequently force it to renew itself. And all its renaissances, if one looks at them closely, were accomplished under foreign influence'.[22] In the same speech he referred to African civilizations 'which stagnated, isolated from lively waters and from the rest of the world, because of the solitudes of the desert and the forest'.[23] Since the 1930s, Senghor has supported a French cultural presence in Africa. His rationalization for this position appeared in a 1937 criticism of African insularity: 'Our concept of the *samba-linguer* (ideal man)...corresponds to something specifically racial: sense of honour, politeness, not devoid of refinement, a mind more subtle than learned...this ideal is beginning to be outdated: it was tainted with a certain disdain for newness, economics, and the exact sciences, to mention only these three deficiencies'. Senghor continued by affirming that these lacunae appear 'more and more serious as time goes on, for here we are solidly attached to the five parts of the world by stronger links than the cables which attach us to them – particularly to France. It is a fact that our destiny is one and the same'. Emphasizing that political and economic competition with other continents was dangerous for the Africa of 1937, Senghor advocated modernization, even westernization – 'if we want to survive'. For the milieu in which Africans of the 1930s were living was no longer African: 'it is also French, it is international; to say it fully, it is Afro-French'.[24]

From 1937 onwards Senghor has hoped that Africans would

'react against the anti-western reaction'[25] and accept French civilization: 'Africans have reacted against "our ancestors the Gauls". This
is common sense. But the character of every reaction is to be undis-
ciplined. It might well be time to react against this reaction'.[26] But
Senghor's suggestion came too early since the French had paid no
attention to the initial reaction and had continued their policy of
assimilation. In fact, African schoolchildren of the 1950s were still
reciting 'our ancestors the Gauls' from standard French schoolbooks
used in the 'colonies'.

Senghor's philosophic reconciliation to France was similar to the
American Negroes' attempt to come to terms with their hostile environment in the New World.[27] The American Negroes as a minority people in a western society had had little choice. The French West
Africans, on the other hand, could have followed a course of cultural nationalism which in turn might have hastened de-Frenchifica-
tion. Senghor's 1937 speech, however, discouraged this cultural
separation.

Premature reconciliation of opposites is a philosophic habit of
Senghor's which is as characteristic of his political and economic
thought as it is of his cultural theories. Each time he has perceived
two ideologies in conflict, he has advocated synthesis. He therefore
tends to be convinced that he has resolved the dichotomy. When he
realized that African nationalism and French colonialism were in opposition, when he saw that Western capitalism and communism
were at loggerheads, Senghor proposed resolution by synthesis. His
solutions – Eurafrica on the one hand, and a new socialism on the
other – were highly idealistic and impracticable.[28]

Senghor's theory of cultural cross-breeding has remained essentially unchanged since the 1930s. His attempt to reconcile the West
and Africa appears over and over in his writings:

> *1946*
> 'In what way can we understand France's civilizing mission? We
> think that no nation is more suited than she to play the role of
> awakening drowsy civilizations and of fertilizing civilizations,
> which, even if young, are not primitive.'[29]

> *1950*
> 'We have to "master our pride", as the American Negro poet said,
> and forget old suffering to render justice to Europe and admit its
> necessity'.[30]
> (Note Senghor's identifying the African's state with that of the
> American Negro.)

> *1958*
> 'We could not return to our former condition, to the original *négri-*

tude. We no longer lived under the *Askias* of the Sonrai, nor even under Chaka the Zulu. We were twentieth-century Parisian students... To be ourselves, we had to incarnate African culture in the reality of the twentieth century.'[31]

1961

'We are, certainly, African Negroes cross-bred with Berbers, born on a certain soil and in a certain climate, with an ancient cultural heritage. But we are men of the twentieth century, fashioned whether we like it or not, by a socializing civilization which is becoming planetary... Our ultimate task is to bring about a symbiosis of our African Negro, or more precisely, Negro-Berber values, and European values – European values because Europe contributes the principal technical means of the emerging civilization. Indeed, all the values from either side cannot be retained....'[32]

In an essay written in 1950, Senghor went so far as to equate the 'liberty of the soul' with 'cross-breeding.'[33]

There has been a development of certain specific themes, but the theory of cross-breeding has remained strikingly unchanged for more than thirty years. Is this constant repetition of the same themes a submission by Senghor to those forces which cause African music and civilization to depend on archetypes and repetition? (This is Senghor's own perception of African civilization.) It is true that Senghor has been called the 'Knight of the *idée fixe*'.[34] Senghor himself has admitted that he is 'obsessed' by a few *idées-forces*.[35] René Maran, Senghor's mentor in the 1930s, put forward an explanation for this obsession: 'The white race has its stains and the black race too. Both, on the other hand, have their own qualities and virtues. To reconcile these two sets of virtues and qualities, to help them reach a synthesis, is this not a task worthy of a great heart? To this accord, to this concilation, to this synthesis, he has dedicated his life'.[36] Senghor's constant preoccupation with cultural integration is perhaps one reason for the repetition in his works. The task of merging cultures is not easy and requires centuries of time. It can only be *begun* during a lifetime. In his haste to accomplish it, Senghor has not realized the enormity of his task.

Senghor has hoped that cross-breeding, once it is no longer felt as such,[37] will develop 'neo-Africanism', a 'new African humanism, which will be the *accord conciliant* of Arabism and *négritude*, the whole enriched by European contributions'.[38] In 1955, speaking of his project for political federation, Senghor declared: '...in the French community each colony can live, its own culture enriched by the French spirit'.[39] One European contribution to the development of a new Africa was the 'historical ethno-sociology of Africa, of the

Africas'.[40] Senghor has relied on the discipline developed by European ethnologists to discover Africa's values: 'We will never understand ourselves – nor will we be understood – if we do not first study ethno-sociology'.[41]

   Unlike his critics, Senghor does not consider his syncretism to be 'a heteroclite assemblage of antagonisms'; it is rather an effort to 'gather complementary virtues together into a dynamic symbiosis'.[42] Senghor suggested this attitude when he wrote the words for the Senegalese National Anthem: '...a single people open to all the winds of the world'.[43] The French political scientist Raoul Girardet has described the ideologies of newly born nations differently: 'It is rarely that one of the new ideologies...does not present an amalgam of elements from the mother country (from varying sources) and from native sources'.[44] The political leaders and artists of the underdeveloped world show this essential trait of 'eclectic comprehension'[45] which allows them to lump together different influences. Senghor's answer to critics such as Girardet was that he had allied African sensitivity, an intuitive understanding of men and things, to European logic...'.[46] This theory enabled Senghor to justify the colonial situation which, according to him, should be a fertilizing intrusion of Europe into Africa.[17]

   It is difficult to understand Senghor's theory of cross-breeding without referring to his personal drama. Senghor has declared: 'A cultural cross-breed needs, as much as does a biological half-breed, an unusual strength of character to enable him to reconcile the many contradictions within him.[48] A poem written in 1939 reveals the same dilemma which bedevilled Claudel and Gide:

> To have to choose! deliciously torn between these
>   two friendly hands
> – A kiss from you Soukeina!...these two antagonistic
>   worlds
> When painfully...ah! I no longer know which is my
>   sister and which my foster sister
>   ......
> When painfully – a kiss from you Isabella! – between
>   those two hands
> That I want to reunite in my own warm hand.[49]

'Trapped between two races, two cultures, two ways of life',[50] Senghor found a way to resolve his dramatic condition, which had troubled him ever since the day in 1914 when he entered the mission school at Joal. René Maran explained how Senghor found a new equilibrium: 'Senghor...is the prototype of what should and will be one day the French-African community. He carries within him two differing cultures which complement each other. And in his heart he carries both France and Africa. He loves both with such a passion that he cannot leave one without giving the other that *dimindra pars animae suae* of the Latin poet'.[51]

Senghor has confused his condition with that of his countrymen.[52] To him the African condition can be reduced to the battle which rages within him: '..."joy and suffering...radiant pleasure and excruciating pain", which is not merely a dualism but is rather a harmonizing of contrary elements to make an original whole. I have said it many times: every great civilization, every real culture is cross-bred'.[53] He showed a relationship between his personal experience and this theory by declaring in 1950: 'As one can well see, even if it is cross-bred, a civilization is not necessarily divided against itself'.[54] This same statement might be re-read as: 'Although I am a half-breed, I have resolved my internal contradictions; I am no longer divided against myself'.

In developing a theory of cross-breeding Senghor has relied on the ideas of Catholic thinkers: the Scholastic method of *sic et non* and Claudel's 'catholicism'. Teilhard de Chardin's influence on Senghor, which dates from 1948, only reinforced the tendencies of the 1930s, as is evident in a speech made by Senghor in 1961:

'...above all do not believe that the militants of *négritude* lack modesty. Today, more than ever, we are conscious of our defects: of the gaps in African civilization. That is why we have always refused to refuse European elements, particularly from France. These are complementary to ours. As Pierre Teilhard de Chardin said, races are not equal mathematically, they are equal complementarily. And the Civilization of the Universal is situated exactly at the crossroads of the complementary values of all individual civilizations. For this reason, my country, Senegal, attempts an original and perhaps unprecedented cultural effort in black Africa. We want to root ourselves deeply in Africanity, of which *négritude* is but an aspect, and, at the same time, remain open to the four winds of the world, particularly to the tradewinds which blow from the North and chase away fevers of the rainy season.'[55]

It is interesting to note that Delavignette was responsible for introducing Senghor to Teilhard's ideas on the complementary character of races. In his 1948 preface to Ousmane Socé Diop's *Karim*, Delavignette quoted the eminent French Africanist Théodore Monod, who himself was quoting Teilhard's ideas on racial questions.[56] Monod wrote: '...for the same reason that a variety of instruments is necessary to a symphony.... This is exactly what Teilhard de

Chardin said when, apropos of the human races, he spoke of "functional diversity", of "essential complementarity", and of "union which differentiates" '.[57]

This theory of cultural cross-breeding is only one aspect of Senghor's *négritude*. Soon after its formulation, and even before Teilhard's writings confirmed it, Senghor formulated a complementary theory of active assimilation: 'Assimilate, don't be assimilated'.

The formulation of Senghor's theory of active assimilation dates from the beginning of 1937. It countered the French policy of assimilation which presupposed a passive Africa. According to Senghor, to co-operate with the French, it was first necessary to be an African. The exaltation of Negro values assured this preliminary condition. After having assured himself of the value of traditional African civilization, Senghor could now accept influences from other civilizations. From his studies he knew that French civilization was the product of centuries of active assimilation of the most diverse elements – first of all Greek-Latin, followed by Spanish, English, Italian, German, Indian, Chinese, and finally African. Senghor saw this as an example to be followed by Africa. It was necessary to integrate France's contribution of modern technology, with its roads and railways, its large factories, and its bridges and dams in reinforced concrete. But in the process of this integration, Africa must remain itself. Just as Senghor hoped to remain African while absorbing French culture and methodology, he wanted Africa to remain African while adopting French technology.

In his study of ethnology, Senghor perceived a certain 'permeability' in the Negro soul which he recognized in his new theory. He described this quality in a pre-War essay: 'The Negro body, the Negro soul is permeable even to imperceptible rhythms, to the solicitations of the world...The Negro is sensitive to words and ideas ...to the sensitive, should I say sensual? qualities of ideas. Clever speaking seduces him and the communist theorist and the hero and the saint at the same time'. All this, Senghor stressed, 'gives the impression that the Negro is easily assimilated, while it is above all he who assimilates'.[2]

In a memorable address given during a brief visit to Dakar in 1937, Senghor first voiced his terse slogan: 'Assimilate, don't be Assimilated'. On 4 September 1937, at the end of a long, hot, humid day, the first African to have obtained the coveted *Agrégation* mounted the steps of the stage of Dakar's Chamber of Commerce. The hall was packed. In the audience was the Governor-General of French West Africa, Marcel de Coppet, several Colonial officials, and a crowd of Whites and young Africans. Senghor hoped that these young people would help him change the relationship between France and the colonial peoples. He addressed himself to the dynamic element in the audience, and in the style of Hamlet he declared:

'To assimilate or not to assimilate, that seems to be the dilemma... I believe that the question does not really exist or rather that it is badly put... For what does one mean by assimilation?... the word has... a double meaning: subjective and objective, passive and active. I could not do better than to compare the cultural phenomenon of assimilation with its biological counterpart. To assimilate a foodstuff is to transform it up to the point of making it one's own flesh and blood. It is to gain by absorbing foreign bodies. One does not become millet or beef, it is the millet or beef which becomes our flesh and blood. Therefore only one kind of assimilation is interesting, and that is the active, *assimilating* assimilation. It is a question of assimilating, not being assimilated.'[3]

Senghor paraphrased Michelet by stating that the foreign elements 'should be but foodstuffs. They enrich a civilization, they give it another quality, but not another direction. It is a question of advancing within one's own framework, of developing oneself while remaining oneself'.[4] Senghor accepted Europe, but on the condition that Europe agree to enrich African culture, not crush it and then substitute itself in the resulting vacuum.

'The Europe of light' was not 'refused and repudiated',[5] but rather it was to be assimilated. Both Senghor and the violent Césaire recognized the value of Europe. Initially their attitude had been hostile, but it rapidly became co-operative. Their goal became a new African civilization which would selectively absorb Western culture.

Senghor's representation of the two kinds of assimilation was based upon the grammatical distinction between passive and active. Senghor, who was trained in philology, treated this notion in his linguistic essays which discuss progressive and regressive assimilation.[6]

Senghor wanted Africans 'to accept themselves, while at the same time remaining ready to welcome the best of what the others offer'.[7] To the European who told him 'Confess at least that we brought you civilization', Senghor answered, 'Not precisely. You brought us your civilization. Let us take from it what is best, what is seminal, and allow us to give you back the rest'.[8]

The influence of Senghor's years at the Sorbonne is clear: 'Is not the great lesson (of those years) the realization that Culture consists in assimilating, like Montaigne, not in being assimilated? That Culture begins when one forgets one's lessons? This... is what makes the grandeur of Rome *vis-à-vis* Athens, the grandeur of Paris *vis-à-*

vis Rome. Believe me, I pondered this lesson for years, while studying at home, turning the pages with a nocturnal hand'.[9] Senghor re-
examined the problem in his 1950 essay: 'Africa questions itself:
subjection or choice?' After showing appreciation for European
civilization, Senghor continued: 'Are we going to be subjected to
Europe, are we going to let ourselves be assimilated passively?'[10]

Senghor's concern was not only philosophic. He was appalled at
what he termed the 'loosening morality among educated Africans'.
The 'rejection of the moral tradition of their fathers' was at fault.[11]
He proposed positive steps to rehabilitate native African values before beginning the task of assimilating French elements.

His first action plan described a system of education for French
West Africa. In an innovative speech Senghor presented his reforms
for education.

'We can, at present, suggest the general principle that the study of
West Africa and France must be the two poles of education in
French West Africa and that this bipolarity, so to speak, should be
found at all levels. As each student progresses, the African pole
will lose its force of attraction, to the benefit of the French pole. It
is a question of starting with the African milieu and civilization in
which the child is bathed. He should learn to know and express its
elements at first in his native tongue and then in French. Little by
little, he will acquire knowledge of the new universe in which he,
as well as his race, will be involved when he becomes a man.'[12]

Ten years later Senghor as a politician was able to implement his
plan. He then promised that 'African education will attempt to give
a culture simultaneously native and French, for I believe that every
civilization results from a cross-breeding'.[13]

The educational reform that Senghor proposed in 1937 required the
child to read works adapted to the French African milieu. To provide
adequate background reading Senghor suggested an 'anthology for
school children which would group the best work of colonial writers,
black and white, as well as writers from the mother country, one
group complementary to, and able to shed light on, the other'.[14] Certain selections would be written in French and, if the author were
African, the piece would appear in his own language.

Senghor attacked French discrimination against African languages
in the educational system. The 'first quality' of the new African
youth 'would be to be Africans by knowledge of Africa, above all by
the sense of Africa'. Senghor proposed in his 1937 speech that the
schoolchildren acquire this sense by 'the study and practice of a
native tongue'.[15] His training as a grammarian and his study of linguistics, similar to that of the Pan-Slavs of the nineteenth century,[16]

were thus intimately linked to this literary 'nationalism', tempered by the theory of cross-breeding.

Senghor continued by stressing the need for the rehabilitation of local languages: 'The élite is called upon by the community as an example and as an intermediary. What respect can it command if it is cut off from the roots of its race? What competence can it have if it ignores its people?'[17] In phrases reminiscent of Delavignette and the *Revue du Monde Noir* he spoke of the cultural advantage of African languages: 'The intellectuals have the mission to restore Negro values in their truth and excellence... by letters above all. There is no civilization without a literature which expresses and sets values. Without written literature, there is no civilization which goes beyond a simple ethnographic curiosity. How can one conceive of a native literature which would not be written in a native language?'[18] Senghor's mission was to persuade his audience to produce a literature which might be used in the enterprise of *enracinement* which he advocated. The fact that this literature was not to be written in French demonstrates the linguistic 'nationalism' (in the Pan-Slav sense) of Senghor's 1937 theory. (It is interesting to note that in 1963 he rejected the linguistic aspect of this 1937 theory.[19] The curious rejection shows a growing moderation in his 'nationalism' while, at the same time, other Africans have gone so far as to translate scientific texts into *Wolof*.)

He continued his 1937 argument by re-appraising the value of a Negro literature in French: 'A Negro literature in French seems possible to me; it is true, Haiti proved it, and other Negro literatures which borrowed a European language have been born: American Negro, Spanish Negro, and Portuguese Negro literature attest to this fact. To be completely candid I would judge it a little premature. Our nation, taken as a whole, is not yet capable of tasting all the beauties of French...'. He was, in fact, critical of African literature in French: 'Such a literature could not express our soul. There is a certain Negro flavour, a certain Negro colour, a certain Negro accent, a certain Negro tonality which is impossible for a European language to express'.

To avoid advocating separatism, Senghor proposed a bilingualism which 'would allow a precise and entire expression of the "new Negro"'. Although scientific works would be written in French, native languages would be used for the 'literary genres which best express the race's particular genius: poetry, theatre, storytelling'.[20] (It is interesting to note that this idea was also repudiated by Senghor in 1963.[21])

To stave off European criticism that indigenous languages lacked richness of expression, Senghor insisted that they 'need only to be manipulated and established by talented writers'. He cited the example of the Malagasy language which had no written rules of grammar a few years previously, and yet had recently become a literary instrument. American Negro patois had also been successfully transformed from argot to literature: Paul Lawrence Dunbar, Langston Hughes, and Sterling Brown 'made American Negro lingo, this poor uprooted slave stammering, into a thing of beauty...'. To support his position he also cited Africanists who praised 'languages like *Manding* for the great facility they give to verbal invention'.[22]

And yet Senghor himself did not write in an African language. It is true that, as a qualified French grammarian, Senghor was capable of using and appreciating all the beauty of the language of Baudelaire and Proust. However, his poetry presents the terrible paradox of expressing the new African consciousness in the language of the white colonist.[23] Although aware of this problem, Senghor has made no effort to employ his native language in writing poetry, except for occasional words used to designate certain aspects of African, or more precisely *Serer*, life: *dyali* (an African troubadour, poet, and musician); *guelwar* (a noble, descendant of *Manding* conquerors); *bolong* (canal or fiord lined by tropical trees); *tann* (flat marshland, saltflats, etc.).[24] But these words are *Serer* and therefore not understood beyond a limited region in Senegal. Because of the veritable tower of Babel which characterizes linguistic Africa, Senghor could not have utilized a single African language to propagate his idea of a *universal* black civilization.

Senghor explains his use of French with no regrets:
'...the French language! Certainly not the Byzantine language of sophists who serve imperialism, but the language of philosophers, the language of poets: a language of liberation and fertilization. On the one hand, the language of philosophers of the eighteenth century: analytical, made for exploding false myths, hard, precise, brilliant as a diamond – on the other hand, the language of Surrealist poets, heavy with saps and juices, dense with striking images and syncopated rhythms, close, after all, to African languages. In brief, a language of destruction and construction, of revolt and of revolution.'[25]

Because of his love of French, Senghor has done less to rehabilitate African languages than did other linguistic nationalists such as the Pan-Slavs in the nineteenth century.

Senghor's proposal for a new education in French West Africa presupposed an 'ethnic personality' for Africans: a civilization (language, tradition, history) 'however humble it might be...It is in this active personality that one finds the necessary prerequisite for active assimilation'. In 1937 Senghor declared that 'no serious individual could deny that African civilizations exist'.[26] Senghor cited the example of the French West Indians of his generation to conclude his 1937 argument:

> 'I will ask...a Césaire, student of the *Ecole Normale Supérieure*, a Monnerot, essayist and critic...What do they tell us? That in the French West Indies there are many diplomas and degrees yet little culture despite their very lively intelligence; that they have a literature, but that it is only the negative and a pale copy of that of the mother country; that when the races of the world stand trial... they will arrive empty-handed; that what is at fault is the education they received because they were never taught the history and civilizations of their African ancestors. Listen to...Léon Damas ...who calls himself "a Negro poet" and who laments, in a rhythm of the tom-tom, that he has instinctively recaptured his nudity, the result of the spiritual stripping following his exile.'[27]

Before leaving for France, Senghor hoped, in September 1937, to form a Senegalese association (*rassemblement*) led by young people like himself,[28] which would help put his theory of active assimilation into practice. This group would be the African branch of the Association of West African Students founded in France in 1934. The young people of the African group would work for the rehabilitation of African languages, the study of African traditions and history, and they would have the task of creating an African literature in native languages. Unhappily the proposed African Association never took shape, and Paris continued to be the centre of the work of rehabilitation until French African independence in the 1960s.

In a speech at the International Congress on the Cultural Evolution of Colonial Countries held in Paris at the end of September 1937, Senghor tried to explain why the work of renewing African civilization had been carried out by Africans who had spent long years abroad. His paper, 'The Resistance of the Senegalese Bourgeosie to the *Ecole Rurale Populaire*', described the Francophilia of the bourgeoisie which, 'perhaps repudiated...what is African'.[29] In fact, the bourgeoisie of the four Senegalese Communes which had metropolitan status knew that their special voting privileges were the result of the French policy of assimilation. To be represented in the French Assembly they had to become black Frenchmen.[30]

Senghor, who had not been born in the privileged communes, was much better placed to understand the aspirations of African intellectuals of native status. The special status of the important Senegalese towns was partially responsible for the lack of awareness of acculturation on the part of the Senegalese youth of the 1930s.

It was not in Africa but in France that he found support for his projected reforms. Senghor defended the concept of the *Ecole Rurale Populaire* before a Parisian audience composed of such eminent Africanists as Pierre Gourou, Melville Herskovits, Robert Delavignette, Germaine Dieterlen, Marcel Griaule, Henri Labouret, Michel Leiris, Marie-Andrée de Sacrée Coeur, and Théodore Monod. (It is interesting to note that Fily Dabo Sissoko, future founder of the RDA party, and Yacine Diallo, future *Député* to the French National Assembly from Guinea, also addressed the Congress.)

In his speech Senghor criticized the Senegalese bourgeoisie for advocating 'educational assimilation'. He reproached them for not understanding the 'Franco-African cultural movement, of which the *Ecole Rurale Populaire* was an expression'. Senghor enthusiastically supported this new school which had been 'born out of a completely modern concept of culture which consisted of "cultivating one's difference" as André Gide wishes'.[31] Senghor accused the assimilationist bourgeoisie of 'excluding the *Ecole Rurale Populaire* and the Africanization of education in general'.[32] He insisted that the bourgeosie *wanted* to be *déracinée*.

His hostility towards the Senegalese bourgeoisie contributed to his refusal to become Inspector of Education in French West Africa, a post which was offered to him by Governor-General de Coppet during his Dakar visit of September 1937.[33] He felt that it would be impossible to find enough support for his educational reforms among influential Senegalese who were resolutely assimilationist. In addition, he knew that he could not carry out educational policies which would be diametrically opposed to everything he had supported since reading Barrès in 1929.

His support of the *Ecole Rurale Populaire* might be considered reactionary. It is possible that Senghor was the unsuspecting tool of those 'colonialists' who were alarmed at the development of an African élite which would have too many of the advantages of European higher education. It should be emphasized that assimilation in the 1930s was a very liberal and progressive idea. The Senegalese bourgeoisie feared that their hard-won gains in the battle for assimilation might be lost if African education differed from the French model.

17. 'Seek Ye First the Cultural Kingdom'

Although by 1937 Senghor had become an activist verbally, he refused to accept the post offered by the Governor-General because he did not want to enter politics.[1] The distaste for politics common to many members of the French intellectual generation of the 1930s was also characteristic of Senghor. Urged to join with French West Indian communists during the early 1930s, Senghor and Césaire both refused to engage in political activities: 'To the handful of young French West Indians who cried out in the name of communism "Politics first", we replied, "Culture first". We must first promote *négritude*'.[2] Barrès, too, had warned: 'Let us first repudiate political doctrines and the parties that they engender'.[3]

Between 1934 and 1936 Senghor regularly contributed to *l'Etudiant Noir*, a purely cultural journal run by some of the young French West Indian intellectuals. Léon Damas, neglecting the *Revue du Monde Noir*, credited *l'Etudiant Noir* with the 'birth of the movement that helped reunite Negroes of French nationality and status with their history, their traditions, and with the languages which expressed their soul...'.[4] *L'Etudiant Noir* placed the cultural awakening of Black students in Paris above political nationalism. *L'Etudiant Noir* had as 'its objective the end of the tribal system, the clannishness which prevails in the Latin Quarter. One ceases to be essentially Martiniquan, Guadaloupan, Guyanese, African, or Malagasy, to become a *black* student. We will end life in hermetically sealed containers'.[5]

Senghor and his West Indian friends hoped to avoid any contact with traditional politics. Young French intellectuals of the 1930s were almost unanimous in their criticism of political parties, of the traditional game of politics, of parliamentarianism. They attacked politics itself. As Emmanuel Mounier and the group behind *Esprit*, Senghor and Césaire avoided giving their movement political overtones. Péguy, one of the principal mentors of this French intellectual generation, influenced their anti-political stance. His position that the political was the contrary of the mystical was paralleled by Senghor and Césaire who believed that the political was the contrary of the cultural.

Senghor's disdain for political institutions appeared in a 1939 essay:

'In today's Western democracies...the legislator is elected, in the best instance, by a party which is an aggregate of material interests, and he makes laws under the dictatorship of a financial oligarchy and for that oligarchy. Legislation is doubly inhuman because it is doubly corrupted. As for the government, despite its police force which grows constantly, it has no authority. Authority reposes on spiritual pre-eminence, but the government is in the hands of overly clever men and puppets, of politicians instead of statesmen.'[6]

Senghor's anti-political position also paralleled that of Surrealists. So antithetical was politics to the Surrealists that André Breton expelled from his group those disciples who let themselves be tempted by politics.[7] Breton was defending the independence of the artist from the surrounding society. As had the young *négritude* movement, the Surrealist movement confronted communism.[8] Jules Monnerot, member of the *Légitime Défense* group, later wrote: 'Surrealism clashed with the communism of the 1930s, like licentiousness against discipline. Discipline, without which, from the revolutionary point of view, there is no possibility of success nor any conceivable victory, challenges the free expression towards which the curve of the history of Western letters has been moving'.[9]

As both the 'spiritualists' and the Surrealists, Senghor discarded politics in favour of the primacy of culture. He stated in 1937: '...the cultural problem in French West Africa is the most serious problem in this hour'.[10] It seems that the black novelist René Maran, who had suffered from the violent criticism levelled against his political stand, counselled Senghor to adopt an apolitical position.[11] A poem by Senghor reflects his substitution of poetical interpretation for political leadership:

> Pardon your great-nephew if he has *tossed away his
>   lance* for the sixteen cents of the *sorong*.
> *Our new nobility is not to dominate our people*, but
>   to be its rhythm and its heart.
> Not to graze our land, but as the grain of millet
>   to rot in the earth
> *Not to be the head of the people*, but rather its
>   mouth and its trumpet.
> *Who could chant you* but your brother in arms, your
>   blood brother?[12]

The Catholic philosopher Jacques Maritain's 'primacy of the spiritual' opposed Charles Maurras' 'Politics first'.[13] The close link between Maritain and Senghor explains Senghor's rejection of Léro. The primacy of the spiritual resulted from the anti-materialism of the French Catholic thinker in the same way that the primacy of culture developed out of the African Catholic's anti-materialism. According to Senghor, Léro's Marxist analysis of West Indian society [14] repelled him because atheistic materialism not only led to involvement with the communist party but also violated African 'spiritualism'.

The pre-eminence of culture in Senghor's philosophy supported the creation of an African literature. It was crucial that Africans be aware of their dignity. In so doing they would have 'gained what is essential',[15] for they would realize that 'African man is the product of a civilization, of an art and of a religion'.[16]

Literature, 'the written word, an instrument of liberation, will be even more an instrument for the rebirth of man at last reconciled to his existence'.[17] Poetry, according to Senghor, was activity which brought salvation: '...for the poet the rhymed word is an act of creation, *poïesis*. Singing of our fratricidal wars, he exorcises them; our revolutions he turns into victories. He restores to us the ample breath of regained salvation, our true being, that which, by love, renders us present in the world, in accord with cosmic forces. He revives purity, that is to say, integrity of being'.[18]

The primacy of culture constituted a first step towards ending the cultural alienation of the Negro. Through his poems Senghor hoped to work for Africa and the black man: 'For the poet's mission is, first and foremost, redemption'.[19]

Que je bondirai comme l'Annonciateur, que je
manifesterai l'Afrique comme le sculpteur de
masques au regard intense.[20]

'What the Negro Contributes' is the title of an essay that Senghor published in 1939. But it is also a theory which he developed after reading the *Revue du Monde Noir*. It is the twin of cultural cross-breeding: Africa accepts European influences on the condition that Europe accept those from Africa:

> 'You have brought to us Africans logical reasoning: we bring to you Europeans, to you Latins, intuitive reasoning by which *négri-tude* is defined, *négritude* being total comprehension of the world, a symbiosis of subject and object... To atheistic materialism we oppose spiritualistic materialism, which is incarnated in History and whose precursor was the Arab-Berber, the African – Ibn Khaldun. *Credo quia absurdum.* Tertullian's sentence, taken up by Saint Augustine... What these two Berbers, these two Africans, mean is that logic by itself is incapable of comprehending reality. That there is a superior reason: this vital *élan*, this intuition of faith in which subject and object are mingled in an amorous embrace.'[1]

This 1962 speech is perhaps closer to Senghor's thought of the 1930s than some of his speeches which date from that period, for in the 1930s Senghor took pains not to shock his European audiences. Certain texts dating from 1939 seem to confirm this. The above text is not anachronistic except, perhaps, in the reference to Berbers. In 1937 he might possibly have used the *Wolof* sage Kotye Barma instead of Saint Augustine.

The attitude towards Senghor's ideas was well summarized in the preface to the proceedings of the International Congress on the Cultural Evolution of Colonial Countries which Senghor addressed in 1937. This preface was the first European summary of Senghor's thought:

> 'The anti-assimilationist ideas were taken up and rejuvenated with great authority by a Senegalese intellectual, Monsieur L. S. Senghor. He contested the right of the civilizing nations to make uniform the human race, under the pretext of civilizing. To teach African Negroes Graeco-Latin humanities would be to misunderstand their fundamental originality, to domineer the genius of their race, to divert them from another possible humanism, more in conformity with their deepest desires and their congenital

aptitudes. To apply to them the mould of a civilization which is neither made for or by them, for which they are not made, would be to commit an error in orientation, a real injustice, that would result in miserable cultural half-breeds [here used pejoratively and not in Senghor's sense], coated with a varnish which would not penetrate because it *could* not penetrate. According to L. S. Senghor, it is our duty, therefore, to discover the paths along which Negro civilization has been progressing, and to ensure that it continues on these paths, while at the same time speeding up its development. We have not believed it necessary to subscribe to this seductive theory.'[2]

The preface continued by attacking Senghor's ideas: ' "Negro Civilization" is a meaningless word and there is no reference to American half-breeds which could convince us that it exists. The "Negro race" understood as an anthropological reality and as the collective author of a given civilization, is a myth'.[3] This is the mood that Senghor intended to combat by publishing his 1939 essay. But the preface was not content with calling Negro civilization a myth: it also attacked the notion of Negro art which it qualified as a 'no less summary myth in which one finds helter-skelter a mass of sculptural, musical, or choreographical productions which have no relation between them'.[4] In his 1939 essay Senghor tried to show the relationship of all the aspects of Negro civilization to each other. He hoped to show not only the unity of Negro culture, but also that Negro civilization, taken as a whole, could contribute to humanity.[5] Senghor was already demanding European recognition of the work done by African slaves. According to Senghor, the European Renaissance was built on the ruins of Negro African civilization, just as American power developed through Negro sweat and blood.[6] Here he echoed the argument of the Communist Theses of 1922.[7]

Senghor's essay was published in an anthology edited by Daniel-Rops, the late French Catholic intellectual and member of the *Esprit* group. Daniel-Rops noted in his preface: 'We feel today among all the errors of our times which are often monstrous that a new humanism is being elaborated. It will be tomorrow's humanism. To that humanism, which technology will certainly make universal, each of the three races can contribute something'. And he concluded: 'This is a "humanistic" requirement, it is, more deeply, a Christian necessity...'.[8]

His Eminence Cardinal Verdier in his introduction to the book recalled a speech by His Holiness Pope Pius xi who, on 28 July 1938, mentioned the racial problem, underlining forcefully that 'Catholic means universal'. The Cardinal repeated that the Church opposed separatism which tended to dislocate the human family.[9] This lesson reinforced the ideas Senghor previously obtained from his reading of Claudel.[10]

In 1937, Senghor had quoted Césaire's phrase: 'the rendezvous [Judgment Day] of giving and receiving' (where Negroes risked arriving empty handed).[11] By 1939 the development of his theory enabled him to write: 'And the black peoples will not come empty handed to the political and social rendezvous'.[12] He had discovered the virtues of traditional society in Africa.[13]

While awaiting the diffusion of the social lessons that African society could give Europe, 'the Negro contribution to the twentieth-century world had been in literature and art in general'.[14] In 1939 Senghor stressed the musical contribution of Negro civilization. Jazz and other Negro music brought a much-needed revitalization to Western music which was 'enfeebled from being based and perpetuated on arbitrary rules which are too constricting'.[15] He later noted with pride that Dvořák, Milhaud and Stravinsky found a source of inspiration in Negro music.[16] Senghor felt that the position of the African in France was similar to that of the Negro in America, at least in regard to the contribution of the dominated culture to the dominating culture. He has referred to 'jazz' as a black art form, for to him the 'supreme gift' of the black man is rhythm: 'It is the only gift that no one disputes, that the man in the street identifies with *négritude*'.[17] Senghor is happy that European young people are 'crazy about jazz, a healthy folly', because there is a need for it in a mechanized world.[18]

Senghor also stressed the European debt to African artistic originality. Picasso's works, among others, showed the influence of African sculpture and of African masks. Picasso often admitted (notably to Senghor himself) that he owed a great deal to African art.[19] Other artists of the Paris School, Vlaminck, Derain, Modigliani, Braque, and Matisse had been influenced by African art, and Senghor, like the *Revue du Monde Noir*, often mentioned this fact.[20]

The development of Surrealism in Western literature was traceable, according to Senghor, to African sources. Rimbaud, the precursor of the Surrealists, was inspired by African mysticism and animism, and even travelled to Ethiopia to experience them.[21] Senghor has thus underlined the importance of Africa in the revitalization of European literature: 'What the Negro brings is the faculty of perceiving the supernatural in the natural, the sense of the transcendental and the active abandon which accompanies it, the abandon of love. It is as ardent an element of his ethnic personality as is animism'.[22] He made the same comments poetically:

Let us report present at the rebirth of the World
Like the yeast which white flour needs.
For who would teach rhythm to a dead world of machines
        and guns?
Who would give the cry of joy to wake the dead and the
        orphans at dawn?
Say, who would give back the memory of life to the man whose
        hopes are smashed? [23]

Senghor later added to his argument that Africa is distinctive from
Europe in the same way that permanence is distinctive from change.
European criticism of repetition in African arts was answered by
pointing to Egyptian art 'which for 4,000 years, presented the same
impassive face'.[24]

An expanded theory of black contributions was developed by
Senghor after 1939. However, the basic notion was quite simple:
Africa could help Europe.

'We do not believe that we are too presumptuous in advancing the
idea that France's colonies, and among them black Africa, as well
as her provinces can help her to discover the richest elements of
her own traditions: the sense of community, the sense of hier-
archy, the feeling of the divine – in any case of the spiritual – the
feeling of an art which plunges its roots in life and which is produced by the soul as much as and more than by the mind.'[25]

This modest proposal contained the idea that Africa could help
Europe get rid of its emphasis on cold rationality. Africa could contribute 'that human warmth'[26] which would thaw out Europe. Senghor at the end of the 1930s had become quite prudent; there was
little trace of the 'unheard of message' which the militants of *négritude* had spoken of a few years before.[27] He declared in a 1944 essay:

'It is not a question of sending France to an African school; it is
not even a question of assimilating African elements of which
French writers and painters have begun to be aware…It is a…
service that Africa can render to France: she can help France to
uncover her original and authentic face that lies beneath the ugliness which modern evolution has superimposed.'[28]

In 1961 he addressed Frenchmen:

'The militants of *négritude*, educated by your Africanists, perhaps
helped awaken in you that human need of sensitivity: of the heart
and of the imagination.'[29]

Senghor also declared that, without outside influences (especially
African), the 'terrible factory' which was Europe would have risked
'functioning on nothing and devouring its own entrails'. According

to Senghor, Europe would always be in need of outside sustenance. The Negro contribution had only begun. Europe should become more conscious of her needs, and Senghor took on the task of reminding her of this situation.[30]

'So that the civilization of tomorrow's world will not finish in a planetary catastrophe – and a moral dissolution would be worse than an atomic one – so that Europe's virtues can ripen into harvests for all, it is necessary that Europe appear at the catholic rendezvous of giving and receiving. It is necessary for her *to assimilate*, I do not say imitate, other civilizations. And those others must assimilate Europe. The old Continent has already perceived this fact. Does she not welcome Gandhi and Shri Aurobindo, jazz music and anonymous sculptures from black Africa as revelations... Already Oriental philosophy shapes Western thought, Negro fervour fires the imaginations of artists, while in Africa and Asia people count "two and two make four".'[31]

In 1961 Senghor was more affirmative: 'Your permanent mission is to open yourselves to all the exotic civilizations...'.[32] It is a question of Europe's assimilating extra-European elements.

In modern times the militants of *négritude* relived the tradition which Balthazar began at the foot of Christ's cradle when he presented, and represented, the unique treasure of the black world.[33] This treasure was the 'Negro attitude' to the world and the Hereafter. In 1939, Senghor claimed that 'the Negro contribution will have been to join with other peoples to remake the unity of man and the world; to link the flesh to the spirit, man to his fellow, the pebble to God – in other words, the real to the surreal'.[34]

According to Senghor, Africa's strength lay in her refusal to disassociate reason from imagination. Africa, in Senghor's view, had not left behind the 'Childhood Kingdom' – that of art and poetry. Africa, long before the Romantics and the Surrealists, had understood that the imagination should be given first place.[35]

Senghor and the other militants of *négritude* participated in the war against technology and the machine age which was waged by many young French intellectuals of the 1930s. Senghor employed the concept of African humanism which had been rediscovered by the group of the *Revue du Monde Noir* to combat those who valued industrialism over humanism. '*Négritude* is essentially made of human warmth.'[36] Young French intellectuals who wrote at this time identified technology with the United States. In 1931 Robert Aron and Arnaud Dandieu wrote *Le Cancer Américain*:

'The American cancer... is the hegemony of rational mechanisms over basic and emotional reality, the source of real human progress

...The Yankee spirit is nothing but exploitation on a gigantic production line based upon the most lamentable error that Europe has
ever committed, the rationalist error.' [37]

Senghor offered a solution to suffering Europe, to the whole industrialized world:

'To the anguished reason of Europe...to the problems posed by
the machine, Africa brings its solution: the sense of life, the joy of
life, that which is daughter of rhythm, of earth forces.' [38]

Senghor worked the theory into one of his poems:

New York! I say, New York! let the black blood flow into
    your blood
So that it might unrust your steel joints, as a life-giving oil. [39]

Senghor responded to the needs of white men. He believed he could
furnish that 'additional nourishment for the soul' which Bergson
had mentioned as necessary for a world at grips with the prodigious
progress of technical innovation. [40]

But, more importantly, the 'human warmth' of Senghor's *négritude*
would prevent the dissolution of the world, for it helped to unify, to
synthesize. Senghor believed that the divisions in the world cried out
for this contribution of love which links what seems opposed. He
noted: 'Beyond artistic virtues, the virtue of love will be the major
African contribution to the construction of a world civilization'. [41]
Senghor singled out the capacity for love as a characteristic trait of
Negro peoples, love even for those who had oppressed the race. [42]
This love would thus serve the cause of reconciling races and continents. Reconciliation through love was a recurring theme of Senghor's political thought in the 1940s. [43]

Senghor also developed the idea of Negro uniqueness mentioned
earlier by Gobineau: 'Emotion is as Negro as reason is Greek'. [44] His
concept of 'Negro reason' is linked to the emotion that he claims is
characteristic of his race. Senghor's ideas on this subject were undoubtedly influenced by his reading of Bergson, as well as other
scholars: Louis Achille of the *Revue du Monde Noir*, the anthropologist Lévy-Bruhl, and Father Placide Tempels in *La Philosophie Bantoue*.
To Senghor, 'Negro reason' is synonymous with *sagesse* (wisdom). [45]
He defines this reason as not having 'the rational form'; it is a reason
which is 'non-logical'. [46] In 1948 Senghor supported his theory by
quoting from a letter which Marx wrote in 1843: 'Reason has always
existed but not always in the rational form'. [47] This reason is intuitive.
Since it is a sensitive reason, an embracing reason (*raison-étreinte*),
it is expressed in emotion – losing oneself in order to identify with
an object – and by myths, the archetypal images of the collective

soul.[48] It is a means of understanding reality by empathy: an embracing reason which plunges beyond material appearances thereby reaching the underlying reality of an object by wedding its rhythms.[49] Senghor's motive for describing 'Negro reason' was to achieve recognition of a 'foreign' type of rationality. In this way, he sought to promote his race, to raise it up from the ignominious state to which it had fallen[50] in the eyes of white men.

Senghor observed that Europe had begun the process of abandoning, at least partially, the ideal of objectivity. He quoted Gaëtan Picon's *Panorama des Idées Contemporaines* to underline this fact:

'We are witnessing the general retreat from the idea of objectivity, and everywhere we find the researcher's personality enters into his work... The light of knowledge is no longer that steady brightness which alights on an object without touching it and without being touched by it: it is rather the flashing of lightning born of mutual embrace, the spark of contact, a participation, a communion.'[51]

Senghor affirmed that this abandoning of 'objectivity' was due to the contact between European reason and 'Negro reason': knowledge through empathy.

'Classical European reason is instrumental by utilization...I say classical, since European reason has now returned to the school of empathy...This Europe, so necessary to the world, is in peril of death...if it does not renew itself through contact with exotic civilizations... The salvation of the world resides in this: that, on contact with exotic civilizations, Europe might come back, certainly not to humility, but to modesty and most of all to that subjectivity which is the source of human warmth.'[52]

The poet in Senghor was responsible for his reinstatement of the non-rational. The Nobel prize winning poet St John Perse, to whom Senghor has often been compared, has explained this reliance on intuition:

'When one measures the drama of modern science discovering, even in mathematical absolutes, its rational limits; when one sees in physics two great key doctrines pose, on the one hand, a general principle of relativity, on the other, a quanta principle of uncertainty and indeterminacy...when one hears the greatest scientific innovator of this century...invoke intuition to the aid of reason and proclaim that "the imagination is the true terrain of scientific germination"...is one not right to hold that poetry is as legitimate an instrument as logic?'[53]

Senghor has expressed very similar thoughts:

'...since the discovery of non-Euclidian geometry, of quanta physics, of wave mechanics, and of relativity, we know today that there are no contradictory categories – that intuitive knowledge is the complement of rational knowledge, even in the sciences – that imagination and reason are "well married", that the dream is a part of reality, and that in any case it is the major condition of the transformation of reality.'[54]

In his book, *La Pensée Sauvage*, the French anthropologist Claude Lévi-Strauss appears to support Senghor's argument. Lévi-Strauss stresses that it is necessary to 'recognize that so-called primitive peoples have been able to develop reasonable methods for inserting ... irrationality in rationality'.[55]

The *négritude* movement, in part a result of the desire to propagate intuitive 'Negro reason' in Europe, is somewhat similar to the phenomenological, existential, and Teilhardian movements. Senghor has noted this relationship between the four movements, all born in the 1930s. He speaks of the 'Great Revolution' which, in reaction to the scientism of the nineteenth century, had shaken all the domains of the mind – of culture, art, literature, science, philosophy. 'From that Revolution were to arise not only the new scientific discoveries – relativity, wave mechanics, quantum mechanics, the theories of the non-continuous and of the indeterminate, but also the new philosophies such as phenomenology, existentialism, and Teilhardism'.[56] Like *négritude*, these movements only made an impact on the intellectual world in the 1940s and 1950s.

The unchanging aspect of the notion of 'Negro reason' is seen by examining a number of Senghor's writings from 1939 to the present:

1939

(discussing the Negro soul) '...sensitivity...without literature between subject and object...without subject or object...The nature itself of emotion...It is an abandon which becomes a need, an active attitude of communion....'[57]

1947

'...Negro reason abhors abstraction, even though it is often capable of it. It attaches itself by preference to the real, "Chinese shadow" of the surreal: it is more practical than speculative, it is wisdom more than science.'[58]

1958

'What distinguishes Negro culture is that it is not animated by a desire to dominate, but rather a desire for symbiosis. It does not analyse...from the outside; it does not destroy things in order to use them for material purposes. It approaches the object by a circuitous route, from within, pouring itself into the object's rhythm, not shaping it, but shaping itself as a soft wax in the object's most secret, most alive corners. Negro reason is born with [*con-naît*]⁵⁹ the object by sympathetic intuition. Its purpose is not utilization, but participation; it is to live with the other a more intense life, more spiritual than material....'⁶⁰

1961

'Negro values opposed those of Europe; they opposed discursive, logical, instrumental reason. *Négritude* was intuitive reason, a loving reason, not the reason of the eye. It was, to be precise, communicating warmth, the image-symbol and cosmic rhythm, which, instead of sterilizing by dividing, fertilized by uniting.'⁶¹

Is not the essence of *négritude* 'part of an important and continuous current of *Western* philosophy, a current which tends to by-pass intellectualism by use of the irrational?' This question, asked by the French literary critic Pierre-Henri Simon, seems to be the most difficult one for Senghor to answer.⁶² In fact, it does not appear that 'Negro reason' is a contribution of the black man; it is a part of all men.

However, this weakness does not invalidate certain elements in Senghor's theory. As the French essayist Claude Roy observed: 'The entry of primitive arts and non-classical cultures into the common domain of humanity is not accomplished by a simple transposition in which the masks and the *tapas* would replace the *kouros* and the paintings, which would in turn be relegated to the dungeons of culture. They must be thought of as enrichments'. He noted that the study of non-European societies could furnish 'a more profound understanding of the movements and rhythms of psychic and social life'. It would 'help us to know ourselves better by enabling us to recognize ourselves in what seemed to negate us'. Claude Roy finished by writing of a 'total humanism',⁶³ thus echoing Senghor's first formulation of 'What the Negro Contributes'.

There is one further difficulty caused by the 'Negro contribution'. Senghor conceived his humanism as an orchestra with Europe as maestro: 'We do not see any inconvenience in Europe being the conductor. We Negroes are content to take care of the drum section'. It is true that he specified the role of the Negroes in the orchestra: 'It is sufficient for us to mark imperiously the basic rhythm, tapping our feet on the ground...'.⁶⁴ But the impression left on his readers is that Senghor, in exaggerating the differences between European and African, relegated Africa to a subsidiary role in the field of technology. Africa would supply the Civilization of the Universal only with its more exotic needs.⁶⁵ By doing so, he would appear to have condemned Africa to continuing unfavourable terms of trade. The parallel between economy and culture seems particularly significant because prices of tropical products have consistently diminished in relation to prices of industrial products on the world market.

African students of the 1960s regard this theory with much hostility, especially the apparent subordination of Africa to Europe by its so-called complementarity. They wish to equal Europe in all fields, and they do not appreciate the 'orchestra' which is a favourite French Catholic metaphor. Cardinal Verdier's preface to the 1939 book in which Senghor's essay appeared had quoted Pope Pius XI, who had said 'There are in musical compositions great variations in which the same leitmotif comes back constantly, but with diverse tonalities, intonations, and expressions...' to show the possibility of a humanism which incorporates the influences of very diverse civilizations.[66] Théodore Monod, quoted by Robert Delavignette in his preface to the Senegalese novel *Karim*, used a similar metaphor: '...for the same reason that a variety of instruments is necessary to a symphony, or the different colours of the palette to the harmony of a painting. And this is exactly what Teilhard de Chardin said when, apropos of human races, he spoke of "functional diversity", of "essential complementarity", and of "union which differentiates". It is not a question of impoverishing humanity by assuring the ascendancy of only one of the possible aspects of human culture, but rather it is a question of allowing each element of the earthly family to bring something to the common concert, to enrich the whole by the best of itself'.[67]

19. The Impact of World War II

The publishing of his essay 'What the Negro Contributes' in 1939 marked the end of a period for Senghor. The beginning of the war led Senghor outside his literary preoccupations and tossed him into military camps. In 1940 the *Agrégé* Senghor left the *Lycée* near Paris where he was teaching to become a 'second-class soldier'[1] in the Regiments of the Colonial Infantry. Although racism in the French army denied him the commission due the holder of a high academic degree, Senghor had to help the French overcome Nazi racism and hate.

> O Lord, heed the offering of our militant faith
> Receive the gift of our bodies, the elect of all
>   these darkly perfect bodies
> Black victims, lightning rods.
> We offer Thee our bodies with those of the peasants
>   of France, our comrades
> Friends till death after the first handshake, the
>   first exchange of words...[2]

On 20 June 1940 Senghor was made prisoner at La Charité-sur-Loire. According to Georges Pompidou, Senghor barely escaped being shot with some other Senegalese. Fortunately a French officer intervened and prevailed on the German officers to help Senghor 'escape this racist massacre'.[3]

From his capture until his release in June 1942 Senghor shared the life of the *stalags* with other colonial troops. In the *Stalag* of Poitiers he met Henri and Robert Eboué, sons of the black Governor of Tchad who was the first high colonial official to rally the Free French.[4] (This encounter was important to Senghor's later political career. He eventually married Eboué's daughter, Ginette, whose family introduced him into the Paris Gaullist milieu.) In 1942 Senghor wrote a poem 'To Governor Eboué' and dedicated it to his co-prisoners Henri and Robert:

> Eboué! You are the rock on which the temple and hope
>   are built.
> And your name means 'the rock'.

I say you are no more Félix but Pierre Eboué...[5]
Eboué! You are the Lion with the brief cry, the
   Lion who stands and says no!

You are the simple pride of my own Africa, the pride
   of a country drained of its sons.
Knocked down cheaper than herrings.
She has only her honour
And three centuries of sweat have not bowed your back.
Eboué. You are the stone that gathers moss, because
   you are set because you are erect.
   ......
Now Africa arises...
Africa made herself white steel,
Africa made herself black sacrifice
That the hope of man might live.[6]

In *Front Stalag 230* Senghor complained of his condition:

I am no longer the official who has authority,
   the *Marabout* with charmed disciples[7]
Europe has flattened me as the ordinary warrior
   under the pachydermal feet of the tanks.
   ......
Mother, I am a humiliated soldier fed on rough millet.
Tell me, O tell me, the pride of my fathers.[8]

During the time spent in *Front Stalag 230*, Senghor turned to the classics for perspective: 'Often at dusk, in the moment of the low and shiny tide of the soul, I felt the need of comforting. Well, it was enough for me to read some pages of French prose. In this French-style garden I found everything in its exact place, illuminated according to its size. And, once again, everything within me regained its place and its assurance: its human size in its own light'.[9]

The African prisoner did not only read French works. 'It was at the end of 1941, I had been in a prison camp at Poitiers for one year...My progress in German had at last enabled me to read Goethe's poetry in the original. It was a revelation which brought me to re-read the great works of the Master with a more attentive eye. In my minuscule library I now placed *Faust* and *Iphigenia* beside the *Aeneid*, Pascal's *Thoughts*, and Plato's *Dialogs*, which had become my bedside reading.' Senghor wrote in 1949 that this reading resulted in a 'veritable conversion'.[10] Nevertheless it seems that the influence of Goethe was much less important than that of French thinkers. Goethe rather reinforced the tendencies already encouraged by Gide who was himself a fervent admirer of Goethe. The 'discordant dualism' of the two writers resolved itself in a 'harmony' which appeared as the 'sovereign purpose' of life.[11]

However, Senghor has continued to insist on the importance of Goethe's works to *négritude*.

'The defeat of France and of the West in 1940 had at first stupefied us, the Negro intellectuals. We soon woke up under the sting of the catastrophe, nude and sober. Here, in the odour of ossuaries and to the noise of execution squads, our hate of reason and cult of blood had led us...Goethe...taught us first the danger of cultural solitude, of falling back on oneself, of the desire to build only on one's own race, one's nation, one's native virtues...Here then is Goethe, back from Italy, rich in new visions, readings, and thoughts. Fruitful uprooting, which enabled him to produce... his masterpieces..."Everyone must be Greek in his own way but must be Greek" Goethe counsels the New Negroes. This is not to say that they must renounce the proud affirmation of their feelings, that they must smother the dark fountains of their blood...they will be the magnificent masters of the earth forces by which *négritude* expresses itself; with them from now on the image will not live by an autonomous force and ruin the idea, the mind will contain the form...Perfect equilibrium between two complementary values, the heart and the head, the instinct and the imagination, the real and the fact: that is the lesson which Goethe extracts for us from ancient art.'[12]

Senghor concluded by developing his earlier themes of the 1930s: 'It is thus, I thought near the barbed wire of the camp, that our most incarnate voice, our most Negro works would be at the same time the most human...Strange meeting, significant lesson. The blind categories of Leo Frobenius had divided us, Negroes from Germans. And now another German had reconciled us. He had wandered from the extreme North in search of the sun. We came from the South to more temperate countries. And now we had met on the shores of the middle sea, the navel of the world...And we tasted the sweetness of the half-caste sea, of the Mediterranean'.[13] Goethe's idea of two worlds merging in one soul increased Senghor's appreciation of German philosophy. 'You [the Germans] have contributed to convince us of the dangers of autarchy, whether economic or cultural.'[14]

It was also inside the barbed-wire enclosure that Senghor had the opportunity to meet African peasants recruited into the French army. They enabled him to renew his contact with sons of Africa which he had lost so many years before.

To Samba Dyouma the poet, and his voice is the colour
 of flame, and his forehead shows the mark of destiny
To Nyaoutt Mbodye, to Koli N'Gom your brother in name
To all those who, at the hour when the long arms are
 sad as branches beaten by the sun
In the evening, grouped shivering around the dish of amity...
Make place for me around the stove, that I may take
 back my still warm seat
Let our hands touch scooping in the steaming rice of friendship
Let the old *Serer* words pass from mouth to mouth like
 a friendly pipe
Let Dargui share with us his succulent fruits – dried
 and perfumed hay!
You serve us your sayings, enormous as the navel of
 prodigious Africa.
Which singer will this eve summon all the ancestors
 around us?...
Your words so naïvely assembled! And the learned laughed
 at them, yet they restore to me the surreal...[15]

The African tales that Senghor heard from his fellow prisoners helped him endure the difficult hours and gave him ancient inspirations. He later remembered the 'long evenings of captivity in the miserable hut and the groups around the stoves. We had our literary evenings, without books, and our shows'. During the storytelling Senghor heard of the exploits of his African forebears. The other prisoners chanted the refrain of the stories. A makeshift *kôra* strummed with a white shell marked the rhythm. 'You sang in your low and warm voice: you sang of the hard combat, the retreat, the captivity, our odyssey and the future return home.'[16]

While a prisoner, Senghor wrote a number of poems and sent them by letter to Georges Pompidou. They were hand delivered by one of Senghor's guards, a German soldier who was formerly Professor of Chinese at the University of Vienna.[17] These poems were later published as *Hosties Noires*.

In June 1942 one of Senghor's West Indian friends pleaded with the French doctors of the hospital of the prison camp of St-Médard-en-Jalles near Bordeaux to rescue Senghor from the 'clutches of the Germans into whose hands he had fallen'.[18] The doctors diagnosed a 'diplomatic' illness and had Senghor discharged.[19] Senghor has said that before his release from prison he had been sent to a punishment camp for having helped some Breton prisoners escape and for having edited anti-Nazi propaganda.[20]

Upon leaving the *Stalag* Senghor went to Paris and shortly thereafter reassumed his functions as *Professeur* in the *Lycée* of the suburb St Maur. He immediately joined a resistance group and hid a Jewish woman and a resistance sniper sought by the Gestapo. Senghor is proud of his activities in the underground which brought him close to danger. After the liberation of Paris, Senghor delivered a case of nitroglycerine bombs to the French police.[21]

The war had stranded a number of black students in Paris and other university towns of France. There was Sourou Migan Apithy, future president of Dahomey; Alioune Diop, future director of the *Revue Présence Africaine*; Abdoulaye Ly, future leader of the opposition in Senegal; Santos and Amorin of Togo; Sankhalé and Diatta of Senegal; Caku of the Ivory Coast; Béhanzin of Dahomey, and the West Indian poets Guy Tirolien and Albert Béville (who wrote under the pseudonym Paul Niger). Missing from France, however, was Césaire who had returned to the West Indies.

The Vichy government organized Colonial Students' Clubs (*Foyers*) and vacation camps. The Imperial *Foyer* of Paris was opened on 8 May 1943 on the Boulevard Saint-Germain. The colonial students in Paris had organized study groups to discuss colonial problems. A news-sheet was published by the organization of *Foyers* from July 1943 on. Senghor contributed his poems to the first issue. He lectured at cultural meetings in the *Foyer* on 'The Problem of Education in French West Africa' and on 'The African Soul and Civilization'.[22] Senghor wrote regularly for the news-sheet which became an official publication of the Secretariat of State for Navy and Colonies of the Vichy government. Eight numbers in all appeared before publication ceased in May 1944. The news-sheet was called *L'Etudiant de la France d'Outre-Mer: Chronique des Foyers* and in its last issue appeared the account of a lecture given by Georges Pompidou, then *Professeur* at the *Lycée Henri IV*. (Pompidou had been invited to speak at the Paris *Foyer* by Senghor.)[23]

Senghor's participation in the colonial student groups in Paris showed that he had not abandoned his old idea of an association[24] to put into effect the cultural theories that he had developed during the 1930s. His ideas were taken up by the new generation of Parisian Negro intellectuals, and it was under the direction of Alioune Diop that the association outlined by Senghor took shape. The 'Cercle du Père Diop' met regularly at the Paris *Foyer*, inviting such speakers as the geographer Pierre Gourou, the economist Jacques Madaule, the ethnographer Marcel Griaule, and the writer Albert Camus.[25]

Students from the colonies agreed about the effect French culture had on them: 'French culture...brings about a crisis in us which can be resolved by one of three different attitudes: resistance, capitulation, adaptation'.[26] Reacting like their older brothers Senghor and Césaire, they in their turn became militants of *négritude*. They also tried to think out their role in the world, realizing that they were as much strangers to traditional African society as they were to Europe.[27] Alioune Diop has described the dilemma of Blacks such as he. 'Incapable of returning entirely to our original traditions or of assimilating ourselves to Europe, we had the feeling that we were constituting a new race, mentally half-caste, but which had not made itself known by its originality and which had scarcely become aware of itself. Uprooted? We were uprooted precisely to the extent that we had not yet thought out our position in the world and had fallen between two societies, without recognized significance in one or the other, strangers to one as to the other.'[28]

It was during the war that the movement of *négritude* began to gather momentum. The young African intellectuals, as their European counterparts, began to question former values which had been upset by the crisis of the 1940s. For Senghor, the war only reinforced his experiences of the 1930s, but for Alioune Diop and the others, it was the war that brought about this reappraisal of European values.

After the 1944 liberation, the 'cercle du Père Diop' of the Vichy period sponsored a lecture series called 'Encounters with Europe'.[29] The group was addressed by great post-war French writers such as Jean-Paul Sartre, Emmanuel Mounier, and the philosopher Gabriel Marcel.[30]

With the liberation, the colonial reforms heralded by the Brazzaville Conference held in January-February 1944 began to be felt in the Negro milieux of the French capital. The new colonial policy gave the public gatherings of 'Encounters with Europe' an increasing importance, for the possibility of African representation in the future Constituent Assembly was in the air. By the end of 1944 colonial officials, including the Minister of Colonies, attended these meetings. Governor Robert Delavignette, Director of the *Ecole Coloniale* which trained colonial officials, often came.

Delavignette, whose writings had helped Senghor in his search for *négritude* during the 1930s,[31] gave Senghor the chair of African Languages at the *Ecole*.[32] (Delavignette later played an important role in Senghor's nomination to his first political post in 1945.[33]) In 1945 Senghor published his essay 'Views on Africa or Assimilate, don't be Assimilated' in a collective work entitled *La Communauté Impériale Française*. The essay was dedicated to Robert Delavignette.[34] Senghor had previously written an analysis of one of Delavignette's books and published it in the *Etudiant de la France d'Outre-Mer*.[35]

The chair of African Languages at the *Ecole Coloniale*, the essay of 1945, and his friendship with Governor Delavignette marked the beginning of a new period in Senghor's life. The parenthesis of the war was closed. There was no question of returning to the *status quo ante*.

From 1939 on Senghor grew progressively more interested in the political organization of traditional African society. He seems to have become aware of the political and social alienation of Africa. An essay written in 1943 but only published in 1945 showed this growing political awareness.[1]

In this essay Senghor also developed certain of his cultural ideas of the 1930s. He wished to suggest the basis of a new cultural policy to the Free French colonial officials. He quoted the great French colonial officer, General Lyautey, who expressed certain ideas similar to those of Gide and Michelet already noted.[2] When the General had been the French Resident in Morocco, he had written: 'What I dream of is that it [Morocco] may become a community of people where men, however diverse in origin, habits, professions, and races, can pursue the search for a common ideal without losing anything of their individuality...'.[3]

Senghor wanted French cultural policy to be reassessed in the light of Lyautey's dream, so that it would encompass the entire French Empire. The solution of the colonial problem was 'at the very basis of the French renaissance'.[4]

'Natives of Africa...we have a profoundly original temperament and soul which is shown in our customs and beliefs. It is possible to convey to us *in toto* the political and social organization of the Mother Country with its *Départements* and *Députés*, proletariat and parties and unions, secular education with its manuals and programmes, etc., etc. It is possible to make us lose our virtues, perhaps our faults. We can be impregnated with the defects of the Metropolitan French. I doubt that it would be possible in that fashion to give us their virtues. The risk is that we should become only pale copies of the French, consumers and not producers of culture.'[5]

Senghor expanded his thought by stating that the Africans were opposed to 'false assimilation which is only identification'. They were 'no less hostile towards the anti-assimilationist trend'. Those opposed to assimilation were tainted by capitalist interests. Senghor repeated his phrase 'Assimilate, don't be Assimilated' which appeared in the sub-title of the essay: 'It is a matter of an active and judicious assimilation which enriches native civilizations and which helps them to leave behind their stagnation or to be reborn out of their decadence'.[6]

In 1944 Senghor applied his theory of active assimilation to religion as well as to society and politics. 'Just as French colonization by its "civilizing" action cannot ignore African civilization, so Catholicism cannot ignore Animism without laying itself open to a serious bankruptcy. In these countries of sandy plains, nothing solid, nothing durable can be built except on the stony foundation of Animism'. The missionary must therefore understand traditional religion.[7] The advice of Delafosse echoes through this passage.

In his essay Senghor also focused his attention on educational reform. He hoped to see more money for education in Africa. He criticized the orientation of the *Ecole Rurale Populaire* which he had warmly supported in 1937 at the International Congress on the Cultural Evolution of Colonial Countries. He now saw the danger of the emphasis placed on manual labour at the expense of intellectual training.[8] Trade schools, on the other hand, should teach European technology while encouraging the 'hereditary manual skills and the recovery of truly African styles'. But the necessity of recovering and maintaining the traditional styles applied above all to the old trades of Africa: leather working, weaving, basketwork, pottery, jewellery. The new craftsmen 'will respond to new needs by making new objects, but they will do so in accord with African aesthetic criteria'.[9]

Senghor went on to criticize the William Ponty Teacher's College for French West Africa. He applauded the placing of 'colonial writers' such as Pierre Loti and Delavignette in the reading lists. But he wanted to see the addition of more controversial writers such as René Maran.[10] He recommended teaching ethnography and linguistics at the College. 'The professors of ethnology would thus add to the personal experience that each student has of Africa by examining it in the light of other experiences; they would give him a sound training in methods of research that would enable him to bring new primary sources which could be used by professors for their texts'. Senghor lamented old Africa's passing and the transformation of languages and customs. He added: 'there is still time to photograph Africa's present face in which its timeless qualities are still so emphatic. Tomorrow it will be too late'.[11] He advocated two specific additions to the curriculum: native language instruction and a course on African humanities. These subjects would aid in the development of a Negro-African literature, 'as has happened in America'.[12] Once again Senghor held up the American Negro as worthy of emulation.

Senghor's 1945 essay was intended to arouse French opinion at a moment when it could play an effective role in the 'rebirth' of all French territory, both at home and overseas. It was Senghor's last publication as a private individual. From this point on he took his case into the political arena.[13]

Although Senghor's activity during the years 1945 and 1946 was primarily political, he managed to publish a volume of poems entitled *Chants d'Ombre* (Shadow Songs) and an essay in the progressive Catholic review *Esprit*.[1] The attention of the French literary world was also drawn to African writing with the emergence of the black cultural review, *Présence Africaine*.

In 1946, Alioune Diop (who was *Chef de Cabinet* of the liberal Governor-General of French West Africa, René Barthes) discussed with Georges Balandier and other Africanists in Dakar the idea of founding an African literary review. Soon afterwards Alioune Diop was elected Senegalese *Counseiller de la République* on the SFIO ticket. With the aid of Governor-General Barthes the young legislator published the first issue of the review in November 1947. Jean-Paul Sartre apparently gave the idea for the title *Présence Africaine*. The Board of Sponsors included Théodore Monod, Director of the *Institut Français d'Afrique Noire* (the Africanist research organization based in Dakar); André Gide, whose books on his travels in the Congo had influenced the *négritude* movement in the 1930s; Jean-Paul Sartre, who gave a systematic analysis of *négritude* in a 1948 essay; Emmanuel Mounier, leader of the group of progressive Catholics who had exerted an important influence on Senghor in the 1930s; the ethnographer and Surrealist Michel Leiris; and the novelist Albert Camus.[2]

Alioune Diop met with this eminent group during the autumn of 1947 in the famous Left Bank café *Brasserie Lipp*. Richard Wright, the self-exiled American Negro writer, and Senghor were also present at the first meetings. The group decided that all political points of view would be included in the review. This explains why names such as Aimé Césaire, communist *Député* from Martinique, appeared beside those of Reverend Father Maydieu, Dominican and Director of the review *Vie Intellectuelle*.[3]

It is noteworthy that many Catholic intellectuals helped Alioune Diop found *Présence Africaine*. A left-wing African student accused the Catholics of 'appropriating this journal which was created for the expression of Negro intellectuals'. Under the 'occult sponsorship' of these French Catholics *Présence Africaine* was born.[4] It is incontestable that liberal Catholics played an important role in the enterprise, but it is an exaggeration to imply that they controlled the review. The influence of the publishing house *Editions du Seuil*, which published Senghor's works as well as those of Mounier and Teilhard de Chardin, should not, however, be underestimated.

Starting in 1947 the literature and thought of the Afro-French was regularly published and commented on. That year Léon Damas published a collection of poems written by overseas 'Frenchmen', *Poètes d'Expression Française* which appeared under the auspices of the *Editions du Seuil*. Following Damas's example, Senghor published his own *Anthologie* of the New Poetry by Black and Malagasy writers. The format was similar to that of the earlier work by Damas, but there was one important difference. The *Anthologie* contained a preface written by Jean-Paul Sartre entitled 'Black Orpheus'. For this reason there was considerable attention given to the book. The public was irresistibly attracted by Sartre.

Sartre tried to grasp the meaning of Blackness. He then developed a systematic presentation of the notion of *négritude* in 'Black Orpheus'. By analysing the 'theory', he crystallized it. 'Immediately', noted the Senegalese historian Abdoulaye Ly, 'the impressions, the subjective opinions of *négritude* seemed to become a doctrine.'[5]

Sartre, in the tradition of the 'committed' thinkers of the eighteenth century, put his talents to the service of a great human cause.[6] Despite the one hundred years that had passed since the abolition of slavery in the French colonies, it was only recently that there had been a conscious effort to understand Blackness as a positive quality. In 'Black Orpheus' Sartre examined the black man's contribution to his own liberation.

Sartre began his preface with disquieting questions: 'What did you expect to find when you took out the gag which silenced these black voices? That they would sing your praises? When these heads that our fathers had forced to the ground straightened up, did you think you would read adoration in their eyes?'[7] It was Sartre's purpose to see white men and their civilization through black eyes. 'I want you to feel, as I, the sensation of being seen'. White men had had the monopoly on 'seeing without being seen.' 'The whiteness of his skin was another aspect of vision, a light condensed. The white man, white because he was man, white like the day, white as truth is white, white like virtue, lighted...all creation.' Through the poetry of the *Anthologie*, 'black men have fixed their gaze upon us'.[8] Poetry was the black man's medium of reinstatement.

According to Sartre, 'Negro poetry in the French language is, in our times, the only great revolutionary poetry'. Because of the colour of his skin, the Negro is 'forced to be authentic: insulted, enslaved, he straightens up, he picks up the word "Nigger" that was thrown at him like a stone, poetically he claims his Negro-ness, in the face of the white man, and with pride'.[9] It is for that reason that the final revolutionary unity, 'which will gather together all the oppressed in the same combat, must be preceded in the colonies' by what Sartre called the 'moment of separation or negativity: that anti-racist racism which is the only way leading to the abolition of the differences between races'. In that moment the poetry of *négritude* was born.

Sartre stressed the notion that there is a difference between white and black proletariats. The Whites profit from colonization, even the white proletariat. Here was a powerful reason to justify the Black's claim to his own separate identity before joining with the proletarians of all races against capitalist exploitation from which they all suffer.[10] The concept of a unique black identity relied heavily on Senghor's notion of the 'Negro soul'. Sartre's definition of *négritude* characterized it as a 'certain quality common to the thoughts and conduct of Negroes'. Negroes could discover their *négritude* in two ways: the Negro could 'make objective certain subjective characteristics' or he could 'interiorize behaviour objectively observed'.[11] Here Sartre had accurately described the process followed by Senghor. In finding his soul the Senegalese poet had plunged within himself to his dreams, to his childhood – and had drawn on the works of Africanists.

After regaining their black consciousness, the poets wanted others to partake of that experience. Their poetry had an evangelical quality. The missionaries of *négritude* had another responsibility which Sartre called 'Orphic': 'It is a quest, a systematic stripping and an asceticism which accompanies a continual effort of searching within oneself'. The poet descends within himself like Orpheus descending into Hades in search of Eurydice, 'chanting his angers, his regrets, or his hates, exhibiting his wounds, his life torn between "civilization" and the old Negro foundation'. When he is at his most lyrical, wrote Sartre, the Negro poet 'achieves what is most certainly a great collective poetry: by merely speaking for himself, he speaks for all black men; it is when smothered by the serpents (of European culture) that he shows himself most revolutionary'. It is then that he undertakes to 'systematically ruin his European attributes, and this mental destruction symbolizes the great taking-up of arms by which the Blacks will break their chains'.[12]

Poetry became the Black's mode of expression and yet language was his nemesis. Sartre defined this dilemma as linguistic. Because of the great number of African languages, black men who had been

transplanted to a new culture found that they could only be understood by their compatriots in a Western language. (The similarity
with Pan-Slavists is striking.)[13] Black poets, however, twisted the
French language until they 'de-Frenchified' the words by breaking
their customary associations: 'It is only when they have disgorged
their whiteness' that the poet adopts these words in his vocabulary.[14]
Sartre pointed to the example of the words 'black' and 'white' as
used by Afro-French poets. 'Black' signifies beauty, 'white' signifies
suffering, pain, hate, etc. By transforming conventional French, the
black poets recovered their 'existential unity'. 'It is necessary therefore for the Negro to die in the context of white culture so he can be
reborn with a black soul.'[15] Although the poetry of *négritude* was
often strong and innovative, there was 'something shrivelled, tense,
and desperate' about it when it attempted 'to recapture folk poetry'.
It was created from the experience of the new Negro and did not
emerge organically out of traditional inspirations.[16]

Until 1948 no one had really tried to define this amorphous, in-
expressible perception called blackness. Sartre began his description
of *négritude* by evoking images of the night. *Négritude* is 'that far
away tom-tom in the nocturnal streets of Dakar, the voodoo cries
which emerge from the airhole of a Haitian hut and slip smoothly
along the road'; it is the Congolese mask. It is a poem by Césaire,
'foaming, bloody, full of snail's mucus, which writhes in the dust
like a worm cut in two'. It is 'that double spasm of ingestion and
excretion' which beats the rhythm of the Negro heart.

Sartre noted that a white man 'cannot speak adequately (of *négritude*) because he does not have the inner experience and because
European languages lack words which allow its description'. *Négritude* is 'in its heart pure poetry'. Sartre supported Senghor's conception of *négritude* in poetry as 'the emotional warmth which gives life
to words, which transmutes word into speech'. Style was more
important than theme as a criterion for *négritude*.

Négritude was not 'a state, nor a definite group of vices and virtues,
intellectual and moral qualities; it was a certain affective attitude towards the world'. Sartre wrote that *négritude* was a feeling and thus a
'clear way of living in *rapport* with the world which surrounds us...
it is a tension of the soul...a way of overcoming the hard postulates
of experience... *négritude*, to use Heidegger's expression, is the being-
in-the-world of the Negro'.[17]

Contrasting the white man and the Negro, Sartre explained that
the white *Homo faber* violates what he analyses by his reason while
the Negro, on the other hand, respects what he tries to understand
'by empathy'. This was a distinction based on Bergson which was

appreciated first by Senghor and later by Sartre. Referring to black poetry as a poetry of 'farmers', Sartre used Nietzsche's definition and styled it as 'Dionysiac' in contrast to European poetry which was 'Apollonian'.[18]

There is a unity in the Negro world which Sartre perceived. Part of that unity comes from the collective past of black men; part comes from the similar reactions of both West Indians and Africans to nature and the supernatural. At times, however, even Sartre had difficulty expressing this ambiguous concept:

'But can we still...believe in the internal homogeneity of *négritude*? And how can we say what it *is*? Sometimes it is a lost innocence which existed only in a distant past, and sometimes a hope which will only be realized in the City of the future. Sometimes it contracts itself in a pantheistic instant with Nature and sometimes it extends itself until it coincides with the whole history of Humanity; sometimes it is an existential attitude and sometimes an objective group of African traditions. Does one discover it? Does one create it?'

It was difficult for Sartre to decide whether *négritude* was predetermined or self-imposed: 'Does the authentic Negro's conduct follow from his essence as consequences follow from a principle, or is one a Negro as the faithful adherent of a religion is a believer, that is to say in fear and trembling, in anxiety, in perpetual fear of not being exactly what one would like to be?'[19] He questioned whether *négritude* was a given fact or a value, 'the object of an empirical intuition or a moral concept'. He asked whether *négritude* was ever authentic 'outside the impulsive and in the immediate'. Was *négritude* a systematic explanation of the Negro soul or a 'Platonic archteype that one can approach indefinitely without ever reaching it?' Sartre concluded that *négritude* was all of these at one and the same time 'and many other things as well'.[20]

In his attempt to define *négritude*, Sartre viewed the Negro as a proletarian: 'Because he has suffered more from capitalist exploitation, he has acquired a heightened sense of revolt and a greater love of liberty. He is the most oppressed, and when he works for his own deliverance, it is the freedom of everyone that he is of necessity pursuing'. This mission constitutes the 'Negro contribution to the evolution of Humanity'. According to Sartre, the Negro wants to abolish ethnic privileges, regardless of their origin; he affirms his solidarity with the oppressed of all colours.

Sartre believed that the 'most ardent poets of *négritude* were also militant Marxists'.[21] This statement did not apply to Senghor. Senghor and the black Marxists did have something in common, however.

They all thought that racial affirmation preceded integral human-ism. Sartre described this process:

> '*Négritude* appears as the second step in a dialectic progression: the theoretical and practical affirmation of white supremacy is the thesis; the position of *négritude* as antithetical value is the moment of negativity. But this moment has no self-sufficiency and the Negroes who use it know that quite well; they know that it pre-pares the synthesis or realization of the human being in a society without races. Thus *négritude* is intended to destroy itself, it is a passage and not an end, a means and not a final end. At the mo-ment when the Black Orpheus most closely embraces his Eurydice, he feels that she vanishes from between his arms.' [22]

Following this line of reasoning Sartre wrote that it was indeed a strange path that these poets took: 'Humiliated, offended, the Ne-groes dig to the most profound depths of themselves to find their most secret pride, and when they at last find it, that pride contests it-self: with a gesture of supreme generosity they abandon it'. And Sartre concluded: '*négritude* is not a condition, it is pure by-passing of itself, it is love'. [23] It is like Senghor's black woman who dies 'to nourish the roots of life'. [24] Because *négritude* exists only in tension, it must, according to Sartre, express itself in poetry. [25]

In his essay Sartre had transformed the idea of *négritude* into a philosophy. The impact of 'Black Orpheus' upon the Afro-French community was dramatic. Sartre had not only crystallized the notion, he had helped to make it a philosophical war-cry. Attracted by the name of the great French writer, many who would never have read the poetry of *négritude* sought to discover this new world of being.

After the publication of his *Anthologie*, which had allowed Jean-Paul Sartre to make such a significant contribution to the enterprise begun in 1929, Senghor limited his cultural activity to the elaboration of ideas first expressed during the 1930s. He began to spend increasing amounts of time in politics, even though he winced at this inevitable reorientation. Beginning in 1945 Senghor served as a *Député* in the French National Assembly. The publication of 'Black Orpheus' coupled with Senghor's entry into political life brought the notions of *négritude* under rigorous scrutiny.

In 1949 Gabriel d'Arboussier, an African politician who at the time was most closely linked to the French Communist Party, was the first to open fire. He violently attacked the theory of *négritude*, which had become a dangerous doctrine in the eyes of the communists. He called it a '*mystification*', a 'diversion from the class struggle', and a racism.[1] D'Arboussier reproached *négritude* for placing the accent on the irrational aspect of life.[2] He used the arguments French communists had employed against Bergson during the 1930s to attack Senghor. The idea of a 'Negro soul' seemed particularly dangerous to D'Arboussier: 'The confusion which consists in putting the West Indian, the American Negro, the Malagasy or the African problem in the same category is nothing but a shocking mystification'. He added that each of these peoples has its own political, social, and cultural problems and that these issues 'cannot be resolved in the same manner'.[3]

Some time later Albert Franklin, an African student member of the nascent *Fédération des Etudiants d'Afrique Noire en France* (FEANF), developed D'Arboussier's line of attack. In 1953 he noted that *négritude* was no longer a simple speculative mental attitude, 'because there are today certain Africans who use it openly or deceitfully to justify their political acts'. Franklin contested the claim of uniqueness in Negro culture and attributed the characteristics of *négritude* (collectivism, rhythm, etc.) to the level of economic development or the living conditions of Negroes. As for Senghor's aphorism 'emotion is Negro as reason is Greek', Franklin wrote: 'We know that reason is not any more Greek than emotion is Negro ...reason and emotion are at the same time Negro, Greek, Yellow, and Red; that is to say, they belong to all humanity...'.[4] Attacking the idea that 'Negro reason is understanding by empathy', Franklin showed that Negroes use the intellect as well as the intuitive.

Franklin criticized Sartre's notion of 'anti-racist racism' which in effect fought fire with fire. Sartre's advice that the Negro should proclaim his *négritude* was erroneous. The only way to destroy racism was to encourage a 'real development of African economy in an independent Africa...'. Franklin believed that prejudice was based on the technical inferiority of the Negro. Once this inferiority was done away with, racial prejudice would soon disappear.[5]

Although Franklin distinguished the West Indian communist *Député* Césaire from 'the mystifiers who live a dreamy and contemplative *négritude* which repudiates reason to espouse the irrational', he cautioned that Césaire risked being confused with them. Franklin ended his essay by noting that the consequence of 'Black Orpheus' was to separate the Africans from the united front of the oppressed against the oppressors. Naturally he advocated continuing close ties with the white proletariat.[6]

Another African critic, Abdoulaye Ly, observed a lack of 'concrete' rapport between *négritude* and the masses of Africa, between the 'black poets and their people'. In 1959 he declared: 'This poetry is linked indirectly to the revolution *par excellence* of our era, to the anti-imperialist revolution in Negro worlds, but it does not express this revolution in its essential aspects'. Abdoulaye Ly examined a passage from 'Black Orpheus' in which Sartre noted that European poetry was often written by 'well-intentioned young members of the middle class who drew their inspiration from their psychological contradictions'. Ly concluded that this description applied to the Negro intellectual of Senghor's generation facing the anti-imperialist revolution in Africa: 'exactly the same'. He criticized the 'non-technological attitude, the lack of preparedness and the neglectfulness of African intellectuals in the practical struggle of the masses'. *Négritude* had been left behind by the struggle for national liberation 'which mobilizes and draws the intellectuals along with all the social classes of Africa in the exaltation of that other poetry, that of militant action'. In Ly's interpretation *négritude* was not the concern of those Africans whom the colonizer did not assimilate. Africans under British indirect rule and the peasant masses of French Africa were not assimilated and had no interest in *négritude*.[7]

The young generation of African students in France during the 1960s approved of these criticisms and added their own linguistic argument: the poetry of *négritude* cannot reach the African masses because they do not read French. To those Africans who reproached

Senghor for writing in French and to those Frenchmen who criticized him for using *Serer* words which they did not understand,[8]
Senghor replied: 'I write in the first place for my people...I think
that it is in touching the Afro-French that we will best reach the
French and, beyond seas and frontiers, other men'.[9]

If Senghor is really writing for his people, it is for those few who
read French and understand all the subtleties of that language. Senghor's poetry, that of an *Agrégé* of Grammar, is filled with archaic
expressions and difficult syntax. In addition to these difficulties for
the ordinary reader, Senghor uses *Serer* words which are not understood outside of Senegal and very likely not understood in some
parts of Senegal itself.

Who, then, was to read this poetry? Senghor said in 1937 that a
Negro literature in French was 'premature'.[10] During the 1940s he
changed his opinion but hesitated advocating Afro-French literature,
which in reality was his own. In 1963 he opposed the wide use of
African languages in poetry, theatre, and the short story thus completely reversing his 1937 position.[11] The young Africans of the 1960
intellectual generation were very hostile to this neglectful attitude.
They have advocated, notably in the *Séminaire* on Negro literature
that the FEANF held in July 1961, a literature which reaches the
masses, a literature in African languages. They have criticized Senghor's generation for its abdication *vis-à-vis* African languages. 'It is
rather strange' wrote a young Congolese 'to learn that the bards of
négritude have until now made no effort to speak Negro, to write in an
African language'. The same student reproached *négritude* for addressing 'European intellectual circles'.[12] A Senegalese student believed
that the neglect of African languages revealed 'a total lack of confidence in the richness of our patrimony and of its possibilities', and
displayed the older generation's 'evident doubt about the advent of
an authentic national culture'. Senghor's poetry had no 'means of
taking root or of gaining an audience among the masses'. Senghor
really addressed 'a new tiny African elite, a few collectors of antique
knick-knacks, or cultivated and refined aesthetes'.[13] These attacks
did not offer solutions to the problem of using an African language
to reach an audience larger than the ethnic group. The African
students' criticism is probably more a function of political antagon-
ism than of hostility to Senghor's work. It is ironic that these criticisms were levelled in French!

Senghor defended his position in 1956 with a query: 'How can we
write for a people composed of ninety per cent illiterates and in a
language which is not its own?...While awaiting the bilingualism
that we advocate and which requires the teaching of an African

language in primary schools along with French, it is necessary to continue writing in French.'[14] In the 'Babel of Linguistic Africa' French possessed the distinct advantage of making one's message understood 'to a greater proportion of our brothers and compatriots, as well as to other men in the world for whom we write as well'.[15]

The African students did not link their rejection of *négritude* solely to the problem of language. Senghor's poetry also lacked the revolutionary qualities necessary to African liberation. The young generation advocated a kind of 'socialist realism' in literature. Senghor, on the other hand, had his party adopt a motion of general policy which 'takes exception to socialist realism as interpreted by Soviet literature of the Stalinist period and recommends African realism which is existential and lyrical...'.[16] This move seemed to be directed against the young Africans who affirmed: 'it is time for our writers and poets to direct their works towards a truly revolutionary realism...'.[17]

Senghor and his generation were accused of being city-dwellers, sons of wealthy, middle-class families, sons of 'feudal lords on the side of colonialism'. According to these young men, 'at the moment of its ideological awakening, [Senghor's generation] had no real contact with African masses and therefore was incapable of expressing the masses' profound aspirations'.[18] Senghor seems to have been aware of this failing. In 1956 he quoted Mao Tse-tung who had said in a speech to Chinese writers that they must write for the people, that it is necessary to 'speak to the people about the pre-occupations of the people'.[19] Senghor's work, taken as a whole, was not written with these ends in mind and therefore cannot be classed as a revolutionary realism.

Senghor's quarrel with socialist or revolutionary realism seems to revolve about relative emphasis to be placed on politics or culture. Senghor agrees with Mao Tse-tung that a modern revolutionary literature should be founded on folk art, but he differs with him when he requires that the 'work be oriented by a political intention, that it be not an end in itself, but a pragmatic means'.[20] Senghor considers politics and art as 'complementary activities' while the communist subordinates 'the latter to the former'. According to Senghor, the communist reverses the proper order when 'he considers politics as an end and art as a means'.[21] Here again Senghor's 'Culture first' of the 1930s appears. It was not until 1957 that Senghor slightly changed his position. Only after the First Congress of Negro Writers and Artists and the *Loi-Cadre*[22] did Senghor admit the pre-eminence of politics in the struggle for African liberation.

Senghor's 'culture first' was also attacked by Frantz Fanon, the French West Indian psychologist who served the cause of Algeria in the long battle against France. Fanon stated that 'it is around peoples' struggles that black African culture takes its substance, and not around songs, poems, or folklore'. Fanon continued by indirectly criticizing Senghor's 'support' of France during the Algerian War:

'Adherence to black African culture and to the cultural unity of Africa is arrived at in the first place by upholding unconditionally the peoples' struggle for freedom. No one can truly wish for the spread of African culture if he does not give practical support to the creation of the conditions necessary to the existence of that culture; in other words, he must first see to the liberation of the whole continent.'[23]

Ezekiel Mphahlele, the exiled South African writer, also criticized the poetry of *négritude* for being a 'romantic rhapsodizing of Africa – Ancestors, naked feet, half-naked women and so on'. He went on to question Senghor's attempt to reconcile a 'near-racist theory' with his 'celebrated humanism'. Stating that '*négritude* means little or nothing' for the black man in countries of British influence or in multiracial communities, Mphahlele concluded: 'The writer in British West Africa does not protest against anything. The writer in multiracial communities finds a lot to protest against as an underdog: this has much to do with the physical fact of discrimination, not with something as abstract and philosophic as cultural alienation'. Mphahlele seemed to misunderstand Senghor's theory of cultural cross-breeding, for he noted: 'Lately, *Présence Africaine* has, unfortunately, been too preoccupied with anthropological creepy-crawlies to devote enough attention to the problems of the artist in his present predicament. It worried me a lot that such a useful institution did not seem to be aware of cultural crosscurrents that characterize artistic expression in multi-racial societies. They seemed to think that the only culture worth exhibiting was traditional or indigenous'. Although Mphahlele blames *Présence Africaine* for a narrow focus, his attack was unjustified because he failed to take into account *négritude*'s theme of cultural cross-breeding. Mphahlele appears as a poor spokesman when he claimed: 'To us in multi-racial communities then, *négritude* is just so much intellectual talk, a cult. Of course, we have not had the misfortune of being educated abroad and being assimilated like our French-speaking friends'.[24] Finally Mphahlele attacked the efficacy of depending on an African cultural renaissance to solve the practical problems facing Africa. Fanon and Mphahlele were preoccupied by the political and racial struggles raging at opposite ends of the African continent – Algeria and South Africa. They criticized *négritude* from the point of view of nationalists involved in destroying the most militant form of Western political intimidation.

Another interpretation of Senghor's *négritude* came from René Ménil, a founder of *Légitime Défense* in 1932, and more recently a member of the political bureau of the French West Indian Communist Party. Ménil updated his long-standing quarrel with Senghor by publishing a long article which appeared in August 1963 in *Action*, the journal of the Martinique Communist Party.

René Ménil analysed what he called a 'reactionary doctrine: *négritude*'. He began by contrasting Negro poetry and *négritude*. Negro poetry expresses 'the historic and social condition of Negroes in modern civilization. More specifically, it describes all the richness of the Negro soul...that is to say, the hate and the joy, the feeling and the hope of the colonized Negro.' But *négritude*, according to René Ménil, was something quite different: 'It is a political doctrine which developed from the racial awakening of intellectuals who were related to the colonial *petite bourgeoisie*, and which had the aim of resolving, in the perspective of that milieu, the problems posed by the struggle for liberation in French colonies...'.[25] To René Ménil, Senghor was the 'principal theorist' of *négritude*. In Senghor, Ménil, found a development of 'mystic and religious themes' that can also be seen in Césaire's pre-1945 work. He accused Césaire and Senghor of exalting 'an anti-intellectualism and a superstitious mysticism', the product of 'reactionary philosophical sources' such as Maritain and Claudel. He was convinced that Catholic intellectuals controlled and directed a considerable number of the militants of *négritude*.[26]

The philosophers from whom Senghor drew inspiration were characterized by Ménil as 'nostalgic for the past and hostile to progress and reason'. He described them in the following manner: 'Faced with the absurdity and the immorality of Western civilization as evidenced in the use of science and technology for the exploiting of man by man...these Western philosophers, most of them spokesmen of the liberal *petite bourgeoisie*, have criticized capitalism in a pessimistic and even outspoken way. But instead of criticizing it lucidly, rationally, or constructively in order to change life by changing institutions – an approach that would have brought them to the revolutionary positions of Marx – they preferred the backward-looking formulations of magic, of religious obscurantism, and advocated a new golden age, a return to nature, a new sort of feudalism. Césaire, Senghor, and their disciples adore Novalis, Frobenius, Bergson, the Surrealists – all of them superstitious spiritualists.'[27]

As Abdoulaye Ly before him, René Ménil stressed the role of Sartre who 'gave form and substance to the still vague and nebulous conceptions' of the Negro poets. 'Sartre was the first to...define the notion of *négritude* and to fix the content in a way that made a coher-

ent system.' Ménil believed that Sartre, 'under the pretext of analysing the prefaced poems', had tossed the poems into a 'magician's hat
and conjured up the Negro in their place! But the Negro in question
is a Negro who resembles Jean-Paul Sartre, a Jean-Paul Sartre whose
colours were darkened and sometimes reversed. He is a very
anguished, a very existentialist, petty bourgeois, picturesque
Negro!' [28]

Senghor's characterization of the Negro's soul and his reason as
something unique to him was false and unreal. Senghor was incapable 'of understanding the Negro psyche as a historic development
and a product of social life. Senghor's Negro was the absolute Negro,
the Negro from nowhere, the Negro outside of social rapports, outside of the real world and the national context.' [29] Senghor's Negro
was 'a noble savage'. Ménil went on to criticize Senghor's racial determinism. 'Reason for the Senghorian Negro is not reason...he
takes reason away from us...to give us better than reason. He gives
us emotion! For emotion is a "superior form of knowing". In brief,
if Whites have reason, will, a power of doing, science, technology,
we Negroes, we have sensation, the gift of myth-making, a magical,
animist, existentialist vision of the world.' Ménil questioned whether
the traits identified by Senghor can be considered as just so many
purely racial elements. The answer was an emphatic 'no!'. 'Contrary
to what Senghor proposed, psychic aptitudes (emotion, logical and
technical aptitude, etc.) should not be considered as a result of race.
They result from historical circumstances, from social conditions
from the structures which determine social class, and from social and
economic practice.' Since his reading of Gobineau, Senghor had considered the 'gift of emotion' as 'an absolute, immutable, eternal trait
of the Negro race'. Ménil insisted, on the other hand, that this trait
was not characteristic of all Negroes or even of all Africans. It could
be found, however, among Africans living under the conditions of
colonialism. Their escape into emotional rather than rational inner
worlds was due to 'the primitive structures of an agrarian economy
and the ignorance maintained in African populations by Western
imperialism'. [30]

René Ménil refused to accept Senghor's notion of cross-breeding
of Negro and white qualities in order to create a 'New Negro'. Senghor's position is weak because he exaggerated the differences between
the races to lay the foundation for his ideal Negro of the future, a
human synthesis of different civilizations, a true cultural half-breed.

In Ménil's view, Senghor had divided human faculties into 'two
radically separated groups which are mutually exclusive'. *Grosso
modo* he saw a Manicheanism with its thesis-antithesis, but failed to

appreciate the synthesis which was essential to Senghor. Ménil in a striking paragraph declared:

'...one [of these two groups] is beneficial and he [Senghor] attributes it to the Whites...On the one hand, emotion, magic, rhythm, imagination, dance, etc. – the Negro's lot. On the other hand, reason, science, technology, the faculty of thinking logically, etc. – the white man's lot. One mentality, the Negro, is the logical opposite of the other, the White. Here we are facing two human worlds which are mutilated and incomplete. The Negro is only the darkened and inverted shadow of the White. Two halves of humanity to one of which certain faculties are lent only on the condition that they be refused to the other. Neither Senghor's Negroes nor his Whites are men, if to be a man it is necessary to enjoy all the aptitudes of sensitivity, reason and practical will, if to be a man it is necessary to be capable of the infinity of operations proper to the human species...To sum up, in the Senghorian theory, it is necessary to add and combine one White and one Negro to have one Man.'[31]

This criticism seems justified in the light of one of Senghor's recent statements: 'The Manichean spirit of the Whites, the spirit of true or false, of all or nothing, the spirit of passion is opposed to the spirit of Africa, that of conciliation by the palaver'.[32] Senghor gives further strength to his critics' arguments by stating that he has no idea of how to describe the identity of Negroes other than by his 'emotion is Negro...'.[33]

A Senegalese student added one more voice to the increasing number of African critics of *négritude*. His article, 'The End of *Négritude*', seemed to level the final blow. 'Until recently most everyone agreed that *négritude* had been, since birth, revolutionary in character. The issue now is whether this "anti-racist racism" will continue to dictate the conduct of Negroes all over the earth.' This student neglected the fact that *négritude* had been attacked by the communist D'Arboussier and the 'progressive' Africans in 1949, and by Albert Franklin, the FEANF leader, in 1953. But one must read on to understand why *négritude* was approaching its end: 'At the present moment it is not colour which should be at the basis of the distinction between men, but rather ideas. Therefore, to advocate *négritude* is to be counter-revolutionary'. He described *négritude* as a veritable 'intellectual bazaar in which one meets a helter-skelter confusion of theories from different schools of thought...'. After noting that Senghor considered emotion a superior form of knowledge, the student continued: 'Today almost all specialists are unanimous in rejecting such a theory. For a long time it has been established scientifically that emotion was the least developed form of know-ledge.' He added that 'those who advocated *négritude* were the only ones to fit their own definition of the Negro' and concluded that the young generation of Africans felt closer to Fidel Castro than to Tshombé, colour notwithstanding.[34]

Attacked by African students more 'nationalist' than he, attacked by Negro Marxists more 'revolutionary' than he, Senghor found himself confronted by Frenchmen who reproached him for his exaltation of Africa. Those who criticized Senghor attacked one or another aspect of *négritude* but did not take the trouble to understand the 'theory' well enough to perceive its complexities. War was waged against *négritude* without precise knowledge of its richness.

These criticisms came during the passionate time of political decolonization. Misunderstandings were inevitable given the irrational nature of *négritude*. During the 1940s, *négritude* became the concern of many Negro intellectuals and it was expressed in as many different ways. *Négritude*, like Marxism, was taken up by men who had very little in common except their adherence to a vague theory, a theory to which they often clung without worrying about the intentions of those who first formulated it.

For a variety of reasons the French intellectual establishment made *négritude* a frequent target of their logic. A right-wing professor of political science Raoul Girardet was able to place *négritude* in the category of systematically anti-Western ideologies. He regarded it as a denial of the heritage of the rationalist and progressive West.[1] Although certain advocates of *négritude* were anti-Western, they only represented one school. The 'theory of cultural cross-breeding' which was characteristic of Senghor's *négritude* lessens the impact of Girardet's appraisal.

Jean Guéhenno, member of the *Académie Française*, described *négritude* as a 'bogeyman's philosophy and poetry'. He found the idea charged with poisons and witchcraft: 'We should erase from dictionaries these big words which ring out like the tom-toms of war. As for me, I cannot any more believe in the virtues of *négritude* than in those of whiteness. The mind has no colour.'[2] Curiously enough, this reasoning was similar to that of the Negro Marxists.

For Roger Bastide, professor of sociology at the Sorbonne, *négritude* in France had become a 'phenomenon of counter-acculturation, and has ended by becoming an apology of African ancestral traditions, whether they be anti-Western, or, on the contrary more Western than even those of the West (which only copied Africa)'.[3] This attitude was based on Cheikh Anta Diop's claim that Western civilization was the direct descendant of the early black civilizations of Egypt.

One of the most violent critics of *négrttude* was Paul-Henri Siriex, former Governor of Overseas France and President of the *Compagnie Française du Haut et Bas Congo*. In his book *Une Nouvelle Afrique*, the former Governor described *négritude* as a 'false inferiority complex'. He spoke of African intellectuals who were tempted to draw inspiration from 'the poisoned sources' of *négritude*. Siriex accused *négritude* of being an 'anti-White racism' and a 'bad cement for a nationalism produced in decadent literary salons or existentialist cellars'.[4]

One of the most developed European criticisms appeared in the great French newspaper *Le Monde* in August 1964. Pierre-Henri Simon, literary critic for the Paris daily, attacked Senghor.[5] He distinguished between what Senghor intended to do and what he actually did. Senghor wanted to write an authentic Negro poetry but his *négritude* 'corresponds to that pole of Western Humanism which re-evaluates the intuitive, the instinctive, the irrational, the mystical; applied to Christianity, it is more Augustinian than Thomist; to logic and ethics, more Rousseauist than Cartesian; to philosophy and history, more Teilhardian than Marxist'.[6] Simon questioned whether the French language was well adapted to expressing the Negro genius: 'We are not always sure that [Senghor] conveys the particular character of Negro rhythm and images: perhaps he has read too much French poetry, lived too long in Paris. Certainly, he uses and abuses words from his native land and language...we must admit that [these words] annoy us in his verbal flow, which is in the high [French] style'. As for the blend of traditional African literary genres which Senghor praised, Simon replied: 'Basically I have remained too Cartesian and too classical to concede willingly that confusion of orders and genres is a sign of progress and an extension of the mind'.[7]

Pierre-Henri Simon dealt his final blow: 'If the reader wants to savour *négritude* in a pure state, without additions or improvements, he can read the first volume of the collection of traditional African Classics'. Simon was referring to the translation of *Nzakara* tribal poetry by a Frenchman, Eric de Dampierre,[8] pointedly ignoring the modern literary efforts of the Afro-French.

By making adjustments to the realities of the colonial world Senghor alienated the young Africans. *Négritude* and Senghor with it became the symbols of conciliation. The more Senghor altered his theory to make it acceptable to the French, the more distance he put between the black anti-Western élite and himself. Yet, for Senghor the defence of *négritude* and the values of African civilization was never so necessary as 'at the moment when understudy-colonizers stood in the wings, hoping to replace France, Great Britain, and Belgium'.[9] For him, *négritude* is a means of pointing to the danger of accepting *en bloc* the Soviet experience as a model.[10] He would rather accept reform in the French colonial context than reject it and fall into the hands of a less familiar hegemony.

In 1962 Senghor willingly admitted that *négritude* was a myth, but he added that free enterprise, democracy, and communism were also 'myths which stir hundreds of millions of men'. The word myth did not have a pejorative connotation for Senghor. The myth of *négritude* was living, dynamic; it 'evolves, given certain circumstances, to become a humanism'.[11] Senghor contrasted false myths which harbour disunity and hate with the true myth of *négritude* which was 'the awareness and expression by sensitive imagery of the problems of a social group, a particular people. In this context it has a didactic value....' [12] Using these arguments Senghor answered the sociologist Paul Mercier who had spoken deprecatingly of the development of 'a veritable mythology around the notion of *négritude*, a kind of "counter racism" which shut out the external world, essentially the Western world...'.[13]

Although European criticism was often addressed to those who emphasized the anti-Western themes of *négritude*, Senghor felt the need to defend it each time it was attacked. Because of Senghor's compulsion to answer these critics, the arguments and counter-arguments frustrate the reader for it would seem that the prosecution and the defence are rarely speaking about the same thing.

As Protestantism has many denominations, *négritude* has many variants. The most successful classification has been made by L. V. Thomas, a professor of philosophy at the University of Dakar who described four distinct types of *négritude*: the suffering, the aggressive, the serene, and the triumphant.[1] Thomas's groupings are, appropriately, emotional descriptions of the Negro's interpretation of his role in the world. They also serve as a catalogue of Negro attitudes and responses to racial discrimination.

The first type of *négritude* is a *Suffering Négritude*. The Negro represents himself to himself as having taken on all human pain; he suffers for all, even the white man. The best example of this tendency is found in Cheikh Hamidou Kane's *Aventure Ambigüe* written in 1961.[2] *Aggressive négritude* is the second type described by Thomas. Having suffered, the Negro revolts. Anger is mixed with virulent anticolonialism. A good example of this *négritude* is A. Tevoedjre's 1958 *L'Afrique Revoltée*.[3] Observing that suffering and anger are not constructive responses, the Negro gives way to appeasement and reconciliation and adopts a *Serene Négritude*. No one has expressed this attitude better than Senghor. The final form that *négritude* takes is as a *Triumphant Négritude*. Once respect for himself and his culture has been restored, the Negro points to his contribution to civilization and asks the West to join him in a proud proclamation of the West's debt to Africa. This triumphant attitude is characteristic of a younger generation than Senghor's. It is particularly well represented by Cheikh Anta Diop's *Nations Nègres et Culture* (1955) which claimed that Negroes founded ancient Egypt, the cradle of the West.[4]

Although Kane, Tevoedjre, Senghor, and Diop each represent one of these types of black awareness, all share some aspect of the others. Their differences lie in the emphasis each places on the various responses to racism. Senghor seems to be at the calm centre of the storm, having unleashed forces which often went beyond his original intentions.

For the purposes of tracing the development of the major exponents of black consciousness, it is useful to distinguish the differences between its primary advocates and to clarify Senghor's position within the framework of the whole movement. The contrast between

Senghor and Césaire reveals the seemingly irreconcilable positions within a single movement.

A critic and friend of Senghor, Aimé Patri, wrote that Senghor and Césaire represented 'the two types of Negro culture distinguished by Frobenius...the frenzied warfare against nature and all forms of human domination (Césaire) and the profound acquiescence, the peaceful harmony with the cosmic powers (Senghor), the "yes" (Senghor) and the "no" (Césaire)'.[5] Another literary critic contrasted them by observing that: 'Where Césaire cries out his horror at the condition of the victims of colonization and preaches revolt, exorcising the chaos created by the "civilizer" with the true believer's supreme confidence, Senghor prefers to charm the monster in a low voice, slowly and ritually, to enchain it with words of seduction and to suggest to it, even now, the promised land of reconciliation'. Senghor's fervour never explodes, 'it is appeased at each impulse'. Unlike the poetry of Césaire, Senghor's is not 'disputatious'.[6] Senghor lacks Césaire's pugnacity and violence.

A more generous evaluation of Senghor was made by a brilliant student of the Paris Ecole Normale Supérieure who wrote that 'the only real defect in Senghor's poetry is that it is remote and rejects the otherness and the complete rupture that Césaire proposes'.[7] An African commented: 'Sometimes Senghor's work induces spontaneous anger. One knows, one feels, that he *could* say what it is necessary to say, but the poet does not say it. Or again...the tone rises to a pitch of virile protest only to subside suddenly into prayer or lamentations.'[8]

The fundamental difference between Senghor and Césaire is Senghor's belief in God and Césaire's atheism: 'God is absent from Césaire's work. There is not a single poem of Senghor's that does not bear the mark of a hidden divinity. Most of the time his poems end with the rhythm of a psalm.' Senghor is a Christian thinker 'who has forgotten to close his missal.'[9]

Senghor's Catholicism sets him apart. His religion is responsible for the *catholic* (universal) love which characterizes his works. This universal love prevents Senghor from advocating violence and consequently distinguishes his work from that of the majority of other black poets. Catholic love is the basis for both his cultural and political theories.

Senghor sees the difference between himself and the more 'revolutionary' poets of *négritude* in the fact that he was less uprooted. Césaire was doubly *déraciné* (a Negro taken from Africa to exile in the West Indies and then exiled from the West Indies to France).[10] Senghor's own experience was similar to that of the Malagasy poet

Ranaivo: 'He passed all his childhood...in Tananarive and its suburbs...He did not go to school before he was eight years old and was therefore aware of his ancestral tradition. This awareness helped him avoid a lengthy period of passive assimilation of French influences.'[11] Those black writers who were more conscious of their uprooting insisted on political liberation from France and preached revolt against the West.[12] Senghor on the other hand, found political separation unthinkable.

Until 1956 Senghor's preoccupation with culture overshadowed the development of his political and economic thought. At the end of the decade political events forced him to reorient his priorities. Even then, his feelings about the pre-eminence of culture influenced his attitudes as a statesman.[13]

The themes of his cultural thought became those of his political thought and of his socio-economic thought. Cultural cross-breeding gave birth to political cross-breeding which took the form of a Federal French Republic. That same cultural theme was at the basis of an economic cross-breeding from which was derived 'the African Road to Socialism'. Senghor's political and economic thinking reflects his desire to 'bridge the gap' and formulate a 'conciliatory agreement'[14] between what seems irremediably opposed: Africa and France, capitalism and communism.

In his Dakar lecture in 1937 Senghor advocated cultural independence for Africa on the one hand and supported political assimilation on the other. 'If you call me a reactionary' he stated in reference to his emphasis on the importance of African traditions, 'I will protest and, distinguishing the political from the cultural, I will propose to you: let us work at making the West African politically a French citizen....'[1] This proposal was relatively progressive at that time. In another 1937 speech Senghor clarified this idea. 'For cultural and social reasons, and not political ones', he supported the *Ecole Rurale Populaire* against cultural assimilation, but he also hoped that his 'compatriots would participate increasingly in the administration of the community.'[2] Until 1943 Senghor believed in the possibility of a certain amount of political assimilation; he wanted it and did not see the contradiction between his cultural and political positions. Addressing the 'colonial students' of Paris in 1943, Senghor discussed the possibility and desirability of becoming Frenchmen: 'To be "a Frenchman above all" is an excellent prescription on the political level where one must place the accent on unity and where Paris must take precedence over the provinces, the head over the heart and viscera'.[3]

The first formulation of Senghor's political theory appears in a 1943 essay dedicated to the colonial Governor Robert Delavignette, whose book *Soudan-Paris-Bourgogne* had influenced the young Senegalese. The essay, part of a collection called *La Communauté Impériale Française*, dealt with the colonial problem 'as nothing more than a provincial problem'.[4] Delavignette's book had already introduced this notion by its very title: Paris linking two equal provinces, the French Sudan and Burgundy. In 1931 the *Revue du Monde Noir* had already treated Africa as a province: 'Different civilizations should be respected in the same way as are the usages and customs of the different provinces of France'.[5]

Barrès's provincialism was the original model for these ideas. It is in Barrès that Senghor's political theory is rooted. Barrès wrote: 'The French nationality is made up of provincial nationalities'. He went on to quote the Provençal poet Mistral's writings on the revitalization of provincial identity. Barrès concluded that a federation would safeguard provincial diversities.[6]

Between 1930 and 1943 Senghor absorbed and reworked these ideas. Africa was not to be integrated purely and simply into France, but rather it was to become a part of a new Federal French Empire. The difference is important. Senghor's new approach to colonial politics cleared the way for the 'accession' of the popular African masses 'to citizenship'. 'It was not, however, a question of drowning the mother country's representatives under the waves of colonial *Députés* who could be representing some seventy-million people.'[7] Senghor proposed an 'Imperial Citizenship', an idea partly advocated by Professor Henri Labouret in the 1930s in the same volume in which an essay of Senghor's appeared.

In 1943 Senghor proposed the creation of 'colonial nations' which would be constituted on the basis of the existing administrative units: North Africa, French Equatorial Africa, French West Africa, the West Indies, Indo-China, and Madagascar. These 'colonial nations' would be governed by a Governor-General, appointed by the mother country, who alone would have executive power and the right of initiative in legislative matters. 'The new Governor-General, however, would need the support of the Federal Assembly to give his projects force of law.'[8] This new political arrangement would have a metropolitan French Governor assisted by a local Assembly. 'In the mother country there would be an "Imperial Parliament" which would contain the representatives of the *Métropole* as well as those from the colonies. Parliament would concern itself with all the problems of general interest: imperial defence, foreign affairs, etc.'

Two themes important in Senghor's cultural thought reappear in his political thought – cultural cross-breeding and active assimilation. France, through her representative, would help Africa, and Africa would help France by sending legislators to a new Parliament. The 'Federation' that Senghor proposed in 1943 strongly resembled the future organization of the French Community of 1958–9. Because Senghor's ideas were in advance of his times, they needed arguments to allay the fears of French conservatives. 'This system…, far from weakening the authority of the mother country, would reinforce it, because it would be based on the consent and love of liberated men, free men. Far from weakening the unity of the Empire, it would reinforce it, because the conductor's task would be, not to drown the voices of the different instruments by shouting them down with his own voice, but rather to direct them in harmony, allowing the smallest bush flute to play its part.'[9]

In this 1943 proposal Senghor hoped to end political alienation in the colonies: 'We saw that the political expression of Africa requires chiefs who represent the people, chiefs chosen by the people'. He noted that there was 'a policy crisis concerning French selection of chiefs which made the colony...or, rather, colonization, ill'. Direct government by the French 'instituted very sincerely in the name of progress constituted, in effect, a political regression'.[10]

Senghor compared the 'former system', that of Negro-African tradition, with French dictatorship. Before French colonization 'all the castes participated in the election of the King and in the administration of the state'. Senghor here made use of his memories of Koumba N'Dofène Diouf, King (*Bour*) of Sine, as well as the work of French ethnography on the kingdom of Sine. It was after Koumba's death that the French gave Sine 'an overall administrator who received his orders from Dakar and Paris'. In the colonial council of Senegal the chiefs named by the Colonial Administration 'were in permanent opposition to the Councillors elected by the citizens (of the four privileged communes)'. Senghor proposed that the new chiefs be intellectuals of the new élite.[11]

Only the election of representatives of the colonial peoples could end the unjust conditions of colonized Africa. In order to effect his programme, Senghor proposed a family vote rather than an individual vote. The election of the parliament would take place in electoral colleges: the village chiefs would designate the representatives of the *cercles* who in turn would designate the representatives of the colonies. The latter would then choose the members of the federal assembly of French West Africa, from which representatives would be sent to the Imperial Parliament in Paris.[12]

The liberation of France in 1944 delayed the publication of Senghor's first important political essay. With its appearance the French politicians who were to apply the ideas of the Brazzaville Conference of January–February 1944 took note of Senghor. These men were selecting the representatives of the Empire to the Commissions which were to prepare the Constitutional Assembly, a measure which had been proposed at the Brazzaville Conference. Governor Delavignette worked for and obtained Senghor's nomination to the political commissions dealing with colonial problems. Senghor was appointed by the Colonial Minister to the Monnerville Commission which sat from 26 March to 6 July 1945 preparing the future representation of the colonies to the Constituent Assembly. The Monnerville Commission included Sourou Migan Apithy, a student at the famous *Ecole Libre des Sciences Politiques* in Paris who later became a *Député* and, eventually, President of Dahomey. Another member was Prince Sisowath Youtevong who, along with Senghor, had published an essay in *La Communauté Impériale Française*.[13] The Monnerville

Commission was Senghor's first step into the political arena. It is significant that Senghor entered politics by appointment and not by election.

Senghor's federalist ideas, his cautious liberalism, and his friendship with the liberal Catholic, Governor Delavignette were the basis
for Senghor's appointment to his first political post. The more
nationalistic Africans opposed the manner in which Senghor acceded
to political realities. Apithy and Senghor were angrily attacked by
Abdoulaye Ly and Louis Béhanzin for having accepted their posts on
the Monnerville Commission. Because their nominations had been
made in Paris without the consultation of Africans, it was inevitable
that Senghor and Apithy would be attacked by the 'young Turks'.[14]

In July 1945, having finished his work with the Monnerville Commission, Senghor sailed to Senegal. His departure from France was
funded by a fellowship from the *Institut Français d'Afrique Noire* so
that he might complete his doctoral thesis on African linguistics.[15]

That same month his friends, his family, and certain Frenchmen
convinced him to become a candidate for the local elections, which
were in part the result of the work of the Monnerville Commission.
Under pressure from his friends Senghor became a member of the
Senegalese branch of the French Socialist Party (SFIO). Only sixteen
hours later and despite heated opposition, the Dakar meeting nomin-
ated him to run for *Député* to the French National Constituent Assembly. It was necessary for Lamine-Guèye, the Mayor of Dakar and
uncontested leader of the Senegalese branch of the SFIO, to face the
anger of his friends and take an unpopular stand in order to have
Senghor's nomination upheld.[16] Opposition to Senghor's nomination occurred because he was considered to be a conservative; it
might also have been because he was a Catholic. Critics pointed out
his long stay in France and implied that he was not a 'true African'.
Ignoring these judgments, Lamine-Guèye chose Senghor because he
hoped that, as the only African to have obtained the academic title of
Agrégé, Senghor might be able to impress the French.

Senghor campaigned successfully with Lamine-Guèye to become
the second Senegalese *Député*. Lamine-Guèye was elected by the
native citizens of the 'four communes' which had elected an African
Député since 1914.[17] This representation in the French parliament
distinguished Senegal from other African colonies which had experienced no previous electoral history. The election of an African
Député from Senegal thus had precedents, but the election of a
second *Député* representing the interior was a result of colonial reforms initiated at the Brazzaville Conference of 1944. Senghor was
elected by the 'subjects' of the interior as their first representative to
the parliament of France.[18]

Senghor was now in a position to pursue the practical development of his theory of 'Imperial Community'. To gain his objectives Senghor began to play the political game. It was by the compromise and log-rolling characteristic of parliamentary life that Senghor gained support for his ideas. Theories which had previously been clear now often became diffuse and almost unrecognizable. The development of Senghor's political theories became dependent on his colleagues: he weighed the opposition before advancing a theory and accepted many modifications in order to allow his ideas to advance fractionally. But the development of his political theories was also dependent upon events. If his political attitude often seemed to change, it was a result of the changing situation in France's overseas territories which had been brought about by the development of the anti-colonial movement in the post-war world.

World-wide anti-colonialism enabled Senghor and other Africans to obtain increasingly generous reforms. Senghor's political style allowed his theories to follow the movement of events. He tried to open a small breech in the wall of the colonial system, which he then progressively widened. It was not Senghor's tactic to make a frontal assault on those who opposed him. He was patient and slow. He began by advocating small reforms which, once put into practice, were immediately declared to be out of date. This was perhaps as characteristic of the French régime as it was of Senghor. France was slow in making reforms. Senghor himself has said that the Fourth Republic was always one reform behind the times.[19]

26. A New Union with France

Soon after his return to France, the new *Député* accepted a seat in the Constitutional Commission of the Constituent Assembly.[1] He also became a member of the Overseas Territories Commission.[2] Senghor was thus directly involved in the development of the Constitution's 'colonial' articles, and it was he who presented the general report on these matters in April 1946. From the outset he stressed 'the contrast between unitary and federalist factions', which led the Constitutional Commission to adopt a 'compromise solution'.[3] In fact, this compromise did not hide the fundamental contradictions of the final text, which led at least one later commentator to question whether these articles 'could ever have been applied'.[4]

The implied contradiction in the colonial relationship with France was created by the notion of the French Republic as being 'one and indivisible'. The proposed Constitution of April 1946, which was rejected in the referendum,[5] stipulated that France 'forms with the Overseas Territories on the one hand and with the Associated States on the other, a freely agreed upon union'. The Constitution then mentioned the 'French Republic, one and indivisible'. As one observer queried: 'How could these two contradictory provisions be reconciled? Were the Overseas Territories freely united to France, or were they part of the French Republic, one and indivisible?'[6]

Other contradictions were inherent in the text. Did the Constitution accord French citizenship to overseas French subjects, or did the text create a French Union citizenship? The law of 7 May 1946, known as the *Loi Lamine-Guèye*, had, it seemed, dissipated the cloud of uncertainty: French citizenship was granted to all former overseas subjects. In the referendum, however, the *Loi* was not applied, inasmuch as colonials, the new citizens, were not allowed to vote their approval of the Constitution. The Constitution, which itself was so liberal in its approach to France's relationship with Overseas Territories, was not approved, since the voice of the new citizens was not heard. A new Constituent Assembly had to be elected and the intricate job of creating a new Constitution had to begin once again.

During the first meetings of the second Constituent Assembly, federalism seemed to predominate. However, the important role played by the 'colonial' delegates frightened the French 'colonialist forces'. In addition the failure of the Fontainebleau Conference on Indochina heightened their fear of colonial revolts. Supported by the right-wing and a portion of the MRP (Social Christian Movement), a group of 'reactionaries and colonialists' met during the summer of 1946 and formed the *Etats Généraux de la Colonisation Française*. The 'colonialists' succeeded in imposing certain of their views on the government, which drew up a text entitled 'The French Union Charter'. Submitted to the Constitutional Commission, this text was to become, with few adjustments, Title VIII of the second Constitution. Upon reviewing Title VIII, delegates from 'overseas France' saw clearly the withdrawal of some of the liberal measures of the April 1946 Constitution and threatened to resign.

As a spontaneous reaction to the deceptions of August 1946 Senghor mentioned possible independence for Africa. It was the only time in his political career prior to 1956 that he called for any kind of separation with France, and even then it seemed more like a threat than a real desire on his part. Senghor asked for equal rights for Africans. He put forward the idea of a federation on the scale of the French Union which would serve until complete independence was attained. This federation would allow Africans 'to quickly assimilate certain modern techniques and to prepare the trained personnel that independence will require'. He assured the Whites of the 'unshakeable will' of colonized peoples to gain their independence. He ended by saying that they were 'ready, in the last resort, to attain their liberty by any means, even by violence'.[7] A few months later Senghor seemed to have changed his mind: he no longer spoke of independence and showed marked hostility to those who supported it.[8]

Before changing his position, Senghor pursued the idea of creating a federation. His objective was the political equality of 'overseas' citizens with metropolitan Frenchmen, not necessarily the equality of the colonies with France. His federation was an adaptation of the Soviet model which combines several republics under the domination of one of them, the federated Russian Republic. In Senghor's 1946 system, metropolitan France would assume the dominant role inside the French Federation. On the juridical level, however, the 'colonial' Republics such as French West Africa and Indochina would be on equal terms with the mother country.

Initially Senghor had hoped to establish this 'Union of Equal French Socialist Republics',[9] but he rapidly abandoned his position when French politicians showed reluctance to support it. Senghor's withdrawal from his progressive stand was due to his pragmatic political attitude. For Senghor, politics was not a religion, a philosophy, nor a science. It did not attempt to discover or reveal an absolute truth. It was the practical business of managing the affairs of men. Politics, according to Senghor, was 'the art of using a method which, by approximations that are constantly corrected, would permit the greatest number to lead a more complete and happy life...'.[10]

Senghor did not want to be doctrinaire. In 1946 he followed the advice of the 'utopian' socialist Proudhon, who wrote in a famous letter to Marx: '...but, for God's sake! After having demolished all *a priori* dogmatisms, let us not attempt in turn to indoctrinate the people: let us not fall into the contradiction of...Martin Luther, who, having overthrown Catholic theology, immediately set himself, armed with a supply of excommunications and anathema, to found a Protestant theology'. Proudhon advised socialists not to make themselves the leaders of a 'new intolerance' or set themselves up as 'apostles of a new religion'.[11] Barrès, too, had warned: 'Let us repudiate...philosophical systems...'.[12]

Consciously eschewing dogmatism Senghor set out to achieve short term successes. He knew that the world changes: what one hopes for today is not necessarily what one would like to have tomorrow. This allowed him a great deal of liberty: he could say along with Stendhal: 'Why do they want me to have the same opinion today as I had six weeks ago? If I had, then my opinion would be my tyrant'.[13]

Events caused Senghor to abandon for a decade any notion of political independence for Africa. At the end of the second Constituent Assembly, the African delegates who had threatened to resign took a positive action to achieve equality for their countrymen. In September 1946, they published a Manifesto summoning a Constituent Congress for a Democratic African Rally (*Rassemblement Démocratique Africain*) on 11, 12, and 13 October 1946.[14] The final version of the Manifesto was drawn up in the council room of the Overseas Territories' Commission at the Palais Bourbon, having previously been drafted at Lamine-Guèye's house in Ermont.[15] Between the publication of the Manifesto and the RDA meeting, the October constitutional Referendum took place. The African meeting was therefore postponed until 18 October 1946.

Between the publication of the Manifesto and the meeting, Marius Moutet, the Socialist Minister of Overseas France, successfully exerted pressure on Lamine-Guèye to prevent his participation at the RDA Congress. Lamine-Guèye, in turn, persuaded his lieutenant, Senghor, who had supported the idea of a Congress, to withdraw as well.[16] According to a Dakar newspaper of 9 October 1946, Senghor and Lamine-Guèye had already made arrangements for their stay during the meeting in Bamako.[17] Their absence ended all hope of creating a single African Party which would unite all parties – the original purpose for the Congress. With the Senegalese abstaining, a united French West Africa seemed more and more difficult to achieve and, correspondingly, the possibility of a Federation of the French Union which would include as a member-state the territories of French West Africa.

There were other reasons why Senghor's 'French Imperial Community' was not a practical possibility. Despite the 'secessionist' language of the African delegates, the Constitution was voted by the Commission, by the Assembly, and then barely missed defeat at the hands of the electorate in the referendum of 13 October 1946.[18] The anomalies contained in the April project reappeared in the new text. The French political scientist Alfred Grosser has noted that there were not only contradictions between the Preamble and Title VIII, contradictions which had been frequently criticized during the Fourth Republic, but there were also inconsistencies within the Preamble itself. Said Grosser: 'the members of the Constituent Assembly juxtaposed the federal idea of equality of national entities and the assimilationist idea of equality of individuals within French territory. The Preamble expressed the inequality of the political entities and the equality of individuals'.[19] There was also the problem of the 'one and indivisible' French Republic which included almost one half of the African continent. These inconsistencies indicated that the delegates had found it impossible to choose from among the different theories: assimilation, federation, association, independence within interdependence. Senghor was faced with the French refusal to grant autonomy to French West Africa. The African Overseas Territories were therefore included in the French Republic and not grouped with the Associated States of Indochina as Senghor had proposed in 1944. His 'Imperial Community' or Federation thus became a dead letter. Instead of opposing what had been done, Senghor acquiesced. But, at the same time, he did not hesitate to try to alter the course of events. From then on it was within the framework of the 1946 Constitution that Senghor worked for an improvement in the status of the African Overseas Territories.

In August 1946 Senghor believed that the 'Imperial Community' could be brought into being 'immediately'.[20] But the Constitution established an 'apprenticeship' within the French Republic before transforming the status of Overseas Territory into that of an Associated State.[21] Senghor accepted this halfway house, a role different from that of Indochina which became a group of 'Associated States', and different from that of the French West Indies which became 'Overseas *Départements*'. Africa's position thus remained ambiguous.

Senghor's acceptance of second-class statehood for French Africa was characteristic of his ability to accommodate political realities. In 1947 at the end of the Second Constituent Assembly, he declared that 'a federation was impossible because it demanded a comparable degree of technical evolution'.[22] Only a few months before, he had stated that a federation could be achieved by uniting regions without the same degree of technical evolution, as in the case of the Soviet Union.[23]

Senghor had now accepted the juridical status of French Africa as a part of the French Republic until these territories attained a sufficiently high technical level to enable them to become part of the French Federation. His subsequent efforts were directed more towards individual civil rights and economic development than towards the immediate revision of the status of French Africa within the Constitution. Senghor oscillated between individual equality and equality of political units. Since the latter seemed difficult to achieve, he continued his efforts in the realm of civil liberties.

The failure of Senghor's plan for a French Federation triggered the re-emergence of his theme 'Culture first'. As already noted, Senghor had been influenced during the 1930s and early 1940s by the anti-political sentiments common to young French intellectuals. Abdoulaye Ly and some of the younger Africans, however, were intensely interested in the future political relationship between France and Africa. In discussions held at Senghor's apartment during World War II the young Africans were impatient with Senghor's insistence that cultural matters have priority over political questions.

In 1945 certain members of the African student group in France began to agitate for political independence from France. Ly and other 'young Turks' wanted to fight for national liberation. Senghor and Alioune Diop, however, devoted their time to the study and exaltation of Negro culture.[1] Senghor confessed in 1961 that he had believed that 'the problem was only cultural, that it was on the level of the individual – or better, the person – and that the colonial problem would be resolved'.[2] This emphasis on individual cultural awakening instead of national liberation dominated Senghor's political thought after his disappointments during the Constituent Assembly. Beginning in 1947, politics became but a means; the arts were the end.[3] Although he admitted after 1956 that it was necessary to give priority to politics,[4] he still refused to militate for political independence. 'We must understand that true independence is cultural independence', he said in 1959.[5] Even in the late 1960s Senghor was heard to observe deprecatingly: 'Politics is but an aspect of culture'.[6]

Senghor's subordination of politics to culture after 1944 included his subordination of the political to the social. His increasing concern for social problems was symptomatic of his growing awareness of the poverty of Africa. 'The political', he constantly reiterated after 1947, 'is but an instrument in the service of the social.'[7] For Senghor, black Africa had no 'political pretensions',[8] only social needs.

One reason for Senghor's emphasis on social and cultural change was the strong influence of the political doctrines of French metropolitan parties. Senghor, first a member of the French Socialist Party, found himself increasingly at odds with his 'boss', Lamine-Guèye. He also did not appreciate the anticlerical position of the

SFIO. Unable to compromise any more, Senghor left the party in 1948 to join the *Indépendants d'Outre-mer*, a grouping of overseas *Députés* linked with the Social Christians of the MRP, who helped in its formation.[9] Strictly speaking, the IOM was not a political party, but a bloc of votes in parliament.[10] He remained with the IOM group until 1956. Both the SFIO and the MRP, metropolitan parties to which Senghor was linked, insisted on the social side of 'colonial issues'. Senghor's anti-nationalist position was, to a certain extent, a reiteration of the policies of the SFIO and the MRP.

The intellectual training received by Senghor also prejudiced his political viewpoint. While at secondary school, Senghor considered himself a 'humanist' and disdained 'practical matters' which seemed to him to be the concern of lesser minds. Something of this attitude remained in Senghor's distrust of the political. Having passed more than half of his life putting politics in second or even third place, it would be difficult to expect him to change his attitude fundamentally. Even when he realized the value of politics intellectually, his inherent belief in the importance of culture and his intense distrust of politics, inherited from the 1930s, prevented him from changing radically. As the Malagasy poet and politician Jacques Rabemananjara justly observed in 1957, Senghor and Césaire are 'first of all poets'. For them, poetry 'precedes and envelops politics, lays hold of it...'.[11]

Viewed in retrospect, the *négritude* movement of cultural liberation seems to have been the precursor of political liberation and a means of gaining it. But for those who formulated *négritude*, the cultural awakening was an end in itself. Senghor's own rationale appeared in an article he wrote about Gandhi: 'Let us not take the Mahatma for a soft dreamer. With a truly Western realism he works for the economic and social liberation of his country, but that liberation itself is a means, not an end. It is from this point of view that he considers colonization less an evil than the symptom of the malady from which India suffers. He invites the colonizer to collaborate with him in the spiritual liberation of the country.'[12] Through his political activity Senghor invited France to help in the spiritual liberation of Africans. His adversaries criticized him for this insistence on economic and social liberation when it was necessary first to eliminate the political domination of France. Senghor's 'idealistic' subordination of the economic and social to the spiritual was called reactionary by his 'materialistic' critics.[13] Attacked by African nationalists, Senghor gained the approval of the French. The moderate demands Senghor made on them jibed with their attempt to keep Africa French through gradual social reform.

28. Independence or Economic Development?

With the realization that France would not support separatist proposals Senghor recast his political objectives and refused to plead for independence for French Africa. As a member of the SFIO, he could not help but be influenced by that party's vigorous rejection of the idea of overseas nationalism. Although the SFIO wanted the African liberated from economic and political oppression, the party's programme stated that this liberation could best be attained without political independence. Members of the French left-wing of Senghor's generation found the word 'nationalist' unpalatable. It provoked a reaction of 'mistrust if not of hostility'.[1] As late as 1958 Guy Mollet wrote that one of the goals of the SFIO was to spare the colonized world the nationalist phase.[2]

After leaving the SFIO to join with IOM group in 1948, Senghor found additional reasons for rejecting independence. The IOM group was strongly influenced by the *Mouvement Republicain Populaire* (MRP) whose 'catholic' ideology was hostile to whatever might lead to separatism. The MRP hoped to unite different parts of the world in much the same way as Claudel, who earnestly sought after a truly 'catholic' world. Senghor and the MRP were influenced by the anti-nationalism of Maritain's *Humanisme Intégral* (1936). Maritain's reply to Charles Maurras' *Nationalisme Intégral* of 1927 showed clearly the opposition of Catholic to nationalist.

Rejecting independence and separation from France, Senghor asked for a series of economic and social reforms. The African Overseas Territories 'could assert their claim to become an Associated State, but what they wanted most of all was to develop their economy and increase the number of schools and hospitals', because 'true independence consists of prosperity and culture'.[3] For a long time, Senghor preferred *'les libertés à la Liberté'* ('prosperity to liberty') and 'the material and moral independence of the individual to the political independence' of his country.[4]

Senghor was not a nationalist. His ideas contrast sharply with those of nationalists such as Sékou Touré, who told General De Gaulle in 1958: 'We prefer poverty in liberty to wealth in slavery'.[5] His ideas also distinguished him from nationalists in English-speaking Africa. Senghor roundly criticized Kwame N'Krumah for being 'too radical' when, in April 1947 at a West African Congress under N'Krumah's leadership, the Africans of the Gold Coast, Sierra Leone, and Nigeria demanded dominion status in the Commonwealth.[6] Until 1960 the nation, whether Senegal or Africa, was not given a central position in his scheme of things; national development took second place to economic development.

For Senghor, even in 1956, to speak of independence was to 'reason upside down with one's feet in the air. It is not reasoning at all'.[7] 'What I fear', said Senghor a few days before the opening of the 1955 Bandung Conference on colonial independence, 'is that, in the future, under the fatal pressure of African liberation, we might be induced to leave the French orbit. We must stay not only in the French Union but in the French Republic.'[8]

To Senghor independence meant violence, and of all things he wanted to avoid violence. His non-violent approach to colonial problems had been inspired in 1944 by the example of Gandhi. He called Gandhi 'the most surprising revolutionary of our time' because he was non-violent and because 'his goal was not political victory, but spiritual victory'.[9] Senghor repeated Gandhi's statement that 'politics consists of compromises'.[10] And, of course, compromise with France meant denial of independence.

Was there really any other course open to a peace-loving man? The brutal crushing of the Malagasy rebellion of 1947 and the Ivory Coast insurrection of 1949–50, not to speak of the wars waged by France against those who dared to attempt to shake off her political domination were all good reasons for abstaining from the sort of political demands made by the 'nationalists'. Using the Malagasy rebellion as his example, Senghor saw a legitimate request for improved status refused with armed terror.[11] In 1947 the Malagasy leaders wanted to change the status of Madagascar from that of an Overseas Territory to that of an Associated State. The repression which ensued must have made Senghor reflect. Given these hard facts, Senghor's distaste for violence obliged him to take the only course of action open: reform of the statute of Overseas Territory inside the French Republic.

29. *Federation as a Solution*

Rejection of political independence did not mean that Senghor accepted complete assimilation. Instead he advocated a new political federation for France and Africa which represented a compromise between assimilation on the one hand and independence on the other.

Senghor's new brand of federalism brought him into conflict with the philosophy of the SFIO party. The SFIO and its Senegalese branch, which was dominated by the men of the 'Four Communes', advocated assimilation. The SFIO was so assimilationist that its African branches were considered the exact equivalent of branches in the French *Départements*. 'French socialism, like communism, did not understand our problems and wished to force them into a plan made by and for Europe. Thus, in order to analyse and transform *our* realities we had to work out and define, if not a doctrine, at least an original political method.'[1] From Senghor's point of view the position of the SFIO would make the Africans merely black copies of their French *confrères*.

Although assimilationism was an important cause of Senghor's philosophic break with the SFIO, the party's militant anticlericalism equally influenced his decision to quit its ranks. Consequently, Senghor was attracted to a party which recognized the importance of religion and advocated a federalist structure to organize the relationship between France and Africa. The MRP was the logical group to turn to.

The ideology of the MRP was influenced by many of the same philosophers who had shaped Senghor's thought in the 1930s. The 'intercessor' for a considerable number of French Catholic intellectuals in the 1930s was Proudhon who had written *Du Principe Fédérateur* in 1863. His influence is seen in Mounier's writing before World War II and in Senghor's as late as 1960.[2] Senghor, Mounier, and their MRP friends rehabilitated the French 'Utopian' Socialist tradition. Referring to Fourier as well as Proudhon, Senghor remarked: 'It is they who converted me to the ideas of federation and co-operation'.[3]

Proudhon's influence was also important to Daniel-Rops and Denis de Rougemont, both liberal Catholics who were associated with the review *L'Ordre Nouveau*. In November 1934 the *revue* devoted an entire issue to the subject of federalism. Much of what these intellectuals expressed in 1934 reappeared in Senghor's postwar writings.

Senghor had previously been attracted to both Daniel-Rops and De Rougemont because of their basic Catholic liberalism, and he found it easy to accept their view of federalism in the 1940s. All adapted Barrès's provincialism. 'It is Federalism which allows the greatest diversity and Federation gives to all a homeland [patrie].'[4]

An important practical federalist proposal was adopted by Senghor during a Congress held in 1948 under the auspices of Mounier's Catholic progressive monthly *Esprit* when Senghor was introduced to Paul Alduy. Alduy had just published his book *Union Française, Mission de la France*[5] and proposed that the federation of 1948 take a different form from what Senghor had proposed in 1944–6. Instead of having Indochina, the French West Indies, and French West Africa as states, the federation of 1948 only included France and the African Overseas Territories. This federation was to be included in a confederal French Union.

Alerted to a solution for the Franco-African political dilemma, Senghor reformed his ideas of federalism and explained his new variant in *Condition Humaine*, a weekly published by his breakaway political organization. The new federalism counteracted the 'Jacobin and Unitarist' tradition[6] of the SFIO politicians for whom centralization was a kind of reflex.

Philosophy was not, however, the only force driving Senghor to a new political position. Other practical considerations influenced Senghor's decision to break with the SFIO. Among them was the logic of Governor Robert Delavignette in explaining the impact that such a break might have on the Muslim leaders of Senegal. Delavignette, who had become Director of Political Affairs in the Ministry of Overseas France, was in a position to persuade the religious *Marabouts* who controlled a large sector of the 'bush' electorate in Senegal to support Senghor. It is no longer a secret that certain French colonial officials supported Senghor and made this support evident to the powerful religious leaders in the interior of Senegal. By breaking with the SFIO Senghor had put himself into a favourable position *vis-à-vis* these Muslims who could deliver electoral support. His new association with the MRP allowed him to criticize the anti-clerical SFIO for its hostility to the idea of religion playing a role in the state.

A second practical consideration of Senghor's was the increasing power of the MRP in the Ministry of Overseas France. An important display of this power came with the replacement of the sfio Governor-General of French West Africa, Béchard, with a man more favourable to the mrp Christian Social position.[7] If Senghor could establish himself successfully with them he would most certainly become an important political figure. Senghor learned the game of staying alive in French politics by trading his votes for political advantage. He learned this lesson well. After the elections of 1951, Senghor made overtures to the rpf (Rally of the French People) by quoting freely from the federalist plans of this Gaullist group, which had made a spectacular showing during the elections, and which seemed capable of playing a highly important role in parliament.[8]

In order to manoeuvre in a French political context, Senghor went so far as to adopt the philosophy of many of the French political leaders and even used their language. Nationalism was an 'outdated weapon'[9] or an 'old hunting gun'.[10] He admitted that in Lenin's time nationalism was an effective instrument in the struggle against imperialism, but the 1950s, a time of jet aircraft and hydrogen bombs, was also a time of constantly increasing interdependence of peoples.[11] According to Senghor and his French friends there was a future only in large groupings; it was useless to demand independence which at best could be but theoretical. The *Indépendants d'Outre-mer* (which Senghor helped form after breaking with the sfio and to which he belonged from 1948 to 1957) wrote into its platform that it was necessary to replace the myth of pseudo independence for small political entities, badly equipped and economically isolated, by the 'myth' of much-needed interdependence.[12] 'In 1950', Senghor declared 'independence is only a myth devised to keep alive an outdated nationalism.'[13] Nationalism was condemned because it created centrifugal currents in a world which above all needed to be united. He announced his 'mystique of equality by co-operation' which would avoid 'independence by secession'.

Senghor fought for equality. The object of his policy was to lessen the inequalities which arose from differences of race and geography. He was by vocation a federalist, for to him federalism was the 'system which establishes equality between countries, even between races'.[14]

Federalism served both Senghor's past philosophical inclinations and his political ambitions. As a new, more highly sophisticated man of politics, Senghor actively set out to create a new relationship between France and her African dependencies.

30. A Federal French Republic

Faced with the fact that the African Overseas Territories were integral parts of the French Republic, Senghor tried to improve their status within the framework of the Republic. Like his friends of the MRP, he was much more dedicated to applying the Constitutional provisions for improvement inside the existing framework than to changing it radically.[1] Senghor was confronted with the place that France had given Africa in 1946 as defined by the Overseas Territory statute. This statute, formulated as a temporary compromise shaped Senghor's political response.

The statute was conceived as a transitory step which should have soon led either to the status of Overseas *Département* (like the French West Indies) or to that of Associated State (like Indochina).[2] The status of the African territories was thus somewhat uncertain: neither Overseas *Département* nor Associated State, but somewhere in between, having the characteristics of both. Because the Indochina War had given a pejorative connotation to the idea of Associated States, and because the African Overseas Territories were juridically part of the French Republic (which gave any attempt to achieve autonomy a secessionist colouring), Senghor constantly stressed his desire to stay within the French Republic. He even wrote that it was dangerous to have constitutionally provided for the possibility of the African Overseas Territories becoming Associated States, for that gave birth to a 'centrifugal current' in the French Republic.[3] His desire was to remain 'not only in the French Union, but in the Republic'.[4] For Senghor in 1953, the 'ultimate step' in the evolution of the African Overseas Territories would be found in their integration into the French Republic.[5]

An important aspect of Senghor's acceptance of the Constitution should be noted. Senghor did not consider the Republic immutable: 'The Republic, proclaimed as being one and indivisible, is so only as far as obligations are concerned', Senghor declared in 1954. 'It becomes divisible whenever there is a question of rights.'[6] To Senghor the notion of a Republic 'one' and 'indivisible' was a hypocrisy.[7] The Republic in Senghor's new political theory would be 'one' but 'divisible', that is to say, federal.[8] In his reform plan the representatives of

43 million overseas citizens of France would cease to be merely 'stage extras'.[9]

From 1948 to 1958 a Federal French Republic remained the keystone of Senghor's thought. Senghor's theory was a design of concentric circles. The innermost circle consisted of the African Overseas Territories regarded individually (Senegal, Ivory Coast, etc.). The second circle represented the individual territories grouped in primary federations and was comprised of French West Africa and French Equatorial Africa. These federations were integrated as states into the Federal Republic which formed the third concentric circle. The Federal French Republic in turn was included in the confederation formed by the French Union – the fourth circle. In the outermost circle the French Union would be part of a federal European Community.

After the French defeat in Indochina in 1954, Senghor paid less attention to that area and the fourth circle. As a consequence he emphasized the last circle by developing the notion of Eurafrica, a third world power, which would rival the United States and the Soviet Union. Senghor was consistently true to federalism and he applied it to the French Republic, the French Union, Europe, and finally Eurafrica.[10]

Just as his theory of passive and active assimilation was based on a grammatical distinction, his conception of a Federal Republic was established on a subtle distinction between the notions of homeland (*patrie*) and nation. The homeland (*patrie*) is formed by people having the same ancestral traditions and, to a certain degree, belonging to the same race. On the other hand, the nation is based on intellectual rather than emotional ties.[11] Senghor believed, as did Barrès, that men belong to nations because of a conscious desire to pursue a common task based upon a common principle.[12] For this reason Senghor described the attachment of Africans to the French Republic as a marriage of convenience.[13] This rationale was Senghor's justification for belonging to two communities which merged without losing their distinctive character.[14]

These ideas did not simply grow out of Senghor's reading of Barrès. They captured Senghor's attention through the writings of Denis de Rougemont, one of the young French intellectuals who in the 1930s had published *L'Ordre Nouveau*. The article by De Rougemont which Senghor used appeared in the review *Fédération* in the September–October 1954 issue.[15] This is but one example of the use Senghor made of ideas developed in the 1930s. The 'Spirit of the 1930s' as described by Jean Touchard[16] was thus perpetuated in Senghor's political philosophy.

To put these ideas into practice required a revision of the Constitution which, Senghor declared in 1953, 'could come in ten, twenty, or thirty years'.[17] Senghor's constitutional revisions would change France, then dominated by Paris, into a 'decentralized' federation. His tactic was to alter the parliamentary relationships by granting more power to the Overseas Assemblies and the Assembly of the French Union.[18] He knew that metropolitan France did not want to see some three hundred African *Députés* at the National Assembly. To avoid France's becoming the 'colony of her colonies', Senghor proposed the creation of a deliberative Federal Assembly that would replace the Assembly of the Union, which had originally been designed as only a consulting body.[19]

Senghor made concessions to economic realities and was perfectly willing to accept the pre-eminence of the mother country.[20] To guarantee that the proposed Federal Executive was not exclusively metropolitan in its objectives or its personnel,[21] the new Federal Assembly would elect the ministers responsible for the affairs of federal interest.

The machinery for administrative decentralization would be established through the creation of local executives in the Overseas Territories. The French Colonial Governor, as head of the Territory, would be assisted by an Executive Council, half of whose members would be named by the Governor and half by the Territorial Assembly.[22] The project was to create 'autonomous management of local affairs by the legitimate representatives of each territory and each group of territories'.[23] There was to be increased African participation on the Federal level and progressively more involvement in political activities on the territorial level.

Both short-term and long-term objectives were included in Senghor's proposals. For immediate purposes he proposed improving the system outlined by the 1946 Constitution to allow a more real 'apprenticeship'. This 'apprenticeship', insured by a modest improvement in the status of Overseas Territory, would lead in the long run to the transformation of the Republic into a Federation. When the innumerable threads of his proposals are untangled, the inevitable logic governing Senghor's thought during the Fourth Republic becomes apparent: the reforms should lead to the construction of a decentralized grouping permanently linking Europe to Africa. In this scheme the Overseas Territories would be dissuaded from demanding independence and from 'turning away from France towards one or the other of the two great powers'[24] which divide the world.

Senghor's Federation was imbued with the 'Girondin' spirit of reinvigorating the provinces by decentralization. Senghor can be considered a modern 'Girondin' opposed to the unitarist 'Jacobins'.[25]

With the passing of time and with the wisdom of hindsight, Senghor's French Federation seems directly counter to modern African historical experience. The immense amount of time and effort Senghor spent on it now seems particularly futile. But perhaps it was responsible for maintaining the dialogue between Senghor and the French, while other Africans chose the path of open hostility and rupture.

An important aspect of Senghor's federalism was the attempt to create a political and economic union between Europe and Africa. He even went so far as to envision French, British, and Belgian federations or confederations uniting each European country to its African territories. Above these federations would be the European Community. This Community would first take the form of a simple association or confederation; the experience gained would then allow development towards a more closely knit federation: Eurafrica.[1]

The idea of European-African union first came to Senghor's attention in 1931 when an editor of the *Revue du Monde Noir* advocated the creation of Eurafrica. The combination of the two continents would remedy the economic crisis paralysing Europe by using the enormous economic potential of Africa to stimulate European business. Africa was described as the saviour of Europe.[2]

Eighteen years passed before the concept of Eurafrica had its first chance to develop as a practical possibility. In 1949 the Council of Europe was created at Strasbourg to lay the groundwork for European unity. Since the African Overseas Territories were juridically within the French Republic, they were automatically included as part of France in the Council of Europe. Senghor discussed African participation in the Council during debates at the French National Assembly in July 1949.[3] His interest in the creation of a united Europe influenced the decision to send Senghor as France's representative to the Council.[4]

Some time after his nomination, Senghor stated that his 'major concern was to bring a united Europe into being',[5] He felt that 'to sustain Europe was to sustain Humanity'.[6] Europe's spirit and civilization had to be preserved for the sake of the world at large.[7] Europe had 'saved Africa during the nineteenth century because she took Africa out of isolation and set that continent on the path to modernization'. Now Africa could help Europe which had lost her dominant position in the world to the two colossi: the United States and the Soviet Union. The establishment of Eurafrica would be the best way of saving Europe and the only way to return her to her rightful rank.

At Strasbourg Senghor emphasized the future relationship of Africa to the European Union. Initially Africa would play a secondary role. In the cultural 'concert' Senghor said that, while Europe would be the conductor, Africa would be content to be responsible for the drum section.[8] Similarly, on the political level, when speaking of the Eurafrican Community, he stated: 'We are willing, in this *mariage de convenance*, to be the pages who carry the bride's veil; we refuse to be the wedding gift, or the dishes which get broken in quarrels, or the dolls to amuse the children of tomorrow'.[9] In exchange for their consent to be the 'pages', Africans asked Europeans to free them from poverty, sickness, and ignorance.[10]

A confidential report written by the colonial governor Roland Pré summarized Senghor's long-term objectives for a union between the two continents. According to Pré, Senghor wanted to obtain 'the mobilization of all European resources for the immediate equipping of Africa'. This endeavour presupposed the establishment of an integrated economy for the entire length and breadth of Eurafrica and a 'massive transfer of industrial activities from one continent to the other'.[11] In addition to this economic interdependence, Senghor was reported to have had specific cultural objectives. The Eurafrican idea 'would definitely assure the integration of the African Blacks into the community of civilized Western peoples'.[12] Senghor, himself the example *par excellence* of the Eurafrican, did not feel at ease either as an African or as a European. It was necessary for him to think in terms of a 'cross-bred' society. His ideas of 'cultural cross-breeding' influenced the Eurafrica project as they had the project for a French Federation.

Senghor carried the notion of cultural interdependence so far as to argue against the founding of a University at Dakar: 'We would have preferred', he stated in 1957, 'our students to go to French Universities'. He added that the French government wanted to found the University of Dakar 'for reasons of prestige' and 'not in response to a wish on our part'.[13] Twelve years earlier Senghor had listed a university at Dakar as a basic African need; but that was in 1945.[14] His new belief in Eurafrican cultural integration caused him to discard such nationalistic and limited African goals.

The objectives described by Roland Pré, however, did not suggest Senghor's overriding reason for promoting a powerful Europe-Africa combination. Senghor believed that a third 'World Force' led by Europe was crucial to the maintenance of balance in a world controlled by the United States and the Soviet Union. Isolated from each other, neither Europe nor Africa individually could resist the blocs.[15] Europe, highly industrialized but lacking natural resources, would be strengthened by economic integration with Africa. One advantage of a union would be the development of hydro-electric power in Africa for European industry. Senghor took this idea from Anton Zischka's *Afrique Complément de l'Europe* (1952).[16] Eurafrica would be the mediator between East and West.[17]

Establishing this third 'World Force' would save Europeans and Africans from 'the Hell of the dollar – and of the Communist Party'.[18] Senghor's adaptation of this idea could be traced to French intellectual preoccupations of the 1930s, years in which many Frenchmen were concerned with keeping a safe distance from both the Soviet Union and the United States. Senghor's slogan 'the Hell of the dollar – and of the Communist Party' echoed the phrase of *l'Ordre Nouveau* which in May 1933 denounced 'Capitalist disorder and Communist oppression'. In fact, *l'Ordre Nouveau* had placed the accent on federalism and European union before World War II. The political scientist Jean Touchard has said that *l'Ordre Nouveau* was for many young French intellectuals the only school of thought of the 1930s.[19]

Senghor, as well as a number of political leaders of the Fourth Republic, was directly influenced by the ideas of *l'Ordre Nouveau* before World War II. The scheme strikingly resembled that of the Gaullists who also wished to attain the same end. Nevertheless Senghor feared that the French would reject the federalist ideas of 'men of good will' such as he. If that happened, he predicted in 1953, twenty or thirty years later he and the other 'Eurafricans' would be considered 'collaborators' by the young generation of Africans. Such a development would cause 'great damage to the two complementary continents'. If Eurafrica were not realized, the young generation would seek 'independence by secession' instead of building on 'equality by co-operation'.[20]

Condemning at the same time the previous form of 'European colonialism' and intransigent 'African nationalism',[21] Senghor proposed one of those middle-of-the-road solutions cherished by prudent politicians such as he: Eurafrica, a cross-bred community that would unite Europe and Africa and serve as a unifying bloc in a world already too painfully divided.

The French political scene formed only one dimension of Senghor's political world. His appointment to the Council of Europe and his seat in the French Assembly did not prevent Senghor from developing a political base in Africa. The political scene in Senegal became an increasingly important dimension in Senghor's career. He learned to deal with new political realities. Traditional leaders directly influenced the electorate, and Senghor saw the phenomenon of collective voting as a springboard to political success in his own country.

Senghor's political activity in Senegal began in 1945 with Lamine-Guèye's decision to have Senghor represent the people of the interior. Lamine-Guèye reserved for himself the role of representing the citizens of the four communes of the coast. With this division of Senegal into political spheres of influence, it was natural that Senghor find the majority of his supporters in traditionalist communities, and it was from this base that he began to work.

However, differences began to divide Senghor from the Senegalese branch of the French Socialist Party. As early as 1937 he had quarrelled with the citizens of the four communes on the question of the *Ecole Rurale Populaire*. This argument reflected his affinity with the peasants and his distrust of the coastal bourgeoisie, a situation paralleled in his own family conflict between his Uncle Toko' Waly and his father.[1] By 1948 disagreements with Lamine-Guèye and disenchantment with the assimilationist ideas of the SFIO caused Senghor to organize his own political party, the *Bloc Démocratique Sénégalais*. As might be expected the BDS was supported by the 'traditional' leaders of the interior. To combat the 'Laminist' votes of the towns, Senghor worked to spread the vote to increasing numbers of peasants in the interior, and between 1948 and the elections of 1951 he devoted himself to enlarging the Overseas Territories electorate. This tactic was used to create a favourable environment for the development of the BDS and it proved successful when Senghor won the 1951 election by an overwhelming majority, thereby eliminating Lamine-Guèye as a major threat.

Senghor's work to extend the vote had an important side effect. The *Grands Marabouts* or Muslim religious leaders who were his primary source of support found their traditional role of leadership expanded into a modern political context. Religious leadership became the foundation for political influence. Senghor had learned from the works of the great Africanist Maurice Delafosse that 'no institution exists in Negro Africa, whether it be social, political, or even economic that does not rest on a religious concept or that does not have religion as its keystone'.[2]

Senghor's political acumen as well as his inherent 'spiritualism' led him to ally himself with the *Grands Marabouts*. In Africa adherence to a political party is less a matter for the individual than for the tribe or the various social groups.[3] The 'collective character of political expression'[4] was noted by Senghor in his essay of 1943 when he advocated a 'family vote' in black Africa. 'I am not a fanatic when it comes to the ballot, which is a European type of election', he wrote. 'Neither do I maintain that each individual should vote. Rather I should like the family to vote as a unit. A collective vote would be in accord with the tradition of black Africa.'[5] When Senghor realized that individuals voted according to the wishes of their *Marabouts* and that the French would continue to insist on European style elections, he wisely accepted individual voting which would, nevertheless, reflect the wishes of the group's leader. As an African observer noted:

'One imagines a little too easily that the large African parties are parties in which all members adhere to the party ideology, the programme written in black and white, and the resolutions of the party congress. In fact, this is not the least true. These parties are not true parties, healthy parties. They are the parties of influential people and are devoted to interest groups rather than the general good. It is not for Senghor nor for Lamine-Guèye that the elector votes. His choice is made by someone on whom he depends and who tells him for whom he shall vote. The important role is played by the *Marabouts*... There exist people for whom the only valid personality, the only one in whom they have full confidence, is the *Marabout*. They only follow orders issued by the *Marabout*.'[6]

The *Marabout* links the small community, the neighbourhood, or the village far out in the bush to the rest of the religious brotherhood and to the world. He plays a role in all the activities of his faithful. He is asked how one should act and is called on to arbitrate disputes and to maintain harmony in his flock. It is completely natural that he is also asked how to vote.[7] An African student's personal experience illustrates well how this characteristic trait of Senegalese politics functions:

'One day I asked a girl from Keur Modou Bineta [village near

Louga] for whom she would vote. She was very surprised by the question. "But", she said to me, "don't you know that the village has Serigne Cheikh M'Backé as *Marabout*?" "So", I answered, for I didn't see the connection or at least didn't want to let on that I saw it. "So" she continued, "he is a supporter of Lamine-Guèye and so the whole village will vote for Lamine-Guèye".'[8]

If this phenomenon of collective voting is common to Africa,[9] the Senegalese case is somewhat special. Colonial conquest destroyed the traditional feudal military structure. A feudal religious society developed, replacing that shaken by the French Governor Faidherbe and his successors. Based on the new religious fanaticism, the power of the chiefs of the great Muslim brotherhoods became enormous.

The *Grand Marabouts* were the 'instruments' of the colonial administration[10] because of the efficient discipline that exists within each brotherhood, particularly the Mouride. The governor of Senegal developed a kind of indirect administration over the Senegalese interior by using the *Marabouts* as political intermediaries. In exchange for administrative favours the *Marabouts* preached attachment to France and her representatives.[11] During the 1940s and 1950s there were signs of excellent relations between Muslim religious leaders and the French administration.[12]

The effectiveness of the *Marabouts* can be seen in the case of the Mouride brotherhood. Between the years 1940 and 1946, Europe needed enormous quantities of groundnuts for vegetable oil. The French governors of Senegal used the influence of the Mouride *Marabouts* in order to fill the demand. The Mourides had a fanatic attitude towards work which well served war-time governors harassed by continual government appeals to increase production of groundnuts. Although manual labour is generally disdained in Africa and in Islam, the Mourides believe that work is the equivalent of prayer and guarantees eternal salvation to the faithful or *talibé*. The Mouride zeal for work made the religious brotherhood an important economic force.[13] It has been estimated that the Mourides alone produce over half of the total peanut crop in Senegal, which is the most important cash crop in the country.[14]

After World War II the religious brotherhoods in Senegal who produced peanuts established agricultural co-operatives. Unfortunately their financial condition deteriorated. To save the co-operatives, the *Marabouts* were forced to appeal to the colonial administration, which then naturally became involved in the day-to-day economic affairs of the brotherhoods. To obtain colonial administration loans, the Mourides relied on the good offices of African politicians. The political support of the *Marabouts* was traded for the pressure that the Senegalese politicians could put on the administration in the interest of the brotherhoods.[15] This log-rolling was essential to Senegalese politics after World War II.

As the number of voters increased, the power of the *Marabouts* grew.[16] From 1945 on, the *Marabouts'* influence extended beyond the interior to the towns. Although much of their activity continued to be agrarian in nature they began to organize and proselytize in urban areas.[17] The Islamic brotherhoods affected the political life of all of Senegal.[18]

The French government's consent to extend the vote to rural masses had been given because of the 'unwavering attachment' of these Muslim religious leaders to France, an allegiance characteristic of most traditional leaders in Africa. The extension of the vote, so important to Senghor's political success, marked another step towards Africans' participation in their own destiny.

Based on its relationship with the tradition leaders, the BDS became Senghor's vehicle for giving life to his concept of a new Africa. In 1939 he had declared that he wished to 'conciliate tradition and progress'.[19] By relying on the Senegalese religious brotherhoods he fulfilled this ambition. Senghor's concept of democracy for Africa was based on the group, not on the individual.[20] By gaining support from religious leaders, Senghor also achieved a synthesis between spiritual and temporal life. He refused to 'mutilate' man as had been done by the Western separation of religion and politics. Senghor's innovation was to preserve tradition and incorporate it into a modern framework.[21]

The year 1955 witnessed two significant attacks on the old colonial order. It was the year of the Afro-Asian Conference at Bandung, which set a deadline for the end of European colonization. It was also the year of rapid acceleration of the Algerian war. Independence movements shook the world.

In this atmosphere Alioune Diop began to criticize the rejection of independence by many African *Députés* over the previous ten years.

'...the withering of arts and literature are but the symptoms of a more profound malaise: the exploitation of a people, the aliena-tion of its liberty. Political leaders (from all parts of Africa) will often say to us, depending on the period, that we must put the emphasis on the economic, or the social, or education, or spiritual training. Many among the Africans believed this in good faith. But in fact all is first conditioned...by the sovereignty of a people's acts and political institutions. I will limit myself to the cultural, but it is easy to show that neither economic take-off, nor social improvements, nor academic progress, nor cultural or spiritual maturity are possible without a people's political sovereignty.'[1]

This was a scarcely veiled attack against what Senghor had main-tained for more than twenty years. Despite Senghor's previous sup-port of Franco-African union, he was now prepared to listen to Diop. His readiness to adopt the new ideas was due to his elimination from the French ministerial post he had held in 1955. Because of RDA success in the elections of 1956 the 'African portfolio' went to Senghor's rival Houphouet-Boigny.

Senghor found himself a leader in the opposition and free to ex-press more radical ideas which were gaining popularity among BDS regulars. His conversion to independence as a political motif, how-ever, was marked by hesitancy and contradiction. It was difficult for Senghor to suppress the old rhetoric entirely. His public statements over the next several years mirrored this conflict between what he had believed and what he now saw happening. He admitted that Diop's criticism at the 1956 Congress of Negro Artists and Writers gave him a 'great irrefutable lesson': 'there cannot be any cultural liberation without prior political liberation'.[2] To ignore the import-ance of political freedom would be to 'follow the partial counsel of paternalists', Senghor noted in his Cotonou speech of 1958.[3] Yet faithful to the ideas of so many of his intellectual generation, it was not until 1958 that Senghor decided to demand independence from France. Until that time he did not want to make concessions to demagogy. Even if Africa had the means of independence such as trained personnel and a stable economy, the question that still remained was whether Africans 'would profit by being independent', he stated as late as 1956. He insisted that Liberia was not really independent[4] and went so far as to say that there was no truly independent nation in the second half of the twentieth century. On the other hand, when confronted with right-wing opinion, he defended the right to independence.[5]

The growth of independence movements in Africa as well as the insistent demands of the young people whom he integrated into his party in 1956 slowly transformed Senghor's thinking. In 1958 Senghor, not wishing to use the word independence, suggested *autodétermination* and *autonomie* for French West Africa. Later in 1958 he went so far as to mention nominal independence as the ultimate form of Africa's political evolution. However, he warned that the fact of independence did not necessarily carry with it 'the content' of true independence.[6] This distrust of independence, common to most French politicians of the Fourth Republic, inhibited Senghor's ability to foresee the future political development of French Africa.

Until May 1958 Senghor continued to advocate the idea of Africa as part of a Federal French Republic.[7] It was only after the fall of the Fourth Republic when new African policies were being formulated by the De Gaulle government that Senghor abandoned his project. Under the pressure of its new younger members such as Abdoulaye Ly, Senghor's party began to speak of independence. (This was the same Ly who, thirteen years earlier, had vigorously attacked Senghor for accepting nomination to the Monnerville Commission.)

Under the pressure from the 'young Turks', Senghor decided to abandon the struggle for autonomy within a Federal Republic and began to advocate independence within a multinational confederation.[8] By July of 1958 Senghor had launched an attack on the concept of a French Federation by arguing that it went against the current of history. Only confederation could solve the problem of French-African relations. As a member of the Constitutional Committee charged with drawing up the new constitution for France, Senghor advocated confederalism.[9] In spite of Senghor's pleadings, the Constitutional Committee remained resolutely federalist. The articles dealing with the French Community reflected this point of view because Senghor's rival Houphouet-Boigny had dominated the debate.

Between 1956 and 1958 Houphouet-Boigny of the Ivory Coast approved the federalist *Loi-Cadre Defferre*, which Senghor attacked. A French federation would allow the Ivory Coast to circumvent the 'screen' of Dakar and link itself directly to France, eliminating dependence on the French West African federation dominated by Senegal. The quarrel between federalists and confederalists was superimposed on the personal rivalry between Houphouet-Boigny and Senghor and the political rivalry between the Ivory Coast and Senegal. It reflected the desire of the Ivory Coast leaders to dissolve the French West African Federation and retain the funds which would have gone to the development of the federal capital, the Senegalese city of Dakar. The proponents of what Senghor called the 'balkanization' of the French West African Federation were federalists when it came to relations between France and Africa, while the supporters of the French West African Federation were confederalists on the level of Franco-African relations.

In the end the proposed Constitution reflected the position of those who supported a French Federation. However, Senghor in a remarkable turnabout urged his constituents to vote *oui* in the French Constitutional Referendum of September 1958. Senghor's *volte-face* caused a rift between him and the 'young Turks' in his party.

Senghor's disconcerting shift regarding the French Federation can be explained by the locus of power in Senegalese politics. Senghor realized the attachment of the Muslim *Marabouts* to the concept of French Federation, and he knew that political setback in the Referendum could threaten his career. The Mouride brotherhood was a powerful 'state within a state' and threatened loss of their support weighed heavily in Senghor's sudden change of heart. Senghor was plagued by his dependence on traditional leaders for electoral support. In contrast, Sékou Touré in Guinea functioned on a new power base: '...when one thinks of the...role played by the Senegalese *Marabouts*...during the Constitutional Referendum, it is tempting to think that it is at the moment (when he *suppressed* the chiefs) that Sékou Touré in fact achieved independence for his country...'.[10] An African observer wrote: 'When it happens that interests diverge, it is often the political leaders who yield, for they have no direct power over the electoral masses. Thus we had an example during the Referendum of 28 September 1958...After the PRA Congress at Cotonou, everyone believed that the UPS (Senghor's party, a section of the inter-territorial PRA) would opt for the *non* at the Referendum. But finally the Executive Committee opted for the *oui*. This reversal can be explained by the role of the "feudal elements", notably the religious ones, who did not have the same view of the common good as did the political leaders.'[11]

The fact that Senghor advocated the *oui* during the 1958 Constitutional Referendum should not, however, be construed as a permanent change in his confederal position. Immediately after the vote, Senghor worked to amend the federalist provisions of the French Constitution. He wished to obtain an independence 'prepared and organized in association' with France rather than embark upon 'the adventure' of immediate independence 'that would only be nominal'.[12]

Senghor's capitulation should not be misunderstood. Throughout his political career Senghor had proceeded with caution, only supporting what seemed acceptable to France. All of Senghor's declarations on Franco-African relations were imbued with the desire to placate French fears of Africa's withdrawal from the French community. By 1958, however, a strictly pro-French policy was no longer tenable. Africa was becoming increasingly nationalistic. France was beginning to weaken her previous 'hard line' towards African independence. Under these conditions it was possible for Senghor to advocate a limited break with France. By 1960 Senghor's confederalist theses were endorsed by a French government no longer willing to oppose an inevitable development. The African dependencies were given their national sovereignty.

Independence, however, was no panacea. Although forced to support independence as a political objective, Senghor remained convinced that true independence lay in 'raising living and cultural standards to the highest possible level'.[13] Political independence had never been an end in itself for Senghor. National sovereignty in a context of poverty or anarchy would be a farce.[14] Returning to his former ideas on *inter*dependence, the 'reality *par excellence*' of the twentieth century, Senghor stressed the futility for a country as small as Senegal to speak of true independence. Even if he accepted the word independence, which he had abhorred for so long, he did not interpret it as anti-French nationalism. He continued to insist that Africans 'by-pass racism, raise themselves above the inferiority complex forced on them by colonialism in order to take part in a great union with France and Europe'.[15]

Despite Senghor's declaration that the 'total independence' of Africa had been one of his 'major concerns since 1946',[16] he was very slow to support publicly any movement to achieve it. His delay was occasioned by an acute awareness of the special nature of underdevelopment in French-speaking sub-Saharan Africa. The scarcity of technicians and limited industrial development were the decisive factors influencing Senghor's political attitude towards independence. Except for two short periods, one following the end of World War II and the other immediately preceding the decade of the 1960s, Senghor held fast to his belief in Franco-African union.

Senghor had developed the notion of a rationalist and technical Europe complemented by an intuitive and agricultural Africa. Victim perhaps of his own theory, he had to advocate a permanent liaison with France. His ideas on means varied, but the ends remained immutable – the linking of Africa and Europe, thereby saving Africa from materialism (American or Soviet), and the eventual modernizing of Africa by the introduction of European methods.

34. Inter-African Federation

If Senghor was a confederalist with regard to the relationship between France and Africa, he was resolutely federalist in his approach
to inter-African politics. In 1944 Senghor had written of the 'colonial
nations' that would make up the French Imperial Community. One
of these 'nations' would be formed by the existing French West
African Federation.

In a 1954 proposal, Senghor still spoke of the necessity of grouping the African territories into large political units that could be
integrated into a French political community, but in this scheme he
proposed that the integrated state be formed by grouping several
territories:

'It is impossible to make a state out of Mauritania and its 500,000
inhabitants...and the same goes for Dahomey, Senegal, even
Sudan.'[1]

He suggested two states : one grouping Senegal, Mauritania, Sudan,
and Guinea with Dakar as capital; the other grouping the Ivory
Coast, Upper Volta, Niger and Dahomey with Abidjan as capital.[2]
One grouping would be dominated by his *Indépendants d'Outre-mer*
and the other by Houphouet-Boigny's RDA. By separating French
West Africa into two units, Senghor was making a realistic concession to the growing importance of the Ivory Coast in French Africa.
This separation reflected the increasing hostility of the Ivory Coast
to continued integration in a West African Federation dominated by
the Senegalese city of Dakar. The economic boom following the
opening in 1951 of the Vridi Canal, which made Abidjan a port,
further fired the Ivory Coast's separatist tendencies.

This rivalry had grown to such proportions by 1956, however,
that Senghor questioned the wisdom of two states emerging out of
the French West African Federation. Enlisting the support of student
and union leaders,[3] Senghor began a campaign against 'balkanization'. This term was used by Senghor to describe the effects of a
colonial reform law introduced into the French parliament by Gaston
Defferre, SFIO Minister of Overseas France. The *Loi-Cadre Defferre*
was the result of a collaboration between SFIO officials in the
Ministry of Overseas France and Houphouet-Boigny of the Ivory
Coast.[4] The *Loi-Cadre* had the effect of diminishing the importance of

Dakar by decentralizing executive power in French West Africa. Senghor's opposition to Houphouet-Boigny and the RDA compounded by his hostility to the SFIO, which had recently supplanted the MRP in the Ministry of Overseas France, contributed to his campaign against the *Loi-Cadre*. The battle was all the more bitter because Senghor had lost his ministerial post in the French government to Houphouet.[5]

Except for his 1954 'concession' Senghor had consistently advocated enormous African political unions which would embrace the different territories of French West Africa as well as the 'brother peoples of Portuguese and British colonies'.[6] At a time when Europe was beginning to talk seriously of economic and eventual political federation, 'it would be vain', declared Senghor, 'to cultivate separatism in Africa'. Africa would be strangled by 'artificial frontiers' cutting off the flow of men and ideas.[7]

A 'United States of Africa' was the logical extension of Senghor's emphasis on African solidarity. In 1950, at the Strasbourg Assembly of Europe, Senghor had supported a proposal by the British Labour Party spokesman MacKay for a United States of Africa. Africa as a single powerful political unit could then enter united into a Eurafrican federation.[8] This United States of Africa was not an anti-European grouping. Senghor remained 'resolutely opposed' to any African 'continentalism' which excluded Europe.

The student and union leaders whom Senghor had drawn to him were less inclined to embrace Europe. They placed their emphasis on the United States of Africa as the ultimate goal. Even so, Senghor remained closely allied to them inasmuch as his opposition to the *Loi-Cadre* concided with the main preoccupation of these 'young Turks' who advocated total African independence. They all sought to preserve a large West African Federation which eventually would become a sovereign state. The passage of the *Loi-Cadre* prevented them from realizing their dream.

The reforms of the *Loi-Cadre* provided for several West African executive departments. The French Governor of each territory presided over the new Territorial Cabinet as President of the Council of Ministers. The Vice-President of the Council was to be an African, and the Ministers were chosen from the Territorial Assembly. The problem of 'balkanization' appeared because of the absence of a federal executive branch on the inter-territorial level for French West Africa taken as a whole. No provision was made for the Governor-General of French West Africa to preside over a cabinet of African ministers at the federal level. Even after the passage of the *Loi-Cadre*, Senghor continued to battle for the creation of a federal executive in Dakar.

The vote of the French Constitution of 1958 made the struggle against 'balkanization' even more desperate. Senghor attempted unsuccessfully to bring about a federation of the different territories. The Federation of Mali was created in January 1959 and grouped four former Overseas Territories. Shortly thereafter, the Mali Federation retained only two territories: Senghor's Senegal and Modibo Keita's Sudan. By 20 August 1960, what remained of the Mali Federation split into two separate states, partly as a result of the wishes of Senghor himself who recognized the growing centrifugal forces in West Africa and the impossibility of reconstituting a French West African Federation.[9]

After the disintegration of the Mali Federation, Senghor abandoned his federal ideas for a more confederal approach.[10] He became increasingly aware of the impossibility of an African federation and went so far as to repel such a seemingly innocuous movement as the inclusion of Gambia in a Senegambian entity.

His failure to bring about a federation on the political level was partly responsible for the emphasis he began to place on economic development. If he has placed so much emphasis during the last few years on the 'African Road to Socialism', it is partly the result of the political disappointments he encountered. But his development of African Socialism was also the result of his growing awareness of the primary importance of economics in the development of Africa.

Since the coming of independence in 1960, it has been essential for Senghor, as for most African leaders, to maintain an ideological framework for solving the problems which face any young nation. The masses believed that once independence had been acquired, a comfortable life would automatically follow. To make the people understand that there is much work to be done before a plentiful society is achieved, Senghor has constantly emphasized economic construction, a kind of 'new frontier' beyond independence and as difficult to attain. With the exception of the period between 1956 and 1960 when Senghor stressed the political necessities of federation, he has consistently pressed for the 'true independence' of prosperity.[1] The emphasis on politics during the period of the *Loi-Cadre* had been exceptional for a man who had long advocated the 'subordination of the political'.

The social dislocations caused by the economic crash of 1929 had originally forced Senghor to re-examine his philosophic emphasis on culture. Although his poems from 1936 to 1940 reflected the social preoccupations and anti-capitalism of the *Front Populaire* Senghor refused to be converted to Marxism. He held fast to the belief 'that the resolution of economic and social questions would not necessarily solve the human problem, that by misplacing values men would risk the loss of their humanity, mistake the means for the ends, smother ideas with materialism...put the soul to sleep under the narcotic of comfort'.[2]

However, the actual formulation of his ideas into a socio-economic theory appeared at the end of World War II when Senghor became a *Député* in the French National Assembly. To develop this theory Senghor drew heavily on the same fundamental themes that had influenced his thought for so many years. Of particular importance were the themes dealing with the rehabilitation of African social tradition and the contribution of the Negro: 'Sense of community... faith in spiritual values, such are the contribution of African socialism and Africa to international socialism...'.[3] In return, European socialist thinking would modernize African social traditions. Implicit in this 'give and take' between these two civilizations is the theme of 'cross-breeding'.

Senghor's new social and economic theory also showed the influence of Delafosse, Barrès, the 'spiritualists' (Péguy, Mounier, and Maritain), and the Surrealists. What Jean Touchard called the French 'Spirit of the 1930s' was the common denominator between Senghor and those who influenced him. Senghor, as already noted, was a 'full member' of this generation of French intellectuals, and he adopted many of their negative themes: anti-individualism, anti-materialism, anti-capitalism, anti-Taylorization, anti-bourgeoisie, and anti-Americanism as well as anti-communism.

Just as he borrowed these anti-Western attitudes from young French intellectuals, Senghor adopted most of his important themes from Westerners and reworked them into an African idiom. In *Les Nègres*, which Senghor read in the early 1930s, the French Africanist Delafosse scrutinized the failures of Western social organization and held up African society as an example for Europe. This idea became the keystone of Senghor's 'African Socialism'. Delafosse used an old theory about the inferiority of African civilization as straw man for his arguments against Western superiority:

'It is from the social point of view that the Africans *give the impression* of being behind us. They are still in the period of unadulterated collectivism known by our ancestors before the Middle Ages, while we have arrived at individualism. The question is to know whether by that [individualism], we have realized definite progress, since many intellectuals among us who are called *avant-garde* demand, as a good thing, the return to collectivism, albeit in a somewhat different form.'[4]

Senghor strengthened Delafosse's position by adding the example of traditional African community concern whereby the extended family provided economic aid and personal support to weaker members. In Africa the old and indigent were not discarded. In 1939 Senghor proudly wrote: 'On Judgment Day the Negro peoples will not come politically or socially empty handed; they will bring their unique contribution to a world divided between democratic individualism and totalitarian gregarianism'.[5] The value of the African family unit was also perceived by Dietrich Westermann in 1937. Two years later Senghor quoted the German ethnographer's *Noirs et Blancs en Afrique*: 'If the Africans succeed in keeping (their institution of the family) intact during the transitional period, in purifying it of its unhealthy elements and in saving it from degenerating, there is no anxiety as to their future'.[6] In much the same way, Karl Marx had argued for using traditional Russian communes (the *mir*) for socialist Russia. It was Westermann, however, who opened the door which led to Senghor's adaptation of Marx's theory of the *mir*.[7]

Senghor said in 1939 that the African family, in dealing with political and social problems, 'has already found the "community spirit" which is still an ideal of today's humanists'.[8]

The foundation of the *extended* African family is the 'communion of Dead and living'[9] cherished by Barrès. Senghor attempted to show the validity of traditional African social organization and tried to preserve it by integrating it into modern civilization. These efforts were inspired by Senghor's reading of Barrès. The African village, which became the practical basis for Senegalese socialism, had become surrounded by a mystical aura similar to that which Barrès wove about rural France. The reason for the emphasis on the village in Barrès and Senghor was that it provided the perfect fulcrum between opposing social tendencies. Barrès wrote: '...now we believe it possible to reconcile (collectivism and anarchy)...in the manner opened by Proudhon...The problem reduced to its most simple expression consists in finding an equilibrium between two elements: collectivism and anarchy, authority and liberty, solidarity and individualism'.[10]

Having been convinced of the validity of African social organization, Senghor went on to attack capitalism: 'The vice of capitalist society is not in the existence of property, which is a necessary condition for the development of the person, but rather that property is not based essentially on work'.[11] African society was more equitable, and Delafosse had pointed out why: 'Work, or more precisely, productive action, is considered as the sole source of property in Negro society'. Critics of capitalism had observed that: 'property is virtually non-existent if natural riches and the means of production remain in the hands of a few individuals'. Africa, in contrast, 'treats property in a humanistic way' as a natural communal value. 'The earth as well as everything it provides – rivers, streams, forests, animals, fish – is a common good divided between families and even sometimes between members of the family, who have it as temporary and usufructuary property.' Senghor concluded on the superiority of African collectivism:

> 'The means of production in general, the instruments for work in particular, are the common property of the family group. This means that the ownership of products is collective, work itself being collective. From this tradition follows the great advantage of everyone being assured materially of the "vital minimum" according to his needs. "When the harvest is ripe" says the *Wolof*, "it belongs to all".'[12]

Under this system 'individual property is regulated and restrained, but not eliminated'.[13]

The influence of Barrès and the Africanists in Senghor's economic and social thinking before World War II was complemented by that of the Catholic humanists Jacques Maritain and Emmanuel Mounier. 'Negroes', wrote Senghor in his 1939 essay, 'if they neglect the *individual*, do not enslave the *person*....'[14] Originally this distinction had been made by the 'Personalist' philosophers Maritain and Mounier, and it is central in Senghor's 'African Road to Socialism'. Twenty years later he continued to insist on this distinction: 'Let us guard against believing that the African communal society ignores the *person* even if it neglects the *individual*'.[15]

It was Maritain, however, who married the concepts of collective and personal property. Senghor quoted from Maritain's *Humanisme Intégral* of 1936: 'For a collective form of property to be an effective aid to the individual, it must not have as its aim depersonalized possession'.[16] Senghor could then point out that 'the African is linked to the object of collective property by the juridical link of custom and tradition: and even more significantly by a mystical link...a man thus feels himself a person – communitary I admit – in dealing with the object of property'.

Maritain's *Humanisme Intégral*, which Senghor was quoting in 1939 and continued to quote in his 1948 essay '*Marxisme et Humanisme*', is certainly a basic source for the 'African Road'. Senghor conceived of a new society as an 'active humanism'. For Senghor as for Maritain, human activities and religion are not separable because 'society must be *intégral* and base itself on an ethic'. To these Catholic theorists 'religion remained the most solid foundation of ethics'.[17] In economics and social matters as in culture, Senghor followed Maritain and gave pride of place to the spiritual by adopting the philosophy of Maritain's 1927 book *Primauté du Spirituel*.

Senghor and the 'Personalists' believed that they had proposed a revolution more profound than what 'revolutionary Marxist literature' had called by that name. Like Mounier and Maritain, Senghor wished to dissociate the Catholic Church from 'reactionaries' in economic matters.[18] Senghor, as the neo-Thomist Maritain, was persuaded that the State had no other end than to assure 'common well-being', which was not to be confused with 'individual well-being'. The State was but an instrument in the service of Man, and for this reason they condemned the hypocrisy of middle-class liberalism that served only the bourgeoisie. Senghor's denunciation of capitalism is based less on economic than on moral and spiritual objections. Senghor's first anti-capitalist sentiments, like Mounier's, proceed from the 'spiritualist' essayist Charles Péguy more than from Marx.

After the 'crash' of 1929 Senghor and Mounier became very hostile to liberal individualism and middle-class democracy. As already noted, they distinguished between the person and the individual. Anti-individualism became a corollary to anti-capitalism and was used by Senghor to rehabilitate 'African collectivism'. Senghor profited from the social and economic difficulties of industrial civilization to reinforce his belief in traditional African social systems.

Anti-capitalism, however, did not lead them to embrace communism. Both Senghor and Mounier were as hostile to the Communist Party and the Soviet experiment as they were to Western capitalism. Senghor denounced both capitalist disorder and communist oppression as 'materialist' systems. Mounier had set the example when he tossed Stalin and Ford into the same sack in June 1934.[19] This double hostility was similar to that of the theorists of Fascism and 'National Socialism'. Senghor's wish to by-pass the opposing forces of capitalism and communism was a desire common to many thinkers of the 1930s who hoped to shun these conflicting ideologies and start 'beyond':[20] '... we can, on the ruins of capitalism and *beyond* communism, construct a new world of souls in which the Divine will rule'.[21] This attitude resembles the 'neither nor-ism' (*ni-nisme*) of the 1930s when many French intellectuals accepted neither right nor left, neither capitalism nor communism. Despite their later denunciation of *ni-nisme* – Mounier chose the left during the 1930s and Senghor did so in 1945 – this spirit still persists in Mounier's 'Christian Socialism' and Senghor's 'African Socialism'.

The non-orthodox character of their socialist philosophies owed much to the essays of Charles Péguy.[22] Péguy 'discerned the *embourgeoisement* of the French working class' and identified 'peasants as the revolutionary force of the twentieth century'. Péguy's popular masses are 'pre-industrial' and therefore his analysis cannot be used by orthodox Marxists.[23] Senghor, on the other hand, does follow Péguy by concentrating on the peasant as the fundamental agent of social change:

I've chosen my toiling black people, my peasant people,
    the peasant race throughout the world.[24]

Senghor shows that Africa has kept those peasant traditions which Péguy looked towards for renewing social harmony. In 1939 he declared that work in Africa was 'not *corvée*, but a source of joy'. In Africa the working of the soil 'is the most noble' kind of labour. There is a mystical link with the earth characteristic of Africans which makes 'the Negro soul remain obstinately peasant'. Senghor points out that the African has remained the pre-industrial man so important to Péguy's ideal society: 'Negro work, Negro rhythm,

Negro joy which is liberated in working and which liberates itself from work'. 'The worker', wrote Senghor concerning Africa's peasant system, 'feels he is someone, not a simple cog in the wheel.'[25]

The influences of the 1930s thus modelled Senghor's socio-economic thinking, but it was only after the war that he developed a coherent system from his readings. It is therefore necessary to cover the war years and the immediate post-war period before analysing the socialist theory which resulted from all these influences.

From the fall of France in June 1940 until he joined the French Socialist Party in 1945, Senghor was subjected to an alien philosophy which marked the brand of socialism he came to espouse under the label of the 'African Road'. The period of the Vichy government in France was an important influence on the development of Senghor's economic and social thought.

The Fascist philosophy attacked both communism and capitalism as 'materialist' systems and envisaged a 'New Order' uniting both nationalism and socialism. The Vichy propaganda theme used to create nationalist feelings was the theme of 'reconciliation of classes which have become equal in their common suffering from the war'. It was constantly reiterated in the press and on the radio, and a people sick and tired of the discomforts of wartime France no longer had the energy to question it.[1]

This idea of reconciliation of all groups within the 'proletarian nation' conflicted with the notion of internal struggle and competition which characterized both capitalism (ruthless competition) and communism (class struggle). Party struggles and class struggles were outmoded. Senghor later used this idea and the theory that there is no proletariat, only proletarian nations. The 'African Socialists' seem to have renewed the fascist idea of proletarian nations which have no proletarian internal class struggle and, in place of the Vichy idea of reconciliation, they have substituted the 'African notion of dialogue'.

The French Neo-Socialists were responsible for much of the Vichy propagandists' concern for all exploited groups: workers, peasants, artisans, tenants, members of co-operatives, and other oppressed categories. Their belief that the socialization of property could be brought about by an immense development of co-operatives attracted Senghor. These 'Neos' proposed to go 'beyond Marxism' and their ideology was summarized up by the Italian Arturo Labriola, who published *Beyond Capitalism and Socialism* in 1946. The fact that the Neo-Socialists also advocated a Eurafrican concept helped to attract Senghor's attention to them.

It was with this fascist intellectual legacy that Senghor entered the French Socialist Party in 1945. One of his reasons for choosing socialism was that he considered Negro-African civilization 'collectivist and communitary: socialist'.[2] As he likes to observe: the African concept of democracy is based on the group, not on the individual.[3]

Immediately after entering the SFIO he began to study the great social theorists whose works helped form the party's creed. 'I began in 1946', he writes, 'to read the works of the French utopians – Fourier, Saint-Simon and Proudhon.' But he adds, 'That year I concentrated on Marx and Engels'.[4] This reading made Senghor aware of the economic determinants of the condition of the colonial population and of the proletarian. Everything seemed to link up: the material poverty of the victim of colonialism had produced his poverty of spirit. 'On reflection, the situation of the African Negro appeared as a typical, clinical case' of alienation.[5]

Saint-Simon, the French utopian socialist, also seems to hold an important place in Senghor's thought. Saint-Simon's distinction between real liberty and formal liberty inspired Senghor to distinguish between real independence and nominal independence. Both Saint-Simon and Senghor placed great faith in artists and men of imagination, whom they believed would proclaim the future of the human species. Senghor, following Saint-Simon, founded the future society on the past, using tradition in the creation of a new world. Saint-Simon's fundamental thesis substituted the exploitation of man by man with the exploitation of the earth by all men and is echoed by Senghor in his 'African Road'. Saint-Simon hoped for human love, for human fraternity which would eventually conquer the globe. 'Saint-Simonism' was an indistinct mixture of socialism and capitalism which were bound together in their common goal before they became brother enemies. Saint-Simon insisted on man as a producer and creator, not as a consumer. With the same emphasis, Senghor wanted the African to become a producer of culture, not merely an imitator or consumer.[6]

Proudhon affected Senghor's specific construction of a socialist society. Proudhon was not 'the man of one party, one idea, one milieu'; he was 'half-peasant, half-worker, half bourgeois', in short, a man 'liking' many different and opposing worlds. His search, like Senghor's, led to a 'third way' between materialism and spiritualism. Proudhon advocated 'progressive socialization of industry by giving an increasing place to the worker in the advantages and prerogatives of the enterprise'. He proposed a 'mutualization' of agriculture by the establishment of co-operatives. The State, in Proudhon's philosophy, was an initiator, a national accountant, and a planner, but it abstained from any direct economic management. Proudhon was at the root of Jaurès' socialism and of the social Christian personalism of Péguy, Mounier, and Maritain.[7] Barrès stated that 'Proudhon's socialism, by combining our national sensitivity and Hegelianism, accommodates the interests of the French, who could never lean towards German collectivism or Russian terrorism, both concepts characteristic of foreign races'.[8] Proudhon's ideas seem to have been incorporated textually into Senghor's programme for Senegalese development.

Senghor read the 'utopian' socialists as well as Marx and Engels because of his association with the Senegalese branch of the SFIO, which remained faithful to socialism of the French nineteenth-century type. Saint-Simon and Proudhon preached a humanitarian and egalitarian socialism which gave the Senegalese of Lamine-Guèye's party the feeling of absolute equality with the Europeans as well as the integral respect of their African personality.[9]

Since Senghor was the *Député* representing the interior, socialism meant reorganizing agricultural production. He simply avoided the question of nationalizing industrial production. Agriculture, the economic sector which employs by far the largest number of people in Senegal, monopolized Senghor's socio-economic thinking. As early as 1944 Senghor had stated that 'the most serious question', the agrarian issue, 'has been at the root of all reform, of all progress'.[10]

In *Reveil*, the organ of the revolutionary RDA, Senghor broached a theory for re-invigorating tradition in the African countryside. 'In taking inspiration from European socialism and African collectivism' Senghor hoped to 'cross-breed modern technique with African humanism'. By doing so he hoped to construct a 'better world than yesterday's colonial world, better also than...the world before European conquest'.[11] This 1947 proposal was basic to Senghor's 'African Road'.

The SFIO wanted countries dependent on France to avoid passing through a nationalist phase.[12] It was also thought that these same countries might be spared the period of proletarianization and all the anguish which came with the nineteenth-century Industrial Revolution. In his preface to Roger Deniau's *Avec Tes Défenseurs* (1947) the SFIO leader Guy Mollet wrote: 'The principal objective of the author and of the group which he formed is to spare civilizations still in infancy the obligation to evolve exactly in the wake of Western experiences, for it is not entirely true that this process is unavoidable everywhere...'.[13]

The source of this deviation from standard Marxism is to be found in Marx's own letter to the Russian Populist Vera Zassúlich. The full text of Marx's letter dated 8 March 1881 was published in the SFIO

journal *La Revue Socialiste* in May 1947. Vera Zassúlich had written
to Marx in February 1881 to ask whether in *Das Kapital* he meant
that agrarian Russia had to pass through all the stages of capitalist
industrial exploitation before hoping to have a socialist revolution.
Near the end of his life, Marx rejected Engels' 1852 declaration that
the Russian peasant commune (the *mir*) was entirely devoid of value
as an eventual basis for socialism. His answer to Zassúlich's question
was that *Das Kapital* applied to Western Europe and that conditions
of Eastern Europe called for different solutions. In 1881 he was convinced that the peasant commune could constitute the *'point d'appui*
for social regeneration in Russia', but if the commune were to function in this role, it would be necessary to rid it of the pernicious influences 'which assail it from all sides'.[14]

After reading Marx's letter in the SFIO review, Senghor began to
draft his theory of 'African Socialism'. At the same time Senghor
broke away from the SFIO to found his new party the *Bloc Démocratique Sénégalais* (BDS). Senghor distinguished his new party from
the SFIO by a new creed. In the first place his party was based on
'African Socialism' and not on 'French Socialism'. In the second
place his new party did not share the anti-clerical orientation of the
SFIO, but was based on a socialism of 'believers': Christian and
Muslim.[15]

Senghor's new party wished to transform 'traditional village organization which was communal into modern collectivist organization without having to pass through the capitalist stages'.[16] Senghor
hoped to graft new economic and technical structures onto the old
African community traditions enumerated by Delafosse: collective
property, labour in common, and complementary functions of age
groups.[17] He proposed agricultural co-operatives both of the producer and consumer variety, based on the extended family and kinship groups in villages.[18] Consequently, he argued that it was not
necessary for the African worker and peasant to form a proletariat in
order that the African socialist society be realized.[19]

Senghor's approach clearly parallels that of the nineteenth-century
Pan-Slavists who hailed the primitive democracy, the agrarian Slavic
sense of collectivity and its brotherly institutions and customs that
were in danger of being distorted by the invasion of class-structuring
from the West. Appreciation of these traditions had led to the Slavic
Populist movement of Alexander Herzen,[20] which was directly responsible for Vera Zassúlich's letter to Karl Marx. Pan-Slavic 'nationalism' had contributed not only to *négritude*, but also to African
Socialism.

The one thing missing in this new social order was religion. Senghor insisted that if it was not necessary to make the African a proletarian, it was equally unnecessary to render him an atheist.[21] From his study of ethnology, Senghor knew that African community traditions were based on religion, and he felt that it was imperative that he reconcile religion and socialism in order to found an agrarian socialist community.[22] Senghor believed that the essential dialogue of the twentieth century was between Christians and Marxists.[23]

In the world of 1948 he saw two European movements which succeeded in reconciling religion and socialism. The first was the British Labour Party, which, according to him, achieved a social revolution while remaining 'most faithful to national tradition, monarchy, and Christianity'.[24] The second example was closer to home. The Catholic intellectuals of the MRP wanted the spiritual to animate the political. Some believe that it was this 'sacred conviction' which created the originality of the French Social Christian party.[25]

Progressive Catholics introduced Senghor to the writings of the Jesuit scholar Teilhard du Chardin. Senghor first became acquainted with Teilhard's ideas in 1948 through the Director of the Dakar *Institut Français d'Afrique Noire*, Théodore Monod, who quoted them.[26] In 1955 the progressive Catholic publishing house *Editions du Seuil* brought out the collected works of the Teilhard du Chardin. The *Editions du Seuil*, which published Senghor's works as well, invited Senghor to join a discussion group analysing Teilhard's philosophy.[27] These discussions helped Senghor accomplish what his reading of the 1930s had begun: the synthesis of modern science and theology, of reason and faith. Teilhard's philosophy enabled Senghor to escape from certain *impasses* by elaborating a theory of socialism without renouncing any of the spiritual values of African Negro civilization. According to Senghor, Teilhard carried the theories of Marx to their logical conclusion, achieving the 'neo-humanism' sought after by the German philosopher. Marx considered only the *homo oeconomicus*. Teilhard, on the other hand, refused to 'mutilate' man by ignoring his spiritual nature.[28] Teilhard helped Senghor resolve the opposition of Marxism and spiritualism, of socialism and Catholicism, conflicts which had occupied him since the 1930s and which had found a partial resolution in the works of Jacques Maritain and Mounier.

It is interesting to linger a moment on the coincidence of the intellectual itineraries of Teilhard and Senghor. Teilhard, like Senghor, reconciled several intellectual points of view, for he was by method and vocation a man of syntheses. He spent a large part of his life pursuing an inner unity before realizing that a synthesis had in fact been created out of the various opposing forces which attracted him.[29]

The two theorists were very much imbued with the philosophy of Saint Thomas Aquinas. All this explains Senghor's natural attraction to the French Jesuit philosopher. The influence of Aquinas is highly significant, since both Maritain's Neo-Thomism and Senghor's partiality to the Thomistic approach prepared the way for Senghor's acceptance of Teilhard.

Senghor believed that 'thanks to the progress of human and physical sciences, thanks to new philosophical currents – phenomenology, existentialism, Teilhardism – socialism will be integrated' into a spiritual humanism.[30] French Marxists, on the other hand, considered this project impossible: 'To consider the philosophy of Father Teilhard as by-passing Marxism, as being an integration of Marxism into a Christian perspective, Teilhard doing for Marxism what Saint Thomas Aquinas did for Aristotelianism, would be to commit a serious error'.[31]

After World War II Senghor had sought a 'third' ideological position somewhere between the Soviet position and the American position – or rather beyond these two 'materialist' attitudes. He did not want to see 'the triumph of American policy in Africa' which would mark the 'downfall of France' and, more seriously, herald 'the triumph of a capitalism and a racism which would lead us...to the destruction of the Earth and to the end of Man's hope'.[32] But neither did he want Africa to fall under the influence of orthodox Marxism: 'Socialist humanism is not in the least based on materialism but on that philosophy of a vital force which gives rise to emotion and dialogue and which is at the basic root of African spirituality'.[33] Senghor knew that 'African peoples are believing peoples and for them socialism is to be the exact opposite of abstract idealism and atheistic materialism. It is an incarnated and living spiritualism'.[34]

Along with a number of other Third World socialists, Senghor admired Marx but could not become an orthodox Marxist.[1] He agreed with Marx's early humanism, he subscribed to Marx's evaluation of capitalism, and he approved of the revolutionary attitude required by Marx. However, these Marxian qualities, which were integrated into Senghor's philosophy, did not make other aspects of the dialectic palatable. The rationalism, atheism, and violence which were fundamental to Marxian dogma were repugnant to him. Of equal significance was Marx's reliance on an industrialized Western European environment as the setting for a world wide proletariat. Senghor had no choice but to reject Marx's ethnocentrism.[2]

Senghor's real introduction to Marx had occurred relatively late in his intellectual life. His reading of Marx had begun with his membership in the SFIO, and the party viewed Marx in its own special way. In 1947 the party review contained an article on Marx by Maximilen Rubel who had published the Zassúlich letter. The article presented a picture of the young Marx as having 'an ethical vision'.[3] Senghor interpreted it as an unavowed spiritualism which he had not discovered in his first readings. Publishing an article in 1948 entitled 'Marxism and Humanism', Senghor defended his new-found insight and accused the Marxist-Leninists of neglecting the humanist side of Marx and betraying the Master's intentions.[4]

Having discovered a new quality in Marx, he was more willing to adopt what he called the 'Marxist method'. This method helped him analyse the 'alienation and dehumanization' produced by the capitalist system: 'Our entire life, our whole society was threatened by the same evil capitalist system that had destroyed European society and which, in Africa, had appeared in the guise of the Colonial Pact'.[5]

Once the villain had been identified, Senghor had no choice but to assume Marx's 'revolutionary attitude': men must not let history take its course, but must actively fashion history by making it conform to nature.[6] African society would not really be valid, Senghor noted in 1947, unless it suppressed classes and castes. Only after passing through the socialist stage would Africans re-discover 'the best of African Negro civilization, its spirit of charity...and its collectivist organization'.[7] Senghor's adaptation of Marx contained a certain optimism: the ending of the many alienations suffered by the colonized African, the abolition of economic *asynchronie*. Senghor refused to see Marx as a doctrinaire thinker. According to him, the great German philosopher had only proposed 'a method of action in service of the total man'. Senghor refused to erect Marxism into a 'catechism'. Had not Barrès counselled: 'Let us first of all repudiate philosophical systems and the parties they engender'?[8] Senghor deplored the fact that so many Marxists, and so many adversaries of Marx, have committed this serious error.

After extracting what he found attractive in Marx, Senghor saw much more to reject. Marx's 'materialism without warmth' had brought 'discursive reason to its ultimate absurdity'.[9] Because of his predilection for the irrationalist thought of Bergson and the 'spiritualists', Senghor could not accept the dogged rationality of Marx. Materialism in the Marxian sense also had no place for God. As explained earlier, atheism was an impossible concept; Senghor could not abandon his faith in God.

Equally impossible for Senghor to accept was Marx's exhortation to violence. The revolution which Senghor envisioned was a peaceful revolution: a 'revolution, not a revolt', as he has constantly reiterated since 1947.[10] The phrase echoes Eduard Bernstein's 'revisionist' concept summarized in the dictum 'evolution, not revolution' popular in the 1930s. His Christianity and the influence of Gandhi's philosophy of non-violence conditioned Senghor's pacifism. In 1962 Senghor justified non-violence by arguing that in Africa 'there was no class struggle. Even in Europe...thanks to a developed social policy...class differences had diminished'.[11]

Senghor tried to recast class struggle in another dimension. 'Today's socialist cannot hold as an ideal the suppression of class inequality within a nation.' Instead he should try to end 'the inequalities which result from the division of the world into developed and underdeveloped states'. This schism is the real problem, but it is not recognized by the 'states which call themselves socialist, in the East or in the West'. Their theorists have not 'been able to renew socialist doctrine'.[12] For Senghor the mission of 'today's socialist must be the elimination of the division of the world into developed and underdeveloped peoples'.[13] The fascist idea of 'have' and 'have-not' nations is very much evident in the new national socialism of Senghor.

The critical weakness of *Das Kapital* exposed by Senghor was Marx's Western European focus. Senghor accused Marx of concentrating his study on Western Europe alone, to the neglect of the rest of the world. Marx wrote *Das Kapital* for the industrialized countries of Western Europe; Africa, possessing few industries, could hardly enter into the Marxist schema. Senghor pointed out that Marx had predicted that socialist revolution would break out in industrialized countries where it did not in fact do so, and that Marx had not foreseen the development of European colonization at the end of the nineteenth century. If Marx had erred so significantly in his analysis of Western Europe, how could his philosophy be applied to an African situation which he could not have understood?

Beginning in 1947 Senghor proclaimed that Africa's evolution 'must not pass through the same stages as Europe, that it is not necessary to make a proletariat of African workers and peasants in order to build the African socialist world...'.[14] After the publication of 'Black Orpheus' in 1948 Senghor appropriated Sartre's argument that a world-wide proletariat did not exist. In Africa there was no proletarian consciousness while in Europe it was beginning to die. He then rephrased Sartre's question: 'Do you really believe that the dock workers of Antwerp feel solidarity with those of... Matadi?'[15]

According to Senghor, Marx's thought invited such criticism, for in his letter to Vera Zassúlich, Marx had observed: 'the conclusions of *Das Kapital* are only valid for Western Europe'.[16] Senghor believed that Marxism should be regarded as 'Graeco-Latin rationalism, re-worked by a Jewish-German mind and adapted to the situation of Western Europe in the middle of the nineteenth century'.[17] Marxist doctrine was not a 'precious pearl that one swallows only to render it unchanged'. Marx's ideas were 'food' which 'must be chewed' before becoming part of the body.[18] Senghor's instinctive resistance to assimilation dominated his reaction to this Western philosophy.

Senghor's attitude towards the Marxist-Leninists was much more hostile than his reaction to Marx. It was these 'scientific socialists' who systematized Marx's thought so that it became a doctrine, 'an illegitimate passage from a rational philosophy of action to a doctrinarian metaphysic'.[19] Senghor's hostility arose because the Marxist-Leninists were guilty of 'cultural imperialism'. They professed a truth that they wanted to be universally accepted. Senghor saw this as just another form of assimilation or a neo-colonialism. 'What was Marxism-Leninism,' asked Senghor, 'but Marxism adapted to the Russian situation?'[20] Having rejected French cultural assimilation, Senghor did not want Marxism from Europe to impose its *weltanschauung* on Africa: 'No, we could not accept an ideology thought out by others and for others, which denied the values of our civilization, of our collective personality. It had to be adapted to our own needs; otherwise, we denied ourselves and passively accepted our extinction, our non-being.'[21]

Using this argument Senghor attacked the Senegalese *Parti Africain de l'Indépendance* (PAI) whose leader Majemout Diop espoused Marxist-Leninism in his *Contribution à l'Etude des Problèmes Politiques en Afrique Noire*.[22] Senghor accused the PAI of too closely following 'orthodox' Marxist thinking, especially in its adherence to the theory of a class struggle in Africa. The PAI, on the other hand, accused Senghor's government of constituting an African bourgeoisie and advocated its violent overthrow. The PAI, which admitted to being communist, was finally outlawed in Senegal. The 1965 split in the PAI between 'Chinese' and 'Russian' tendencies[23] did not change the nature of these 'African Communists'. The Russian wing still applied the idea of class struggle to Africa and the Chinese wing continued to advocate violence.

If Senghor's ideological position is easily distinguished from that of Majemout Diop and the other African Communists, it is much more difficult to see where it differs from that of Abdoulaye Ly, former head of the PRA-S opposition party who at various times has been a member of Senghor's government. Abdoulaye Ly, like Senghor, dismissed both capitalism and communism as incapable of providing workable solutions to Africa's problems. His *Masses Africaines et l'Actuelle Condition Humaine*[24] and *l'Etat et la Production Sénégalaise*[25] show striking similarities to many of Senghor's later pronouncements. Ly's ideas come from the *Groupe Africain de Recherche Economique et Politique* (GAREP), which was formed in Paris by a few African students with Trotskyite leanings, who met from 1945 to 1956. Ly has been derided as an 'anarcho-Trotskyist, anti-Leninist, and knight of the modern peasant revolution' by his orthodox Marxist rival Majemout Diop.[26]

Although Senghor denied it, some of Abdoulaye Ly's ideas may have influenced him when Ly was Minister of Production in the first black Senegalese government in 1957–8.[27] Ly joins Senghor in severely criticizing Lenin and Stalin for having considered the underdeveloped countries as being merely supporting forces, and he, too, wishes Marxism to be placed in a planetary perspective. He is also close to Senghor in his upgrading of the role of the peasant in the underdeveloped countries: both regard the peasant as the 'true proletarian' of the twentieth century. They both are suspicious of the proletariat of capitalist countries and the parties which represent this group.

But Ly's style differs radically from Senghor's. Ly seems much more intransigent on matters of doctrine than does Senghor. Senghor's 'doctrine' is not really a doctrine. His economic theories are adapted and altered according to the specific problem at hand, in much the same way as his political theories are affected by practical considerations. Until recently the nature of the difference between Ly and Senghor was perhaps the difference between a theorist with no responsibilities and a statesman faced with the innumerable 'hard facts' of reality. Thus Ly could criticize, while Senghor defended, the close link between Senegal and France which associated Senegal to both the French Community and the European Common Market. Ly advocated neutralism, while Senghor continued to commit himself and his country to 'a people whose revolutionary, whose proletarian conscience is most developed' – not the Russians or the Chinese, but the French, 'the most revolutionary by temperament'.[28]

The Gallic influence is highly characteristic of Senegalese politicians whether or not they are pro-French. Most of the perspectives of French socialist thought can be found institutionalized in Senegal. Abdoulaye Ly represents the anti-communist, anti-SFIO weekly *Observateur*;[29] Lamine-Guèye the SFIO, Majemout Diop the French Communist Party, his dissident lieutenants the Chinese Communists, Mamadou Dia the left-wing Catholic weekly *Témoignage Chrétien*, and Senghor the Social Christian MRP. The doctrinaire aspect of Marxist thinking has been altered by each to fit his own world view and to allow him to create an African programme.

The African syncretic approach to Islam and Christianity was echoed in Senghor's transformation of Marxism. Africa could not accept any of these dogmas without adapting them to local conditions. Just as Islam or Christianity was blended with animism, Senghor had to reconcile Marxism and African agrarian institutions. The 'African Road' has been described as 'a doctrine which is still confusedly seeking for itself, an amalgam of very diverse elements' both foreign and native.[1] The most vital sources of contemporary Catholic thought – Mounier, Teilhard de Chardin, Father Lebret of *Economie et Humanisme* and the economist François Perroux – were joined with the African Negro sources which Senghor had helped re-discover in the works of Delafosse.[2]

An everyday symbol of this syncretic process is the boubou dress worn by elegant Senegalese ladies: the material comes from Europe, but the style is original to Africa. For Senghor, what is important is the creative activity of transforming Marxism, Islam, Christianity – or the cloth – so that something new is produced, something clearly African. Thus, the African is not assimilated but rather converts the imported idea or article for his own use. The French sociologist Georges Balandier has noted the relationship between Senghor's socio-economic thinking and the African approach to foreign religion.[3]

Senghor's social and economic ideas show a striking similarity to those of the leaders of other developing countries. According to Balandier, the preamble of the Indian Second Five-Year Plan reveals as diverse sources of inspiration as 'the African Road': agrarianism inherited from Gandhi, 'social welfare' inherited from English economic thinking, and a reinterpretation of Marxism. Like Senghor, the Indian theorists proclaim a socialism 'respectful of traditional and native fundamental values that denies the class struggle and atheism'.[4] Arab Socialism, developed by Nasser's friend Mohammed Hassenein Heykal, follows the same pattern. In fact, Senghor quotes Heykal to show that such an approach is possible. A generalized phenomenon, a similar situation of underdevelopment incites the theorists of the 'third world' to develop solutions such are syncretic, non-dogmatic, and respectful of native values. The pragmatism or empiricism of Senghor's socio-economic approach is thus analogous to most of the 'syncretic socialisms' of developing countries. But in sub-Saharan Africa he seems to have been the forerunner. The young generation of Africans paid tribute to Senghor by imitating his approach, even while refusing to accept the fact that he is responsible for their ideas.

An example of those influenced was Catholic intellectual Joseph Ki-Zerbo from the Upper Volta. Ki-Zerbo's ephemeral *Mouvement Africain de Libération Nationale* (MLN) linked 'African Socialism' and 'African Personalism'. For the MLN, African Socialism was 'modernized Negro collectivism'. The members wanted to 'modernize basic African structures, not adapt socialism to Africa, but adapt Negro African socialism to modern requirements'. As in the case of traditional collectivism, this group of young Africans affirmed that modern Africa had only to reform structures which existed well before colonization. The Manifesto of Ki-Zerbo's movement spoke of the African village as the basic cell of production, but its collectivist structures would be 'reviewed and renewed' by certain improvements such as a plan for production, credit, self-financing. The MLN's 'African Personalism' insisted that traditional Africa had a Personalist concept of society. Like Mounier and Senghor, Ki-Zerbo and his colleagues in turn made the distinction between 'individual' and 'person', society serving the latter while being served by the former.[5] Ki-Zerbo's dependence on Senghor for many of the MLN's ideas is clearly visible in comparing his movement's pronouncements with these lines written by Senghor in 1949: '...this action should permit the Senegalese countryside to transform its old collectivist organization to modern collectivist organization without having to pass through the capitalist stages'.[6]

The transformation of Senegalese society began with an economic plan developed under the auspices of Father Lebret and his group *Economie et Humanisme*. They were sensitive to the values inherent in traditional Senegal and set out to avoid overturning the whole society: 'It will be essential not to make a frontal attack on traditional beliefs and the spirit which animates them, but instead introduce into them the elements necessary to develop them. Obstacles to evolution will thus be eliminated from the interior, and the very structure of society will serve as a framework for, and root of, progress itself.'[7] This was a plan elaborated not by revolutionaries but rather by 'intellectuals who were, by definition, audacious in thought and prudent in action'.[8] It was to produce, in Senghor's words, a 'peaceful revolution',[9] a 'revolution, not a revolt'.[10] There was no need to espouse class struggle and violence as the means necessary for this revolution.[11] The example was set by the experience of Great Britain which 'without violence and while respecting democracy had achieved the most profound social revolution in Western Europe'.[12] It was thus on the basis of the old social order that Senghor and the economic planners hoped to found a new order.[13] Senghor believed that the one means by which a government could prevent a revolution 'was to accomplish it itself by just means'.[14] Senghor defended his empirical and prudent socialism with an argument similar to that of Catherine 11 who replied to the criticism of a *philosophe*: 'You work on paper, and paper is always patient. I, Empress, must write on the infinitely sensitive skins of human beings'. He was acutely conscious of the fact that he worked with men, not things. Regardless of Senghor's insistence that the economic plan was a blueprint for social revolution, the left wing continued to describe Senghor's socialism as timid reformism.[15]

The major fault in Senghor's economics lay in the internal contradictions of the 'African Road'. These contradictions arose because Senghor's socialism was eclectic and because his economic and social thinking was realistic rather than doctrinal. 'Only a Religion', claimed Senghor, 'can pretend to base itself on a doctrine'.[16] What he called 'non-dogmatic' might be more accurately described as opportunistic or, at best, pragmatic. One of the most serious inconsistencies appeared in his multiple explanations of the relationship of the individual or person to the group or community. In 1944 Senghor advocated the family vote in order to give expression to Africa's traditional anti-individualism. Two years later when he asked for political equality and voting rights for Africans, he was confronted with his 1944 position,[17] and he thereupon dismissed 'collective forms' of African civilization.[18] In 1944, he deplored the 'too absolute subordination of the person to the community' in 'Negro collectivism'.[19] In 1963 he praised the 'collectivism' of African societies, calling them 'communalist' or 'communitarist'.[20] According to this revised conception, the individual 'becomes a person by and in society, a society which is not collectivist, that is to say a heterogeneous grouping of individuals, but rather communal...'.[21] From these successive standpoints Senghor unsuccessfully tried to reconcile the traditional European emphasis on liberating the individual – humanitarian liberalism – and its apparent negation – 'African collectivism' or 'communitarism'. His reliance on 'personalism' only partly resolved this contradiction.

Because of Senghor's willingness to bend his theory to meet the needs of the moment, the 'African Road' remained open to continual re-interpretation. Depending on the circumstances, Senghor could hasten or delay important processes of social transformation. In this intellectual framework Senegal embarked on a socialist path which attempted to avoid ideological commitment to any previously defined system.

It must be remembered that the practical expression of Senghor's African Socialism awaited the autonomy granted by the *Loi-Cadre* in 1956. Up to that time the French colonial administration planned and controlled the Senegalese economy. Senghor's role was limited to lobbying for increases in the fixed price of peanuts, the principal cash crop. Since the very existence of Senegal is linked to the price and production of this commodity, 'when the peanut progresses, everything progresses'.[1] Senghor promised: 'Produce peanuts, and I will produce good policies'.[2] Ruth Schachter Morgenthau has remarked that the rapid advance of Senghor's BDS party was in part due to the rise in world market prices for peanuts during the Korean War.[3]

The Senegalese dependence on external decisions to determine prices explains Senghor's numerous speeches prior to 1956 in which he excoriated the 'colonial pact'.[4] Senghor reserved his most violent language for the subject of the low prices paid for tropical products. Declaring in 1947 that 'we wish less to get rid of the tutorship of the mother country than of the tyranny of international capitalism',[5] Senghor revealed his essentially verbal anti-capitalism. During the years from 1945 to 1960 Senghor lashed out at the 'trusts'[6] and called capitalism 'half-blind, hateful, trembling in the enclosure of its privileges'.[7] It was particularly the 'vegetable oil trusts' under 'the sway of Unilever' that Senghor castigated when the prices of peanuts dropped.[8] These trusts were 'feudal financial groups' who wished 'to reserve colonies for themselves as privileged preserves in which they bought cheaply while selling manufactured products at prices far above the world averages'.[9] A perceptive remark made with respect to the French Socialist Party seems, however, to be applicable to Senghor's action *vis-à-vis* the oft-decried trusts: 'The language, so surprisingly violent, differs little from that of the Communists. But, as often noted, the revolutionary vocabulary is an empty shell'.[10]

Senghor has admitted shortsightedness of the pre-1956 period. 'In fact, under the colonial régime, what were our means of thinking, of speaking, of acting? In brief, what was our policy? It was irresponsible... We were only preoccupied... with obtaining a little more "territorial revenue" without worrying about development, or even economic growth.'[11] Nothing lasting was done to remake the system against which he railed.

Senghor's first significant step towards radical change in the economic institutions of Senegal was to invite the development group *Economie et Humanisme* and its leader Father Lebret to undertake a study of the Senegalese economy. Senghor's socialism required a development plan which would increase the economic rhythm of the country. In 1960 Lebret's Twenty-five Year Plan, which attempted to put into practice Senghor's ideas on reviving the traditional co-operative, was presented to the Senegalese government. 'Agriculture', Senghor had declared in 1958, 'will be progressively planned until completely socialized on the basis of democratic co-operatives.'[12] By this socialization, Senghor hoped to light in each Senegalese peasant 'that flame of active fraternity which is found in revolutionary socialism', and to inculcate in him that spirit of practical organization which European techniques had created.[13]

In the 1940s and 1950s something similar had been tried in Senegal, but the co-operatives established then had failed because of corruption. 'When we created peasant co-operatives', he declared in 1963, 'it was the middle class who exploited them for their own profit. As for salaried workers' co-operatives, the only ones which succeeded were those established by the colonizers, who had, more than we Africans, the sense of the common good.'[14]

Notwithstanding previous failures, co-operatives were central to the new Plan. Starting in 1960, the government of Senegal began to institute the provisions outlined by Father Lebret. To activate the 'weak dynamism of the traditional economy of Senegal',[15] the Plan advocated the creation of a peasant élite. The Senegalese government undertook the training of young leaders or rural *animateurs*. However, training selected peasants was not the only means for increasing productivity. It was necessary to reform 'progressively but radically' the commercial structures which had created the country's dependence on private interests linked to foreign trade'. Such reform required that the government be given the authority to establish guidelines for controlling production and exchange; that it be empowered to organize the markets of agricultural products in order to use prices as an incentive for expanding food crops; and that it help the peasants organize their own co-operatives in order to give them the chance of ridding themselves of profiteering middlemen.[16] In brief, it was necessary to redirect and reorganize the entire economy. Senghor charged his Prime Minister, Mamadou Dia, with the task of carrying out the proposals.

Mamadou Dia had been Senghor's faithful lieutenant since the

1948 split with Lamine-Guèye. In 1957 Senghor selected Mamadou Dia to hold the post of Vice-President of the Council of Ministers under the provisions of the *Loi-Cadre*. After the 1958 Referendum, Dia became Prime Minister. Senghor did not assume the Presidency of Senegal until after the Mali split-up of August 1960. Senghor as head of state retained Dia as head of government, an arrangement which allowed Senghor to formulate the major policies but to delegate their implementation to the Prime Minister.

Since Dia was an economist, he instituted radical reforms designed to break the back of 'neo-colonialism', which one observer has described as 'imperial preference, plus monoculture, plus balkanization'.[17] Reforms of such a wide-reaching nature could not help but crystallise opposition on the part of those who profited by the former arrangement. Dia soon felt the wrath of the Senegalese commercial middle-classes and their European allies. The tensions between Dia and the commercial interests led to a crisis in December 1962, which brought about the elimination of Dia as well as his position. The *Moniteur Africain du Commerce et de l'Industrie*, mouthpiece for French-speaking West Africa's European economic interests, applauded the action taken by Senghor to delay the rapid execution of the Senegalese Economic Plan. The *Moniteur* accused Dia of 'brutally countering' the efforts of European commercial houses to develop the private sector. According to the *Moniteur*, the Dia government's proposal to grant co-operatives the monopoly for importing merchandise of 'primary necessity to the rural sector...meant the almost total disappearance of African commerce, beginning with small commerce'. The *Moniteur* summed up the events of the summer of 1962:

> 'It was the whole of the private sector, including potential investors, who felt threatened. Lack of confidence spread; never had so much money been transferred to Europe...the downfall of Dia, the man who had been implementing the Plan...became the *sine qua non* for the success of this Plan...We can say, without hesitation, that Senghor's new governmental group gives total and entire confidence to investors.'[18]

The Muslim, Dia had been supported by many of the Catholic planners of the *Economie et Humanisme* group. He was removed by Senghor, a Catholic, who was supported by those who wished to slow up the commercial reforms, including a large number of Muslim leaders. Senghor once again showed his prudence by refusing to support an economic revolution which appeared to be too rapid, given the strength and weight of its opponents. He did not abandon the Economic Plan; he was merely going to proceed in a less brusque manner than had his former lieutenant. Senghor had decided in favour of those who would maintain a certain economic stability in the country.

It appeared that Senghor was inadvertently working to further the development of a Senegalese bourgeoisie. His action seemed all the more surprising since, from 1948 onwards, he had warned the Senegalese against the 'native feudal elements' or 'Negro exploiters' who could, as had native capitalists in Egypt, supplant white colonizers. He was conscious of the fact that 'oppression' could 'change colour' but still remain oppression,[19] and yet he persisted in serving the interests of the commercial minority. He clearly distinguished his policies from those of the so-called 'revolutionary' African leaders: N'Krumah, Modibo Keita, and even his own former lieutenant Mamadou Dia, who all hoped to radically reform the economies of their countries. In doing so he remained in power while each of them succumbed to coups led by conservative forces.

40. A Role for Foreign Capital

Regardless of Senghor's plan for socialism in Senegal, the 'African Road' permitted the economic coexistence of private and public sectors. It contained the contradictory notion that real independence would result from increasing the amount of private investment in Senegal.[1] Never, claimed Senghor, had he opposed 'capital investment' – only the capitalist system.[2] As a realist, Senghor saw that his country could not industrialize without the help of French private capital. He declared in 1952 that it 'would be a bad policy to kill the goose who lays golden eggs'. Since French public investment would increasingly dwindle, it would be necessary to rely on private capital.[3] It is no wonder that ten years after the first formulation of 'African Socialism', the Senegalese Plan declared that achieving the objectives of the Plan would 'be greatly facilitated by the investment of private capital'.[4] 'This is our socialist stand', declared Senghor. 'We have chosen...to socialize the rural economy, to regulate Mines and Industry, to leave freedom in the hands of Commerce and Banking.'[5]

Although Senghor was a vocal critic of capitalism, he accepted it in practice, at least in so far as crucial sectors of the economy were concerned. He was quick to justify this apparent conflict by formulating one of those 'conciliating agreements' which are so characteristic of his thought. As did the Catholic theorists Mounier and Teilhard de Chardin, he tried to resolve the opposition between nationalization and capitalism in what he calls 'socialization'. From the moment Senegal achieved internal autonomy under the *Loi-Cadre* of 1956, Senghor began to speak of 'socialization'. He wished to 'socialize' the infrastructure of the economy: the means of communication and the sources of energy. For private investors 'socialization' meant that with each major capital investment came the obligation to provide certain social services such as centres for apprentices, worker's housing, and medical dispensaries. At the same time he was encouraging private investment, Senghor insisted that the State make its own investment in Senegal in order to regulate and organize the infrastructure.[6] This form of socialism was meant to reassure Europeans who had invested in Senegal,[7] that they had no reason to fear the nationalization programmes which habitually followed accession of colonial countries to self-government.

For labour, 'socialization' meant a new co-operation between unions and management by the institution of workers' councils in each enterprise, and by the introduction of bilateral conferences between government and management as well as between government and labour.[8] The *Mater et Magistra* of Pope John XXIII later spoke the same language.

There was a great difference between Senghor's socialist ideas as expressed in his speeches and as put into practice. The desire to replace capitalist structures by socialist structures, expressed during the Congress of Senghor's party in 1958, seems to have come up against the practical realities of Senegal.[9] Forty-five per cent of the 92 billion CFA francs necessary for financing the Senegalese Economic Plan had to be requested from private sources.[10] In addition, Senegal lacked the number of experienced engineers necessary to operate her industries. To have socialism, it is first necessary to have socialists, men trained to manage industries effectively and honestly. Throughout French-speaking Africa this remains a serious handicap.[11] Finally, the economic and social condition of Senegalese workers did not warrant the socialist measures applied in Western Europe. Senghor argued that the worker in Senegal was privileged and not a true proletarian. Because of his income he constituted an affluent social group when compared with the peasant. It was natural, therefore, that Senegalese socialism take direct responsibility for radically changing the lot of the neediest members of the society. Consequently the 'African Road' concentrated on the collectivization of agriculture rather than on the nationalization of industry.

Even before Senghor began to apply his theory of socialism, the critics of his ideas began sharpening their pencils. On two previous occasions Senghor's thinking had encountered opposition. As was the case for *négritude* and Federation, Senghor's 'middle of the road' socialism came under harsh scrutiny from both the right and the left.

The majority of right-wing criticism came from the European trading houses and the African middlemen. Since 1956 Senghor had been under pressure from these private investors who contested every move towards government control of industry, commerce and banking. Their attacks eventually provoked the 1962 crisis in which Mamadou Dia was stopped from pursuing the socialist objectives embodied in the Economic Plan.

Criticism from the right was based primarily on the practical application of the socialist Economic Plan, while criticism from the left was more concerned with the validity of Senghor's socialist ideology. Among the first to criticize the 'African Road' from the left was the late Russian Africanist Potekhin. In May 1961 Potekhin observed that the 'partisans of "African Socialism" underestimated by far the degree of social differentiations to which African society had arrived'.[1] He maintained that 'It was wrong to deny absolutely the existence of an African national bourgeoisie, as did the proponents of "African Socialism" '.[2] Potekhin contrasted universal 'Scientific Socialism' with 'African Socialism', which he accused of being influenced by the 'reactionary' socialists of Britain and France.[3] Writing for *The African Communist*, Professor Potekhin argued that 'the social philosophy of most African intellectuals...was marked by an idealistic eclecticism containing an odd mixture of different or even contradictory views on society, the laws of its development, and man's inner world'.[4]

These criticisms were carried further by the *Parti Africain de l'Indépendance* (PAI), which had been banned in Senegal: 'To fool the masses, the Senegalese bourgeoisie has found nothing better than its so-called African Socialism or African Road to Socialism. The theorists of this socialism are nothing but Populists when they deal with peasant problems, and timid reformers in all other matters. They speak of socializing the countryside, but not the towns; they believe they are "nationalizing" foreign property by refusing foreign investment unless it comes within the framework of their alleged Plan; and they think that they can plan production although it is essentially unplannable because of its capitalist and anarchical nature'. The P A I declaration concluded: 'This socialism, which safeguards the interests of the native and foreign bourgeoisie, is nothing more than an African form of capitalism in the neo-colonial era'.[5] The P A I accused Senghor of using this theory 'to intoxicate the African working class', to 'delay its class consciousness, and thus to put the brakes on the development of the only authentic socialism, Marxist-Leninist Socialism'.[6]

Another Senegalese communist noted that it is precisely those who belong to the bourgeoisie, or who aspire to it, who most vehemently deny the existence of a class structure in Africa.[7] He quoted a study by a union which claimed that the 'Ministers and *Députés* (about one hundred persons) absorbed one per cent of the national revenue.[8] He concluded: 'he who denies the existence and the role of this bourgeoisie in our country denies the possibility of organizing an effective battle for a democratic and profound change in Senegal'.[9]

René Ménil, French West Indian communist and former member of the *Légitime Défense* group of the 1930s, criticized Senghor for confusing different political notions about the evolution of societies. According to Ménil, Senghor equated the primitive commune with socialism, and the African palaver with parliamentary democracy that had developed out of European middle-class revolutions. In Ménil's view Senghor had depicted the African Negro as a being with 'true socialism within him: he has it in his blood somehow'. Ménil quoted Senghor: 'It is a fact: a community collectivism, which is the true form of socialism, has long existed in African society and in its groups'. He then observed ironically: 'You see that it is not Karl Marx who will teach Senghor what socialism is because "the true form of socialism" existed in African primitive tribes well before the birth of capitalism and of Marx himself!' Ménil ended his argument by attacking Senghor's position *vis-à-vis* proletarian solidarity: '...[Senghor] is afraid of solidarity with revolutionary Whites but forgets [his] distrust of the West the moment it is a question of playing footsie with the reactionary forces of white Europe!'[10] This criticism had already been voiced by the young black Marxist Albert Franklin in 1953: 'Certain [proponents of *négritude*] would like the Negroes to reject the extended hand of the white proletariat...'.[11]

Senghor had also been criticized by Franklin for idealizing 'Negro collectivism'. Senegalese traditional village society was alleged to contain elements of exploitation.[12] An American critic Ruth

Schachter Morgenthau further challenged Senghor's reliance on the traditional economy as a basis for modern socialism. Observing that village solidarity in Africa is based on kinship, she argued that modern co-operatives must be founded on contract, employees being selected on the basis of merit in order to avoid nepotism. Professor Morgenthau censured the 'African Road' for neglecting some important issues and for failing to answer such questions as whether traditional institutions would be totally or partially integrated, which aspects of kinship would be used, and what role the spirit of community would play.[13] The basic inconsistency in Senghor's 'humanistic' socialism pointed out by Ruth Morgenthau was Senegal's use of police repression, press censorship, and bureaucratic dictatorship to achieve social change.[14]

The most exhaustive and the most revealing analysis of the 'African Road' came from those charged with applying the theory to reality. It was therefore not the Marxists but rather the progressive Catholic planners linked to Father Lebret's *Economie et Humanisme* who launched the most damning attack. They knew that 'the middle-class traders and civil servants who dominated (the Senegalese National Assembly) were by no means ready to understand or to support the process of socialist transformation to which the Dia Government with Senghor's support had led Senegal, beginning in 1959'.[15] Dia had agreed with the economic planners that 'despite the government's efforts, traditional commerce still controlled a sector of the peanut production and oligopolies still controlled the importing of essential consumer commodities. Because of this double dependence, foreign mercantilist capital remained the true master of the game and the winner of all the matches'. Dia and the economic planners had announced: 'The government has resolved to remedy this situation, for it has lasted long enough and cannot continue without completely discrediting the party which allows it to continue'.[16]

Consequently they began to limit the power of a number of private interest groups: 'the "traders" who would be replaced by co operatives; the *Marabouts* who reigned over the Muslim brotherhoods and who drew considerable profits from the monoculture of peanuts; the foreign commercial companies; the Senegalese personnel of foreign companies who, within the existing commercial framework, were ready to occupy the higher echelons, to "Senegalize" the field', and who were especially likely to feel discontented. 'A point of crisis, a breaking point, had been reached; the [socialist] enterprise underway required a change of social structures if it were to continue.'[17] In the end, however, the private interest groups

obliged Senghor to get rid of Dia and to slow down the application
of the Plan, if not to abandon its most 'revolutionary' provisions.
Once Dia was out of the way, Senghor allowed African and French
private enterprise freer rein. His decision to encourage private enterprise to continue was defended by pointing out the 'serious dis-
organization of trade in the interior as a consequence of the socialization of commerce'.[18]

Having had to go on the defensive, Senghor reflected with bitterness on his former associates, Dia and the economic planners. The
heartbreaking irony for Senghor was that much of the criticism
levelled at him was published in *Esprit*, the progressive Catholic
organ which originated with Emmanuel Mounier and which was so
influential in Senghor's early thinking. Senghor replied to the criticism of *Esprit* by stating: 'Certain intellectuals of the "centre left"…
"progressive Christians" have asked us to undertake, in Africa, without capital or technical personnel, the socialist experiment that they
could not, and would not, undertake in France'. 'They treat us,
virtually, as things', he notes, 'and their insults often come close to
racism.'[19]

Senghor wrote of his disappointment: 'I must observe that since
Mounier's death, the review *Esprit* has very much deteriorated. This
review represents the French Left which has not yet abandoned a
form of intellectual colonialism. It secretes a mixture of "Jacobin"
spirit and missionary zeal that is typically French. This Left wishes
to be our *maîtres à penser*: above all, it refuses to let us think by ourselves.' And he concludes: 'On the contrary, my ambition has always
been to use the lessons of teachers to seek my own way'.[20] Senghor's
reaction to *Esprit* is very similar to what Césaire wrote to Maurice
Thorez in 1956: '…in Europe, in all parties, from the extreme right
to the extreme left, is ingrained the habit of doing for us, the habit of
thinking for us, in short, the habit of refusing us the right to our own
initiative…which is, in the last analysis, the right to a personality'.[21]

It seems nevertheless that *Esprit*'s attitude was justified, for in
Senegal no journal took the initiative of criticizing the government or
of clarifying the facts of the crisis of 1962. Until freedom of the press
is regained in Senegal, it will be necessary to find credible news reports in the French or foreign press, which is more impartial, to say
the least, than is the local press. Whatever his reaction to *Esprit*'s
article, Senghor recommended that his Ministers read it.[22]

Senghor had initiated his socialist programme under heavy cross-
fire. The 'right', linked with the old commercial system, hoped to
prevent real socialization of commerce, while the socialist 'left' denounced Senghor's 'African Road' as too timid and too willing to

protect the interests of a tiny middle class minority. Navig ating between this Scylla and Charybdis, Senghor steered a cour se which
hoped to reconcile opposites and which purported to be empirical
and realistic. Only the future can tell whether this choice of a 'middle
way' was the right one.

Conclusion

At the time this intellectual portrait of Léopold Senghor was begun, scholars had already explored the nature of political parties in Africa, of the policies of colonial powers, of nationalist movements – but there had been little analysis of the individuals, who, in the last analysis, had created these organizations, thought out these policies, and initiated these movements. Since the debate on Plekhanov's study, *The Role of the Individual in History*, many historians have subscribed to his thesis that the individual is shaped by 'forces' (ideological, economic, political, institutional, etc.). It cannot be denied, however, that forces of history are set in motion by individuals. This study is an attempt to analyse the dialectical mechanism of men and forces in the light of a recent African example.

In order to do this it was necessary to examine, as accurately as possible, the contribution of an important public figure. Léopold Sédar Senghor seemed one of the best candidates for study. Several reasons motivated this choice. First, Senghor's life spans the three eras which coexist in Africa: traditional civilization, colonial rule, and the period of decolonization and independence. Secondly, Senghor was as much preoccupied with culture as with politics and economics. Finally, Senghor incarnates a type of man produced by the clash of the modern industrial and the traditional civilizations. The study of his life, of his thought, is of special value, since it can serve to shed light on the experience of many men of his generation, men who have had neither the ability nor the opportunity to divulge their innermost thoughts.

One of my first problems in coping with a subject such as Senghor was that of limiting the scope of the study. My resolution was to focus primarily on Senghor's philosophy. But in order to do this it was obviously necessary to know something of his life and the influences upon it. It was by studying these influences on Senghor's intellectual development that a partial answer to the principal question of the role of the individual in history could be found. Senghor, the individual, is original only in his synthesis of these influences. The selection and organization of these different ideas and attitudes into a harmonious whole was Senghor's contribution to the history of ideas.

But his role does not stop there. The application of his theories to the realities of the African situation, his ability to act as an intermediary between theory and practice, is yet another aspect of the man. The formulation and modification of theories in the light of his close contact with the African scene, the creation of organizations to put these theories into practice – these are just two of the many functions which define Senghor's unique role in the history of decolonization.

If French-speaking Africa has taken a certain course during the last three decades, this course cannot help being somehow a function of Senghor's work. He acted at times as an accelerator for certain concepts, as a brake for others: thus, by formulating his theory of *négritude* during the 1930s, he acted as a powerful agent in the progress towards independence; on the other hand, there were moments during the 1950s when he set himself up as a barrier to independence.

However, one must not overlook the events that shaped the history of the 'Third World'. Decolonization received much impetus from the granting of independence to India, from the Indonesian, Indochinese, and Algerian wars, and gained further ground with the independence of Ghana, and the rapid evolution of the United Nations African Trust Territories of Togo and Cameroun. The economic conditions of underdevelopment and the steps taken by nationalist movements after Bandung also helped to further the process. In the final analysis, these forces and events determined the direction of Africa's evolution much more than did her political leaders.

Nevertheless, the more immediate processes of Africa's development remain linked to the thought and actions of her leaders, and among them, Léopold Senghor. The solution of the dilemma of the role of the individual in the contemporary history of Africa lies, perhaps, in the notion of time. If, in the long run, it seems that a certain evolution was necessary and inevitable, that it would have taken place whether or not certain individuals had acted, it is nevertheless true that in the short run the influence of these individuals appears determinant. Everything would seem to depend on the length of the period studied. When dealing with a matter of centuries, certain inherent trends take on increasing importance, the individual only participating as a brake or an accelerator. On the other hand, if one is concerned only with a few decades, the role of the individual seems to grow until it becomes crucial.

In our frame of reference, post-colonial Africa, individuals frequently were responsible for introducing a broad ideology into the

African milieu. It was necessary for a few individuals to assume almost total responsibility for translating ideology into political programmes inasmuch as the size of the African élite was limited in comparison with that of so-called developed nations. The *élite* in Africa was often so small that opposing attitudes were represented by one or by a few individuals at the most, while in Europe there were large parties or organizations with numerous leaders. Therefore ideological battles frequently became a question of single combat – Senghor *v.* Lamine-Guèye, Senghor *v.* Abdoulaye Ly, Senghor *v.* Houphouet-Boigny. It is even conceivable that differences in temperament obliged these men to define themselves with respect to each other by formulating conflicting political theories. A great many Africans supported these theories more because of personal relationships with their progenitors or for private gain than because of ideological conviction. The personification of political tendencies seemed to play an important role during the years under consideration. A few individuals were able to impose their conception of the future because they had the advantage of creating from scratch most of the institutions necessary to a modern nation. In a period of a few years, Senghor and his close associates have been responsible for setting up organizations that have existed for centuries in European nations. In Europe the development of such institutions was not the work of a few men over a well-defined period but, on the contrary, was the product of the work of several generations who slowly but surely perfected the heritage of centuries.

However, the originality of programmes instituted by these individuals was limited by the fact that colonial, underdeveloped environments called for almost identical solutions. It was no wonder that governments in French-speaking Africa began to resemble one another. The limited range of options available caused the single party or dominant party system to become the rule, eliminating previous multi-party systems. The individual leader facing problems could not really impose *his* solution. The case of President Senghor seems to confirm the hypothesis, for, having initially favoured the existence of opposition parties, he came to realize that this was impossible in Africa. Ethnic divisions and the absence of Western electoral habits prevented loyal opposition. This handicap was revealed in a Senegalese White Paper on the Presidential and Legislative Elections of 1 December 1963. This White Paper bore witness to the failure of democratic elections because opposition parties had resorted to violence during voting – something that had happened repeatedly in Senegal and elsewhere in Africa.[1]

European-style democracy, so dear to Senghor for a time, failed because the situation and condition of the country made the practical application of Senghor's liberal ideas impossible. A country, even a political party, cannot be manipulated like a theory. From the moment Senghor leaves his desk, the complex reality of Senegal prevents the practical application of his ideas. This situation occasions his pragmatism and willingness to drop programmes he previously defended. No matter what his ideological position, the African leader of today is obliged to follow a narrowly defined course, which is revealed in the increasing similarity of policies, even in widely separated areas of the continent. The break-up of the attempted Mali and East African federations was only one example of leaders adopting similar policies and bowing to forces beyond their control.

At the same time that Senghor first tried to defend *négritude*, Jomo Kenyatta was writing his *Facing Mount Kenya*. As Georges Balandier has pointed out, *Facing Mount Kenya* might be considered the work of a supporter of *négritude*. After all, Kenyatta also tried to rehabilitate the African society which Europeans were disrupting, and he also had an idealized concept of African life very much in the European tradition of the 'noble savage'. In Kenyatta's protest, Europe thus remains present, even if he does not actually mention it. Kenyatta's praise of the Kikuyu tradition in 1937 resembles Senghor's use of *Serer* society to defend his idealization of traditional Africa in 1939 and 1943.[2] Both men, independently, developed a similar thesis. In view of this coincidence, it is tempting to hypothesize that if Senghor had not developed *négritude* someone else would have come up with something quite similar.

Despite the fact that Senghor might not have been indispensable to Africa, he was the herald of a new life. The conception of the new African society, proclaimed by Senghor in his theories of *négritude*, Federation, and the 'African Road to Socialism', seems to constitute an echo (on the intellectual level) of native religious messianism, which also was a reaction to dependence on Europe. Georges Balandier has observed that these 'modern political doctrines possess a messianic accent'.[3] In fact Senghor proposed a society free from exploitation and in which Europeans and Africans would find harmony. As Senghor states: 'the great design of the Senegalese government – which has a policy of multi-national, multi-cultural, multi-religious integration' is achieving the Civilization of the Universal.[4] He thus promises the world a sunny future, with Africa playing the role of a missionary attempting to spread the warmth of his love.

One of the most interesting aspects of Senghor's theories is that they have escaped from his control. Both *négritude* and the 'African

Road to Socialism' are now in the common domain. They have been developed and transformed by other Africans and constitute ideological forces which shape men's minds all over Africa. Julius Nyerere's *Ujmaa* or African Socialism, N'Krumah's 'Consciencism', Kenyatta's 'African Socialism' all seemed attempts to compete with Senghor in the battle for Africa's minds, to end Senghor's monopoly of creative thought. Might not one of the Senegalese President's most important contributions be the setting in motion of a whole series of African ideological movements?

Notes and References

INTRODUCTION

1. Léopold Senghor, 'Discours au Comité d'Etudes pour le Développement de la Culture', *Dakar-Matin*, 16 juin 1962, 6 (cols. 6–7).
2. L. S. Senghor, *Poèmes* (Paris, Seuil 1964) p. 135. I have used this most recent edition of Senghor's poems for my references. Where possible I will use the recent English translation for footnotes, but many of Senghor's poems do not appear in that edition.
3. The Argentinian sociologist Gino Germani invented this useful term for his famous definition of underdevelopment. He used it in a technological or geographic context to mean the employment of products of the most recent technology alongside centuries-old methods, or developed regions in close proximity to 'retarded' areas. *Asynchronie* can also be defined as the simultaneous existence of what is non-contemporary with what is new. For a summary in French see Jean Lacouture and Jean Baumier, *Le Poids du Tiers Monde: Un Milliard d'Hommes* (Paris, Arthaud 1962) pp. 16–17.
4. At times strict adherence to chronology is abandoned. It is therefore necessary to consult the chronology included in the appendixes at the end of the book.
5. Armand Guibert, *Léopold Sédar Senghor* (Paris, Seghers Collection Poètes d'Aujourd'hui no. 82, 1961), and Armand Guibert, *Léopold Sédar Senghor: l'Homme et l'Oeuvre* (Paris, Présence Africaine 1962). For Senghor's youth I have often referred to these biographies, which were by a poet friend of Senghor's. These works confirmed many facts that I had obtained in Senegal during the summer of 1960. A recent biography in English by Irving Markowitz does not deal with this area in depth.
6. Lilyane Kesteloot, *Les Ecrivains Noirs de Langue Française: Naissance d'une Littérature* (Brussels, Institut de Sociologie Solvay 1963). (Thesis for the degree of Doctor of Romance Philology: University of Brussels.) This dissertation helped me in my analysis of the theory of *négritude*.
7. Senghor's thought has given birth to a certain amount of intellectual clash. What is venerated by certain of his adherents is hotly contested by his opponents. It is useful to present both sides of this debate at a moment when it is still raging.
8. The expression was used by François Mauriac, 'Bloc notes', *L'Express*, 28 juillet 1960, 32.

CHAPTER ONE

1. This term appears often in Senghor's poems. See, for example, Léopold Sédar Senghor, *Selected Poems*, translated and introduced

by John Reed and Clive Wake (New York, Atheneum 1964) pp.
67, 75. These translators use 'Kingdom of Childhood' to express
the idea.

2. See the definition above (Introduction, note 3). I employ the expression also for the juxtaposition of traditional and modern religions or for the coexistence of traditional African sagacity and
modern European education dispensed in Western-type schools,
etc.

3. Senghor, *Selected Poems*, p. 7. My translation.

4. Ibid., p. 4.

5. Ibid., p. 9.

6. Stephen H. Roberts, *History of French Colonial Policy 1870–1925*
(London, King 1929) pp. 329–30.

7. Senghor, *Selected Poems*, p. 12. Poem written at the country home
of Georges Pompidou's parents-in-law, Château-Gontier, October–
December 1939.

8. Senghor, *Poèmes*, pp. 15–16. Poem written in the 1930s. My italics.

9. Guibert, *Senghor* (Seghers) pp. 10–11.

10. *Paris-Dakar*, 14 novembre 1960, 1 (col. 3). See also W. J. M.
Mackenzie and Kenneth Robinson *Five Elections in Africa: A Group
of Electoral Studies* (Oxford, Clarendon Press 1960) p. 311. Kenneth
Robinson, author of the chapter on Senegal, accompanied Senghor
during the electoral campaign of 1957.

11. Interview with M. and Mme Jean Collin (*née* Senghor), Dakar,
8 August 1960.

12. Senghor, *Poèmes*, p. 19.

13. A kind of harp, used by Senegalese minstrels or *griots* to accompany
their tales.

14. Name of the king of the region.

15. Ceremonial drums.

16. River in Senghor's native region. This poem is typical of those
influenced by the thought of Barrès who valued regionalism (see
below).

17. Senghor, *Selected Poems*, pp. 14–15.

18. Ibid., p. 30. Poem written at Tours, France in 1936. These memories were part of the origin of Senghor's *négritude* theory; they also
played a role in his monarchist tendencies during the 1920s (see
below).

19. Ibid., p. 18.

20. Senghor, *Poèmes*, p. 160. Written in Strasbourg, France, 24 September 1954.

21. Ibid., pp. 148–9.

22. Senghor, *Selected Poems*, p. 63.

23. Ibid., p. 92. *Tanns* are sand-flats along the Senegalese coast south
of Dakar.

24. Senghor, *Poèmes*, p. 82. Poem written during World War II.

25. See below, chapters 5, 9, 10.

26. Senghor, *Poèmes*, p. 160.

27. Senghor in *Dakar-Matin*, 29 mai 1961, 3 (cols. 7–8).

28. See below, chapters 32, 36.

29. Interview with L. S. Senghor, Dakar, 1 August 1960.

30. In his 1937 lecture at Dakar after he obtained his *agrégation* (roughly

equivalent to the PH.D.), Senghor stated: 'It is as a Sine peasant that I hoped to speak this evening.' Senghor *Liberté I*, p. 11.
31. See *Clarté*, 6 juin 1947, 1 (opposition newspaper published at Dakar).
32. Interview with Charles Diène Senghor (brother), Dakar, 24 August 1960.

CHAPTER TWO

1. Senghor, 'La poésie Négro-Africaine', lecture given 10 May 1947 in the presence of Marius Moutet, Minister of Overseas France. Summary in *Climats*, 22 mai 1947, 5 (cols. 2–5). Edouard Basse affirms that Senghor still chants these strange canticles. (Interview.)
2. For a description of the effects of this type of education see Paul Mercier, 'The evolution of Senegalese elite', *UNESCO Bulletin of Social Sciences* 8 (3) 1956, 451.
3. Senghor speaking on the subject of culture, but it can be applied to his life as well. Senghor, *Liberté I*, p. 12.
4. Senghor, *Selected Poems*, p. 23.
5. Ibid., p. 81.
6. Senghor, *Poèmes*, p. 189.
7. Ibid., p. 174.
8. Condotto Nenekhaly Camara, 'Conscience nationale et poésie négro-africaine d'expression française' (Paris, Fédération des Etudiants d'Afrique Noire en France, Séminaire sur la littérature, 5 and 6 July 1961) mimeographed documents.
9. Interview with Charles Diène Senghor, Dakar, 24 August 1960.
10. Senghor, *Liberté I*, p. 126. Written in 1952.
11. Interview with Charles Diène Senghor, Dakar, 24 August 1960. Georges Le Brun Keiris, specialist on African questions for the French Social Christian party (M.R.P.) has well described the cultural shock: 'Two worlds of profoundly different essence and ethic clash, and to the degree that we have penetrated Africa, within the Africans themselves'. See his 'Afrique entre deux civilisations', *Preuves* 83, janvier 1958, 7.
12. Senghor, *Selected Poems*, p. 13.
13. Interview with Ambassador Birago Diop, Dakar, 17 August 1960.
14. Interview with Leopold Senghor, Dakar, 1 August 1960.
15. Maurice Barrès, *Les Déracinés* (Paris, Plon 1922) p. 22. See chapter 5 for Senghor's experience with Barrès.
16. Armand Guibert's interview with Senghor, *Léopold Sédar Senghor* (Présence Africaine) pp. 143–4. The term 'conciliatory agreement' was borrowed by Senghor from Leo Frobenius *Histoire de la Civilisation Africaine* (Paris, Gallimard 1952) p. 351. (This is the third edition of a book Senghor originally read in 1936.) Frobenius used the term to show the fusion between 'Hamitic' and 'Ethiopian' civilizations. My italics. See below, chapter 12, for Senghor's experience with Frobenius.
17. Interview with Charles Diène Senghor, Dakar, 24 August 1960. See also *Revue du Monde Noir* 2, décembre 1931, 56–7.
18. Interview with Charles Diène Senghor, who spoke of Léopold's stubbornness. 'He was afraid of no one and defied them all at

times.' Senghor himself has described his bellicose nature: '...I was infernal. I fought all the time. And my best fight was the same day as my first communion.'

19. Interview with Léopold Senghor, Dakar, 1 August 1960.
20. Interview with M. Carrère, Professor of English Literature at the Université d'Aix-Marseille, France, Paris, 2 October 1960. See below, chapter 3, for Senghor's monarchism.
21. Interview with Léopold Senghor, Dakar, 1 August 1960.

CHAPTER THREE

1. Interview with Edouard Basse, Dakar, 24 August 1960. For quote see Senghor, *Liberté I*, p. 11. Kotye Barma was a *Wolof* philosopher and moralist who lived in the middle of the seventeenth century. He is the hero of many stories in *Wolof* oral tradition. For Senghor's experience with Marx, see below, chapters 35, 36, 37.
2. See above in the Introduction, pp. xii. Pantheon question in my interview of Senghor, Dakar, 17 August 1960.
3. See below, chapter 10, for a discussion of Senghor and Maritain. This influence also results in Senghor's 'anti-politics' during the 1930s, his submission to Muslim religious leaders, etc. See below, chapters 17, 27, 28, 31, 32, 37.
4. L. S. Senghor, 'La résistance de la bourgeoisie sénégalaise à l'école rurale populaire', *Congrès International de l'Evolution Culturelle des Peuples Coloniaux 26–27–28 septembre 1937: Rapports et Compte Rendu* (Mâcon, Protât Frères 1938) p. 42.
5. Senghor, 'Discours au Lycée Delafosse', *Dakar-Matin*, 10 juillet 1962, 6 (col. 4). This influences his idea of primacy of culture.
6. Guibert, *Senghor* (Seghers) pp. 35, 53. I quote Guibert who is a poet and a literary critic and who, better than any other analyst, has revealed the meaning of Senghor's poetry.
7. Senghor, quoted by xxx, 'Nous avons lu pour vous', *Paris-Dakar*, 8 mai 1954, 6.
8. Aimé Patri 'Léopold Sédar Senghor' in L. S. Senghor, *Anthologie de la Nouvelle Poésie Nègre et Malgache de Langue Française* (Paris, P.U.F., 1948) pp. 147–8. Hereafter cited as *Anthologie*.
9. Interview with Leopold Senghor, Dakar, 1 August 1960.
10. Senghor, *Liberté I*, p. 87.
11. Ibid., p. 87.
12. Interview with Charles Diène Senghor, Dakar, 24 August 1960. See also Senghor, *Pierre Teilhard de Chardin et la Politique Africaine* (Paris, Seuil 1962) p. 18. Hereafter cited as *Pierre Teilhard*.
13. *Clarté*, 6 juin 1947, 2 (opposition paper published at Dakar).
14. Interview with Dr Louis P. Aujoulat, former French Minister, former leader of the *Indépendants d'Outre-Mer* (I O M) parliamentary group which Senghor joined in 1948, Paris, 24 January 1961.
15. Interview with Charles Diène Senghor, Dakar, 24 August 1960 and *Journal Officiel de l'Afrique Occidentale Française* 1246, 28 août 1928, 509.
16. Interview with Charles Diène Senghor, Dakar, 24 August 1960.
17. This ironic phrase is quoted from Léon Damas, *Poètes d'Expression*

Française 1900–1945 (Paris, Seuil 1947) p. 29. Damas, with Aimé Césaire and Senghor, was one of the first 'militants of *négritude*'. Information also based on my interview with Hyacinthe Lat Senghor, Dakar, 13 July 1960.

18. Interview with James Benoît, former Secretary to Senghor, Dakar, 20 July 1960.

19. Jean Suret-Canale, *Afrique Noire: Ere Coloniale 1900–1945* (Paris, Editions Sociales 1964) pp. 562–3.

20. Interview with Abdoulaye Ly, leader of the Senegalese opposition party, *P.R.A.-Sénégal*, Dakar, 5 July 1960.

21. Interview with Charles Diène Senghor, Dakar, 24 August 1960.

22. Senghor, 'Discours de Fatick', *Afrique Express*, 5 mars 1961, 24.

23. Senghor, *Liberté I*, p. 312. Speech at the City Hall of Paris during his official reception, 20 April 1961.

24. L. Senghor to J. L. Hymans, letter of 22 October 1963, 3.

25. Senghor, 'Le lycée de l'amitié', *Le Figaro Littéraire*, 18 mai 1963, 15. Articles by Thierry Maulnier and Paul Guth appear in the same issue. See also Senghor, *Liberté I*, pp. 403–6 and P. M. Kaymor, 'Le B.D.S....', *Condition Humaine*, 10 février 1955, 2 (Kaymor was a pseudonym used by Senghor in certain articles in his party newspaper).

26. Senghor, 'Mon ami Georges Pompidou', *Afrique Express*, 29 mai 1962, 13.

27. Thierry Maulnier, 'Loin des Censures et des Consignes', *Le Figaro Littéraire*, 18 mai 1963, 15.

28. Senghor, 'Mon ami Georges Pompidou', 13 and *Liberté I*, p. 405. For other influences of Georges Pompidou, crucial in the making of *négritude*, see below, chapters 5, 14.

29. Senghor, 'Comment nous sommes devenus ce que nous sommes', *Afrique Action*, 30 janvier 1961, 17 and Senghor, *Pierre Teilhard*, pp. 17–18.

30. Interview with Senghor, Dakar, 16 August 1960.

31. Leon Damas, *Poètes d'Expression Française*, pp. 12–13. Damas quotes Léro's Manifesto, *Légitime Défense*. Damas's book contains quotes from the original published in 1932 and long since disappeared. See below, chapter 9 for Léro's influence, which Senghor denies in his letter of 5 December 1964 (in the appendixes). It appears, nevertheless, that the Manifesto did add something to Senghor's realization of his acculturation. All these ideas are similar to Price-Mars', see chapter 12.

32. Ibid., p. 15. Senghor is not alone. The Malagasy poets Rabemananjara and Rabearivelo also began by imitating the great French poets of the last century. Césaire also did so. See Senghor, *Anthologie*, pp. 179, 193.

33. According to Georges Balandier, 'La littérature noire de langue française', *Présence Africaine*, 8–9, mars 1950, 398.

34. Senghor, 'Que chacun balaye devant sa porte...', *Paris-Dakar*, 7 Sept. 1959, 4.

35. Senghor, 'Deuxième congrès...', *L'A.O.F.* 23 mai 1947, 1.

36. François Mauriac, 'Chronique', *L'Express*, 13 octobre 1960, 40.

37. Senghor, 'Fédération et confédération', *Marchés Tropicaux du Monde*, 30 Août 1958, 2025–7.

38. See Georges Balandier, 'La Littérature noire...', 398.
39. Senghor, 'Le lycée...', 15.
40. Senghor in *Paris-Dakar*, 14 mai 1955, 6.
41. According to the expression used by Ulli Beier, 'Les intellectuels africains et le concept de la "personalité africaine"', *Comprendre: Revue de Politique de la Culture*, 21–2, 1960, 142.
42. Interview with Léopold Senghor, Dakar, 1 August 1960; L.S. Senghor, 'Discours', *Revue de la Communauté France-Eurafrique*, oct.–nov. 1959, 13.
43. Interview with Hyacinthe Lat Senghor, Dakar, 13 July 1960.
44. Interview with Abdoulaye Ly, Dakar, 8 July 1960.
45. L.S.Senghor to J.L.Hymans, letter of 22 October 1963, 3. This attitude was common to many French Catholic intellectuals in the 1930s.
46. Senghor, *Liberté I*, p. 91.
47. Aimé Césaire, Alioune Diop, Edouard Glissant, Jacques Rabemananjara, 'Les Africains peuvent étonner le monde', *Afrique Action* 27 mars 1961, 22. (Round table of Negro intellectuals.)
48. Senghor, *Pierre Teilhard*, pp. 18–19.
49. These words, used to describe a phase in Mahatma Gandhi's life are equally applicable to Senghor. See Raoul Girardet, 'Influence de la métropole dans la formation d'une idéologie de l'indépendance', in *Les Pays nouvellement indépendants dans les Relations Internationales* (Paris, Centre d'Etudes des Relations Internationales Colloque des 21–27 novembre 1960, mimeo.), pp. 1–4.
50. Jean-Paul Sartre, *Black Orpheus* (Paris, Présence Africaine 1963), p. 18.
51. Interview with Senghor by Henri Dupuy, 'Deux poètes noirs à la constituante', *Renaissances* 20, 20 avril 1946, 154.
52. Jacques Rabemananjara, 'Europe and ourselves', *Présence Africaine* 8, 'The First International Conference of Negro Writers and Artists', June–November 1956, 27.
53. Mamadou Dia, *Paris-Dakar*, 9 sept. 1958, 4 (col. 6).
54. Guibert, *Senghor* (Seghers) p. 22.
55. Ibid., p. 21.
56. Senghor, *Selected Poems*, p. 16.
57. Senghor, *Poèmes*, p. 41.
58. For Gandhi's experience see Girardet, op. cit., pp. 1–4. See below for details on these influences.
59. B.Malinowsky, *Dynamics of Culture Change* (New Haven, Yale 1945) p. 153.
60. Frantz Fanon, *Peau Noire, Masques Blancs* (Paris, Seuil 1952) p. 125. Fanon's work is prefaced by the existentialist Francis Jeanson.
61. Senghor, *Selected Poems*, p. 19.

CHAPTER FOUR

1. Senghor, *Nationhood and the African Road to Socialism* (Paris, Présence Africaine 1962) p. 8. (Translated by Mercer Cook, U.S. Ambassador to Senegal. I have used this edition although a more recent translation has been published by Praeger.)

2. L. V. Thomas, 'Une idéologie moderne: la négritude, essai de synthèse psycho-sociologique', *Revue de Psychologie des Peuples* 4, 1963, 394. This essay seems to be the most exhaustive attempt to approach the reality of *négritude*. See a short summary in *Afrique Nouvelle*, 7–13 juin 1963, 8 (col. 3).

3. See below for the influence of 'irrationalist' philosophers: Barrès, Bergson, the Surrealists, etc. Aimé Césaire has admitted that he is far from mastering the term; he does not remember whether it was Senghor or he who used it first around 1936. (xxx, 'Césaire et la négritude', *La Vie Africaine*, 19 nov. 1961, 33.)

4. Senghor, *Official Visit of the President of the Republic of Senegal to Great Britain: Lecture given by H.E. the President of the Republic of Senegal at St Anthony's College, Oxford University, 26th October 1961* (London, Bradbury Agnew Press 1961) p. 6.

5. Senghor, *Liberté I*, 8. (Senghor admitted this fact only in 1964.)

CHAPTER FIVE

1. L. S. Senghor to J. L. Hymans, letter of 22 October 1963. Neither Guibert, literary biographer of Senghor, nor Lilyane Kesteloot, who published her thesis on French-speaking Negro writers, mentioned this crucial influence on *négritude*. Senghor lengthily described Barrès's impact on him in an interview for a French television programme: 'Portrait – Souvenir de Barrès' broadcast 22 June 1962.

2. Maurice Barrès, *Scènes et Doctrines du Nationalisme I* (Paris, Plon 1925) pp. 93 ff. The mystique of the village, another of Barrès's contributions was at the root of Senghor's socio-economic thought. See below, chapter 35.

3. See above, chapter 1.

4. Senghor, *Selected Poems*, p. 30.

5. Senghor, *Poèmes*, pp. 45–6.

6. Ibid., p. 184.

7. Ibid., pp. 9–10.

8. Senghor, *Selected Poems*, p. 5.

9. Senghor, *Liberté I*, p. 114. (Lecture on American Negro poetry given in 1950.)

10. Senghor, *Poèmes*, p. 148.

11. See above in the Introduction and below in Chapter 15 for examples of this synthesizing spirit characteristic of Senghor's approach to the opposition of France and Africa, capitalism and communism, etc.

12. Guy de Bosschère, 'Une poésie d'enracinement', *l'Unité Africaine*, 9 janvier 1962, 17 (cols. 4–5). I have used the original words *enracinement* and *déracinement*, which signify 'rooting' and 'uprooting'.

13. Maurice Barrès, *Scènes et Doctrines...*, pp. 81–2, 87, 93, 98. This decentralizing 'provincialism' which opposes French centralism was highly significant in Senghor's later political theory of Federa-

tion. See below chapters 25, 29, for Barrès's influence on Senghor's political thought.

14. Barrès quoting Mistral in *Scénes et Doctrines*..., p. 81.
15. See below, chapter 12, for the other influences in the idea of the Negro soul.
16. See above, chapter 2.
17. Senghor, *Selected Poems*, p. 17.
18. J.Price-Mars, *Ainsi parla l'Oncle* (Compiègne, Bibliothèque Haitienne 1928) p. 194. See below, chapter 12, for Price-Mars' influence on Senghor.
19. Jean-Paul Sartre, 'L'enfance d'un chef', *Le Mur* (Paris: 1939 – *Livre de Poche* edition, 1962) pp. 224–5.
20. Césaire quoting Gide in xxx, 'Césaire et la négritude', *La Vie Africaine* 19, novembre 1961, 33.
21. Anne Guérin, 'Aimé Césaire: le cannibale s'est tassé...', *l'Express*, 19 mai 1960, 35. (Interview with Césaire.)
22. Senghor, *Liberté I*, 116, 120; and Senghor, 'La bourgeoisie...', p. 42.
23. Senghor, 'Déclaration au colloque du collège d'Europe', *Afrique Express* 35, 25 sept. 1962, 10. Senghor has often quoted Gide. See for example his 1939 essay reprinted in *Liberté I*, pp. 26, 37. See also Senghor, 'The spirit of civilization of the laws of African Negro culture', *Présence Africaine*, 8–10, june–nov. 1956, 51–2.
24. Anne Guérin, 'Aimé Césaire...', 35.
25. Senghor, *Selected Poems*, p. 8.
26. See Claude Martine, *André Gide par lui-même* (Paris, Seuil 1963) pp. 15–16. Senghor reacted against Barrès in his theory of crossbreeding. For a rapid analysis of Gide and Barrès see Encyclopédie de la Pléiade, *Histoire des Littératures* III (Paris, N.R.F., 1958) p. 1259.
27. See chapter 8 below.
28. An interview with Césaire quoted in 'Césaire et la négritude', *La Vie Africaine* 19, novembre 1961, 33.
29. Senghor quoted this from memory. See Senghor, 'Rapport sur la méthode du parti', *Condition Humaine*, 31 mai 1956, 3 (col. 1).
30. Senghor, 'Discours', *Moniteur Africain du Commerce et de l'Industrie*, 30 mars 1963, 11 (col. 2).
31. See below, chapters 25, 26, 29 for Senghor's political formulation of these ideas. For Michelet and Mazzini, see the rapid survey in Jean Touchard, *et al.*, *Histoire des Idées Politiques: Tome Second, Du XVIIIème à Nos Jours* (Paris, Thémis 1962) pp. 535–7.

CHAPTER SIX

1. Taken from a study by Jean Touchard, 'L'esprit des années 1930: une tentative de renouvellement de la pensée politique française', *Tendances Politiques dans la Vie Française depuis 1789* (Paris, Hachette: Colloques Cahiers de Civilisation, undated reprint, 1960?) p. 89. For the thought of the 1930s, I have often referred to this brilliant and original study by Touchard. The study also sheds light on the socio-economic thought of the period, influential in Senghor's 'African Road to Socialism'. See below, chapter 35.

2. 1929 marks Senghor's reading of Barrès; 1948 is the date of the first publication of Sartre's 'Black Orpheus' which systematized *négritude* into a global theory.
3. Touchard, 'L'esprit...', pp. 90–1.
4. See below, chapter 10, for Maritain's contribution. Senghor mentioned *Ce qui Meurt et ce qui Naît* by Daniel-Rops in a 1939 essay. See *Liberté I*, p. 22.
5. Mounier to Martinaggi, letter of 1 April 1941, quoted in *Mounier et sa Génération* (Paris, Seuil 1955) pp. 82–3.
6. Touchard, 'L'esprit...', p. 100.
7. Louis-Jean Finot, 'Egalité des races', *La Revue du Monde Noir* 1, novembre 1931, 3–4.
8. Touchard, 'L'esprit...', 99.
9. Senghor, 'Défense de l'Afrique noire', *Esprit* 112, 1 juillet 1945, 237.
10. Touchard, 'L'esprit...', 101.
11. For these influences on the 'African Road to Socialism' see below, chapter 35.
12. Arthur Rimbaud, *Oeuvres* (Paris, Classiques Garnier 1960) pp. 213, 216–17 (taken from *Mauvais Sang – Une Saison en Enfer*). See also p. 457. Senghor quotes this poem in a 1952 essay, see *Liberté I*, p. 128. He read it first in the 1930s.

CHAPTER SEVEN

1. The phenomenon of the attraction of the 'savage' is not only characteristic of Rimbaud. At the beginning of the century Yeats was obsessed by myths, magic, and symbols. It was his means of combating the machine-age, and also, perhaps, English colonialism. Yeats had sounded the collective subconscious before Jung had named it; he glorified the irrational before Freud discovered its primordial role. See below, chapters 9 and 10 for the contribution of irrationalists, spiritualists, etc.
2. Girardet, 'Influence de la metropole...', pp. 1, 4–5.
3. Ibid., pp. 1, 4–5.
4. *La Dépêche Africaine* 9, novembre 1928, 6. 6,000 copies of this issue were published, which gives an idea of the extent of its influence among 'exotic' milieux in Paris. The paper preceded the *Revue du Monde Noir* in awakening Senghor's West Indian friends to colonial injustice. See next chapter for the themes of the *Revue*.
5. See the *Revue du Monde Noir* 2, décembre 1931, 56–7. See above, end of chapter 2 and chapter 3.
6. whose *Anthologie Nègre* in which Cendrars organized and classified by subject a series of African stories, fables, poems, songs and legends, was published in 1921 and whose *Les Petits Contes Nègres pour des Enfants Blancs* was published in 1929.
7. whose commentaries on Negro art attracted public opinion in 1931.
8. René Maran, *Batouala: Véritable Roman Nègre* (Paris, Albin Michel 1921 – definitive edition, Paris, Albin Michel 1938) p. 11. By 1938, 189,000 copies had been sold.
9. Senghor quotes the *Retour du Tchad* in which Gide wrote that European popular songs are 'poor, simple, rudimentary' compared with African songs. See Senghor *Liberté I*, p. 37.

10. According to Guibert, *Senghor* (Seghers) p. 21 and Claude Roy, *Arts Sauvages* (Paris, Robert Delpire 1957) p. 92. For a discussion of Surrealism see chapter 9.
11. Léro quotes Rimbaud, for example, in 'Evelyn', *Revue du Monde Noir* 2, décembre 1931, 35. For a discussion of Léro, see below, chapter 9. Senghor has contested the fact that Léro influenced him, see Appendixes, letter of 5 December 1964.
12. Senghor, 'Les idées et les lettres: René Maran l'homme et l'oeuvre', *L'Unité Africaine* 46, 21 mai 1960, 12. Paulette Nardal wrote me a long letter substantiating these ideas (letter dated 17 Nov. 1963).
13. Lilyane Kesteloot in her study (op. cit., pp 20, 63–4) noted the importance of the *Revue du Monde Noir*; she, however, was unable to obtain copies of the *Revue*. I found the six numbers published between 1931 and 1932 at the Bibliothèque Nationale in Paris. I hope to shed some new light on the origins of *négritude* in describing in detail the important influence of the *Revue*. Etienne Léro and Jules Monnerot published poems in the *Revue du Monde Noir* 2, décembre 1931. Ménil contributed to the issue of January 1932.
14. MacKay contributed to the first number in December 1931. See chapter 11 for American Negro influence on Senghor. Locke published 'Negro spirituals' in the April 1932 issue. See chapter 11 for his influence. Hughes contributed to the January 1932 issue. See influence on Senghor in chapter 10. Maran contributed to the January 1932 issue. Price-Mars contributed to January 1932 issue. See influence on Senghor, chapter 12. Excerpts from Delafosse's works appeared in the December 1932 issue. See below, chapter 12 for his influence on Senghor. A translation of Frobenius appeared in the March 1932 issue. His works were not translated into French until 1936. See below chapter 12.
15. *Revue du Monde Noir* 3, 60; *Revue du Monde Noir* 4, 40.
16. See *Revue du Monde Noir* for the first months of 1932.
17. *Revue du Monde Noir* 6, 60.
18. *Revue du Monde Noir* 3, 60.
19. Senghor, 'Les idées et les...', 12.
20. P. Nardal to J. L. Hymans, letter of 17 November 1963.
21. P. Nardal, 'Eveil de la conscience de race', *Revue du Monde Noir* 6, avril 1932, 29. I have used my own translation from the French in all quotations from the *Revue*. An English translation of each article does appear in the Revue. See Appendixes for Paulette Nardal's translation of her important article on 'Race Consciousness' quoted here.
22. Emile Sicard, 'Mutual ignorance', *Revue du Monde Noir* 2, 3.
23. Senghor, *Liberté I*, p. 94. (1950 lecture).
24. Senghor in *Paris-Dakar*, 24 janvier 1961, 1 (col. 3).
25. Abdoulaye Ly maintains this is true of Senghor. Senghor considers this hypothesis insulting. See Appendixes, Senghor's letter of 5 December 1964.

CHAPTER EIGHT

1. P. Nardal to J. L. Hymans, letter of 17 November 1963.
2. *Revue du Monde Noir* 1, novembre 1931, 2.

3. It is interesting to note the curious itinerary of these American Negro ideas of the 1920s. Having left America for Paris, these ideas contributed to the cultural nationalism of West Indians. They in turn influenced the Africans who later helped spur the American Negro revolution of the 1960s.

4. My italics. Quoted by Grégoire-Micheli, 'La mentalité des noirs est-elle inférieure?', *Revue du Monde Noir* 2, décembre 1931, 27.

5. See below, chapter 17.

6. See below, chapter 27. It also continues a previous current in Senghor's thought. See above, chapter 3.

7. Senghor, 'The spirit of civilization, or the laws of African Negro culture', *Présence Africaine* 8–10, June–November 1956, 51. (English translation of the papers presented at the First Congress of Negro Writers and Artists.)

8. Paulette Nardal, 'Eveil de la conscience de race', *Revue du Monde Noir* 6, avril 1932, 25. See Appendixes for the complete article.

9. Ibid., 29.

10. Ibid., 26–8.

11. See Joseph-Henri Georges, 'Magie Noire par Paul Morand', *Revue du Monde Noir* 1, novembre 1931, 57. Senghor quoted this same proverb in an essay published in 1956, showing the permanence of the ideas he obtained from those who contributed to the *Revue*. See Senghor, *Poèmes*, p. 155.

12. G. D. Périer, 'La poésie ethnique: la riposte poétique des noirs', *Revue du Monde Noir* 6, avril 1932, 46–7.

13. Ibid., 47. My italics.

14. P. Nardal, *Revue du Monde Noir* 6, avril 1932, 25–7. Senghor quoted Sieburg's book in his 1944 essay. See *Liberté I*, p. 42.

15. Paulette Nardal, 'Eveil de la conscience de race', 29–30.

16. Ibid., 31. The novel appeared in instalments in the *Revue de Paris*.

17. Baye-Salzmann differed from Senghor in that he was a member of a prominent family of Saint-Louis-du-Sénégal, one of the four Senegalese towns which were considered as parts of metropolitan France. These families traditionally sent their sons to study in France. Senghor, it will be remembered, came from a part of Senegal considered as a colonial area.

18. P. Baye-Salzmann, 'L'art nègre, son inspiration, ses apports à l'Occident', *Revue du Monde Noir* 5, mars 1932, 48.

19. Ibid., 45.

20. Ibid., 46.

21. Philippe de Zara, 'L'Eveil du monde noir', reprinted from the *Dépêche Tunisienne* of 24 December 1931 and published in the *Revue du Monde Noir* 4, février 1932, 3–4.

22. Pierre B. Salzmann, 'L'Art nègre', *Revue du Monde Noir* 4, février 1932, 48.

23. P. Baye-Salzmann, 'L'Art nègre, son inspiration...', 45.

24. Ibid., 45.

25. Sartre, *Black Orpheus*, p. 49. See also Georges Le Brun Keiris, 'L'Afrique entre deux civilisations', *Preuves* 83, janvier 1958, 9.

26. Paulette Nardal to J. L. Hymans, letter of 17 November 1963. Senghor quotes many of the critics of Negro art mentioned in his 1939 essay: Paul Guillaume and Thomas Munro, *La Sculpture*

Nègre primitive and Georges Hardy, *L'Art négre*, published in 1927.
27. Paulette Nardal to J.L.Hymans, letter of 17 November 1963.
28. Louis Th. Achille, 'L'Art et les noirs', *Revue du Monde Noir* 1, novembre 1931, 53, 54, 56.
29. L.S.Senghor, 'Constructive elements of a civilization of Negro-African inspiration', *Présence Africaine*, 24–25, Feb.–May 1959, 268. (English translation of the original French issue.) See also XXX 'Les états-unis d'Afrique noire', *Paris-Dakar*, 18 août 1958, 4 (col. 7).
30. Grégoire-Micheli, 'La mentalité...', 27.
31. Paulette Nardal, 'Eveil de la conscience de race', 31.
32. Paulette Nardal to J.L.Hymans, letter of 17 November 1963. See also *Revue du Monde Noir* 4, février 1932, 60.
33. Finot, 'Egalité des races', 5.
34. Zara, 'L'Eveil...', 3–4.
35. Ibid.
36. Paulette Nardal to J.L.Hymans, letter of 17 November 1963.
37. Senghor, 'Comment nous sommes...', 17. See below, chapters 9, 17, 27 for a description of this controversy and its consequences.
38. Paulette Nardal to J.L.Hymans, letter of 17 November 1963.
39. Ibid.
40. Karl Marx, 'Le panslavisme' in *Oeuvres Politiques* (Paris, A.Costes 1930) VI: 199–201. Article in *Neue Oder Zeitung*, 24 April, 1855.
41. See below chapters 11 and 16 for Senghor's study of ethnology and African languages.
42. L.S.Senghor, 'La civilisation négro africaine' in M.El Kholti *et al.*, *Les Plus Beaux Ecrits de L'Union Française et du Maghreb* (Paris, La Colombe 1947) p. 233.
43. Marx, 'Le panslavisme', op. cit., pp. 199–201.
44. Marx, 'Le panslavisme', op. cit., 199–201.
45. Ibid.
46. See below, chapter 22. For a recent analysis of the relationship of Pan-Slavism and Pan-Africanism see Hans Kohn and Wallace Sokolsky, *African Nationalism in the Twentieth Century* (New York, Van Nostrand 1965). See also Kohn's earlier *Pan-Slavism*.

CHAPTER NINE

1. Jane Nardal, 'Pantins exotiques', *La Dépêche Africaine* 8, octobre 1928, 2. (4,000 copies of this issue were printed, indicating a large audience of West Indians and Africans.) Senghor also befriended Soupault.
2. Senghor, *Pierre Teilhard*, p. 19. See also Senghor, 'Comment...', 17.
3. This phrase recalls the title of a book by the right-wing Nationalist French author and friend of Charles Maurras, Léon Daudet. It is used by Senghor in *Pierre Teilhard*, p. 19.
4. See previous chapter.
5. Touchard, 'L'esprit...', 90. André Breton, as a result of the general upsets of World War II, discovered Aimé Césaire in the West Indies in 1942. See on this subject, Jean-Louis Bedouin, *20 ans de Surréalisme 1939–1959* (Paris, Denoël 1961) pp. 31–7.

6. See above chapter 3.
7. Quoted by Damas, op. cit., p. 11; Damas, op. cit., p. 14.
8. Manifesto of *Légitime Défense* quoted by Kesteloot, op. cit., p. 25. Kesteloot obtained some excerpts of the Manifesto from Léon Damas. I quote her quotation, and from the excerpts published by Damas in his study, *Poètes*, op. cit.
9. Surrealists' letter to Paul Claudel quoted in 'Chronique Littéraire', *L'Express*, 6 oct. 1960.
10. Damas, op. cit., pp. 14, 15–16.
11. Ibid., pp. 15–16.
12. Ibid., p. 16. Senghor feels he was not influenced by Léro. See Appendixes, Senghor's letter of 5 December 1964.
13. See below, chapters 10 and 14.
14. Jean-Paul Sartre, *Black Orpheus*, p. 35.
15. Senghor, *Poèmes*, p. 155.
16. Senghor, *Anthologie*, p. 49.
17. Ibid., p. 55.
18. Senghor, *Liberté I*, pp. 33–4.
19. For a discussion of the importance of this attitude in Africa see Georges Balandier, 'Littérature de l'Afrique et des Ameriques noires' in *Encyclopédie de la Pléiade, Histoire des Littératures* I: *Littératures anciennes orientales et orales* (Paris, N.R.F. 1955) pp. 1536–67. See also Kesteloot, op. cit., pp. 49–50.

CHAPTER TEN

1. Senghor quoted by xxx, 'Claudel, Péguy et l'Afrique noire', *Le Figaro*? le 14 juin 1947 (clipping at Editions du Seuil, 27 rue Jacob, Paris).
2. Jean Touchard, 'L'esprit...', 105. Senghor was directly influenced by Proudhon somewhat later. See below, chapters 26, 27, 36 for Proudhon's federalism and socialism in Senghor's theories. See chapter 35 for Péguy's influence on Senghor's socialism.
3. Paul Thibaud, 'Le colloque d'Orleans a mis en valeur le "genie polyphonique" de Péguy', *Le Monde*, 16 sept. 1964, 10 (cols. 1–2).
4. Interview with Senghor, Dakar, 17 August 1960. (Question on his personal Pantheon.)
5. Senghor, *Pierre Teilhard*, p. 19.
6. See above, chapter 1.
7. Senghor, *Pierre Teilhard*, p. 19.
8. See Jean Lacroix' article on Lévi-Strauss' *La Pensée Sauvage*, 'La philosophie', *Le Monde*, 27 nov. 1962, 17.
9. These quotations are taken from Jean-Paul Sartre's *Reflexions sur la Question Juive* (Paris, Gallimard 1954). I have used the edition in the collection Idées, N.R.F. 1961, 140–2.
10. *Encyclopédie de la Pléiade, Histoire des Littératures* III, p. 1279.
11. Paul Claudel, *Le Soulier de Satin* (Paris, Gallimard 1944) p. 116.
12. Ibid.
13. Ibid., 42. This quotation inspired two French students who later became Africanists, Paul Mercier and Georges Balandier. See Georges Balandier, *Tous Comptes Faits: Roman* (Paris, Le Pavois

1947) p. 155. See also Georges Balandier and Paul Mercier, *Lettres sur la Poésie* (Paris, les Cahiers Littéraires 1943) p. 50.

14. For Senghor's use of Claudel's *con-naissance* see Senghor, 'Constructive elements of a civilization of Negro-African inspiration', *Présence Africaine*, 24–25 (translation of the Second Congress of Negro Writers and Artists reports) 268.

15. Senghor quoted by xxx, 'Claudel, Péguy...'.

16. Jean Guéhenno, *La France et les Noirs* (Paris, Gallimard 1954) p. 75. See also Senghor, *Poèmes*, p. 157.

17. Ibid., p. 157. According to Guéhenno, St John Perse's poetry also resembles the *Dogon* cosmogonies. St John Perse is also considered important as an influence on Senghor's later poetry. It appears that all three poets are inspired by the same type of source: religious mysticism. St John Perse influenced Senghor only after 1945.

18. See above, chapter 5, for Gide and Goethe.

19. See below, chapter 22, for D'Arboussier's criticism of Senghor which uses the same terms as Politzer's criticism of Bergson.

20. See below, chapter 10.

21. *Encyclopédie de la Pléiade, Histoire des Littératures* III, pp. 1252–5.

22. Senghor to Hymans, letter of 22 October 1963, 2.

23. Pierre-Henri Simon, 'La vie littéraire', *Le Monde*, 20 janvier 1965, 9.

24. The title of a book published by Maritain in 1927. See below, chapters 17, 27.

25. Senghor quotes Maritain's *Humanisme Intégral* in his essay of 1939. See *Liberté I*, p. 30.

26. P. Baye-Salzmann, 'L'art nègre...', p. 45–8.

27. Maurice Delafosse, *Les Civilisations Négro-Africaines*, quoted by Hubert Deschamps in *Les Religions de l' Afrique Noire* (Paris, P.U.F. 1954) p. 5.

28. Georges Le Brun Keiris, 'L'Afrique entre...', p. 5.

29. Ibid., p. 5.

30. Senghor to Hymans, letter of 22 October 1963, 3.

31. Note the similarity of his critical loyalty to the Church and his attitude towards France after the years at the Lycée *Louis-le-Grand*. See above, chapter 3.

CHAPTER ELEVEN

1. Senghor, 'Par ce signe', *Condition Humaine*, 30 nov. 1948, 1 (cols. 7–8).

2. See above, chapter 1.

3. W. E. B. Du Bois, *The Souls of Black Folk* (Chicago 1903) p. 3.

4. Ibid.

5. L. S. Senghor, 'La poésie Négro-américaine' (typed copy of a 1960 lecture, courtesy of Senghor) p. 21.

6. See Jean Wagner's exhaustive study of American Negro writers, *Les Poètes Nègres des Etats-Unis : le Sentiment Racial et Religieux dans la Poésie de P. L. Dunbar à Langston Hughes (1890–1940)* (Paris, Istra 1963) pp. 169–74. See also Senghor, *Liberté I*, pp. 104–21.

7. Senghor quoted Locke's works in his 1939 essay. See *Liberté I*, p. 36.
8. See Senghor's 1939 essay reprinted in *Liberté I*, p. 27, Senghor's 1939 poem reprinted in *Poèmes*, p. 37 (in the English translation the word *négritude* was replaced by blackness), and Césaire's 1939 *Cahier d'un retour au Pays Natal.*
9. See Senghor's allusion in his poem of 1939, *Selected Poems*, p. 17.
10. Senghor quotes this phrase in his Dakar lecture of 1937, *Liberté I*, p. 21.
11. See below, chapter 12, for Africanists' influence on *négritude*.
12. Senghor, *Liberté I*, p. 116.
13. Senghor, *Liberté I*, p. 108.
14. Senghor, 'Il y a une négritude', *Preuves* 86, avril 1958, 36.
15. Senghor in his 1939 essay reprinted in *Liberté I*, pp. 24–5.
16. See below, chapter 18, for 'Negro reason'. See below in chapters 22, 23 for criticism of this idea in the 1940s and 1950s.
17. Senghor, *Liberté I*, p. 25.
18. Ibid., p. 31.
19. Interview with Abdoulaye Ly, Dakar, 8 July 1960; *Clarté* 117, 23 mai 1947, 2.
20. Senghor, *Liberté I*, p. 27. My italics.
21. See below, chapters 25 ff.
22. See above, chapter 8.
23. See below, chapter 14.
24. Claude MacKay, 'America', *Revue du Monde Noir* 1, nov. 1931, 38. Senghor quoted this poem in his unpublished lecture on American Negro poetry, pp. 21–2. My italics.
25. Senghor, *Liberté I*, p. 33.
26. Ibid., p. 27.
27. Interview with Senghor, Dakar, 17 August 1960. See below, chapter 14, for a poetic expression of this attitude.
28. See below, chapter 14.
29. Paulette Nardal, 'Une noire parle à Cambridge et à Genève', *Revue du Monde Noir* 1, novembre 1931, 37.
30. Senghor, *Liberté I*, p. 22.
31. See below, chapters 17, 27.
32. Claude MacKay, 'America', *Revue du Monde Noir* 1, novembre 1931, 38 and Langston Hughes, quoted by Senghor in *Liberté I*, p. 115. I am translating back to English from the French to show how these lines appeared to Senghor.
33. Senghor, *Liberté I*, p. 120.
34. Senghor to Alain Badiou, letter of 20 February 1957, and interview with Senghor, Dakar, 8 July 1960.
35. Etienne Léro quoted by Léon Damas, *Poètes*, pp. 13–16.
36. Ibid., pp. 14–15.
37. Senghor, *Liberté I*, pp. 117–18.
38. Senghor, *Selected Poems*, p. 8.
39. Paulette Nardal, 'Une noire...', 37.
40. Langston Hughes, 'Moi aussi', *Revue du Monde Noir* 3, jan. 1932, 34. Senghor quoted this poem in his unpublished lecture 'Poésie Négro-américaine', 22. The last line might have been inspired by the *Song of Songs*: 'Black I am, and beautiful'.

41. See above, chapter 8.
42. Grégoire-Micheli, 'La mentalité...', 26. Compare this quote with Senghor's ideas and formulation of these ideas.
43. *Manifeste, Thèses et Résolutions adoptés par les Ier, IIe, IIIe et IVe Congrès de l'Internationale Communiste 1919–1923: Textes Complets* (Paris, Bibliothèque Communiste juin 1934) 'Thèses sur la question nègre', p. 184. Abdoulaye Ly affirmed that these ideas were a powerful factor in the development of *négritude*. Interview of Abdoulaye Ly, Dakar, 8 July 1960. For Senghor, these ideas took on increasing importance after the *Front Populaire* of 1936. See below, chapter 14.

CHAPTER TWELVE

1. Senghor, *Liberté I*, p. 107.
2. Senghor quoted by Philippe Decraene in *Le Panafricanisme* (Paris, P.U.F. 1959) p. 17.
3. In the *Revue du Monde Noir*, Guy Zuccarelli quoted from *Ainsi Parla l'Oncle*. See 'Docteur Price-Mars', *Revue du Monde Noir* 3, jan. 1932, 22–5.
4. Ibid., 24.
5. Jean Price-Mars, *Ainsi Parla l'Oncle...essais d'Ethnographie* (Compiègne, Bibliothèque Haitienne 1928) p. 220.
6. Ibid.
7. Ibid., pp. I, II, III, IV, 190–1.
8. Ibid., p. IV, 221, 187.
9. Ibid., p. 190.
10. Ibid., p. 5.
11. Guy Zuccarelli, 'A stage in Haiti's evolution', *Revue du Monde Noir* 5, mars 1932, 28–31.
12. Price-Mars', *Ainsi*, pp. 64–5.
13. See Philippe Decraene's analysis of Price-Mars in *Le Panafricanisme*, 16–17 and Robert de Billy, 'L'Amerique Latine et l'Afrique', *Le Monde*, 30 novembre 1960, 11.
14. Senghor, *Liberté I*, p. 83. Autobiographical essay written in 1949.
15. M.Delafosse, *Les Noirs d'Afrique* (Paris, Payot 1922). I use the passages quoted by Grégoire-Micheli, 'Is the mentality of negroes inferior to that of white men?', *Revue du Monde Noir* 2, dec. 1931, 23–6.
16. Ibid., 23–6.
17. Senghor, *Liberté I*, p. 26.
18. Delafosse, *Les Nègres* (Paris, Rieder 1927) p. 9.
19. Leo Frobenius, 'Le spiritisme dans l'intérieur de l'Afrique', *Revue du Monde Noir* 5, mars 1932, 19–24. The above note is taken from comments of P.Desroches-Laroche introducing the article, p. 19.
20. Senghor, *Liberté I*, pp. 83–4 (essay on the 'Message of Goethe to the New Negroes' first published in 1949).
21. Mme de Staël, *De l'Allemagne* (Paris, Marcel Didier 1956) pp. 40–2, 100.
22. The possibility that Mme de Staël influenced Senghor was raised by a delegate to a Cannes' meeting of Africans and Europeans.

See Paris-Dakar, 9 oct. 1959, 3 (col. 6). For N'Diaye's phrase see Senghor, *Liberté I*, p. 91. This vocabulary is Senghor's in his later theories. See below, chapters 15, 16. My italics.

23. Leo Frobenius, *Histoire de la Civilisation Africaine* (Paris, Gallimard 1952) p. 15. (Third edition of the book first published in 1936.) Senghor often quotes this passage. See *J.O.A.N.C.*, 21 mars 1946, 945, where Senghor affirms that Frobenius was the first to have a 'vision in depth' of *négritude*. See also Senghor in *Paris-Dakar*, 6 oct. 1960, 1.

24. Senghor, *Liberté I*, pp. 22–3. 1939 essay.

25. Senghor, 'Rapport', Congrès Constitutif du P.R.A. mimeo documents, 1958.

26. Aimé Césaire, *Cahier d'un retour au pays natal* (Paris, Présence Africaine 1956) 68, 71. (Poem written in 1939.)

27. Ibid., 83.

28. Senghor, *Liberté I*, p. 24.

29. Senghor, 'La contribution négro-africaine à l'édification d'une civilisation mondiale', *Liberté de l'Esprit* 41, juin–juillet 1953, 143. Comte de Gobineau, *Essai sur l'Inegalité des Races Humaines*, livre II, chap. VII, Paris, 1853–5.

30. Senghor often quotes from Keyserling's *Méditations Sud-Américaines* (p. 82). See Senghor, *Liberté I*, p. 70 and Senghor, 'Constructive elements...', 269.

31. Lévy-Bruhl, 'Morceaux choisis', *L'Education Africaine: Bulletin de l'Enseignement de l'A.O.F.* 97, juillet–septembre 1937, 201, 205. I use this source as Senghor was a regular subscriber to this review. See *Liberté I*, p. 77.

32. See above, chapter 1.

33. Senghor to Hymans, letter of 22 October 1963, 3. See chapter 15.

34. Ousmane Socé, *Mirages de Paris* (Paris, Nouvelles Editions, 2nd ed. 1948) p. 180.

35. Senghor, *Liberté I*, p. 40.

36. Robert Delavignette, *Soudan-Paris-Bourgogne* (Paris, Grasset 1935) p. 25.

37. Ibid., p. 216.

38. Ibid., p. 242, 244. Senghor quoted this passage in his 1944 essay. See *Liberté I*, p. 43.

39. Delavignette, *Soudan...*, pp. 10, 248. See below for Delavignette's influence in Senghor's 'cross-breeding', chapter 15. See below for Delavignette's role in Senghor's political career, chapter 25. I have begun to move from strict adherence to chronology in this chapter.

40. Senghor quotes Valéry in *Liberté I*, p. 96.

41. Senghor, 'La civilisation négro-africaine', in El Kholti, op. cit., 233.

42. XXX, 'Césaire et la *négritude*', *La Vie Africaine*, 19, nov. 1961, 33.

43. Senghor, 'Comment nous sommes...', 17.

44. Césaire *et al.*, 'Les Africains...', *Afrique-Action*, 27 mars 1961, 22.

45. Ibid.

46. Senghor, *Liberté I*, p. 99.

47. Senghor in *J.O.A.N.*, 4 août 1947, 3889.

48. Senghor (speech at the Sorbonne 1961) in *Liberté I*, p. 316.

49. Senghor, 'La Critique des livres: *Les Sao Légendaires* par Marcel Griaule', *l'Etudiant de la France d'Outre-Mer* 6, février 1944, 15.

50. Senghor, *Liberté I*, pp. 28, 32. (1939 essay).
51. XXX, 'Césaire et la *négritude*', p. 33.
52. Senghor (speech at Paris 1961), *Liberté I*, pp. 313–14.
53. Senghor (speech at the Sorbonne 1961) in *Liberté I*, p. 316.
54. See Claude Lévi-Strauss, *La Pensée Sauvage* (Paris, Plon 1962) p. 323. See also Jean Lacroix' analysis, 'La philosophie: la pensée sauvage', *Le Monde*, 27 nov. 1962, 17 (col. 2).
55. Senghor, 'Défense de l'Afrique noire', *Esprit* 112, 1er juillet 1945, 237. Senghor quotes A. Labriola, *Le Crépuscule de l'Occident*.
56. A final source in that search was Father Placide Tempels' *La Philosophie Bantoue* published in French by Présence Africaine in 1947. Tempels' book reinforced currents already present from 1932 on.
57. These terms were used by the pro-western French literary figure, Roger Caillois. They are quoted by Aimé Césaire in his violent *Discours sur le Colonialisme* (Paris, Présence Africaine 1955) p. 58.

CHAPTER THIRTEEN

1. Senghor, 'Comment nous sommes...', 17. It is interesting to note that the fascist influence can also be found in Senghor's economic thought. His anti-capitalism coupled with anti-communism is similar to the fascist theory as explained by the Italian political theorist Alfredo Rocco, 'The political doctrine of fascism', *International Conciliation*, No. 223 (Oct. 1926) 393–415. See below, chapters 35, 36.
2. Senghor, *Pierre Teilhard*, pp. 20–1. The former director of the *Ecole Coloniale*, Georges Hardy, in his *Art Nègre* published in 1927 reproduced a photograph of a statue from the Ivory Coast called the 'Eldest son of Heaven and Earth'. Senghor read the book which helped give him pride in the early days of his race.
3. Senghor in *Dakar-Matin* 37, 19 mai 1961, 8 (col. 5).
4. Senghor in *Dakar-Matin*, 4 février 1963, 1 (cols. 1–2).
5. Senghor quoted from *Préhistoire et Protohistoire de l'Egypte* edited by the *Institut d'Ethnologie* of the University of Paris. See L. Senghor, *Eurafrique: une Opinion* (1953 lecture) (Paris, Section de Documentation Militaire de l'Union Française 1953) p. 9.
6. Senghor, 'Constructive elements...', 264.
7. Senghor, *Liberté I*, pp. 84, 85.
8. Senghor, *Selected Poems*, p. 30.
9. Georges Pompidou to J. L. Hymans, letter of 12 Nov. 1963.
10. Interview with Senghor, Dakar, 1 August, 1960.
11. Senghor, *Pierre Teilhard*, p. 21.
12. Senghor, 'La négritude', *Revue de la Communauté France Eurafrique*, oct.–nov. 1959, 13.
13. Césaire, *Cahier d'un retour...*, pp. 47–8.
14. Senghor, *Liberté I*, p. 315. (Speech at Paris 1961.)
15. Césaire, *Cahier d'un retour...*, pp. 47–8.
16. Senghor, 'Comment nous sommes...', 17. See next chapter for contrary influences which led to the moderation of early ideas.
17. Senghor, *Liberté I*, p. 12.

18. Ibid., p. 13.
19. xxx, 'Césaire et la *négritude*', 33.
20. Senghor, *Liberté I*, pp. 316–17. (1961 speech at Paris.)
21. Senghor, *Revue de la Communauté France-Eurafrique*, oct.–nov. 1959, 13.

CHAPTER FOURTEEN

1. Jean-Paul Sartre, *Black Orpheus*, p. 11.
2. Senghor, *Pierre Teilhard*, pp. 21–2.
3. Senghor to Hymans, letter of 22 October 1963. This group was of sf10 tendency. It will be remembered that the French Socialist Party broke with the Communists in the 1920s and since then has been relatively moderate.
4. Senghor, 'Mon ami Georges Pompidou', *Afrique Express* 29, 25 mai 1962, 13.
5. Georges Pompidou to J.L.Hymans, letter of 12 November 1963.
6. Senghor, 'C'est Georges Pompidou qui m'a converti au socialisme', *Le Figaro Littéraire*, 12 mai 1962, 4.
7. Interview with Milka Lodetti Boyer, *agrégée de Philosophie* and one of Senghor's colleagues during the period of the *Front Populaire*, Paris, 14 November 1963.
8. Interview with Senghor, 1 August 1960.
9. Senghor to the Turkish Ambassador, Dakar-Matin, 18 October 1963, 1 (cols. 2–3).
10. See below, chapter 25, for the importance of this fact in his political career.
11. Interview with Milka Lodetti Boyer, Paris, 14 November 1963 and Milka Lodetti Boyer to Hymans, letter of 16 November 1963.
12. Guibert, *Senghor* (Seghers), p. 24.
13. Interview with Milka Lodetti Boyer, Paris, 14 November 1963.
14. Senghor, 'Biographie' (typed note submitted by Senghor to the Editions du Seuil when he first published his poems in 1945) and Senghor, 'Discours à la Conférence Constitutive de la Centrale Syndicale de Mali', Dakar mimeo, 4 April 1960, p. 1.
15. Interview with Milka Lodetti Boyer, Paris, 14 November 1963.
16. Senghor, *Selected Poems*, p. 32. My italics.
17. Ibid., p. 31. A *guelwar* is a noble warrior.
18. Ibid., p. 23.
19. Chateau-Gontier Oct.–Dec. 1939.
20. Senghor, *Selected Poems*, p. 14. See below, chapter 35 for this influence.
21. Senghor *Anthologie*, p. 55.
22. Senghor *Selected Poems*, p. 71.
23. Ibid., p. 23.
24. Ibid., p. 23. See above, chapter 11 for American Negro influence in this lack of hatred.
25. Senghor, *Selected Poems*, pp. 7–8.
26. Césaire, *Cahier*, pp. 74–5. See below, chapter 24 for a comparison between Senghor and Césaire.
27. See Damas, *Poètes*, p. 136.

28. Senghor, *Anthologie*, p. 55.
29. See below, chapters 24, 25.
30. Senghor, *Selected Poems*, pp. 48–51.
31. *Paris-Dakar*, 18 juillet 1959, 1 (cols. 1–2).

CHAPTER FIFTEEN

1. Senghor to Alain Badiou, letter dated Paris, 20 February 1957. (Private collection.)
2. See below, chapters 25, 35.
3. *L'Etudiant Martiniquais : Organe de l'Association des Etudiants Martiniquais en France*, nouvelle série, no. 1, mai 1934, 2.
4. Ibid., 2.
5. Ibid.
6. Ibid. Here it is necessary to underline the fact that Lilyane Kesteloot's sources did not include this type of document written before World War II.
7. Ousmane Socé, *Karim : Roman Sénégalais suivi de Contes et Légendes d'Afrique Noire* (Paris, Nouvelles Editions Latines 1948) p. 105. First published in 1935. Original edition not at Bibliothèque Nationale.
8. Ousmane Socé, *Mirages de Paris* (Paris, Nouvelles Editions Latines 1937) p. 183.
9. Senghor, *Liberté I*, p. 92. (Written in 1950.)
10. See above, chapter 1.
11. Senghor, *Liberté I*, p. 92.
12. H. M. Bernelot-Moëns, 'Can humanity be humanized', *Revue du Monde Noir* 4, février 1932, 11.
13. E. Sicard reporting on the future Dahomean Ambassador B. Ig. Pinto's speech at the colonial exhibition, *Revue du Monde Noir* 1, nov. 1931, 62.
14. H. M. Bernelot-Moëns, 'Can humanity...', 10.
15. Senghor, *Liberté I*, p. 92. (Written in 1950.)
16. Senghor, *Liberté I*, p. 357. (Speech at Rome.)
17. Thus the theories of Federation and the 'African Road to Socialism' were grafted on the complementary theories which made up Senghor's *négritude*. See below, Part III.
18. Senghor, 'Rapport au Congres P.R.A. à Cotonou', mimeo, 1958. p. 23.
19. Senghor, 'La vraie civilisation', *Notre Republique: Organ de l'U.N.R.–l'U.N.R.–U.D.T.* 70, 22 février 1963, 6.
20. Senghor, 'Comment nous sommes...', 17.
21. Senghor, *Liberté I*, p. 84.
22. Senghor, 'Le problème culturel en A.O.F.', *Essais et Etudes Universitaires : Edition Lettres* 1, 1945, p. 47. This paragraph is not in Senghor's recent re-printing of the essay.
23. Ibid., p. 47.
24. Senghor, *Liberté I*, pp. 13–14.
25. Ibid., p. 17.
26. Ibid.
27. See above, chapter 11.

28. See below in chapters 30, 37 for these proposals.
29. Senghor in *J.O.A.N.C.*, 21 mars 1946, 945.
30. Senghor, *Liberté I*, p. 89.
31. Senghor, 'Rapport au Congrès P.R.A. à Cotonou', mimeo, 1958, p. 22.
32. Senghor, *Nationhood*, p. 9.
33. Senghor, *Liberté I*, p. 98.
34. Guibert, *Senghor* (Seghers), p. 31.
35. Senghor, *Liberté I*, p. 7.
36. René Maran, 'Léopold Sédar Senghor et l'Afrique noire' (clipping at Editions du Seuil, 27 rue Jacob, Paris).
37. Senghor in the discussion, *Présence Africaine* 8–10, June–Nov. 1956, 219 (English translation of the 1st International Conference of Negro Writers and Artists).
38. Senghor, 'Discours', *Le Petit Matin*, 20 oct. 1961, 5 (col. 1) (Tunis newspaper). The term *l'accord conciliant* is taken from Frobenius.
39. Senghor in *J.O.A.N.* 18 février 1955, 810. See below, Part III.
40. Senghor, 'Discours', *Le Petit Matin*, 20 oct. 1961, 5 (cols. 6–7).
41. Ibid., 1 (cols. 6–7).
42. Quoted by Georges Larché in 'Ce que l'Afrique attend de l'Europe', *Paris-Dakar*, 24 mai 1955, 1.
43. *Paris-Dakar*, 18 juillet 1959, 1 (cols. 1–2).
44. Raoul Girardet, 'Influence de la métropole...', 1–10.
45. According to the expression used by René Tavernier in 'Le poète reconcilié', *l'Unité Africaine* 9, 6 mars 1962.
46. Senghor, 'La voie sénégalaise', *Jeune Afrique*, 19–25 nov. 1962, 26.
47. See above, chapter 12.
48. Senghor, *Liberté I*, pp. 96–7.
49. Senghor, *Selected Poems*, 13.
50. Georges Balandier, 'Erreurs noires', *Présence Africaine* 3, mars–avril 1948, 402.
51. René Maran, 'Un poète de l'union française', *Les Nouvelles Littéraires*, 22 mai 1947, 1–5.
52. See Senghor, *Liberté I*, p. 357. '...telle est *ma* situation, *notre* situation'.
53. Senghor, 'Preface à la "Phrase Ensemble" d'André Breton', *Présence Africaine* 4, mai–juin 1948, 687. Note the influence of Goethe and Gide.
54. Senghor, *Liberté I*, p. 96.
55. Senghor, *Liberté I*, p. 318.
56. This preface dates from 1948 and not from 1935 as Lilyane Kesteloot implied, op. cit., p. 106.
57. Robert Delavignette, 'Preface' in Ousmane Socé Diop, *Karim* (1948 edition).

CHAPTER SIXTEEN

1. In this chapter I use interchangeably 'assimilate', 'integrate', 'absorb', for the French word *assimiler*.
2. Senghor, *Liberté I*, pp. 23–4.

3. Senghor, 'Le problème culturel en A.O.F.', 47. Paragraph not reprinted in *Liberté I.*
4. Ibid., p. 47.
5. Raoul Girardet, 'L'influence de la métropole...', 1–4.
6. Senghor, 'Harmonie vocalique en serère: dialecte du Dyegumène', *Journal de la Société des Africanistes* T.XIV, 1944, 19.
7. Senghor, 'Discours d'Achimota au Ghana', *Paris-Dakar*, 18 février 1961, 6 (col. 7). It is quite possible to use this quotation to illustrate Senghor's ideas in 1937, for they remained constant.
8. Senghor, *Liberté I*, p. 40 (1944 essay).
9. Senghor, *Liberté I*, p. 316 (1961 speech).
10. Ibid., pp. 87–9.
11. Ibid., p. 15.
12. Ibid., p. 14.
13. Senghor in *J.O.A.N.C.*, 21 mars 1946, 946.
14. Senghor, *Liberté I*, p. 16.
15. Ibid., p. 17 and Senghor, 'Le problème culturel...', 50.
16. See above, end of chapter 8.
17. Senghor, *Liberté I*, pp. 18–19.
18. Ibid., p. 19.
19. Ibid., p. 19 (note).
20. Ibid., p. 19.
21. Ibid., p. 19 and note.
22. Ibid., pp. 19, 20.
23. Sartre touches on this problem in his *Black Orpheus*, pp. 22 ff.
24. For a complete list of translations of *Serer* words used by Senghor, see *Selected Poems*, pp. 95–9.
25. Senghor, 'Discours de reception de l'Ambassadeur de Haiti', *Paris-Dakar*, 20 janvier 1961, 6 (col. 4).
26. Senghor, 'Le problème culturel...', 47. (Not reprinted in *Liberté I*.)
27. Senghor, *Liberté I*, p. 20.
28. xxx, Interview with Senghor, *Paris-Dakar*, 4 septembre 1937, 1.
29. Senghor, 'La résistance de la bourgeoisie sénégalaise à *l'Ecole Rurale Populaire*', *Congrès International de l'Evolution Culturelle des Peuples Coloniaux 26 27 28 septembre 1937: Rapport et Compte rendu* (Paris, Exposition Internationale de Paris 1937, 1938) p. 42.
30. This fact is at the source of Senghor's break with Lamine-Guèye in 1948, see below, chapter 27.
31. Senghor, 'La résistance...', 40–2.
32. Ibid.
33. Interview with Senghor, Dakar, 16 August 1960.

CHAPTER SEVENTEEN

1. Interview with Senghor, Dakar, 1 August 1960.
2. Senghor, 'Comment nous sommes...', 17.
3. Barrès, *Scènes...*, p. 86.
4. Damas, *Poètes*, p. 30.
5. Damas quoted by Kesteloot, op. cit., p. 91. As already noted, Kesteloot also exaggerated the importance of *Légitime Défense* and Léro. Her admission of her inability to obtain the *Revue du Monde*

Noir, which I found at the *Bibliothèque Nationale*, accounts for certain of her distortions. My discovery of the *Revue du Monde Noir* and the announcement of the Association of West African Students thus seems to challenge certain of Kesteloot's historical affirmations.

6. Senghor, *Liberté I*, p. 31.
7. Yves Dupleissis, *Le Surréalisme* (Paris, P.U.F. 1961) pp. 15–17.
8. Jules Monnerot, *La Poésie Moderne et le Sacré* (Paris, Gallimard 1945) pp. 86–7, 88, 91.
9. Ibid., p. 91.
10. Senghor, *Liberté I*, p. 11.
11. Interview with Madame René Maran, Paris, 11 October 1963.
12. Senghor, *Poèmes*, p. 56. Poem dedicated to L. G. Damas and written in Paris, April 1940. Note the influence of André Gide's *Si le grain ne meurt* in the phrase about the grain of millet. My italics.
13. See above, chapter 10.
14. Senghor, *Anthologie*, p. 49. See above, chapter 9.
15. Senghor, *Liberté I*, p. 152. (1953 speech.)
16. 'Manifeste de la Société des Artistes Africains', *Paris-Dakar*, 27 decembre 1958, 3 (col. 5).
17. Senghor *Liberté I*, pp. 198–9.
18. Ibid., p. 200.
19. Senghor, 'La voie prophétique de la jeune poésie suisse', *Présence* (Genève), été 1957, 31. (Passage not included in the reprint *Liberté I*.)
20. Senghor *Poèmes*, p. 26.

CHAPTER EIGHTEEN

1. Senghor, *Liberté I*, pp. 356–7. (Speech at Rome 1962.)
2. Denis Blanche, 'Preface' in *Congrès International...*, pp. 18–19.
3. Ibid., p. 19.
4. Ibid.
5. See above, chapter 12.
6. Senghor, 'The spirit of civilization...', *Présence Africaine* 8–10, June–November 1956, 51. (English translation of 1st International Conference of Negro Writers and Artists.)
7. See above, chapter 11.
8. Daniel-Rops, 'Preface' in S. E. le Cardinal Verdier *et al.*, *L'Homme de Couleur* (Paris, Plon 1939) p. 11. (Preface signed: 'the Editors'.)
9. S. E. le Cardinal Verdier, 'Introduction', in ibid., p. 111.
10. See above, chapter 10.
11. See above, chapter 16.
12. Senghor, *Liberté I*, p. 33.
13. For Negro contributions to the socio-economic domain see below, chapter 34.
14. Senghor, *Liberté I*, p. 33.
15. Ibid., p. 36.
16. Senghor, 'La contribution...', 143–4, 145.
17. Ibid., 145.
18. Senghor, *Liberté I*, p. 310 (1961 speech.)
19. Senghor, 'La contribution...', 144.

20. Senghor, 'Les voix et voie...', 225. See above, chapter 8.
21. See above, chapter 6.
22. Senghor, *Liberté I*, p. 27 (1939 essay).
23. Senghor, *Selected Poems*, p. 9. (Poem written in the 1930s.)
24. Senghor, 'Discours', *Dakar-Matin*, 27 mars 1963, 3 (cols. 4–5).
25. Senghor, *Liberté I*, p. 68 (1944 essay).
26. Ibid., p. 317.
27. See above, chapter 13.
28. Senghor, *Liberté I*, pp. 68–9.
29. Ibid., p. 318. (Speech at the Sorbonne, 1961.)
30. Senghor, 'Les voix et voie...', 219.
31. Senghor, 'La contribution négro-africaine à l'édification d'une civilisation mondiale', *Liberté de l'Esprit* 41, juin–juillet 1953, 143. The title of this essay is a function of the subject of the chapter.
32. Senghor, *Liberté I*, p. 319. Note the influence of Barrès' *The Inspired Hill*: 'There are certain places where the Spirit blows'.
33. Jacques Rabemananjara, 'Le poète noir et son peuple', *Présence Africaine* 16, oct.–nov. 1957, 15.
34. Senghor, *Liberté I*, p. 38. See above, chapter 10, for Claudel's influence on the notion of the great chain of being: pebble to God.
35. Senghor, *Liberté I*, p. 157 (1954 essay).
36. Senghor in *Paris-Dakar*, 16 février 1961, 6 (col. 3).
37. Robert Aron and Arnaud Dandieu, *Le Cancer Américain* (Paris, Rieder 1931) pp. 15–17, 82.
38. Senghor, 'La contribution...', 146.
39. Senghor, *Selected Poems*, p. 79. (Written in the 1950s.)
40. Senghor in *Dakar-Matin*, 10 juillet 1962, 6 (col. 4).
41. Senghor, 'La contribution...', 146.
42. Senghor, *Liberté I*, p. 26. See also Senghor, 'Socialisme et developpement ou la voie sénégalaise', supplement à *Developpement et Civilisations*, décembre 1962, pp. 1–2. For American Negro influence on this idea see above, chapter 11.
43. See below, chapter 24.
44. Senghor quoting Gobineau, *Liberté I*, p. 24 (1939 essay).
45. Thomas Hodgkin, *Nationalism in Colonial Africa* (London, Muller 1956).
46. Senghor, 'Marxisme et humanisme', *La Revue Socialiste* 19, mars 1948, 206.
47. Ibid., 206.
48. Senghor, *Visit...Oxford*, p. 7.
49. Senghor, 'Comment nous sommes...', 17.
50. Paraphrasing Alioune Diop in 'Le sens de ce congrès: discours d'ouverture', *Présence Africaine Deuxième Congrès*, 44. (See English translation *Second Congress of Negro Writers and Artists*, p. 48.)
51. Senghor, 'Comment nous sommes...', 17.
52. Senghor, 'Les voix et voie de l'Afrique noire', 220, 224–5.
53. St John Perse, 'Réponse: éloge de la poésie', *Le Monde*, 11–12 décembre 1960, 16. (Speech at Nobel Prize ceremonies.)
54. Senghor, 'Rapport', *Condition Humaine*, 31 mai 1956, 2 (col. 4). These writings of the 1950s and 1960s are very much in the spirit of the statements made by Senghor in 1939 and therefore do not violate chronology.

55. Lévi-Strauss, *La Pensée Sauvage* (Paris, Plon 1961).
56. Senghor, 'Comment nous sommes...', 17.
57. Senghor, *Liberté I*, p. 23.
58. Senghor, 'La civilisation négro-africaine' in El Kholti, op. cit., p. 215. (Passage not included in *Liberté I*.)
59. Senghor has used here the Claudelian term *con-naître* (to be born with, to know). See above, chapter 10.
60. Senghor, 'Il y a une *négritude*', *Preuves* 86, avril 1958, 36.
61. Senghor, *Pierre Teilhard*, p. 20.
62. Pierre-Henri Simon, 'La vie des lettres: pour et contre: Pierre Teilhard de Chardin', *Le Monde*, 11 avril 1962, 10 (col. 5). For other criticism see below, chapters 22, 23.
63. Claude Roy, *Arts Sauvages* (Paris, Robert Delpire 1957) pp. 92, 95.
64. Senghor, 'Les voix et voie...', 225.
65. See criticisms below, chapters 22, 23.
66. Verdier, 'Introduction' in Verdier *et al.*, *L'Homme de Couleur*, p. 111.
67. Delavignette, 'Preface' to Socé, *Karim*, p. 15.

CHAPTER NINETEEN

1. Senghor, *Poèmes*, p. 68.
2. Senghor, *Selected Poems*, p. 36.
3. Georges Pompidou to J.L. Hymans, letter of 12 November 1963, p. 1. See also Senghor in *Paris-Dakar*, 17 décembre 1959, 3 (col. 3).
4. Senghor, 'Biographie' (typed note at Editions du Seuil, 27 rue Jacob, Paris).
5. Pierre in French means stone as well as the proper name Peter.
6. Senghor, *Selected Poems*, p. 38.
7. Senghor referred here to his years as Professeur in French *Lycées*. A *Marabout* is an Islamic teacher.
8. Senghor, *Poèmes*, p. 81.
9. Senghor in *Dakar-Matin*, 25 avril 1961, 3 (cols. 7–8).
10. Senghor, *Liberté I*, p. 83.
11. See Jean Delay *La Jeunesse d'André Gide* (Tome 2: d'André Walter à André Gide) (Paris, Gallimard 1957) p. 277. Also see above, chapter 5.
12. Senghor, *Liberté I*, pp. 85–6.
13. Ibid., p. 86.
14. Senghor, 'Discours', *l'Unité Africaine* 1, 14 nov. 1961, 8 (col. 2).
15. Senghor, *Poèmes*, pp. 83–4.
16. Senghor, *Liberté I*, p. 78. (Written in 1947.)
17. Georges Pompidou to J.L. Hymans, letter of 12 November 1963.
18. Sylvère Alcandre, *L'Emancipation des Peuples Colonisés* (Paris, Editions Europe–Colonies 1949) I, p. 173. Alcandre had some influence among educated Africans in the 1940s because he demanded independence.
19. Senghor, 'Biographie' (at Editions du Seuil, 27 rue Jacob, Paris).
20. Senghor in *J.O.A.N.*, 11 mai 1951, p. 5074.
21. Senghor to Hymans, letter of 5 December 1964, pp. 7–8. Senghor, 'Biographie' and *J.O.A.N.*, 11 mai 1951, 5074.

22. *L'Etudiant de la France d'Outre-mer : Chronique des Foyers* 1, juillet 1943, pp. 26–7.
23. *L'Etudiant de la France d'Outre-mer* 8, avril–mai 1944, last page.
24. See above, chapter 16.
25. Senghor, *Liberté I*, pp. 55, 298. Interviews with Alioune Diop and Senghor.
26. Kothj Barma, 'L'étudiant de la France d'Outre-mer', *L'Etudiant de la France d'Outre-mer* 1, juillet 1943, 3. The author of the article who took as pseudonym the name of the *Wolof* sage of the seventeenth century is Alioune Diop. (Interview of Alioune Diop, Paris, 28 December 1963.)
27. Alioune Diop, 'Niam N'Goura ou les raisons d'être de présence africaine', *Présence Africaine* 1, oct.–nov. 1947, 8.
28. Ibid., 8.
29. Me Robert Bailhache, 'Alioune Diop affirme sa foi dans l'avenir de la culture négro-africaine', *l'Unité Africaine* 1, 15 mai 1959, 11.
30. Interview with Alioune Diop, Dakar, 27 August 1960.
31. See above, chapter 12.
32. Interview with Governor-General Delavignette, Paris, 29 November 1960. Interview with Alioune Diop, Dakar, 27 August 1960.
33. See below, chapter 25.
34. Senghor, *Liberté I*, p. 39.
35. *L'Etudiant de la France d'Outre-mer* 4, décembre 1943, pp. 16–17.

CHAPTER TWENTY

1. See below, chapter 24, for a discussion of the political proposals.
2. See above, chapter 5.
3. Senghor, *Liberté I*, p. 39.
4. Ibid., p. 39.
5. Ibid., p. 43.
6. Ibid., pp. 44, 45.
7. Ibid., p. 56.
8. Ibid., pp. 63–4.
9. Ibid., p. 64.
10. Ibid., pp. 65–6.
11. Ibid., p. 66. A lecture by Pierre Alexandre of the Paris *Ecole Nationale des Langues Orientales Vivantes* at the *Maison Française des Pays et Etats d'Outre-mer* in 1964 showed that this matter still preoccupies Africanists in the 1960s.
12. Ibid., p. 68.
13. At this point strict adherence to chronology is sacrificed so that, in the next four chapters, the later development of *négritude* can be discussed. Chapter 25 will take up the thread of events from 1945 onwards.

CHAPTER TWENTY-ONE

1. 'Défense de l'Afrique noire', *Esprit* 112, 1er juillet 1945, 237–48.
2. Me Bailhache, 'Alioune Diop...', 11, and my interview with Alioune Diop, Dakar, 27 August 1960.

3. XXX, *Présence Africaine 1947–1958* (Condé-sur-Noireau, Calvados, Imprimerie Condéenne 1958). Brochure distributed by *Présence Africaine*.

4. Condotto Nenekhaly-Camara, op. cit., p. 6.

5. Abdoulaye Ly, 'Sur le nationalisme dans l'Ouest-Africain', *Publications du P.R.A.-Sénégal* 1, Dakar, août 1959, p. 21. Lecture given at the 'Séminaire des Jeunes', Bamako, 10 August 1959, by the leader of the legal opposition in Senegal, friend of the militants of *négritude*, but member of a younger generation and hostile to their theory.

6. C.A. Julien, 'Avant Propos' in Senghor, *Anthologie*, p. VIII.

7. Jean-Paul Sartre, *Black Orpheus* (Paris, Présence Africaine 1963) p. 7. This is a recent translation of the preface to Senghor's *Anthologie*. I refer to it, but use my own translation from the original.

8. Ibid., p. 7.

9. Ibid., pp. 11, 15.

10. See below, chapter 22.

11. Ibid., p. 17.

12. Ibid., p. 21.

13. See above, at the end of chapter 8.

14. Ibid., pp. 25–6.

15. Ibid., p. 31.

16. Ibid., p. 32.

17. Ibid., pp. 40, 41.

18. Ibid., pp. 44–5, 49.

19. Ibid., pp. 57–8.

20. Ibid., pp. 58–9.

21. Ibid., pp. 57, 59.

22. Ibid., pp. 59–60.

23. Ibid., pp. 61, 62.

24. Senghor, *Selected Poems*, p. 6.

25. Sartre, *Black Orpheus*, p. 63.

CHAPTER TWENTY-TWO

1. Gabriel d'Arboussier, 'Une dangereuse mystification: la théorie de la négritude', *Reveil* 375, 1 août 1949, 1 (cols. 6–8); *Reveil* 376, 8 août 1949, 3 (cols. 2–5); and *Reveil* 378, 22 août 1949, 3 (cols. 4–8).

2. Ibid., also see above, chapter 10.

3. Ibid., 22 août 1949, 3 (cols. 4–5).

4. Albert Franklin, 'La négritude: réalité ou mystification?', *Présence Africaine* 14, décembre 1953, 287, 289, 293.

5. Ibid., pp. 294–5, 298–9.

6. Ibid., pp. 301–303.

7. Abdoulaye Ly, 'Sur le nationalisme...', 17, 21–2.

8. See below, chapter 23.

9. Senghor, 'Appendice', *Chants pour Naëtt: Poèmes* (Paris, Seghers 1949) p. 46. He wrote precisely the same thing in 1961, substituting

'French-speaking Africans' for 'Afro-French'. See Senghor *Poèmes,* p. 245.

10. Senghor, *Liberté I,* p. 19.
11. Ibid., p. 19 (note 2).
12. J. Van den Reysen, 'Reflections sur la littérature africaine' (Paris: mimeographed documents of the *F.E.A.N.F. Séminaire* on literature, 1961), p. 1.
13. Mame Pathé Diagne, 'Remarques sur chants d'ombre et hosties noires' (Paris, mimeographed documents of the *F.E.A.N.F. Séminaire,* 1961), p. 5.
14. Senghor, 'Rapport sur la méthode du parti: socialisme et culture', *Condition Humaine,* 31 mai 1956, 3 (col. 4).
15. Ibid.
16. xxx, '8ème Congrès du B.D.S.: Motion de politique générale', *Condition Humaine,* 31 mai 1956, 1–2.
17. Edmond Ferly, 'Les poètes antillais et la négritude' (Paris, mimeographed documents, *F.E.A.N.F. Séminaire* 1961), p. 4.
18. Mustapha Bal, 'L'homme noir dans la poésie' (Paris, mimeographed documents *F.E.A.N.F. Séminaire* 1961), p. 1.
19. Senghor, 'Discussion', *Présence Africaine 1st Conference,* pp. 70–1.
20. Senghor, 'Rapport', *Condition Humaine,* 31 mai 1956, 3 (col. 1), 2 (col. 1).
21. Ibid., p. 2 (col. 4).
22. See below, at the beginning of chapter 32.
23. Frantz Fanon, *The Damned* (Paris, Présence Africaine 1963) p. 189.
24. Ezekiel Mphahlele, 'African Culture Trends' in Peter Judd, *African Independence* (New York, Dell 1963) pp. 132–9 and Ezekiel Mphahlele, *The African Image* (London, Faber 1962) pp. 25–7, 40. See also Ezekiel Mphahlele, *Remarks on négritude* (mimeographed document, University of Dakar 1963) which is included in the Appendixes.
25. René Ménil, 'Une doctrine réactionnaire: la négritude', *Action: Revue Théorique et Politique du Parti Communiste Martiniquais* 1, août 1963, pp. 37, 38.
26. Ibid., pp. 38, 44–5.
27. Ibid., pp. 44–5.
28. Ibid., p. 39.
29. Ibid., p. 40.
30. Ibid., pp. 41, 42, 43.
31. Ibid., pp. 49–50.
32. Senghor, *Messages* (Dakar, Grande Imprimerie Africaine 1962) p. 15.
33. Senghor, *Liberté I,* p. 260.
34. Ibrahima Signaté, 'Fin de la négritude', *Jeune Afrique,* 24 février 1964, 28. A recent Ghanaian critic accuses Senghor of writing 'French poetry...interlarded with odd African allusions'. See Willi Abraham in *Africa Report,* July 1964, 17.

CHAPTER TWENTY-THREE

1. Raoul Girardet, 'Influences de la métropole...', pp. 1–4.
2. Jean Guéhenno, *La France et les Noirs* (Paris, Gallimard 1954) pp. 121–3. See also p. 48.

3. Roger Bastide, 'Variations sur la négritude', *Présence Africaine* 36, 1er trimestre 1961, 8.
4. Paul-Henri Siriex, *Une Nouvelle Afrique* (Paris, Plon 1957) pp. 226–7.
5. See above, at the end of chapter 18 for Simon's earlier criticism.
6. Pierre-Henri Simon, 'La vie littéraire', *Le Monde*, 12 août 1964, 8 (col. 2).
7. Ibid., 8 (col. 4).
8. Ibid., 8 (col. 5).
9. Senghor in *Paris-Dakar*, 20 janvier 1961, 6 (cols. 3–4).
10. See below, at the beginning of chapter 37.
11. Senghor, *Official Visit...*, p. 9.
12. Senghor in *Afrique Express*, 5 mars 1961, 14.
13. Paul Mercier, 'Evolution des élites sénégalaises', *UNESCO Bulletin International des Sciences Sociales* 8 (3), 1956, p. 459.

CHAPTER TWENTY-FOUR

1. L. V. Thomas, 'Une idéologie moderne: la négritude', *Revue de Psychologie des Peuples* 18 (3), 1963, 246–72, and 18 (4), 367–98. See especially 256–65.
2. Cheikh Hamidou Kane, *L'Aventure Ambigüe* (Paris, Julliard 1961).
3. A. Tevoedjre, *L'Afrique Revoltée* (Paris, Présence Africaine 1958).
4. Cheikh Anta Diop, *Nations Nègres et Culture* (Paris, Présence Africaine 1955).
5. Aimé Patri, 'Deux poètes noirs en langue française', *Présence Africaine* 3, mars–avril 1948, 379.
6. Guy de Bosschère, 'Une poésie d'enracinement', *l'Unité Africaine* 5, 9 janvier 1962, 17 (cols. 4–5).
7. Alain Badiou, 'La poésie de L. S. Senghor', *Vin Nouveau* 2, janvier 1957, 78.
8. Abacar N'Diaye, 'Léopold Senghor, chantre de la négritude', *l'Unité Africaine* 27, 9 janvier 1960, 12.
9. Ibid., p. 12.
10. Interview with Senghor, Dakar, 1 August 1960.
11. Senghor, *Anthologie*, p. 207.
12. This distinction was made by Immanuel Wallerstein in *The Evolution of Pan-Africanism as a Protest Movement* (Revised version of a paper delivered at the American Political Science Assn. Congress, St Louis, Missouri, 1961. Mimeo.) pp. 12–13.
13. See below, chapters 27, 33.
14. As that which Frobenius stressed about Ethiopian and Hamitic civilization in his *Histoire de la Civilisation Africaine*.

CHAPTER TWENTY-FIVE

1. Senghor, *Liberté I*, p. 13.
2. Senghor, 'La résistance de la bourgeoisie sénégalaise à l'école rurale populaire', pp. 43–4.
3. Senghor, 'La critique des livres: *Les Pionniers de l'Empire* de René Maran', *l'Etudiant de la France d'Outre-mer* 8, avril 1944, 24–5.

4. Senghor, *Libertè I*, p. 40.
5. E. Sicard, 'Une manifestation à l'exposition coloniale de Vincennes', *Revue du Monde Noir* 1, novembre 1931, 61.
6. Maurice Barrès, *Scènes et Doctrines du Nationalisme* (Paris, Plon 1925) I, 80, 81, 98; II, 250, 253. See above at the beginning of chapter 5. for Batrès' influence and his provincial ideas.
7. Senghor, *Liberté I*, p. 59.
8. Ibid., p. 60.
9. Ibid., p. 60. I am using the term 'mother country' interchangeably with the French term *Métropole*.
10. Ibid., p. 58.
11. Ibid., pp. 57, 58. For recent work in this field see Martin Klein, *Islam and Imperialism in Senegal* (Edinburgh University Press 1968).
12. Ibid., pp. 59–60, a *cercle* was the equivalent of a district.
13. *J.O.R.F.* (*Ordonnances et Décrets no. 79*), 4 avril 1945, 1861–2 (List of members of the commission.) See also *J.O.R.F.*, *Assemblée Consultative Provisoire*, 2ème Séance du 29 juillet 1945, 1612 (Monnerville report), and *Paris-Dakar*, 3 janvier 1956, 4, which mentions Senghor's role in this appointing body.
14. Interviews with Abdoulaye Ly, Dakar, 8 July 1960 and Governor-General Delavignette, Paris, 29 September 1960.
15. *J.O.A.O.F.* 2162, 5 mai 1945, 322 and *J.O.A.O.F.* 2165, 26 mai 1945, 389.
16. *l'A.O.F.* (organ of the Senegalese branch of the SFIO) 2258, 14 octobre 1948, 1 (col. 2) and 2261, 4 novembre 1948, 1 (col. 7).
17. These communes were Dakar, Rufisque, Gorée, and Saint-Louis-du-Sénégal. The first Negro *Député* was Blaise Diagne who, in 1916, obtained the affirmation of the statute of the Negro Citizens of the Four Communes by sending African troops to defend France. Blaise Diagne was replaced in 1934 by Galandou Diouf, whose death in 1945 left the place open for Lamine-Guèye. See G. Wesley Johnson's work on early twentieth-century Senegalese politics.
18. Senghor obtained 15,095 of the 19,126 'subject' votes. Lamine-Guèye obtained 21,528 votes of the 25,439 'citizen' votes. This shows the reduced size of the electorate during the first elections.
19. Senghor, 'Pour une solution fédéraliste', *La Nef* 9, juin 1955, 148.

CHAPTER TWENTY-SIX

1. Assemblée Nationale Constituante élue le 21 octobre 1945, *Séances de la Commission de la Constitution: Comptes-rendus analytiques*, p. 8. On 19 February 1946 Senghor replaced André Philip, who became a Minister. See also Ruth Schachter Morgenthau *Political Parties in French-Speaking West Africa* (Oxford, Clarendon Press 1964) p. 85, note 3. Professor Morgenthau's exhaustive study of the political developments allows me to concentrate on intellectual developments. For party politics consult her outstanding account.
2. *Paris-Dakar*, 20 décembre 1945, 1. I have translated *territoires d'outre-mer* as 'overseas territories'.
3. *J.O.A.N.C.*, 12 avril 1946, 1713.

246 Notes and References

4. François Borella, *L'Evolution Politique et Juridique de l'Union Française depuis 1946* (Paris, Pichon et Durand-Auzias 1958) p. 39.
5. See below.
6. Borella, *Evolution...*, p. 40.
7. Interview with Senghor by Julien Teppe, 'La condition humaine – allons-nous perdre nos colonies?', *Gavroche: Periodique de Paris* 102, 8 août 1946, 7.
8. See below, chapter 28: 'Refusal of Political Independence 1947–1956'.
9. Senghor in *J.O.A.N.C.*, 18 septembre 1946, 3791.
10. Senghor, 'Rapport sur la méthode du parti', *Paris-Dakar*, 3 juillet 1953, 3.
11. P. J. Proudhon, *Correspondance de P. J. Proudhon* (Paris, Librairie Internationale A. Lacroix 1875) 11, 198–9. (Letter of 17 May 1846 to Marx.)
12. Barrès, *Scènes et Doctrines...*, I: 86.
13. Stendhal, *Le Rouge et le Noir* (Paris, Livre de Poche 1958) p. 264.
14. 'Manifeste du rassemblement démocratique africain' in *Le Rassemblement Démocratique Africain dans la Lutte Anti-Impérialiste* (Paris, les Imprimeries Rapides 1948) p. 24.
15. Alain Djammet, 'Note sur l'évolution politique du RDA' in Association Française de Science Politique, *Table Ronde de Mars 1959* (Paris, mimeo, at 27, rue St Guillaume 1959) p. 1. Also see paper by Le Rolle in ibid.
16. *Le Rassemblement Démocratique Africain...*, p. 18.
17. *Paris-Dakar*, 9 octobre 1946, 2.
18. I have not gone into the details of the October 1946 Constitution because Borella, op. cit., pp. 43–57, as well as Morgenthau, op. cit., pp. 48–54, covered this terrain quite thoroughly. I am dealing only with those aspects which shed light on Senghor's thought.
19. See Alfred Grosser, *La Quatrième République et sa Politique Extérieure* (Paris, Armand Colin 1961) pp. 246–51.
20. Julien Teppe's interview with Senghor, loc. cit., p. 7.
21. Senghor in *J.O.A.N.*, 4 août 1947, 3889.
22. Senghor, 'Les Négro-Africains et l'Union Française', *Reveil*, 24–8 avril 1947, 1 (cols. 3–8).
23. Senghor in Assemblée Nationale Constituante, *Séances de la Commission de la Constitution*, 3 juillet 1946, p. 37.

CHAPTER TWENTY-SEVEN

1. Interview with Abdoulaye Ly, Dakar, 8 July 1960.
2. Senghor to De Gaulle, *Dakar-Matin*, 26 avril 1961, 3 (cols. 5–6).
3. Senghor, 'Rapport...', *Condition Humaine*, 31 juin 1956, 2.
4. Senghor, 'Rapport au Congrès de Cotonou', mimeographed document, Cotonou Congress of the PRA, 1958, p. 27
5. Senghor, 'Discours', *l'Unité Africaine*, 1 août 1959, 8.
6. Senghor in *Dakar-Matin*, 30 juin 1961, 3 (cols. 5–8) and 3 février 1962, 4 (col. 3), etc.
7. Senghor, *Liberté I*, p. 60. See also Senghor's articles in *Condition Humaine*, especially during the years 1952 and 1953.

8. Senghor, 'Il faut que la France entre dans l'Union Française', *Paris-Dakar*, 13 novembre 1952, 6.
9. See below for the problem of assimilation in the split with Lamine-Guèye. Morgenthau, op. cit., pp. 139–45, goes into the details of the split as to personalities, conflicts, etc. I will not repeat her observations in the hope that the reader will complement my study with her brilliant analysis.
10. See Morgenthau, op. cit., pp. 93 ff.
11. Jacques Rabemananjara, 'Le poète noir et son peuple', *Présence Africaine* 16, octobre–novembre 1957, 19.
12. Senghor, 'La critique des livres: *Le Pelerinage des Sources* par Lanza del Vasto', *l'Etudiant de la France d'Outre-mer* 5, janvier 1944, 15.
13. That is the opinion of Abdoulaye Ly, head of the legal opposition in Senegal and a 'non-orthodox Marxist'. See below, chapter 41, for the political criticisms of these 'materialists'.

CHAPTER TWENTY-EIGHT

1. Albert Memmi, *Portrait du Colonisé precédé du Portrait du Colonisateur* (Paris, Buchet-Chastel 1957) p. 41.
2. Guy Mollet, *Bilan et Perspectives Socialistes* (Paris, Plon 1958) p. 45.
3. Senghor, 'Il faut que la France entre dans l'Union Française', *Paris-Dakar*, 13 novembre 1952, 6.
4. xxx, 'Résolutions sur la politique générale des indépendants d'Outre-mer', *Condition Humaine*, 25 février 1953, 1–2.
5. Sékou Touré to De Gaulle, Speech of 25 August 1958 quoted by Jean Lacouture in *Cinq Hommes et la France* (Paris, Seuil 1961).
6. Senghor, 'Lettre de Londres', *l'A.O.F.* 23 mai 1947.
7. Senghor, 'Confédération et fédération', *Condition Humaine*, 14 avril 1956, 1–2.
8. Senghor, 'Il faut rebatir l'Union', *Paris-Dakar*, 31 mars 1955, 1 (col. 6).
9. Senghor, 'La Critique des livres: *le Pelerinage des Sources* par Lanza del Vasto', *l'Etudiant de la France d'Outre-mer* 5, janvier 1944, 15.
10. Senghor in *J.O.A.N.C.*, 11 avril 1946, 1714.
11. Senghor, 'L'avenir de la France...', 422.

CHAPTER TWENTY-NINE

1. Senghor, *Nationhood and the African Road to Socialism*, p. 9.
2. Senghor, *Nationhood*, p. 109.
3. Senghor to Hymans, letter of 22 October 1963.
4. Barrès, *Scènes*, 11, 250, 253.
5. Senghor, 'L'Union française, mission de la France' (analysis of Alduy's book), *Condition Humaine* 14, 5 octobre 1948, 1 (cols. 4–6). The book was prefaced by Guy Mollet, but it was less the book than the explanation made during the *Esprit* Congress which influenced Senghor. It is not necessary to detail the project because it only became Senghor's after the two men talked.
6. Senghor in *J.O.A.N.C.*, 11 Avril 1946, 1714.

7. For details see Morgenthau, op. cit., pp. 96–7.
8. Senghor quoted the federalist projects of R P F. *Député* Raymond Dronne in the 5th Congress of the B D S 3–5 July 1953. See Senghor, 'Rapport sur la méthode du parti: socialisme, fédération, religion', *Condition Humaine*, 18 juillet 1953, 2. See also *Condition Humaine*, 21 octobre 1953, 1.
9. Senghor, 'Il faut que...', p. 6.
10. Senghor in *J.O.A.N.*, 6 janvier 1953, 31.
11. Senghor in *J.O.A.N.*, 30 juin 1950, 5310.
12. X X X, 'Le programme des 10 M', *Paris-Dakar*, 9 juillet 1951, 6.
13. Senghor in *Paris-Dakar*, 10 novembre 1950, 2.
14. Senghor, 'Contre le courant centrifuge de l'état associé, une seule solution: la République Fédérale Française', *Marchés Coloniaux du Monde* 4 avril 1953, 1006.

CHAPTER THIRTY

1. This phrase was used to characterize the African policy of the M R P by Bruno de Saint-Victor in *Les Partis Politiques Français et l'Evolution de l'Afrique Noire sous la I Ve République* (unpublished manuscript in the library of the *Institut d'Etudes Politiques* of the University of Paris, 1960) p. 65.
2. Senghor, 'Pour une République Fédérale Française', *Le Monde*, 4 juillet 1953, 4 (cols. 1–2).
3. Senghor, 'Contre le courant centrifuge...', 1005–7. Also see Senghor in *J.O.A.N.*, 18 novembre 1953, 5429.
4. Senghor, 'Il faut rebatir l'union', *Paris-Dakar*, 31 mars 1955, 1 (col. 6–7).
5. Senghor, 'Contre le courant...', 1006.
6. Senghor in *Paris-Dakar*, 10 avril 1954, 6.
7. Senghor, 'L'avenir de la France dans l'Outre-mer', *Politique Etrangère* 4, août–octobre 1954, 420.
8. Senghor in *Paris-Dakar*, 17 février 1953, 3.
9. Senghor in *J.O.A.N.*, 30 novembre 1954, 5618.
10. Senghor in *Paris-Dakar*, 23 septembre 1957, 2 (col. 7).
11. Senghor, *Nationhood*, pp. 22–3.
12. Senghor, 'Pour une solution fédéraliste', *La Nef* 9, juin 1955, 148–61. See also an analysis of the article in B. de Saint-Victor, 'La réforme du Titre V I I I de la Constitution de 1946', Assn. Françse. de Science Politique, *Table Ronde de Mars 1959* (Mimeographed documents at Institut d'Etudes Politiques in Paris) p. 8. See also Senghor, 'Les nationalismes d'Outre-mer et l'avenir des peuples de couleur', *Le Mali*, 4 décembre 1959, 5–11.
13. Senghor in *Paris-Dakar*, 16 octobre 1946, 1.
14. Senghor, 'Pour une solution fédéraliste', pp. 148–61.
15. Senghor expressly quoted the article. See Senghor, *Nationhood*, p. 22.
16. See above, chapter 6 and below at the end of chapter 31.
17. Senghor in *Paris-Dakar*, 17 février 1953, 1.
18. Senghor, 'Appel', *Condition Humaine*, 5 octobre 1948, 2 (cols. 7–8).

19. Senghor, 'Pour une République Fédérale…', *Le Monde*, 4 juillet 1953, 4.
20. Interview with Senghor in *Paris-Dakar*, 30 août 1947, 1.
21. Senghor in *J.O.A.N.*, 17 juin 1954, 2996.
22. Senghor, 'Rapport…', *Condition Humaine*, 18, juillet 1953, 2.
23. Senghor in *J.O.A.N.*, 17 juin 1954, 2996.
24. Senghor, 'L'avenir de la France…', 422.
25. Senghor, *Nationhood*, p. 23, refers to the Girondins who were federalists and wished to maintain the provinces.

CHAPTER THIRTY-ONE

1. Senghor, 'Le destin de l'Afrique est conditionné par celui de l'Europe et inversement', *Paris-Dakar*, 22 décembre 1953, 8.
2. Louis-Jean Finot, 'Egalité des races', *Revue du Monde Noir* 1, novembre 1931, 5–6.
3. Senghor in *J.O.A.N.*, 9 juillet 1949, 4487.
4. Daniel de Bergevin, Editor-in-chief of *Paris-Dakar* in an interview with Senghor, 'L'Assemblée Européenne de Strasbourg et l'Union Française', *Paris-Dakar*, 6 septembre 1949, 1.
5. Senghor in *Paris-Dakar*, 9 janvier 1953, 1.
6. Senghor in *Paris-Dakar*, 16 mars 1953, 1.
7. Senghor in *J.O.A.N.*, 9 juillet 1949, 4488–9.
8. Senghor, 'Les voix et voie…', p. 219.
9. Senghor in *Paris-Dakar*, 9 janvier 1953, 6.
10. Senghor in *J.O.A.N.*, 9 juillet 1949, 4489. See also Senghor in *Paris-Dakar*, 31 mai 1954, 6.
11. Gouverneur Roland Pré to Minister of Overseas France, 'Rapport confidentiel' letter from Bobo-Dioulasso, 7 October 1952, p. 3. (Aujoulat Archives.)
12. Ibid., p. 3.
13. Senghor in *Paris-Dakar*, 15 février 1957, 4 (col. 6).
15. Senghor in *Paris-Dakar*, 10 novembre 1950, 2. See also Senghor in *Paris-Dakar*, 31 mai 1954, 6.
16. See for example Senghor, 'Les nationalismes d'Outre-mer et l'avenir des peuples de couleur', p. 9.
17. Senghor in *J.O.A.N.*, 18 novembre 1953, 5250.
18. 'parti unique' in the text. See Senghor in *Paris-Dakar*, 28 mars 1953, 6.
19. Touchard, 'L'Esprit…', 106.
20. Senghor in *Paris-Dakar*, 9 janvier 1953, 1.
21. Senghor, 'Le destin…', 8.

CHAPTER THIRTY-TWO

1. See above, at the end of chapter 16 for Senghor's hostility to the bourgeoisie of the towns. See also above, chapter 1, for the 'bourgeois' versus 'peasant' in Senghor's youth.
2. Maurice Delafosse, *Les Civilisations Négro-Africaines*, quoted by Hubert Deschamps in *Les Religions de L'Afrique Noire* (Paris, P.U.F. 1954) p. 5.

3. Léo Hamon, 'Introduction à l'étude des partis politiques de l'Afrique française', *Revue Juridique et Politique d'Outre-mer* 2, avril–juin 1959.

4. François Luchaire, 'Les grandes tendances de l'évolution politique en Afrique noire', *Revue Française de Science Politique* 9 (3), septembre 1959, 591.

5. Senghor, *Liberté I*, pp. 59–60.

6. Abdou Diouf, *L'Islam et la Société Ouoloff* (Paris, unpublished manuscript at the Institut des Hautes Etudes d'Outre-mer 1959) pp. 111–13.

7. Michel Villeneuve, 'Les Mourides' in *Le Plan pour le Sénégal établi par la C.I.N.A.M.* (Dakar, Grande Imprimerie Africaine, mimeographed, 1960) p. 1–5–(27).

8. Diouf, op. cit., pp. 112–13.

9. There are many examples of co-operation between modern and traditional leaders. In Mali, for example, political parties must come to terms with the powerful initiation society known as *Komo*. In Guinea and in the upper Ivory Coast, the R D A consolidated its hold by using a similar society, the *Poro*. (Balandier, *Afrique Ambigüe* (Paris, Plon 1957) p. 249.)

10. J. Suret-Canale, 'Les fondements sociaux de la vie politique africaine contemporaine', *Recherches Internationales* 11–12 (22) 1960, pp. 41–3.

11. *Paris-Dakar*, 26 novembre 1951 and 21 novembre 1951.

12. *Paris-Dakar*, 7 janvier 1953, 4 (visit of Grand Khalife to District officer).

13. F. Quesnot, 'Influence du Mouridisme sur le Tidjanisme' in Centre de Hautes Etudes Administratives sur l'Afrique et l'Asie Modernes, *Notes et Etudes sur l'Islam en Afrique Noire* (Paris, Peyronnet 1962) pp. 122–3.

14. Bourlon, 'Actualité des Mourides', *L'Afrique et l'Asie* 46, 2ème trimestre 1959, 25–6.

15. Pierre Duran, *Notes sur le Mouridisme* (Paris, unpublished manuscript at the Institut des Hautes Etudes d'Outre-mer, 1954) p. 68.

16. Bourlon, 'Actualité...', 26.

17. Villeneuve, 'Les Mourides', p. 1–5–(27).

18. See below, chapter 33, for the *Marabout's* role in changing Senghor's mind during the campaign for the French Community of 1958. See below, at the end of chapter 41 for the *Marabont's* role in the 1962 crisis.

19. Senghor, *Liberté I*, p. 32.

20. Senghor, 'Discours à Accra', *Paris-Dakar*, 16 février 1961, 6 (col. 3).

21. For a thorough study of the *Marabouts*, see Quesnot, op. cit., pp. 127–94. See below, chapters 33 and 41 for the consequences of Senghor's reliance on this sector.

CHAPTER THIRTY-THREE

1. Alioune Diop, 'Le congrès des écrivains et artistes noirs', *Paris-Dakar*, 27 octobre 1956, 4 (cols. 4–7).

2. Senghor, 'Culture et politique', *l'Unité* 4, 4 décembre 1956, 2.

3. Senghor, 'Rapport sur la doctrine et le programme du parti', Congrès Constitutif du PRA, juillet 1958, mimeographed documents, p. 27.
4. Senghor, 'Confédération et fédération', *Condition Humaine*, 14 avril 1956, 1–2.
5. Senghor in *Paris-Dakar*, 13 octobre 1956, 4 (col. 3).
6. Senghor, 'Rapport...', PRA mimeographed documents, 1958, p. 20.
7. Senghor in *J.O.A.N.*, 13 mai 1958, 2266–7.
8. Senghor, 'Discours au colloque de Cannes le 2 octobre 1959', *Paris-Dakar*, 10 octobre 1959, 1 (col. 4).
9. See *Travaux Preparatoires de la Constitution: Avis et Débats du Comité Consultatif Constitutionnel* (Paris, La Documentation Française 1960).
10. Robert Jumeaux 'Préface' in Sékou Touré *Guinée: Prélude à l'Indépendance* (Paris, Présence Africaine 1958) p. 7.
11. Diouf, op. cit., pp. 113–14. For a detailed analysis of the pressures exerted by France in favour of the *oui* see William J. Foltz, *From French West Africa to the Mali Federation* (New Haven, Yale 1965) pp. 91–5.
12. Interview with Senghor in *Le Regroupement* 7, février 1959, 3–4.
13. Senghor, 'Préface' to *Manuel du Militant U.P.S.* quoted in *l'Unité Africaine* 2, 28 novembre 1961, 2.
14. Senghor in *Paris-Dakar*, 23 janvier 1959, 1 (cols. 1–2).
15. Senghor in *Paris-Dakar*, 23 février 1959, 1 (col. 8).
16. Senghor to De Gaulle in *Le Monde*, 20 mars 1962, 8 (col. 4). See also Senghor, 'La vraie civilisation: un métissage culturel', *Notre République: Organe de l'U.N.R.-U.D.T.* 70, 22 février 1963, 6.

CHAPTER THIRTY-FOUR

1. Senghor, 'L'avenir...', 424.
2. Ibid., 424.
3. André Blanchet's interview with Senghor, *Paris-Dakar*, 10 octobre 1957, 2.
4. Interview with M. Espinasse, Conseiller Technique to the French Minister of National Defense, former assistant to Gaston Defferre at the Ministry of Overseas France, Paris, 19 octobre 1960.
5. Ibid.
6. Senghor, 'Le Deuxième Congrès de l'Afrique Occidentale', *l'A.O.F.*, 23 mai 1947, 1 (cols. 5–6).
7. Senghor (Ivory Coast visit) in *Paris-Dakar*, 14 septembre 1953, 6.
8. Senghor, 'Conférence au Rialto', *Paris-Dakar*, 7 novembre 1950, 1. See also interview of Senghor in *Paris-Dakar*, 10 novembre 1950, 2.
9. For a detailed analysis of the break see William J. Foltz' brilliant study, *From French West Africa to the Mali Federation* (New Haven, Yale 1965).
10. Foltz, op. cit., p. 183, used a misquoted speech of Senghor's at Oxford. Senghor did not 'group *federalism* together with colonization and capitalism', but rather *'feudalism'*.

CHAPTER THIRTY-FIVE

1. See above, chapter 28.
2. Senghor, *Liberté I*, p. 100 (1950 article).
3. Senghor, 'Message au Congrès Méditerranéen' (Florence, 1961 mimeo).
4. Maurice Delafosse, *Les Nègres* (Paris, Rieder 1927) p. 12.
5. Senghor, *Liberté I*, p. 33.
6. Ibid., p. 28.
7. See next chapter.
8. Senghor, *Liberté I*, p. 29.
9. Ibid., p. 29.
10. Barrès, *Scènes*, 11, p. 251.
11. Senghor, *Liberté I*, p. 29.
12. Ibid., pp. 29–30. See Delafosse, *Les Nègres*, p. 44.
13. Ibid., p. 30.
14. Ibid., p. 30.
15. Senghor, *Nationhood*, p. 120, or *Liberté I*, p. 275.
16. Senghor, *Liberté I*, p. 30. He quoted this work again in 1959, which shows the continuity of his thought. See *Liberté I*, p. 275.
17. Senghor, 'Rapport au 5ème Congrès du BDS', *Condition Humaine*, 18 juillet 1953, 6.
18. Senghor quoted Mounier in this respect, see Senghor, 'Marxisme et humanisme', *La Revue Socialiste* 19, mars 1948, 205, 215.
17. Emmanuel Mounier, *Oeuvres Tome I 1931–1939* (Paris, Seuil 1961) p. 278.
20. See Touchard's analysis, op. cit., p. 105. 'Au-delà' in French.
21. Senghor, 'Rapport moral', *Condition Humaine*, 28 mai 1952, 2.
22. See above, chapter 10.
23. Paul Thibaud, 'Le Colloque d'Orleans à mis en valeur le "Génie polyphonique" de Péguy', *Le Monde*, 16 septembre 1964, 10 (cols. 1–2).
21. Senghor, *Selected Poems*, p. 14. See above, chapter 14.
25. Senghor, *Liberté I*, pp. 30, 31.

CHAPTER THIRTY-SIX

1. See the wartime experience described by Georges Balandier, *Tous Comptes Faits: Roman* (Paris, Le Pavois 1947). For the classical statement of fascist doctrine see Alfredo Rocco, 'The political doctrine of fascism', *International Conciliation*, no. 223 (Oct. 1926) pp. 393–415. Many of Rocco's ideas bear a striking resemblance to those of Senghor.
2. Senghor, 'Eléments...', 277.
3. Senghor, 'Discours à Accra', *Paris-Dakar*, 16 février 1961, 6 (col. 3).
4. Senghor to Hymans, letter of 22 October 1963, p. 4.
5. Senghor, *Liberté I*, p. 101.
6. See Jean Lacroix, 'La philosophie: un nouveau Saint-Simonisme', *Le Monde*, 8–9 mars 1964, 14 (col. 1).
7. See Jean Bancal, 'Proudhon, prophète du 20ème siècle?', *Le Monde* 24–25 janvier 1965, 1 (cols. 4–6).

8. Barrès, *Scènes*, p. 251.
9. R.Fleury, 'Les partis politiques en AOF (1945–1958)', *Marchés Tropicaux du Monde*, 28 août 1958, 2037.
10. Senghor, *Liberté I*, p. 61.
11. Senghor, 'Les Négro-africains et l'Union Française', *Reveil* 201–2, 24–28 avril 1947, 3 (cols. 6–8).
12. See above, at the beginning of chapter 28.
13. Guy Mollet, 'Préface' in Roger Deniau, *Avec tes Défenseurs* (Paris, Edition de la Liberté 1947) p. 11.
14. Karl Marx, 'Lettre à Véra Zassoulitch du 8 mars 1881', published with a facsimile in Maximilien Rubel, 'Karl Marx et le Socialisme Populiste Russe', *La Revue Socialiste* 11, mai 1947, 544–59.
15. See the brilliant analysis of African Socialism by Ruth Schachter Morgenthau, 'African Socialism: Declaration of ideological independence', *Africa Report* 8 (5), May 1963, 4.
16. Senghor, 'Rapport sur la méthode du parti', *Condition Humaine* 37, 26 avril 1949, 2 (col. 4), and Senghor, 'Avec tes défenseurs', *Condition Humaine* 6, 10 mai 1948, 2 (col. 8).
17. Senghor, 'Message au Congrès Méditerranéen', Florence 12–25 mai 1961, mimeo, p. 4.
18. Senghor, 'Rapport...', *Condition Humaine* 37, 26 avril 1949, 2 (col. 4).
19. Senghor, 'La "doctrine" du BDS', *Condition Humaine* 101, 24 juin 1952, 1 (cols. 1–2).
20. Waclaw Lednicki, 'Pan-Slavism' in Feliks Gross, ed., *European Ideologies* (New York 1948) pp. 860, 863 (R.Gonella brought this to my attention).
21. Senghor, 'La "doctrine"...', op. cit.
22. For this importance of religion see the beginning of chapter 32 above.
23. Senghor, 'Marxisme et humanisme', *La Revue Socialiste* 19, mars 1948, 201.
24. Senghor, 'Rapport moral 5ème Congrès du BDS', *Condition Humaine*, 18 juillet 1953, 2–6.
25. B.de Saint-Victor, op. cit., pp. 17–18.
26. R.Delavignette quoted Monod (who quoted Teilhard) in his preface to Ousmane Soce's *Karim*. T.Monod also quoted Teilhard in an article in *Présence Africaine* in 1950.
27. Senghor to Hymans, letter of 22 October 1963.
28. Senghor, *Pierre Teilhard de Chardin et la Politique Africaine* (Paris, Seuil 1962) pp. 33–4. See also *Paris-Dakar*, 29 avril 1960, 6 (col. 7).
29. See Jean Lacroix, 'Une thèse de Mme Madaule: Teilhard et Bergson', *Le Monde*, 9–10 juin 1963, 13.
30. Senghor, 'Rapport Cotonou, juillet 1958', *Le Regroupement* 5, 1 novembre 1958, 4.
31. Roger Garaudy, *Perspectives de l'Homme ; Existentialisme, Pensée Catholique, Marxisme* (Paris, P.U.F. 1959) p. 196.
32. Senghor, 'L'avenir de la France...', 426.
33. Senghor, 'Message à Florence', mimeo, 1961.
34. Ibid.

CHAPTER THIRTY-SEVEN

1. See Aristide Zolberg's interesting commentary in William Friedland and Carl Rosberg, ed., *African Socialism* (Stanford 1964) pp. 113–27, and the volume of speeches published in 1963 by Présence Africaine under the title *Colloque du 3 au 8 décembre 1962*. These studies allow me to concentrate on Senghor's theories without analysing the 'African Socialist Movement' as a whole. See also Ernest Milcent, 'Prochain Colloque...', *Le Monde*, 23 novembre 1962, 20.

2. Senghor, 'Rapport', *Condition Humaine* 37, 26 avril 1949, 2.

3. Maximilien Rubel, 'Un inédit de Marx: le travail aliéné', *La Revue Socialiste* 8, février 1947, 154–68. See also the excellent analysis of African Socialism made by Georges Balandier and the members of the Section Afrique of the Paris *Fondation Nationale des Sciences Politiques*, 17 January 1961. (Mimeo at the library, 27 Rue St Guillaume, Paris.)

4. Senghor, 'Marxisme et humanisme', 201, 215–16.

5. Senghor, 'La "doctrine" du BDS', *Condition Humaine* 101, 24 juin 1952, 1.

6. Senghor, 'Le Bantou, l'argent, et la civilisation', *l'A.O.F.*, 15 juillet 1947, 2 (cols. 1–2). See also Senghor, *Pierre Teilhard*, p. 21.

7. Senghor, 'Nous disons: révolution, non révolte', *l'A.O.F.*, 21 février 1947, 1.

8. Barrès, *Scènes*, p. 86.

9. Senghor, *Pierre Teilhard*, p. 22.

10. Senghor, 'Nous disons: révolution, non révolte', *l'A.O.F.*, 21 février 1947, 1.

11. Senghor, 'Discours à la Chambre de Commerce de Cotonou', *Afrique Express* 33, 25 juillet 1962, 2.

12. Ibid., 2.

13. Ibid., 2.

14. Ibid.

15. Senghor, 'Rapport', *Condition Humaine* 37, 26 avril 1949, 2.

16. Senghor, 'La "doctrine" du BDS', 1 (cols. 1–2).

17. Senghor, *Pierre Teilhard*, pp. 24–5, 26.

18. Senghor, 'Rapport', *Condition Humaine* 37, 26 avril 1949, 2.

19. Senghor, 'La "doctrine" du BDS', 1.

20. Senghor *Pierre Teilhard*, p. 26.

21. Ibid., p. 26.

22. Published by Présence Africaine in 1958.

23. On the split see Pierre Biarnes, 'Un groupe de communistes pro-Chinois s'est constitué au Sénégal', *Le Monde*, 15 mai 1965, 5 (cols. 1–2).

24. Published by Présence Africaine in 1956.

25. Published by Présence Africaine in 1959.

26. Majemout Diop, *Contribution à l'Etude des Problèmes Politiques en Afrique Noire* (Paris, Présence Africaine 1958), p. 12.

27. For Senghor's denial see appendixes, Senghor to Hymans, letter of 5 December 1964.

28. Senghor, 'Rapport', *Condition Humaine* 37, 26 avril 1949, 2 (col. 1).

29. The PSU (Parti Socialiste Unifié) is situated at the extreme left,

but falls short of the Communist Party's position. The *Observateur*, formerly *France-Observateur* is close to that group.

CHAPTER THIRTY-EIGHT

1. According to the expression used by Georges Balandier in 'Diversités et inégalités mondiales', *Monde Uni* 28–29, octobre 1959, 7.
2. See the analysis in the article 'Congrès Constitutif du PFA', *Présence Africaine* 32–33, juin–septembre 1960, 202.
3. See G. Balandier, 'Les mythes politiques de colonisation et de décolonisation en Afrique', *Cahiers Internationaux de Sociologie* 23, juillet–décembre 1962, 95–6.
4. Balandier, 'Diversités...', 7.
5. See J. Ki-Zerbo *et. al.*, *Manifeste du Mouvement Africain de Libération Nationale: Libérons l'Afrique – Etats-Unis d'Afrique Noire, Socialisme Africaine* (Paris, Imprimerie du Courier du Commerce 1958) pp. 8–9, 10–12.
6. Senghor, 'Rapport', *Condition Humaine* 37, 26 avril 1949, 2.
7. *Plan du Sénégal: Rapport Général* (1ère partie, Chapître 7: Facteurs humains du développement) p. 1–7–(6).
8. Senghor, 'Comment nous sommes...', 17.
9. Senghor in *J.O.A.N.*, 30 juin 1950, 5310.
10. Senghor, 'Nous disons...', loc. cit.
11. Senghor, 'Rapport', *Condition Humaine* 54, 2 mai 1950, 1–2.
12. Senghor, 'Rapport', *Condition Humaine*, 18 juillet 1953, 2, 6.
13. Senghor, *Liberté I*, p. 60.
14. Senghor, 'La Côte d'Ivoire ou l'avenir...', *Condition Humaine*, 21 février 1950, 2. See also Senghor in *J.O.A.N.*, 27 novembre 1950, 81, 82.
15. Albert-Paul Lentin, 'Le Sénégal dans la solitude', *Libération*, 28 mars 1961, 6.
16. Senghor, 'La "doctrine" du BDS', *Condition Humaine*, 24 juin 1952, 1.
17. Senghor, *Liberté I*, pp. 59–60.
18. Senghor in *J.O.A.N.C.*, *Commission de la Constitution*, 26 février 1946, 452.
19. Senghor, *Liberté I*, p. 53.
20. Senghor, 'Réponse au nonce', *Dakar-Matin*, 3 février 1962, 4 (col. 3). See also Senghor in *Paris-Dakar*, 16 février 1961, 6 (col. 3).
21. Senghor in *Dakar-Matin*, 25 avril 1961, 3 (cols. 5–7).

CHAPTER THIRTY-NINE

1. Senghor in *Paris-Dakar*, 21 octobre 1952, 1.
2. Senghor in *Paris-Dakar*, 18 février 1952, 1.
3. For an exhaustive scholarly study of the history of Senghor's party see Ruth Schachter Morgenthau's *Political Parties in French-Speaking West Africa* (Oxford 1964). See p. 152 for her statement on peanuts.
4. See, for example, *J.O.A.N.*, 8 avril 1954, 1911; *J.O.A.N.*, 4 mars 1954, 643.

5. Senghor, 'Les négro-africains et l'Union Française', *Reveil*, 24–28 avril 1947, 3 (cols. 6–8).
6. Senghor in *J.O.A.N.C.*, 5 avril 1946, 1534.
7. Senghor, 'Défense de l'Afrique noire', 248.
8. Senghor in *Paris-Dakar*, 15 décembre 1952, 2.
9. Senghor in *Paris-Dakar*, 19 février 1954, 1.
10. B. de Saint-Victor, op. cit., pp. 10–11.
11. Senghor, 'Rapport sur la politique générale: IVème Congrès de l'UPS' (Dakar, mimeo, octobre 1963) p. 4. It is interesting that during the 'colonial period', Senghor adhered to the French myth that colonialism had ended after World War II. In the 1960s he reversed this position.
12. Senghor, 'Rapport à Cotonou' (Cotonou, mimeo, 1958) p. 29.
13. Senghor in *J.O.A.N.C.*, 21 mars 1946, 945.
14. Senghor 'Rapport sur la politique générale: IVème Congrès de l'UPS' (Dakar, mimeo, 1963) pp. 4–5.
15. IRFED, *Le Sénégal en Marche: Le Plan de Développement* (Malines, Belgium, Editions Créations de Presse: Cahiers Africains no. 5, 1962) p. 23.
16. Ibid., p. 39. For a discussion of *Animation Rurale* in Senegal, see David Hapgood, *Africa: from Independence to Tomorrow* (New York, Atheneum 1965) pp. 113–33.
17. Albert-Paul Lentin, 'Le Sénégal dans la solitiude', loc. cit.
18. XXX, 'Sénégal: retour de la confiance...', *Le Moniteur Africain du Commerce et de l'Industrie* 64, 22 décembre 1962, 1. (The director of this publication is Pierre Biarnes, also correspondent of Paris' *Le Monde* in Dakar. Recent articles on Senegal in *Le Monde* therefore appear less revealing than when Ernest Milcent or Philippe Decraene reported.)
19. Senghor, 'L'Union française, mission de la France', *Condition Humaine* 14, 5 octobre 1948, 3 (col. 1) and Senghor in *Paris-Dakar*, 29 mars 1952, 2.

CHAPTER FORTY

1. See Senghor, 'Fédération et industrialisation', *Condition Humaine*, 27 janvier 1955, 1 (cols. 1–2), and Mamadou Dia in *Paris-Dakar*, 29 juillet 1958, 1 (cols. 3–4).
2. Senghor in *Condition Humaine* 37, 26 avril 1949, 2 (col. 4).
3. Senghor, 'Rapport', *Condition Humaine* 99, 28 mai 1952, 1. See also Senghor, *Nationhood*, p. 77.
4. IRFED, op. cit., p. 117.
5. Senghor, 'Rapport: IVème Congrès de l'UPS' (Dakar, mimeo, 1963) p. 68.
6. Senghor, 'Dément catégoriquement...', *Paris-Dakar*, 19 octobre 1956, 1.
7. Ibid., 1. This was a response to Touzard (President of the Chamber of Commerce of Saint-Louis-du-Sénégal) and Touzard's speech voicing the apprehensions of the business community. For that speech see *Paris-Dakar*, 4 octobre 1956, 1.

8. Senghor, 'Rapport au Congrès de Cotonou' (Cotonou, mimeo, 1958) p. 30.
9. Mamadou Dia at Cotonou, *Paris-Dakar*, 29 juillet 1958, 1.
10. xxx, 'Sénégal: retour de la confiance', *Moniteur Africain*, 1. This is the equivalent of $167,600,000 out of $368,000,000.
11. See René Dumont, *L'Afrique Noire est Mal Partie* (Paris, Seuil 1962) pp. 231–6.

CHAPTER FORTY-ONE

1. I. Potekhin, 'Observations sur le "Socialisme Africain"', *La Nouvelle Critique* 126, mai 1961, 128.
2. Ibid., 129.
3. I. Potekhin, 'On African socialism: a Soviet view', in Friedland and Rosberg, eds., *African Socialism* (Stanford 1964) pp. 97–112.
4. I. Potekhin, 'African Socialism', *The African Communist*, October–November 1964, 32 ff. See also pp. 14 and 46.
5. Parti Africain de l'Indépendance, 'Sénégal: le programme du PAI'. *France Nouvelle: Hebomadaire Central du Parti Communiste Français*, 880, 29 août–4 septembre 1962, 19.
6. Ibid., 19.
7. Will MacLorin, 'La bourgeoisie sénégalaise dans la condition du néocolonialisme', *La Nouvelle Revue Internationale: Problèmes de la Paix et du Socialisme*, octobre 1962, p. 32. See also xxx, 'Sénégal and the African Party of Independence', *The African Communist* 2 (3), April–June 1963, 49.
8. Will MacLorin, op. cit., pp. 45–6.
9. Ibid., p. 39.
10. René Ménil, 'Une doctrine réactionnaire: La négritude', 41, 42, 48.
11. Franklin, p. 303.
12. Ibid., p. 289.
13. Ruth Schachter Morgenthau, 'African socialism: declaration of ideological independence', *Africa Report* 8 (5), May 1963, 3–4.
14. Ibid., 5.
15. Paul Thibaud, 'Document: Dia, Senghor, et le socialisme africain', *Esprit* 320, septembre 1963, 339.
16. Mamadou Dia, *Nations Africaines et Solidarité Mondiale* (Paris: P.U.F. 1960) p. 111 (translation available published by Praeger).
17. Thibaud, 'Document: Dia...', 343.
18. Pierre Biarnes, 'L'economie sénégalaise...', *Le Monde*, 28 février–1 mars 1965, 5 (cols. 3–5).
19. Senghor, 'négritude et civilisations greco-latine ou démocratie et socialisme', lecture given at Strasbourg, 20 November 1964, mimeo, p. 31. (Given to me by President Senghor during his visit to Paris in 1964.)
20. Senghor to Hymans, letter of 22 October 1963, pp. 2–3.
21. Aimé Césaire, *Lettre à Maurice Thorez* (Paris, Présence Africaine 1956) pp. 12–13.
22. Khar N'Dofène Diouf and Habib Thiam, 'Lettre ouverte à M. Jean-Marie Domenach, Directeur de la Revue *Esprit*', *l'Unité Africaine* 82, 30 janvier 1964, 13 (col. 1). Both authors are members of the

Senegalese government. This letter was reproduced in a subsequent issue of *Esprit*.

CONCLUSION

1. *Livre Blanc sur les Elections Présidentielles et Législatives du 1er Décembre 1963* (Dakar, Ministère de l'Intérieur du Sénégal 1964).
2. See Senghor, *Liberté I*, pp. 25, 47–54.
3. Georges Balandier, 'Les mythes politiques de colonisation et de décolonisation en Afrique', *Cahiers Internationaux de Sociologie* 23, juillet–décembre 1962, 95–6.
4. Senghor, 'La France et nous', *Le Monde*, 8 juin 1965, 9 (cols. 1–4).

Appendix I

A Short Chronology of Léopold Sédar Senghor's Life

1906 Born at Joal, Senegal
1906–28 Youth in Africa: becomes an Acculturated African
1913 Attended Catholic school at Ngasobil, having spent
    seven years of his life with the peasants from whom he
    learned traditional wisdom
1920 Attended Libermann Seminary in Dakar, having been
    assimilated by his Catholic schooling; Catholic in-
    fluences: Saint Thomas Aquinas
1925 Attended Dakar *Cours Complémentaire* (*Lycée* level
    training), after being dropped from the Catholic
    Seminary
1928 Through influence of one of his teachers obtained
    scholarship to continue literary studies in France
1928–40 Higher education and teaching in France
1928 October: Arrived in France; attended prestigious *Lycée
    Louis-le-Grand* in Paris; read Paul Claudel and Charles
    Péguy
1929 Friendship with present President of France, Georges
    Pompidou, his fellow student; began reading Barrès
    which led to the theory of a return to African-Negro
    sources: the cult of Ancestors and the Soil; met Blaise
    Diagne, *Député* of Senegal
1930 Failed oral exam for entry to *Ecole Normale Supérieure*;
    reaction against Western Civilization; read Bergson
1931 Worked with *Revue du Monde Noir* West Indians: im-
    portant influences on his cultural thought. Paris Colonial
    Exhibition helped rehabilitate African Negro culture;
    enthusiasm for Negro arts in Paris. Licencié ès lettres
1934 President of the Association of West African Students;
    developed theory of cultural cross-breeding; read
    American Negro poets. Friendship with Aimé Césaires
1935 Obtained *Agrégation* degree in Grammar; became a
    naturalized Frenchman; influence of Governor Robert
    Delavignette's theories

1936	Compulsory military service in French army; read ethnographers, especially Frobenius, published in French in that year
1936	Taught at *Lycée Descartes* in Tours (Loire Valley); joined *Front Populaire* groups; activity in teachers' union; first poems with Africa as central subject
1937	Vacation spent in Africa; gave speech on 'Let us assimilate, not be assimilated' in Dakar; asked to head French West Africa's school system by *Front Populaire* Governor -General; refused and returned to France
1938	*Professeur* in *Lycée* in suburban Paris; continued study of ethnology by attending courses at the Sorbonne
1939	Published essay 'What the Negro Contributes'
1940–4	*World War II*
1940	Military service; captured at La-Charité-sur-Loire; prisoner of the Germans; met Eboué brothers and Senegalese peasants in the *stalags*
1942	Released from camp; returned to teaching at Paris suburban *Lycée*
1943	Wrote in overseas students' *Bulletin* sponsored by the Vichy government; meetings at the *Foyer Impérial* in Paris with Abdoulaye Ly, S. M. Apithy, Alioune Diop, etc.
1943–4	Wrote essay for *La Communauté Impériale Française*; resistance activities
1945–60	*Towards the Presidency*
1945	Published essay in *Communauté Impériale Française*; named by Governor Robert Delavignette *Professeur* at *Ecole Coloniale* (school for training colonial officials). May: named to Monnerville Commission which studied colonial representation for future Constitutional Assemblies September: returned to Africa; decided to campaign along with Lamine-Guèye to obtain a seat in the Constituent Assembly; published first volume of poems *Chants d'Ombre* October: elected by the subjects of the interior to the French Assembly
1946	Worked in *Commissions de la Constitution* (for both the April and October Constitutions of the French Fourth Republic; decided not to go to Bamako R D A Congress, remaining a faithful member of the Senegalese branch of the French Socialist Party (S F I O); married Ginette

Eboué, daughter of former Negro Governor-General of French Equatorial Africa; read Socialist theorists: Proudhon, Saint-Simon, Fourier, Marx, Engels, etc.

1947   Disagreements with Lamine-Guèye and the SFIO.

1948   March: started publishing a separate weekly, *Condition Humaine*
September: left SFIO to found BDS (*Bloc Démocratique Sénégalais*) joined IOM (*Indépendants d'outre-mer*) group, allied with Catholic MRP in French Parliament; formulated theory of 'African Socialism'; formulated theory of Federal French Republic; Jean-Paul Sartre's 'Black Orpheus' systematized *négritude* theory in Senghor's *Anthologie* (of New Negro and Malgasy Poetry in French)

1949   Elected to European Assembly at Strasbourg; began European unity battle; Senghor anti-nationalist and for great intercontinental federations, Eurafrica.

1951   BDS won both Senegalese seats in the French National Assembly; Senghor's action in extending the vote to the people in the interior helped give his party grass roots support; mobilization of aid from Muslim *Marabouts*

1955   Member of Edgar Faure Government in France; continued to refuse independence and to work for a Federal French Republic

1956   Senghor's inter-territorial group lost in elections; meteoric rise of the RDA; Houphouet-Boigny in French Government replacing Senghor; Senghor in opposition to Houphouet-Boigny and SFIO (Mollet) Government's *Loi-Cadre* granting autonomy to each territory; rivalry Senegal–Ivory Coast.

1957   Continued battle against Houphouet-Boigny and *Loi-Cadre*; more progressive tendency in BDS, which changed name to BPS. Marriage to second wife, Colette

1958   De Gaulle proposals for French Community; Houphouet for Federation, Senghor for Confederation
September: Senghor decided to vote *oui* to Constitution at last minute under French and local pressures (*Marabouts*); split in party, the 'left' leaves to form PRA–S.

1959   Foundation of Mali Federation; movement towards confederalism in French Community because of Sékou Touré's *non* and Guinean independence; renewal of theory of African Socialism

1960   Break-up of Mali Federation; Senghor President of
            Senegal in September; worked with Mamadou Dia in
            a tandem

1960–70   President of Senegal

1962   Pressures from Senegalese middle-class and European
            capitalists caused December crisis and revision of Plan,
            slowing up of African Socialism; Dia imprisoned;
            Senghor took over as head of government

1963   Electoral crisis; imprisonment of Abdoulaye Ly,
            leader of legal opposition
            Senghor continually attempted to bring African nations
            together in loose confederal groupings; less emphasis
            on federalism in West Africa; increasing restrictions
            on opposition parties; less emphasis on French
            Community

1965   April: Abdoulaye Ly released from prison, showing
            Senghor's moderation *vis-à-vis* opposition

1966   April: Festival of Negro Arts in Dakar: apotheosis of
            négritude

1970   Recreates the position of Prime Minister and appoints
            Abdou Diouf to the post

Appendix II

Le Président de la République no. / 1413 / pr / sp
République du Sénégal
Un Peuple – Un But – Une Foi

Dakar, le 22 octobre 1963

Cher Monsieur,

I have received your long letter.

I am very willing to give you the information that you request.

(1) I have written few letters which can inform you, usefully, on the evolution of my ideas, of my doctrine. In fact, my love letters could not contribute very much, and they are private.

It is a fact that I have always preferred expressing my ideas in lectures, essays, or articles rather than in letters.

(2) You are right to insist on the influence of Jacques Maritain on me. This influence of Maritain came between 1932 and 1940. To him it is necessary to add, as you have done, Pierre Teilhard de Chardin. I began to read Teilhard de Chardin in 1950, and especially in 1955 with the publication of his works by my publisher, Pierre Flamand, 'Editions du Seuil'.

(3) Certainly, Emmanuel Mounier, with the *Revue Esprit*, also influenced me, but less than Maritain and Teilhard de Chardin.

I must observe that, since Mounier's death, the management of the *Revue Esprit* has greatly deteriorated. Even now, I am in conflict with it. It is the same problem which turned me against the French left-wing. In fact, it is still not decolonized. It secretes a mixture of 'Jacobin' spirit and missionary spirit, typically French. This left-wing wants to impose its *maîtres à penser* on us; above all, it refuses to let us think by ourselves. On the contrary, my ambition has always been to use the intellectual instruments supplied by my French masters to seek my own way.

(4) The influence of Aujoulat was nil on me. On the contrary, Robert Delavignette greatly helped me to discover the virtues of intellectual cross-breeding.

(5) You write: 'In 1945, you opted for the left-wing. Is it again Mounier's decision which influenced you here?'

In fact, I opted for the left-wing about 1930. It was the year that I lost my Catholic faith. I had been profoundly struck by the gulf which existed between the doctrine and the life of European Christians, between Christ's word and the acts of the Christians.

It was Georges Pompidou, present French Prime Minister, who converted me to socialism. He was my best friend in the *Lycée Louis-le-Grand*. In 1931, when I entered the Sorbonne, I became a member of the *Etudiants Socialistes*. It was natural that, elected *Député* in 1945, I be a member of the SFIO Socialist group.

(6) I never read *L'Ordre Nouveau*; but, I began, in 1946, to read the works of the French utopians – Fourier and Proudhon. They converted me to the ideas of federation and co-operation. But, I read above all, starting that year, Marx and Engels.

(7) I read Barrès very early, in the class of *Première Supérieure* at the *Lycée Louis-le-Grand*, under the influence of Georges Pompidou. This was in 1929. It was Barrès who helped me in my search for authenticity and *négritude*.

(8) I did not read the book by Roger Deniau. It was in Marx that I found the theory of the *mir*.

(9) I became impregnated with dialectic thought by reading Marx and Engels at the same time: that is to say in 1945–6.

Here, very simply, *cher Monsieur*, are the answers I can give to your questions.

I am sending you, by the same mail, my lecture entitled *Théorie et Pratique du Socialisme Sénégalais** and my last *Rapport* to the Fourth Congress of the UPS entitled *Planification et Tension Morale*.

Believe, *cher Monsieur*, in the assurance of my best sentiments.

Léopold Sédar Senghor

P.S. I enclose a bibliography.

Le Président de la République   no./1261/pr/sp
                                          Dakar le 11 septembre 1964
Cher Monsieur,

I have received your letter of 5 September 1964. I should have been very moved by your letter had you not, at the same time, pronounced some severe judgments.

On this last point, reassure yourself. As you may imagine, I receive almost every day by the *Argus de la Presse* a parcel of criticisms of my policies or my poetry. Consequently, I have accustomed myself to receive the most severe criticisms with

* The lecture Senghor mentions has been translated and published in the recent edition of Senghor's social writings: Senghor *On African Socialism* (New York, Praeger 1964).

equanimity. It is an excellent way to keep cool-headed and to prevent taking oneself for God the Father.

What moves me is the interest you have taken in my life and my work and the place I have taken in your thought and research. You see, I am now aware of new responsibilities, and I worry about not deceiving you.

I probably will receive the manuscript that you mention. In fact, packages arrive, always, after letters. You can be sure that I will read your work with the greatest attention. I will not fail, after reading it, to let you know what I think.

Reassure yourself, once again, that when someone submits to me a critical study about myself, I only worry about establishing the facts. As Monsieur Beuve-Méry, Director of *Le Monde*, has said: 'facts are sacred; commentary is free'. Once facts are solidly established, the critic can only enrich the writer by revealing to him certain aspects of his personality, of which he himself, the writer, was unaware.

Be assured, *cher Monsieur*, of the expression of my very attentive sentiments.

Léopold Sédar Senghor

Le Président de la République   no. / 1324/pr/sp
Dakar le 7 octobre 1964

Cher Monsieur,

On my return from Brazil, I found the manuscript of your thesis awaiting me.

I have gone through it, rapidly it is true. Your manuscript interested me greatly and, believe me, nothing shocked me. It is true that nowadays writers or political figures cry that they are insulted when they are not given the epithet of 'genius'.

I intend to read your manuscript, clear-headedly, during the week I will spend in France, at the end of November. I will then be able to write to you more pertinently.

Accept, *cher Monsieur*, the assurance of my *sympathique* sentiments.

Léopold Sédar Senghor

Le Président de la République   no. / 1620 / pr / sp
                                               Dakar, le 5 décembre 1964

Cher Monsieur,

As I promised you during our last meeting on 24 November
1964, I intend to impart, in a written form, my reflections on your
thesis entitled: *'L'Elaboration de la Pensée de Léopold Sédar Senghor:
Esquisse d'un Itinéraire intellectuel'.*

Do not expect me to convey, precisely, value judgments on
your thesis. When critics consult me on their work, I have the
habit of making observations bear more on facts than on ideas. As
says Hubert Beuve-Méry, Director of *Le Monde*: 'Facts are sacred;
commentary is free'.

I wish, nonetheless, to tell you, by means of introduction, how
much I was struck by the extent of your information. You have
read prodigiously and you have interviewed an amazing number
of persons.

That said, I believe the major outline of your thesis to be very
accurate; more exactly, its main threads or, if you prefer, its
idées-forces.

The introduction and the conclusion of your thesis are excellent
because they contain what is essential. Indeed my personality, as
much as I can see clearly into it, is dominated by certain biological
and sociological factors, that you have excellently analysed at the
beginning of your work. Indeed, I was first, by my family and in
the sociological context of my childhood and my adolescence, a
torn being: torn between my father's family and my mother's family,
between family education and the scholarly disciplines imported
from Europe. You wrote excellent things on that and there is no
need for me to go over them.

I believe, equally, that your conclusion is very accurate. Indeed,
if I have some originality, it is less in the ideas that I have expressed than in the synthesis, rather, the *symbiosis* which I have
made of them. That takes care of my compliments.

Surely, I do not only have compliments to make, even if I hold
myself strictly to the level of *facts*. It is very natural, you are young,
you have not yet a long experience with men, and you are writing
a *thesis*.

A thesis, it is the genre which wills it, must be balanced to
respond to the wishes of those 'dear professors'. There should be
neither too much praise, nor too many criticisms.

The author who is the object of the thesis must be neither a
'genius', nor an imbecile, neither a pure creator, nor a pure
imitator.

The defects of your thesis seem to me to be of two kinds. Firstly, you have systematized your 'hypothesis' too much, to make of it, really, a 'thesis', thus a postulate more than a reality. In the second place, you have attributed to me certain moral attitudes which the facts contradict and which are, after all, in contradiction with the moral picture you painted of me elsewhere.

I. I indicated to you the influences to which I had been exposed. In truth, when I reflect on the matter, I discover that I exaggerated these influences a bit, this being true particularly of Barrès, of Price-Mars, of Bergson, of Saint-Simon. In any case, you were mistaken to add to them other influences: Etienne Léro, Alioune Diop, Abdoulaye Ly, not to mention the MRP group and the Socialist group.

In the first place, the living have always influenced me very little. Most of the time, they served me as a *reagent*, if not as a repellent. My natural movement has been to define myself with respect to them. Among the living, the only real influence that I might have undergone was that of Emmanuel Mounier.

To remain in the domain of the living, I will take the example of Etienne Léro and of *Légitime Défense*. What was our *reaction* – for it was more rightly a matter of reaction to than of accepting their influence? *Légitime Défense* drew our attention to the problem of surrealism and to that of the primacy of politics. But, if we were induced to read the surrealists more attentively, the attitude of *Légitime Défense* led us, at the same time, to read them with a critical eye and in a defensive position. And because Léro and Ménil affirmed: 'Politics first', we were pushed by temperament, and to distinguish ourselves, to respond: 'Culture first'.

As for Abdoulaye Ly, he couldn't influence me for the good reason that, being my junior, he always considered me as the more or less secret adversary whom it was necessary to bring to the ground. And then, he was a very bad Minister, who had aggravated the deficit of the co-operatives. As for his revolutionary attitude, it was not until 1958 that he openly demanded 'immediate independence', which at that moment no longer presented any danger.

I have said above that my originality, as you say, consisted less in the novelty of the ideas expressed than in the symbiosis of these ideas. I believe that it is true, although in such matters, one can say the same thing of all creators. It is La Bruyère who observed that, already two thousand years ago, everything had been said. And it is Musset who responded to his critics by this quip: 'Even in planting cabbages you, are imitating someone.'

That said, I believe we furnished something new in defining
négritude, that is to say the values of civilization which are those
of the Negro world. Thus, in linguistics I discovered, in the
languages of the Sénégalo-Guinean Group, a means of economy
and of replacement which I have called *l'expéditif*. Thus again, as
I had occasion to tell you in person, all ethnologists and
Africanists that I had read denied that there might be an 'African
Negro Poetry', that is to say a properly African *prosodie* and
métrique, that is to say that a mathematical formulation could be
given to each African Negro poem – at least in the languages of
the Sénégalo-Guinean Group. You will find the brief demonstration of it in my article entitled: '*Langage et Poésie Négro-Africaine*'
(*Liberté I*, pp. 159–73).

Starting with African Negro *prosodie* and *métrique*, I renewed my
analysis, now studying the related arts: sculpture, painting,
music, dance. I then observed, concretely, that all African Negro
arts presented the same characteristic traits. These can be resumed
in the formula: 'Unity in diversity' or 'harmonious *ensemble* of
parallelisms and asymmetrics which translates the system of vital
forces into rhythmic images'. (cf. in *Liberté I* the article entitled:
'*L'Esthetique Négro-Africaine*'.)

However, before analysis confirmed my hypothesis, I had already
had the intuition. It has almost always been so, my readings nourish
my intuitions. And if I have made use of quotations, it is, most
often, less to give me new ideas than by a professor's habit and to
confirm intuitions or experiences already lived. After my discovery
of African Negro *prosodie* and *métrique*, I entered into a lengthy
correspondence with Reverend Father Tournay, Professor of
Assyro-Babylonian at the Biblical University of Jerusalem, to find
a confirmation of my discoveries in the comparison with the old
languages of the Near East. *Négritude* was such a scandalous thing
in the years 1932–1933 that it was necessary for us to present it as
a phenomenon which was not 'monstrous', but normal.

And then, you should have investigated the very idea of the
symbiosis: in studying more profoundly, that is to say, by analysing,
with more precision, the phenomenon of symbiosis. You have
done so with relevance, nevertheless. But in pushing the analysis
further, you would have discovered that the elements of the
symbiosis cannot be reduced to the elements which compose it; in
other words, that the half-breed or the fruit of grafting is not
simply the addition of the component elements, but something
new. You should have pushed the analysis even further and showed
that, if there is influence, this is neither *linear*, nor one-sided, but

ambiguous and *dialectic*. The influence does not act by action, but
by reaction. Faced with an influence, I have always assimilated
what resembled me and rejected what was contrary to my nature.
I have the impression, I have the sentiment, that my personality
was shaped when I was twenty and Father Lalouse, Director of
the *Collège*-Seminary Libermann, told me that priesthood was not
my vocation. Indeed, in the Seminary I had become a sort of
Secretary-General of black seminarists. I obstinately combated
the insinuations of Father Lalouse who wished to make us believe
that our parents were 'savages' and that we had no civilization.
By family tradition, I felt confusedly that this was false, that we
had an original civilization. In short, all the influences that I
subsequently accepted were those which tended to confirm me in
my conviction, and I have always rejected influences which were
contrary. You see that it is the very notion of *influence* that you
should have penetrated more deeply by discussing it.

II. But what really shocked me, I confess to you, are the moral
judgments, which facts and the portrait of my personality that
you paint elsewhere contradict.

(a) You write: 'Another goal of this group might have been the
search for equality. Senghor says that certain Negroes tried to
have themselves accepted by white society by exalting Negro values. It is
possible that this attitude was his during a certain period'. I find
the hypothesis somewhat insulting. But that is not the most serious
matter. It contradicts the facts because, since my years at the *Lycée*,
I have always been accepted, without any reticence, by white
society. Although I do not like to make confidences, the one or
two amorous deceptions of which one of your informers spoke
did not come from white society, but from black society. As I
have said elsewhere – and you have reproduced my words – in
this period of exalting *négritude* I found the white woman to be
savourless.

(b) You write: 'He *says* he entered the clandestine CGT and the
Front National Universitaire. In this capacity he *says* he successively
hid in his apartment Jews, then a sniper pursued by the Gestapo.
His apartment served at the same time, according to Senghor, as
a depot for explosive bombs'.

My dear Sir, since you wrote the French Prime Minister and he
answered you, you could have, not granting faith to my words,
asked him about the facts that you mention and that you doubt.

Indeed, I was decorated with the 'Medal of Franco-Allied
Recognition' and I have membership in the 'Association of Former
Voluntary Combatants for the Resistance'. The Prime Minister

could have had you let into the Chancellery or Office of the 'Association of Former Voluntary Combatants for the Resistance' where there are certificates showing I belonged in fact to the Resistance.

For more precision, I did not hide 'Jews', but a young woman, who was, at the same time, Jewish, Communist, and of Russian origin. Her maiden name was Ella Raitz. She is now Madame Rivière, having married Marcel Rivière, nephew of Jacques Rivière, whose sister, Marie-France Rivière, works at the Office of French Radio and Television. In addition, I sheltered at my house, for several weeks, Manuel Bridier, whose Resistance pseudonym was 'Fontaine', and who has insulted me quite a bit these last two years in *France-Observateur* under the pseudonym of Braundi. He had, in fact, brought to my apartment a case of nitroglycerine bombs. I took the case to the Police *Commissariat* of the 12th *Arrondissement* near the City-Hall, after the Liberation of Paris.

I am surprised at your doubt, for all these affirmations are easily verifiable, and I regret that you didn't verify them.

(c) You write: 'But the crisis of December 1962 seems to shed more light on the functioning of the Plan than the studies written about it. In this vein it is absolutely indispensable to read the article inspired by the planners who left Senegal after Mamadou Dia's fall and written by Paul Thibaud... The response of the Senegalese Government does not seem to invalidate very many facts reported by Thibaud'.

Here, my dear Sir, you are greatly in error. To convince you, I will send you in a few days the text of the controversy which opposed us to the *Revue Esprit*, texts which are preceded by an *Introduction*. The *Rapport sur la Conjoncture Economique au Sénégal*, which I gave you, proves abundantly that I have not been the 'valet of the Capitalists' as you suggest following Paul Thibaud. Not only has the *Office du Commercialisation Agricole* not been suppressed by me, but its structures have been reinforced and its competence extended.

I am also sending you my *Rapport* to the last Congress of the UPS which will inform you, more than Thibaud's article, on the difficulties of planning the economy in Senegal.

And then those who inspired Thibaud's article are not former planners. Father Lebret, who is the real planner, is still working for the Government. As for Messrs. Chagneau and Baillache, the two 'informers', the first had already left Senegal before December 17, 1962. As for the second, he wished to remain to 'serve' me. It is I who thanked him.

Above all, do not believe, *cher Monsieur*, that I hold a grudge against you for the three last not-too-favourable judgments that you made concerning me. You have been a bit the victim of your youth and of the intoxication of the falsely-leftist milieux of Paris. African Socialism cannot be accomplished in Paris, in the editorial offices of newspapers, but in Africa in the middle of the difficulties that three hundred years of the Negro slave trade and colonization have willed to us.

It remains that your thesis, once again, is accurate in its major lines of thought. Despite the few defects that I have noted, it is a remarkably informative work, written with a remarkable will to be objective.

Let my letter not discourage you, but encourage you in your knowledge of Africa.

I remain at your disposal, in the future, for any information you might have need of on Senegal.

Believe, *cher Monsieur*, the assurance of my very attentive sentiments.

Léopold Sédar Senghor

P.S. I enclose

1e A technical note from Father Lebret dated 11 March 1964.

2e A note from the IRFED on the preparation of the Second Plan.

3e A personal letter from Father Lebret (10 March 1964).

4e A letter from me to Father Lebret.

5e My *Rapport* to the last Congress.

Appendix III

Le Premier Ministre   *Paris, le 12 novembre 1963*

Cher Monsieur,

My engagements make it quite impossible for me to see you.
I deeply regret this; I would have been happy to have welcomed
you. In addition, I do not keep personal papers and consequently
do not possess any of Senghor's letters dating from before he
became a public figure.

The only things I can tell you are the following: I knew him at
Louis-le-Grand in 1929 where we were both boarding, and in the
Khâgne class which prepared students for the *École Normale
Supérieure*. For two years we sat on the same benches and we be-
came friends. At the time Senghor was a scholarship holder from
Senegal and had as his legal guardian in Paris Monsieur Diagne,
Député from Senegal, who had been a Minister. We, of course, had
very numerous conversations, as students, have on, all the problems
of the world and the other-world. I was myself an admirer of Jean
Jaurès and Léon Blum and it is possible that I influenced him in
this direction.

Afterwards, I entered the *École Normale*. Senghor, who had not
been admitted owing to bad luck at the competition, was at the
Cité Universitaire, where he prepared for the *Agrégation*. We
continued to have a close personal relationship.

When the war came, he was drafted and mobilized rather late.
Made a prisoner at La-Charité-sur-Loire, he was almost shot
along with a few other Senegalese. It was the intervention of a
French officer, who spoke with the German officers, that
avoided a racist massacre.

While a prisoner in a camp in the south-west of France, Senghor
was able to send me a few letters and poems that he wrote in his
camp, by the intermediary of one of his guards, a German soldier
of Austrian extraction and who I remember was Professor of
Chinese at the Faculty of Vienna. Senghor was liberated afterwards,
came back to Paris as *Professeur* in the *Lycée* at Saint-Maur and we
took up our normal relationship. In particular, he came several
times to spend his vacations with us at my father-in-law's home.

My father-in-law was a doctor in Château-Gontier in the Mayenne. After the liberation, Senghor entered political life and, from then on, you know as much as I do about his life.

All ties of friendship aside, I have always had the greatest esteem for his intelligence, for his poetic talents and for his qualities of the heart, and I was not in the least surprised, from the moment that the evolution of the African countries became what it was, that he played a great rôle in his country.

This is all I can tell you. I regret not to be able to do more.

Believe, I pray you, *Cher Monsieur*, the assurance of my very cordial sentiments.

Georges Pompidou

Appendix IV

Article by Paulette Nardal which appeared in English
in the *Revue du Monde Noir*, April 1932

The Awakening of Race Consciousness

I shall study this awakening more especially among the Antillian
Negroes. Their attitude towards racial problems is certainly being
modified. A few years ago, we might even say a few months ago,
certain questions were simply taboo in Martinica. Woe to those who
dared to broach them! One could not speak about slavery or proclaim one's pride of being of African descent without being considered as an overexcited or at least as an odd person. Such concerns
roused no deep chord in the mature or in the young Antillians'
thought. It is a fact that this almost disdainful indifference seems to
be transforming itself into a wondering interest among the older
generation and into a genuine enthusiasm among the younger.

However, certain Antillians had already been stirred to race consciousness, but this was the result of having left their small native
islands. The uprooting and the ensuing estrangement they felt in the
Metropolis, where Negroes have not always been so favourably received as they have been since the Colonial Exhibition, had given
them a real Negro soul, in spite of their Latin education. Yet they
never made articulate this state of mind.

The general attitude of the Antillian Negroes towards race problems, which is no different from that of the Aframericans, can obviously be explained by the liberal spirit which characterizes the politics
of France towards coloured peoples. Sicburg's book *Is God French?*
contains, among other things, a very sensible remark upon the power
of assimilation of the French genius. According to him, the lack of
colour prejudice among the French is due to the fact that they are
certain to transform the mind of any coloured man into a truly
French one in a comparatively short time. Besides, it was natural
that the Antillians, who are generally half-castes of Negro and White
descent, imbued with their Latin culture and ignorant of the history
of the black race, should in the end return to the element that
honoured them most.

Quite different was the situation among the American Negroes.

Though they are not of pure African origin either, the deliberate scorn with which they have always been treated by white Americans incited them to seek for reasons for social and cultural pride in their African past. Because they were obliged, immediately after the abolition of slavery, to try to solve their difficult race problem, the race question became the keynote of their concerns.

It would be interesting to find out how this situation has influenced Aframerican literature. As it is the case with all vanquished peoples, three periods may be noted in the intellectual evolution of the American Negroes. First, an indispensable period of acquisition during which the Negroes imported from Africa had to master a strange language and adapt themselves to a hostile environment. It is the period of absorption of the white element by the Negroes. From a purely literary point of view, the American Negroes can only be the docile imitators of their white models. Only certain slave narratives retain all their original freshness and genuine emotion, because they were written in dialect. The anti-slavery struggle saw the outburst of a literature of controversy and moral protest. Many orators of that time achieved real success. The poetry of that epoch was characterized by increasing appeals to pity. Of that period there remains a considerable number of documents and memoirs which from a historical point of view are undoubtedly valuable. Then, from 1880 on, we witness the accession of the Negroes to real culture. Two opposing tendencies make themselves felt. On one side, Dunbar, poet and novelist, who used both dialect and the English language, represents, if we may say so, the school of racial realism. On the other hand, Du Bois continued as it were, the literature of social protest by advocating equal civic and cultural rights for Negroes and Whites. But it is owing to the influence exerted by Braithwaite that the modern writers, without discarding the racial themes and the emotional intensity due to their ancestral experiences, took them as the starting point of their inspiration and gave them a universal purport. It is important to note that they abandoned the Negro dialect in favour of the forms and symbols of traditional literature. The poems of Claude MacKay which were published in this Review have acquainted our readers with this new attitude, and more recently, those of Langston Hughes have shown how young Negro writers, rejecting all inferiority complex, 'intend to express their individual dark-skinned selves without fear or shame'.

This interesting intellectual evolution of the American Negro leads us to ask ourselves what stage of his own development his Antillian brother, who lived in a comparatively favourable environment, has reached. If racial concern can hardly be found in the literary production which followed the abolition of slavery in the Antilles, it is because the 'great forefathers' were busily claiming equal liberty and political rights for the different categories of the black race living on the Antillian soil. Among the following generation of writers, we might cite the Martinicans, Victor Duquesney, Daniel Thaly, Solaving, the Guadaloupean Oruno Lara, and many Haitian poets. They were at the phase of conscious imitation of the literature of the conquering race. But if the intellectual evolution of the Aframericans was rapid, that of the Antillians might be called prodigious. Romanticism was then reigning in European literature. The productions of the Antillian writers were in no way inferior to those of the contemporary French writers, not to speak of such Antillian geniuses as the Dumas and José Maria de Heredia.

If we examine the works of these precursors, we certainly meet with the glorification of their small far-away motherlands, the 'Isles of Beauty' (exoticism was already the fashion), but no race pride is to be found there. Indeed, they speak lovingly of their native islands, but it happened that a stranger celebrated them in a still more felicitous way and accorded to the racial types more appreciation and real attachment. Their successors continued to derive their inspiration from Occidental or purely Metropolitan themes.

However, between that period and the present one, may be classed a generation of men whose racial tendencies had literature, politics, or humanitarian concerns as a starting point. Certain ideas were being launched. The theories of Marcus Garvey were commented upon. The first Pan-Negro Congress was organized. To literature we owe *Batouala* by René Maran, to whom was awarded the Goncourt Prize in 1920. Yet throughout this 'novel of objective observation', as the author himself called it in his preface, rings a pronounced indignation. Then came the first Negro journal of Paris, *The Continents*, which lasted only a few months. We must also mention an essay entitled 'Hermattos' by a young man from Guiana, who enjoyed a certain success in his time. The first Negro paper of long standing was *La Dépêche Africaine*, whose director wrote a much appreciated history of Guadelupa under the monarchy. In this journal, the movement which was to culminate in the *Revue du Monde Noir* was sketched out. In the Antilles we find the remarkable works of M. Jules Monnerot, published as *A Contribution to the History of Martinica*, and more recently *Galleries Martiniquaises*, a valuable source of documents in which racial questions are treated with more frankness than usual by M. Césaire Philémon.

It can readily be observed that in none of these works are theoretical problems studied for themselves. These productions remain the tributaries of Latin Culture. In none of them do we find the expression of a sincere faith in the future of the race and the necessity of creating a feeling of solidarity between the different groups of Negroes living throughout the globe.

However, parallel to the isolated efforts above mentioned, the aspirations which were to be crystallized around the *Revue du Monde Noir* asserted themselves among a group of Antillian women students in Paris. The coloured women living alone in the Metropolis, until the Colonial Exhibition, have certainly been less favoured than coloured men, who are content with a certain easy success. Long before the men, these women felt the need of a racial solidarity which would not be merely material. They thus became conscious of race. The feeling of uprooting which they experienced, which was so felicitously expressed by Roberte Horth in 'A Thing of No Importance' contributed to the second number of the *Revue du Monde Noir*, was the starting point of their evolution. After a period of obedient imitation of their white models, they may have passed through their period of revolt, just as their American brothers. But, as they grew older, they became less strict, less *ultra*, since they came to understand the relativity of all things. At present their position is midway between the two extremes.

As their ideas developed, their intellectual curiosity applied itself to the history of their race and of their respective countries. They thus came to regret the absence of such interesting matters in the educational programmes of the Antillian schools. Instead of despising their unheeding brothers or laying aside all hope about the possibility of the black race ever being on a par with the Aryans, they began to study. And as a matter of course, when the occasion came to select a subject for an essay or a thesis, their choice went to the black race. For the first time one of them took 'The Life and Works of Mrs Beecher Stowe (Uncle Tom's Cabin – Puritanism in New England)' as a subject for the *Diplôme d'Etudes Supérieures d'Anglais*. Later on, another student studied Lafcadio Hearn's works on the Antilles. A student of French selected the poems of John Antoine Nou and the works of Reverend Father Labat. It must be said that at that time the Aframerican writers were still unknown in France. But the interest of the Antillian Negroes in their own race had been aroused. We are informed that certain students are preparing memoirs on the American Negro writers and poets, who, in spite of their evident value, had hitherto been left out in the different surveys of American literature published by French university professors.

Let us hope that the students coming up for degrees in history and geography will avail themselves of the riches which the black race and the African continent offer to them. Let us hope also that they will give us the opportunity to analyse in this review some masterful doctoral theses. In this field, they have had two distinguished precursors: M. Félix Eboué, *Administrateur-en-Chef des Colonies*, a contributor to the *Revue du Monde Noir*, who for long years has studied the ethnology of certain African peoples; and M. Grégoire Micheli, a member of the International Institute of Anthropology who contributed remarkable articles to this review and is an erudite specialist of the ancient religions of South America. Moreover, we know that René Maran's latest novel *Le Livre de la Brousse*, a translation of which is to be published in America, constitutes a real and splendid rehabilitation of the African civilization. It can be considered the masterpiece of this celebrated Negro writer.

It is worth noticing that some of our young friends seemed to have arrived spontaneously at the last phase, as observed by us, in the intellectual evolution of the American Negroes. If, on one hand, they continue to treat purely occidental subjects, it is in an extremely modern form. On the other, they begin to bring into relief characteristic racial themes, as our readers will soon be able to see for themselves in a series of poems we are going to publish.

Should one see in the tendencies here expressed a sort of implicit declaration of war upon Latin culture and the white world in general? It is our duty to remove such a misapprehension. We are fully conscious of our debts to the Latin culture and we have no intention of discarding it in order to promote I know not what return to ignorance. Without it, we would have never become conscious of our real selves. But we want to go beyond this culture in order to give our brethren, with the help of white scientists and friends of the Negroes, the pride of being the members of a race which is perhaps the oldest in the world. Once they become aware of their past history, they will no longer despair of the future of their own race, part of which seems, at the present time, to be slow in developing. They will give to their slower brothers a helping hand and try to understand and love them better.

Paulette Nardal

[This document constitutes tangible evidence of the moment when American Negro ideas first filtered to French-speaking Negroes, thus starting the chain of events leading to the theory of *négritude*. It is for that reason that I have reproduced it *in extenso*.]

Appendix V

A Left-wing African Student's Opinion of the Present Study.
In the January 1965 issue of *L'Etudiant Sénégalais*, published by a group of Senegalese students affiliated with the FEANF, appeared a critique of my study on Senghor. It is perhaps valuable to read some of the lines written by a former high officer of the FEANF in order to see what such a project means for youthful Africans. After President Senghor's reaction, I feel it is only fair to give the podium to the opposition.

A Thesis on Senghor: The Itinerary of a Black-Skinned Frenchman by Diogomaye (pseudonym of Amady Dieng, former Vice-President of the FEANF).
7 November 1964, at nine o'clock an audience...at the Sorbonne... listened with interest to the defence of a thesis...on 'The Evolution of the Thought of L. S. Senghor: Outline of an Intellectual Itinerary'. This is the work of a young naturalized-American historian, Jacques Hymans...His enterprise is not without difficulty: to present a thesis on a living man and in addition the 'first magistrate' of Senegal involves making a choice from among numerous risks (turning his thought in the direction of academic, if not official, conformity...) Hymans has sometimes succeeded in finding appropriate techniques to give us certain truths. Thus, he has succeeded in putting distance between himself and the habitual fauna of *griots* who scamper about the former French *Député*, now President of Senegal. The thesis is full of interest. It merits reading, but it is not devoid of certain defects.
    M. Senghor, according to the information taken from Hymans' thesis, does not belong to the 'peasant race', as he likes to have one believe...In fact, Senghor belonged to a very rich family of traders who made their fortune on the backs of the Senegalese peasants by making enormous profits and by the practice of usury...
    He refuses to assume his condition of an oppressed man to devote himself to his racial condition...His theory of *négritude* took on the allure of a consolation, of an evasion, or an escape...Senghor undertook a so-called 'return to the source' which can be summarized as a cocktail of theories gathered in anthropological works. He does not

return to his 'labouring people', but creates for himself a mystical Africa all decked out in the colours of colonial exoticism...

Hymans' work is full of interest, although it is subject to serious criticism. It can be used for a much more profound work on Senghor. Some of his ideas are original, certain of his *rapprochements* are daring. Certain documents he uses are precious for us.

Hymans is an American; he can have a much more critical attitude to Senghor who is devoted to the interests of certain French business circles. But it was very difficult for him to be entirely objective on Senghor before the authorities of the Sorbonne. Nevertheless, he has succeeded, not without cleverness, to have us discover certain aspects of Senghor's personality. We can regret greatly the absence of an historical analysis of the social and political struggles which could better shed light on Senghor's thought. Hymans was not able to devote a critical study to the influence of enthnologists or philosophers (Lévy-Bruhl, Delafosse, Tempels, Bergson, etc.) on Senghor. The intellectual timidity of the author, who, in order to criticize Senghor, hides behind the authority of other persons or personalities, contributes to weakening the vigour of the thesis.

Hymans' thesis calls for certain observations on the rôle of African intellectuals and particularly of African students. Certainly the social climate of the United States can carry research on Africa to a very developed level (there are enormous interests to safeguard or to implant in Africa). But it is necessary to recognize that, despite material and social difficulties, it is important for African intellectuals to assume their task of combatant in the fullest sense of the term. That implies our presence on the front of culture which we should not leave to non-Africans the possibility of monopolizing. Hymans' thesis has incontestable merits, but it would have gained in depth, in density and in richness if it had been developed by African intellectuals in the fullest sense of the term.

Diogomaye

Remarks on Négritude. Made at the Conference on African Literature in French and the University Curriculum held at the Faculté des Lettres, University of Dakar, 26–29 March, 1963, by *Ezekiel Mphahlele.*

Yesterday I was personally attacked by someone who, because of my views against *négritude*, associated me with 'colonialism, neo-colonialism and imperialism'. He charged me, in effect, with hindering or frustrating the protest literature of *négritude*, its mission. If I had not exiled myself from South Africa five years ago, after having lived for 37 years in the South African nightmare, I should either have shrivelled up in my bitterness or have been imprisoned for treason. My books have been banned in South Africa under a law that forbids the circulation of literature that is regarded as 'objectionable, undesirable or obscene'. So, you see what things I have been called in my life; my body itches from the number of labels that have been stuck on me! As for what I really am, and my place in the African revolution, I shall let my writings speak for me.

We in South Africa have for the last 300 years of oppression been engaged in a bloody struggle against white supremacy – to assert our *human* and not African dignity. This latter we have always taken for granted. During these three centuries, we the Africans have been creating an urban culture out of the very condition of insecurity, exile and agony. We have done this by integrating Africa and the West. Listen to our music, see our dancing and read our literature both in the indigenous and English languages. The bits of what the white ruling class calls 'Bantu culture' that we are being told to 'return to' are being used by that class to oppress us, to justify the Transkei and other Bantustans. And yet there still survive the toughest elements of African humanism which keep us together and supply the moral force which we need in a life that rejects us.

If you notice the two segregated sections of a town like Brazzaville, Congo, you cannot fail to see the sterile and purposeless life of the Whites in their self-imposed ghetto as distinct from the vibrant and vigorous life of the black community. The Blacks have reconciled the Western and African in them, while the Whites refuse to surrender to their influence. This is symbolic of the South African situation. The only cultural vitality there is is to be seen among the Africans: they have not been *uplifted* by a Western culture but rather they have reconciled the two in themselves. This is the sense in which I feel superior to the white man who refuses to be liberated by me as an African. So, anyone who imagines that we in South Africa are just helpless, grovelling and down-trodden creatures of two worlds who have been waiting for the 'messiah' of *négritude*, does not know anything about what is going on in our country. My detractor, as an American Negro who would like to teach us how to feel African, cites the entry of James Meredith into Indiana University as symbolic of the triumph of the Negro's *négritude* in Mississipi [*sic*]. Are we really to believe that the US Federal Army went to Indiana to make it possible for Meredith to sing the blues or gospel songs? Surely his entry is to be seen as part of the Negro's campaign to be integrated socially and politically in the American population; to assert his human dignity. Of course, I am quite aware of certain – and luckily they are few – non-African Blacks and Whites who come crawling on their bellies into this continent as it were, prepared to be messengers or lackeys of some of us, prepared to eat the dust under our feet in self-abasement in an attempt to identify with Africa. Such people are prompted to do this out of a guilt complex whereby they seek to bear the sins of past colonizers who, they imagine, we associate them with. Elsewhere I have warned against this ugly self-abasement because it prevents the 'patient' from criticizing adversely anything the African says or writes, ripe, raw and rotten. I fully agree with James Baldwin when he says, in a brilliant and most moving essay in a recent issue of *The New Yorker* (17 Nov. 1962), that the Negro must solve his problem inside America, not by a romantic identification with Africa. I appreciate also his remark that the Negro refuses to be integrated 'into a burning house', i.e., the American social and political life that is sadly misguided, in which Whites do not believe in death. And yet he also says that White and Black in the US need each other badly, that the white American needs to be liberated from himself but can only do this when he has liberated the Negro. After this, integration must come. Although he appreciates the Black Muslims, he foresees that one day he may have to fight them because they are such a menace.

Now to *négritude* itself. Who is so stupid as to deny the historical fact of *négritude* as both a protest and a positive assertion of African cultural values? All this is valid. What I do not accept is the way in which too much of the poetry inspired by it romanticizes Africa – as a symbol of innocence, purity and artless primitiveness. I feel insulted when some people imply that Africa is not also a violent continent. I am a violent person, and proud of it because it is often a healthy human state of mind; someday I'm going to plunder, rape, set things on fire; I'm going to cut someone's throat; I'm going to subvert a government; I'm going to organize a *coup d'état*; yes, I'm going to oppress my own people; I'm going to hunt down the rich, fat black men who bully the small, weak black men and destroy them; I'm going to become a capitalist, and woe to all who cross my path or who want to be my servants or chauffeurs and so on; I'm going to lead a breakaway church – there is money in it; I'm going to attack the black bourgeoisie while I cultivate a garden, rear dogs and parrots; listen to jazz and classics; read 'culture' and so on. Yes, I'm also going to organize a strike. Don't you know that sometimes I kill to the rhythm of drums and cut the sinews of a baby to cure it of paralysis?... This is only a dramatization of what Africa can do and is doing. The image of Africa consists of all these and others. And *négritude* poetry pretends that they do not constitute the image and leaves them out. So we are told only half – often even a falsified half – of the story of Africa. Sheer romanticism that fails to see the large landscape of the personality of the African makes bad poetry. Facile protest also makes bad poetry. The omission of these elements of a continent in turmoil reflects a defective poetic vision. The greatest poetry of Léopold Sédar Senghor is that which portrays in himself the meeting point of Europe and Africa. This is the most realistic and honest and most meaningful symbol of Africa, an ambivalent continent searching for equilibrium. This synthesis of Europe and Africa does not necessarily reject the Negro-ness of the African.

What have we to say about 'benevolent dictatorship'; chauvinists, peasants who find that they have to change a way of life they have cherished for centuries and have to live in the twentieth century? Let me italicize again: an image of Africa that glosses over or dismisses these things is not a faithfully conceived one; it restricts our emotional and intellectual response. An image of Africa that only glorifies our ancestors and celebrates our 'purity' and 'innocence' is an image of a continent lying in state. When I asked the question at the Accra Congress of Africanists last December how long our poets are going to continue to bleat like a goat in the act of giving birth, I was suggesting that Ghanaian poets should start looking inward, into themselves. Now I am being accused of encouraging 'artistic purity' by asking writers to cease protesting against a colonial boss that has left their country. What is 'artistic purity'? Am I being asked to lay the ghost of *l'art pour l'art*? Surely meaningful art has social significance or relevance and this very fact implies social criticism –

protest in the broadest sense of the word. Gorky, Dostoïevsky, Tolstoy, Dickens and so on did this, but they were no less Russian or English; certainly they were much more committed than *négritude* poets. They took in the whole man. Camara Laye's *Le Regard du Roi*, Ferdinand Oyono's *Le Vieux Nègre et la Médaille* and Mongo Beti's *Le pauvre Christ de Bomba* are not bullied by *négritude*. They are concerned in portraying the black-white encounter, and they do this, notwithstanding, with a devastating poetic sense of irony unmatched by any that one sees in the English novel by Africans (there are fascinating works in the three main Bantu languages in South Africa which are of the same standard). I am suggesting here that we as writers need to be emancipated from ourselves. *Négritude*, while a valuable slogan politically, can, because its apostles have set it up as a principle of art, amount to self-enslavement – *autocolonisation*, to quote a French writer speaking of African politics and economics. We should not allow ourselves to be bullied at gun-point into producing literature that is supposed to contain a *négritude* theme and style. For now we are told, also, that there is *un style négro-africain*, and that therefore we have to sloganize and write to a march. We are told that *négritude* is less a matter of theme than style. We must strive to visualize the whole man, not merely the things that are meant to flatter the Negro's ego. Let it not be forgotten, too, that *négritude* has an overlap of nineteenth-century European protest against machines and cannons. In the place of the cuckoo, the nightingale, the daffodil, Africa has been dragged to the altar of Europe. *Négritude* men should not pretend that this is an entirely African concept.

Several of us, as a result of the physical and mental agony we have been going through in South Africa, have rejected Christianity or any other religion as a cure for human ills. But if I wrote a poem or novel expressly to preach against religion without my seeing the irony of the good and bad done in the name of religion; if I omitted the irony of Christians and educated Africans who still revere ancestral spirits, and several other ironies and paradoxes, then it would not be a lasting work of art. I think that a writer who is too sure about his rejection of the use of a god can be as overbearing as the one who is too sure about his need of an existence of a god, like Browning. I say, then, that *négritude* can go on as a socio-political slogan, but that it has no right to set itself up as a standard of literary performance. There I refuse to go along. I refuse to be put in a Negro file – for sociologists to come and examine me. Art unifies even while it distinguishes men; and I regard it as an insult to the African for anyone to suggest that because we write independently on different themes in divers modes and styles all over Africa, therefore we are ripe victims of balkanization. But then I speak as a simple practising writer, not as a politician or a philosopher, or a non-African Africanist who is looking for categories and theories for a doctorate thesis. I refuse to be put in a dossier. And yet I am no less committed to the African revolution, to the South African freedom fight. The South African, East African and English-speaking West African do not worry over *négritude* because they have never lost the essence of their Negro-ness. Again, let *négritude* make the theme of literature if people want to use it. But we must remember that literature springs from an individual's experience, and in its effort to take in the whole man, it also tries to see far ahead, to project a prophetic vision, such as the writer is capable of, based on contemporary experience. It must at least set in motion vibrations in us that will continue even after we have read it, prompting us to continue inquiring into its meaning. If African culture is worth anything at all, it should not require myths to prop it up. These thoughts are not new at all. I have come to them after physical and mental agony. And this is of course not my monopoly either. It is the price Africa has to pay. And if you thought that the end of colonialism was the end of the agony, then it is time to wake up.

The fear that university teachers who distrust *négritude* or reject it as a principle of art may exclude from the syllabus literature inspired by this school, does not do justice to them. And the suggestion that they have a grave responsibility when they decide which African authors have to be taught is insulting to their intelligence. Why should they feel more responsible than they have been in the teaching of French? Is African writing in French not French literature? I am sure university teachers can be trusted to distinguish literature from a sociological or anthropological document that masquerades as literature! They can examine actual texts, can't they? Why should *la littérature engagée* be so spoiled as to want to be judged by different standards from those that have been tested by tradition?

We acknowledge that *négritude* as a socio-political concept defines the mind of the assimilated African in French-speaking territories. The British never set out to assimilate their colonial subjects. They hate to see people come out of their culture to emulate them (the British). They like the exotic African, not the one who tries to speak, walk and eat like them. They love Africans in museum cases, so they left much of African culture intact. But literature and art are too big for *négritude*, and it had better be left as a historical phase.

Bibliographical Notes

Rather than provide a conventional bibliography I have relied on the
Notes and References to give bibliographical information the reader
might require and have substituted instead a more informal review of
the major sources for the study of Senghor.

I. Senghor's writings translated into English
To understand Senghor's most intimate thoughts it is absolutely
essential to read his poems, which reveal his inner conflict. They
also help to build up a picture of Senghor's childhood. Many of his
best poems have been collected and translated in a single volume.
An interesting introduction by the translators precedes the poems.
(Senghor, Léopold Sédar *Selected Poems*, translated and introduced
by John Reed and Clive Wake. New York : Atheneum 1964. See also
Senghor, L. *Prose and Poetry*. London: Oxford 1965.)

Senghor's political and socio-economic thinking is revealed in
Mercer Cook's (former US Ambassador to Senegal) preface to, and
translation of, several of his long lectures of the 1960s. Two of these
lectures (with an introduction by Senghor written after the breakup
of the Mali Federation) have been published several times. I have
used an earlier volume published by Présence Africaine. (Senghor,
Léopold Sédar *On African Socialism*, translated by Mercer Cook. New
York: Praeger 1964.)

Two earlier lectures focusing on Senghor's cultural thought are
found in the English translations of the Congresses of Negro
Writers and Artists held in 1956 and 1959 by Présence Africaine.
(Senghor, Léopold Sédar 'The spirit of civilization, or the laws of
African Negro culture'. *Présence Africaine* 8–10, June–November
1956, 51–64. See also the speeches by Senghor during the discussion
period, pp. 70–2, 73–4, 218–19. Senghor, Léopold Sédar 'Constructive elements of a civilization of African Negro inspiration',
Présence Africaine 24–25, February–May 1959, 262–94.)

II. Important background material on Senegal and Senghor published
in English
One should begin the background study with the history of political
parties in French-speaking Africa since 1944 gathered patiently by

Professor Morgenthau of Brandeis. This study is a definitive work on the subject and includes a great many comments on Senghor's political activity. Reference is made easy by the splendid index. (Morgenthau, Ruth Schachter *Political Parties in French-speaking Africa*. London: Oxford University Press 1964.) I have not repeated many of the titles in Professor Morgenthau's bibliography.

An impressive survey of Senegal's history, geography, ethnic groups, social structure, health, education, arts, religion, political background (structure of government, political dynamics, foreign relations), economic background (agriculture, industry, labour, trade, financial and monetary system), etc. has been published for the United States Department of the Army. An extensive bibliography follows each chapter. This unclassified document is available from the US Govt. Printing Office. (*U.S. Army Area Handbook for Senegal*. Prepared by Foreign Area Studies Division, Special Operations Research Office, The American University, Washington, DC: August 1963.)

A global study of African Socialism enabled me to focus on the unique aspects of Senghor's thought. This brilliant series of studies, which includes a translation of a 1961 speech by Senghor (pp. 264–266), contains an exhaustive bibliography on African socio-economic thinking. (Friedland, William H. and Rosberg, Carl G. Jr., eds. *African Socialism*. Stanford University Press 1964.) A brief study of Senghor's socialism is also to be found in Skurnik, W. *Journal of Modern African Studies*, March 1965, 49–69.

A good analysis of the period of the Mali Federation gives many details on the end of the French West African Federation and Senghor's rôle in the final dissolution. This study also helps show the 'forces' and groups which submerge the individuals acting on the political scene. (Foltz, William J. *From French West Africa to the Mali Federation*. New Haven: Yale University Press 1965. Foltz has also published an essay on Senegal in Coleman, J. and Rosberg, C. *Political Parties and National Integration in Africa*. Berkeley: Univ. of Calif. Press 1964.)

A general survey of Pan-Africanism and *négritude*, including many documents on these subjects, is very helpful in putting Senghor's activities into an African perspective. (Kohn, Hans and Sokolsky, Wallace *African Nationalism in the Twentieth Century*. Princeton: Van Nostrand Anvil Books 1965.)

For those who cannot read the classic study on French-speaking Negro poetry in French, there is a translation of Jean-Paul Sartre's 1948 preface to Senghor's *Anthologie*. (Sartre, Jean-Paul *Black Orpheus*. Paris: Présence Africaine 1963.) This translation is by S. W. Allen.

Another survey of Senegal in English concentrates on the history of the area under French rule. (Crowder, Michael *Senegal: A Study in French Assimilation Policy*. London: Oxford University Press 1962. 2nd revised edition, New York 1967.)

Two studies of Senegal by political scientists complement the previously mentioned sources. (Milcent, Ernest 'Senegal', in Gwendolen Carter, ed. *African One Party States*. Ithaca: Cornell Press 1962. Robinson, Kenneth 'Senegal' in William Mackenzie and Kenneth Robinson *Five Elections in Africa: A Group of Electoral Studies*. London: Oxford University Press 1960.) Interesting, thoughtful work on Islam and politics in Senegal has been accomplished. (Behrman, Lucy C. *Muslim Brotherhoods and Politics in Senegal*. Cambridge: Harvard University Press 1970.)

One of the earliest, perhaps the pioneer, study of French West Africa should still be read with care. (Thompson, Virginia and Adloff, Richard *French West Africa*. Stanford: University Press 1957.) An updating of the study directed at students of the High School or Junior College level is now available. (Adloff, Richard *West Africa: The French-Speaking Nations*. Holt-Rinehart 1964.) A brief history is also available. (Hargreaves, John D. *West Africa: the Former French States*. Englewood Cliffs: Prentice-Hall 1967.)

Two articles provide excellent short coverage of basic aspects of Senghor's thought. (Morgenthau, Ruth Schachter 'African socialism: declaration of ideological independence'. *Africa Report* 8 (5) May 1963, 3–6. xxx 'People to watch: between France and Africa', *The Times* (London) 13 August 1959, p. 9: 6–7.)

A history of the literary movements in West Africa in general is: July, Robert W. *Origins of Modern African Thought: Its Development in West Africa during the Nineteenth and Twentieth Centuries*. New York: Praeger 1967.

Opposition to *négritude* in English is primarily expressed by English-speaking Africans. (Mphahlele, Ezekiel *The African Image*. London: Faber and Faber 1962. See especially pp. 25–43.)

More objective analyses of Senghor's literary activities are found. They are the work of professional critics. (xxx *'Négritude* in a changing world and poet of Senegal', *The Times Literary Supplement*, 21 September 1962; Guibert, Armand 'Léopold Sédar Senghor', *Encounter* (London) February 1961; Moore, Gerald *Seven African Writers*. London: Oxford University Press 1962. Wauthier, Claude *The Literature and Thought of Modern Africa: A Survey*. New York: Praeger 1967. Jahn, J. *A History of Neo-African Literature*, trans. by O. Coburn and U. Lehrburger. London 1968.)

The most recent attempt to analyse Senghor's ideology appeared after the present study went to press. (Markovitz, Irving *Léopold Sédar Senghor and the Politics of Négritude*. New York: Atheneum 1969).

III. Senghor's writings and speeches published in French
A. Poems 1936–64

Chants d'Ombre. Paris: Seuil 1945. Contains poems from the 1930s.

Hosties Noires. Paris: Seuil 1948. Contains poems of 1930s and 1940s. Wartime poems predominate.

Chants pour Naëtt. Paris: Seghers 1949. Love poems, later re-published in *Nocturnes*.

Ethiopiques. Paris: Seuil 1956. Contains some examples of Senghor's finest writing.

Nocturnes. Paris: Seuil 1961. Contains, under the title 'Chants pour Signaré' a slightly changed version of 'Chants pour Naëtt' and several hitherto unpublished elegies.

Poèmes. Paris: Seuil 1964. Re-publication in a single bound volume of all of Senghor's poems and some of his translations of traditional African poetry.

B. Lectures and Essays 1937–45

Liberté I: Négritude et Humanisme. Paris: Seuil 1964. Contains most of Senghor's cultural works published in reviews and journals from 1937 to 1964.

'Le problème culturel en AOF' in *Essais et Etudes Universitaires: Editions Lettres* I, 1945, pp. 44–53. Senghor's 1937 lecture at Dakar. Some parts not contained in the re-edition entitled *Liberté I*.

'La résistance de la bourgeoisie sénégalaise a l'école rurale populaire', pp. 40–4 in Congrès International de l'Evolution Culturelle des Peuples Coloniaux 26–27–28 septembre 1937, Exposition Internationale de Paris 1937 – *Rapports et Compte-Rendu*. Paris: Protât Frères (Macon) 1938. Lecture not included in the re-publication of Senghor's works entitled *Liberté I*.

'Ce que l'homme noir apporte', pp. 292–314 in S.E.le Cardinal Verdier *et al. L'Homme de Couleur*. Paris: Plon 1939. See the introductions and prefaces as well as Senghor's article.

Several articles, poems, and essays published in *L'Etudiant de la France d'Outre-mer: Chronique des Foyers*. Published monthly in Paris between June 1943 and May 1944. Collection at the *Bibliothèque Nationale* in Paris.

'Vues sur l'Afrique noire ou assimiler, non être assimilés', pp. 57–98 in Robert Lemaignen, Léopold Senghor, and Prince Sisowath Youtevong *La Communauté Impériale Française*. Paris: Alsatia 1945.

Essay written in 1943–4; publication delayed by the liberation of Paris in 1944.

'Défense de l'Afrique noire'. *Esprit* 112, 1er juillet 1945: 237–48. Essay written in Paris, 1 May 1945. Not included in the republication entitled *Liberté I*.

c. Articles in Political Newspapers published in Senegal from 1945 to 1970. Senghor's speeches in the French Assemblies from 1945 to 1958

Various articles published in *l'A.O.F.*: *Echo de la Côte Occidentale d'Afrique – Organe de la Fédération S.F.I.O. de l'A.O.F.* Articles appeared from 1945–8. Criticism of Senghor in this journal appeared after 1948. See also articles under the name of Diamano Silmang, Senghor's pseudonym. This newspaper had a circulation of 5,000 copies during the period, but since more readers in Africa use a single issue, Senghor's articles reached around 20,000 people.

Various speeches published in Assemblée Nationale Constituante élue le 21 octobre 1945 – *Séances de la Commission de la Constitution: Comptes-rendus analytiques imprimés en exécution de la résolution votée par l'Assemblée le 2 octobre 1946.* Paris: Imprimerie de l'Assemblée Nationale Constituante 1947.

Various speeches published in Journal Officiel de la République Française – *Débats Parlementaires Assemblée Nationale: Compte Rendu in extenso des séances, questions écrites et réponses des Ministres à ces questions.* I have used the abbreviation *JOAN* to indicate this series of parliamentary debates. See the index for the years 1945–58 under Senghor for his speeches.

Various interviews, speeches, articles published in *Paris-Dakar* (September–October 1937, then 1945–61). Daily newspaper appearing in Senegal and other French West African Territories. Circulation about 21,000 numbers. Clientèle 60 per cent African, 40 per cent European. Probable number of readers (due to Africans passing a paper from hand to hand) 210,000. This paper is part of a chain of African papers owned by Charles de Breteuil interests. The articles on French Parliament debates by Max Jalade are very lively, much more revealing than the *JOAN*. Certain phrases cut from the *JOAN* are reproduced in Jalade's articles. The climate of the debate is also described. See, for example, Jalade, Max 'Le débat sur les relations economiques', *Paris-Dakar*, 10 avril 1954, p. 6.

Various interviews, articles, speeches published in *Dakar-Matin* which replaced *Paris-Dakar* after independence in 1961. It must be noted that *Dakar-Matin* is much less impartial than was *Paris-*

Dakar, since Senghor became President of the Republic. Towards the end of the 1950s *Paris-Dakar* became less and less hostile to Senghor, opposition becoming more and more the lot of left-wing elements. During the 1940s *Paris-Dakar* tried to remain neutral in the political struggle between African parties; this paper progressively rallied to Senghor's camp, becoming a 'governmental sheet' with the arrival of independence and the transformation in the title.

Various articles, interviews, speeches published in *Condition Humaine: Au Service de la Révolution Sociale* from 1948 to 1956. *Condition Humaine* was the weekly party organ of Senghor's BDS founded in 1948. Senghor wrote in it under his own name and also under the pseudonym Patrice Maguilen Kaymor. This organ gives a good idea of the life of the party. Mamadou Dia's speeches were usually printed *in extenso* in addition to Senghor's.

Various articles, interviews, speeches published in *l'Unité*, a weekly which took over when *Condition Humaine* stopped in 1956.

Various articles, interviews, speeches published in *Le Regroupement*, a weekly which took over when *l'Unité* folded. *Le Regroupement*, which reflected the change in Senghor's approach for the period 1957–9, showed that a change in Party name brought with it a change in the name of the party newspaper. (This is the period when Senghor's party on the inter-territorial level was called *Parti du Regroupement Africaine*.)

Various articles, interviews, speeches published in *l'Unité Africaine*, a weekly which took over when *Le Regroupement* folded. This is the official organ of the *Union Progressiste Sénégalaise* (UPS), Senghor's party to this date.

Various articles, speeches, and interviews in *Afrique Nouvelle* from 1947 to 1966. *Afrique Nouvelle* is published by the White Fathers in Dakar. For an analysis of the papers above cited see Mackenzie, W. J. M. and Robinson, Kenneth E. *Five Elections in Africa: A Group of Electoral Studies*. London: Oxford University Press 1960, pp. 367–74.

Various speeches published in *Travaux Préparatoires de la Constitution du 4 octobre 1958: Avis et Débats du Comité Consultatif Constitutionnel*. Paris: La Documentation Française 1960.

D. Articles, Essays and Writings on Culture 1946–70

'La civilisation négro-africaine', pp. 165–262 in El Kholti, M. *et al. Les Plus Beaux Écrits de l'Union Française et du Maghreb*. Paris: La Colombe 1947. Part of Senghor's contribution appears in the republication *Liberté I*, but much of the article does not.

Anthologie de la Nouvelle Poésie Nègre et Malgache de Langue Française précédée de Orphée Noir par J.-P. Sartre. Paris: PUF 1948. Senghor wrote the little prefaces to each selection. These prefaces, which shed light on his own thought, are not reprinted in the collection *Liberté I*.

I have not mentioned below many essays from 1948–64 which appear in *Liberté I*.

'La contribution négro-africaine à l'édification d'une civilisation mondiale'. *Liberté de l'Esprit* 41, juin–juillet 1953, 143–6.

'L'apport de la poésie nègre' in *Témoignages sur la Poésie du demi-siècle*. Brussels: La Maison du Poète 1953.

'Il y a une négritude'. *Preuves* 86, avril 1958, 36–7.

'Les voix et voie de l'Afrique noire'. *Comprendre: Revue de la Politique de la Culture* 21–22, 1960. Published in Venice by the European Society of Culture: 'Round Table of Civilizations: the entry of Africa into History'.

'Comment nous sommes devenus ce que nous sommes'. *Afrique Action* 16, 30 janvier 1961, 16–18. Important autobiographical revelations.

'Rapport sur la doctrine du parti'. *Documents du Congrès Constitutif du P.R.A.* Cotonou, Dahomey: mimeographed, 1958. A part of this report is autobiographical. It can be consulted at the Fondation Nationale des Sciences Politiques in Paris.

'La négritude est un humanisme'. *Voyage Officiel du Président de la République du Sénégal en Grande Bretagne.* (Brochure printed by the Bradbury Agnew Press on the occasion of Senghor's visit to the United Kingdom. This is a speech Senghor gave at Oxford, St Anthony's College, 26 October 1961. English translation included.)

'La préhistoire et les groupes ethniques', pp. 5–51 in Parti de la Fédération Africaine – *Séminaire organisé à l'occasion du Congrès de l'Union Nationale de la Jeunesse du Mali: Dakar les 16, 17, 18, et 19 mai 1960.* Dakar: Imprimeric Fédérale du Mali 1960.

'De la négritude: psychologie du négro-africaine'. *Diogène* 37, janvier–mars 1962, 2–16.

'Mon Ami Georges Pompidou'. *Afrique Express* 29, 25 mai 1962: 13.

'Une maladie infantile des temps modernes'. *La Nef* 19–20, septembre–décembre 1964, pp. 7–10. Article on racism.

E. Articles, Essays, and Political Writings in Books, Papers, and Journals published in France 1946–69

'Interview' in Teppe, Julien 'La condition humaine...' *Gavroche* 102, 8 août 1946, 7.

'Discours prononcé à la Sorbonne le 27 avril 1948', pp. 11–18 in Monnerville, G. *et al. Commémoration du Centenaire de l'Abolition de l'Esclavage.* Paris: PUF 1948. 'Contre le courant centrifuge de l'etat associé, une seule solution: La République Fédérale Française'. *Marchés Coloniaux du Monde* 386, 4 avril 1953, 1005–7.

'Eurafrique: une opinion'. Paris: CEAA mimeographed, 1953, 10pp. (Lecture given at the *Centre d'Etudes Asiatiques et Africaines* on 27 May 1953.) The CEAA was attached to the *Section de Documentation Militaire de l'Union Française.*

'L'avenir de la France dans l'outre-mer'. *Politique Etrangère* 4, août–octobre 1954, 419–26. Issue devoted to the French Republic's Overseas Territories' problems.

'Pour une solution fédéraliste'. *La Nef* 9, juin 1955, 148–61. Issue devoted to the problem of the *Union Française*, from Colonialism to Association.

'Pour une république fédérale'. *Etudes Sociales Nord-Africaines: Aspects Internes des Problèmes Algériens.* Cahier no. 53 juillet–août 1956, 1–8.

'Pour une Communauté Franco-Africaine'. *Les Cahiers de la République: Revue bimestrielle de Politique* 7, mai–juin 1957, 64–8.

'La lucidité et la franchise, conditions de la communauté franco-africaine', pp. 5–9 in Milcent, Ernest *L'A.O.F. entre en Scène.* Paris: Témoignage Chrétien 1958.

'Vers l'indépendance dans l'amitié'. *Les Cahiers de la République: Revue bimestrielle de Politique* 16, novembre–décembre 1958, 52–58.

'Les nationalismes d'outre-mer et l'avenir des peuples de couleur'. *Le Mali: Organe Central du Parti de la Fédération Africaine* 4, décembre 1959, 5–11. See a reprint of this article in *l'Encyclopédie Française* t.XX, 1959.

Allocution du Président de la République du Sénégal à la XVIème Session de l'Assemblée Générale des Nations Unies tenue le 31 octobre 1961. Paris: Présence Africaine 1961.

I have not repeated the various publications of Senghor's two long lectures which are translated under the titles of *Nationhood and the African Road to Socialism* (used in the footnotes) and *On African Socialism.*

F. Articles, Essays and Socio-Economic Writings 1947–70

'Les négro-africains et l'union française'. *Réveil* 201–2, 24–8 avril 1947, 3.

'Marxisme et humanisme'. *La Revue Socialiste: Culture–Doctrine–Action* 19, mars 1948, 201–16.

'Message au congrès de Florence'. Florence, Italy: mimeo. 1961.
Pierre Teilhard de Chardin et la Politique Africaine. Paris: Seuil 1962.
Lecture sent by Senghor to the Association of Friends of P.
Teilhard de Chardin meeting at Vézelay, France, Septembre 6–14
1961.
'Socialisme africaine et développement ou la voie sénégalaise'.
Développement et Civilisations numéro spécial décembre 1962,
'Sénégal an 11 par lui-même', 1–7.
'C'est Georges Pompidou qui m'a converti au socialisme'. *Le Figaro
Littéraire* 12 mai 1962, 4.
Théorie et Pratique du Socialisme Sénégalais. Dakar: mimeo. décembre
1962. Lecture given to the Séminaire des Cadres Politiques de
novembre–décembre 1962.
Rapport sur la Politique Générale. Dakar: mimeo. octobre 1963. Report
given at the 1vth Congress of the UPS held in Dakar October 10–
12, 1963.
Démocratie et Socialisme. Dakar: mimeo. novembre 1964. Lecture
given at the *Palais de l'Université*, Strasbourg, 20 November 1964
on the occasion of Senghor's being made *Docteur Honoris Causa*
at the University of Strasbourg. (President Senghor gave me the
last few mimeographed documents which are to be found also in
the Senegalese newspapers *Dakar-Matin*, *l'Unité Africaine*, etc.,
as are most official declarations.)

G. Articles on Linguistics
'Les classes nominales en Wolof et les substantif à initiale nasale'.
Journal de la Société des Africanistes XIII, 1944.
'L'harmonie vocalique en Sérère (dialecte du Dyéguème)'. *Journal
de la Société des Africanistes* XIV, 1944.
'L'article conjonctif en Wolof'. *Journal de la Société des Africanistes*
XVII, 1947.
La Dialectique du Nom-Verbe en Wolof. Dakar: mimeo. 1961.
Discours d'Ouverture: Semaine Linguistique. Dakar: mimeo. 12 avril
1962, 11pp.

H. Stories
With Sadji, Abdoulaye *La Belle Histoire de Leuk-le-Lièvre: Cours
élémentaire des Ecoles d'Afrique Noire*. Paris: Hachette 1953.
I. Recent anthropological and cultural writing
Les Fondements de l'Africanité ou Négritude et Arabité. Paris: Présence
Africaine 1967.

IV. Books and articles in French which contribute background information on Senghor's life and cultural thought

Three recent studies have used and developed material first analysed
in the unpublished French version of the present work. Of these the
best general biography is that by Milcent and Sordet. (Milcent, E. and
Sordet, M. *Léopold Sédar Senghor et la naissance de l'Afrique moderne.*
Paris: Seghers 1969; Rous, Jean *Léopold Sédar Senghor, un Président de
l'Afrique nouvelle.* Paris: Didier 1967.)

Another recent study has been published by an African. (Mezu,
S. O. *Léopold Sédar Senghor et la Défence et Illustration de la Civilisation
Noire.* Paris, Didier 1968.)

Two earlier biographies of Senghor were written by a literary
critic, poet, and friend of the Senegalese President. Both biographies
contain extensive bibliographies, selections of Senghor's poetry and
prose. The biographies are somewhat too enthusiastic and lack
scholarly impartiality. Senghor's political career and his political and
socio-economic thinking are almost entirely absent from these
studies. The analysis and criticism of the poems are revealing and
help to make these works accessible to the uninitiated. A long
interview is included in the Présence Africaine biography, as is a
series of criticisms of Senghor's poetry by other writers. For
amateurs of graphology, the two biographies contain samples of
Senghor's handwriting. The author states that he submitted these
samples to a noted graphologist who confirmed many of the points
he had made in the two works. (Interview with Armand Guilbert,
Paris: 31 October 1963.) (Guibert, Armand *Léopold Sédar Senghor.*
Paris: Seghers 1961; and Guibert, Armand *Léopold Sédar Senghor.* Paris:
Présence Africaine 1961.) Excellent illustrations help the reader to
visualize moments of Senghor's life.

A published doctoral dissertation constitutes a first attempt at a
synthesis of the development of *négritude*. The author was not
always able to base her study on texts dating from the 1930s, relying
excessively for that period on the opinions of Léon Damas (see
below). The arguments she uses to counter Senghor's 'revolutionary' critics are not convincing. The author's qualities reside more in
literary analysis than in historical description. I adopted some of the
methodological approaches of the author, but trod warily when it
came to evaluating the conclusions which her method led her to
make. (Kesteloot, Lilyane *Les Ecrivains Noirs de Langue Française
Naissance d'une Littérature.* Brussels: Institut Solvay 1963. 3rd revised
edition, 1967.)

Certain judgements which Kesteloot makes are based on a valuable book written by one of the founders of the *négritude* movement,

which contains a selection of poems of colonial writers that the editor knew personally from the 1930s on. The introduction attempted to trace the beginnings of the French-speaking Negro cultural movement, but it was not exhaustive, as Kesteloot's thesis purports to be. No mention was made of the *Revue du Monde Noir*, nor of Paulette Nardal's salon. Senghor's *Anthologie* followed on the heels of this earlier collection of colonial writing. (Damas, Léon G. *Poètes d'Expression Française: 1900–1945.* Paris: Seuil 1947.)

A brilliant analysis of Senghor's poetry was made by a young French student of the *Ecole Normale Supérieure* in 1957. In a letter addressed to its author Senghor declared that the article was one of the best criticisms of his work that he had read. This article influenced the above-cited works of Guibert, but it indulges in much less flattery of Senghor than do Guibert's somewhat biased accounts. (Badiou, Alain 'La poésie de L. S. Senghor'. *Vin Nouveau* 2, janvier 1957, pp. 67–79.)

For a comparison of Senghor and Césaire there are several interesting articles dating from the 1940s. (Patri, Aimé 'Deux poètes noirs en langue française'. *Présence Africaine* 3, mars–avril 1948, 379. Balandier, Georges 'Erreurs noirs'. *Présence Africaine* 3, mars–avril 1948, 402 ff. Balandier, Georges 'La littérature noire de langue française'. *Présence Africaine* 8–9, mars 1950, 393–402. Patri, Aimé 'Leopold Senghor' in Senghor, Léopold. *Anthologie*, pp. 147–8.)

It is interesting, but difficult, to consult the work of the 'Journées d'Etude de la Littérature Négro-Africaine' held by the Fédération des Etudiants d'Afrique Noire en France (FEANF) July 5–6 1961. These mimeographed essays constitute a good sampling of the opinion of the younger generation on Senghor's works, as well as those of Césaire and the other French-speaking Negro writers. Césare, more 'revolutionary' than Senghor, seems to curry more favour with the generation of the 1950s and the 1960s.

Several published interviews give a glimpse of other French-speaking Negro writers' experience with *négritude* and its origins. Memories of the 1930s and 1940s are prevalent in these interviews. (Guérin, Anne 'Aimé Césaire: le cannibale s'est tassé...'. *l'Express* 19 mai 1960, 35. XXX. 'Césaire et la négritude'. *La Vie Africaine* 19, novembre 1961, 33. XXX. 'Les Africains peuvent étonner le monde'. *Afrique-Action* 24, 27 mars 1961, 22. Round Table of Negro Intellectuals: Alioune Diop, Jacques Rabemananjara and Aimé Césaire.)

The collection of the *Revue du Monde Noir* at the Bibliothèque Nationale in Paris is indispensable for tracing the origins of Senghor's thought. It is necessary to complement these documents with a recent study on the French intellectual generation of the 1930s. It is surprising to find so many of the preoccupations of this generation echoed in the West Indian and African students' concerns. The description of the intellectual climate of those times is incomparable. (Touchard, Jean 'L'Esprit des années 1930: une tentative de renouvellement de la Pensée politique française', pp. 89–120 in: Colloques: Cahiers de Civilisation. *Tendances Politiques dans la Vie Française depuis 1789*. Paris: Hachette 1960.) I have used a reprint given me by the author who is *Secrétaire-Générale* of the *Fondation Nationale des Sciences Politiques* in Paris.

Two developed accounts coming from the time when *négritude* was being formulated can be found in the novels written by one of the Senegalese students who lived in Paris at the same time as Senghor and Césaire. (Socé, Ousmane *Karim: Roman Sénégalais suivi de contes et légendes d'Afrique Noire*. Paris: Nouvelles Editions Latines 1935, and *Mirages de Paris*. Paris: Nouvelles Editions Latines 1937.)

For an account of *négritude* after 1945 there is Sartre's classical analysis above cited. A series of violent criticisms are highly significant, especially those written by French-speaking Blacks who have known Senghor at different moments of his life. (D'Arboussier, Gabriel 'Une dangereuse mystification: la théorie de la négritude'. *Réveil* (organ of the RDA when it was linked with the French Communist Party) 375, 376, 378 of the 1, 8, and 22 août 1949. Ménil, René 'Une doctrine reactionnaire: la négritude'. *Action: Revue Théorique et Politique du Parti Communiste Martiniquais* 1, août 1963, 37–50.) Ménil who has been opposed to Senghor since the 1930s also has attacked Lilyane Kesteloot's study. (Ménil, René 'A propos d'une étude sur la poésie noire'. *Action: Revue Théorique et Politique du Parti Communiste Martiniquais* 2, décembre 1963, 35–42.)

The evident malevolence of Ménil is paralleled by that of Abdoulaye Ly. But Ly doesn't criticize from the orthodox Communist point of view as does Ménil. (Ly, Abdoulaye 'Sur le nationalisme dans l'Ouest-Africain'. *Publications du P.R.A.-Sénégal* 1, Dakar, 9 août 1959, 34 pp.)

Less unfavourable criticism can also be found. The former Senegalese Minister of Information and poet-friend of Senghor wrote a dithyramb on Senghor's poetry before he was ousted from the government. (Diakhate, Lamine 'Une brilliante littérature pleine de promesses: essai sur la poésie de L. Sédar Senghor'. *Paris-Dakar* numéro spécial ND, avril 1961, 45–7.) This article is truly written in *griot* tradition, as the title indicates!

An article full of pleasing expressions and useful insights was written on Senghor and on Guibert's analyses of his works. (De

Grandpré, Pierre 'Léopold Sédar Senghor et la poésie noire'. *Le Devoir* (Montreal), 25 novembre 1961, 13.

A recent study by a philosopher-sociologist constitutes the best scientific work on the notion of *négritude* and its complexity. The historical aspect is almost entirely absent, however. Definitions of the term are listed and the author tries to distinguish the various 'moments' of *négritude*: mystifying *négritude*, episodic *négritude*, eternal *négritude*, *négritude* oriented towards the past, *négritude* prospecting the future, painful, suffering *négritude*, aggressive *négritude*, etc. (Thomas, L. V. 'Une idéologie moderne: la négritude'. *Revue de Psychologie des Peuples* 3ème trimestre 1963 and 4ème trimestre 1963, 246–72, 367–98; and 'Senghor à la recherche de l'homme negre'. *Présence Africaine* 54, 2ème trimestre 1965.)

A global history of African reaction to the European hypothesis of Africa's cultural *tabula rasa* was compiled and published. It includes almost 150 black authors working in many disciplines: historians, poets, theologians, jurists, economists, novelists, ethnologists, etc. (Wauthier, Claude *L'Afrique des Africains*. Paris: Seuil 1964. An English translation has been published under the title: *The Literature and Thought of Modern Africa: a Survey*. New York: Praeger 1967.)

A French literary critic's approach to Senghor and *négritude* is very revealing of the hypothesis that this movement is part of a general European reaction to Western civilization. (Simon, Pierre-Henri 'La vie littéraire: présence africaine'. *Le Monde*, 12 août 1964, 8.)

Two studies of other black poets help place Senghor's poetry in a tradition. (Wagner, Jean *Les Poètes Nègres des Etats Unis*. Paris: Istra 1963. Kesteloot, Lilyan *Aimé Césaire*. Paris: Seghers 1962.)

A series of judgements on Senghor's poetry since 1945 has been collected in a dossier which one can consult at the Editions du Seuil, 27 rue Jacob, in Paris. One can see what a welcome this new kind of poetry received by reading the different commentaries. Among the most interesting are: Testas, Pierre 'Chants d'ombre'. *L'Université Syndicaliste* 10–25 juin 1945; Emmanuel, Pierre 'Les jeunes poètes'. *Temps Présent*, 3 août 1945. Y.L. 'Chants d'ombre'. *Paru*, novembre 1945; Decaunes, Luc 'Hosties noires'. *Cahiers du Sud* 292, 1948; Guibert, Armand 'Chants pour Naëtt'. *Monde Nouveau Paru* 49, 1949; Braen, Helmut 'Tam-Tam Noir'. *Stuttgarter Zeitung*, 23 April 1955; Blasco, Ricardo 'Poètes noirs et malagaches', excerpt from the *Index des Arts et des Lettres* (Madrid), 91, 1955; Grosjean, Jean 'Ethiopiques'. *La Nouvelle Revue Française*, juin 1956; Stierlin, Henri 'L. S. Senghor et la poésie noire'. *La Tribune de Genève*, 13 mai 1956; Larche, Georges 'Ethiopiques'. *La Presse du Cameroun*, 20 août 1956; Juin, Hubert 'L. S. Senghor'. *Combat*, 28 juin 1956; Chabaneix,

Philippe 'Ethiopiques'. *La Mercure de France*, 1 juin 1956; Berger, Pierre 'Léopold Sédar Senghor parle d'amour dans le chaos'. *Démocratie 60*, 8 septembre 1960; Guibert, Armand 'Avec Léopold Sédar Senghor chef d'état africaine et poète française'. *Le Figaro Littéraire*, 15 avril 1961; Guibert, Armand 'Léopold Sédar Senghor et la poésie noire'. *Le Devoir* (Montreal), 25 novembre 1961; Furter, Pierre 'Senghor, poète de la méditation'. *La Gazette de Lausanne*, 6–7 janvier 1962; Tavernier, René 'Léopold Sédar Senghor ou le Poète Réconcilié'. *Preuves-Informations* 147, 6 février 1962; Guibert, Armand 'L'apprentissage de la liberté, un entretien avec L. S. Senghor'. *La Gazette de Lausanne*, 21–22 juillet 1962.

Two unpublished dissertations have been devoted to Senghor's poetry. (Lambert, Paul *Léopold Sédar Senghor: Poète de l'Unité*. Léopoldville: Lovanium University 1960 and N'Diaye, Simone *L'Image dans la Poésie de L. S. Senghor: Expression de l'Ame Africaine*. Dakar: University of Dakar 1960.)

A recent analysis of Senghor's poetry, its themes, techniques and qualities is the work of a French critic. (Leusse, Hubert de *Léopold Sédar Senghor, l'Africain*. Paris: Hatier 1967.)

To place Senghor's cultural reaction in perspective an important essay by a French right-wing Political Science professor should be consulted. This essay underlines how much European ideas influenced the 'nationalists'. (Girardet, Raoul 'Influence de la Métropole dans la formation d'une idéologie de l'Indépendance' in *Centre d'Etude des Relations Internationales Colloque des 26–27 novembre 1960*. Paris: mimeographed 1960. Rapport no. 1. Available at the library of the Institut d'Etudes Politiques, 27 rue St Guillaume, Paris.)

V. Books and articles in French which contribute background information on Senghor's political life and thought

Strangely enough, studies on Senegal and French-speaking Africa from the point of view of the political scientist are much more complete in English than in French. Nothing like Ruth Schachter Morgenthau's study nor like the *U.S. Army Area Handbook* exists in French, at least to my knowledge.

Ernest Milcent, who published a biography of Senghor in 1969 (see above, p. 295) and also wrote the section on Senegal in Gwendolen Carter's *African One-Party States* (see above, p. 288), has published a general study of Senegalese politics. It is the work of a journalist with much Senegalese experience; for over ten years he directed the Catholic sponsored weekly *Afrique Nouvelle*. (Milcent, Ernest *Au Carrefour des Options Africaines: Le Sénégal*. Paris: Editions du Centurion 1965.) This book brings up-to-date some of the material from the author's previous study on French-speaking Africa's politics and includes material from an article published by the author in 1960. (Milcent, Ernest *l'A.O.F. entre en Scène*. Paris: Témoignage Chrétien 1958. Milcent, Ernest 'Forces et idées-forces en Afrique Occidentale'. *Afrique Documents* 51, mai 1960, 51–64.)

Some studies in French, less complete than similar English language efforts, are nevertheless useful for the history of African parties in Senegal. (Fleury, R. 'Les partis politiques en AOF: 1945–1958'. *Marchés Tropicaux du Monde*, août et septembre 1958.) Fleury reveals many facts ignored up to the time of his article, but he attributes certain trends to African political life which seem unconvincing, notably that of bi-partism. In the light of more recent work on Africa, this article seems dated in its approach to the study of African politics.

One of the most important histories of the French Union is contained in a published doctoral dissertation. The analysis of African party politics and the French colonial establishment is still valid. (Borella, François *L'Evolution Politique et Juridique de l'Union Française depuis 1946*. Paris: Librairie Générale de Droit et de Jurisprudence R. Pichon et R. Durand-Auzias, 1958.)

In order to understand certain sociological aspects of the evolution of political parties in Senegal it is very useful to consult the works of Paul Mercier. Almost all the authors who published studies on Senegal have referred to these articles. (Mercier, Paul 'Evolution des élites Sénégalaises' UNESCO *International Social Science Bulletin* 8 (3), 1956, 448–60. Mercier, Paul 'La vie politique dans les centres urbains du Sénégal: étude d'une période de transition'. *Cahiers Internationaux de Sociologie* 27, 1959, 55–85.

As for the influence of the Mourides and the *Marabouts* on Senegalese political life, there are many studies which help to explain this peculiar phenomenon. A recent study by a Senegalese student looks at the movement from within (Cheikh Tidjane Sy, 1969). A penetrating earlier study was put out by the Centre which trains French officials dealing with Islam. (CHEAM *Notes et Etudes sur l'Islam en Afrique Noire*. Paris: Peyronnet 1962.) The articles by A. Bourlon and F. Quesnot deal with the Senegalese *Marabouts*. Several unpublished studies are of crucial importance. (Diouf, Abdou *L'Islam et la Société Ouoloff*. Paris: typed study presented to the *Ecole Nationale de la France d'Outre-mer*, 1959. Duran, Pierre. *Notes sur le Mouridisme*. Paris: typed study presented to the *Ecole Nationale de la France d'Outre-mer*, janvier 1954.) These studies can be consulted (along with numerous other similar studies produced by French or African officials trained at the school) by obtaining permission from the Director. *Institut des Hautes Etudes d'Outre-mer*, 2, rue de l'Observatoire, Paris. The Institut is the former school for training colonial officials.

Another unpublished study which was essential to the present work is one of the many similar efforts available at the *Institut d'Etudes Politiques* 27, rue St Guillaume, Paris. This study was written by a future French government official, who, because of his contacts, was able to piece together the basic philosophy of several of the French political parties on African questions. (Saint-Victor, Bruno de *Les Partis Politiques Français et l'Evolution de l'Afrique Noire sous la IVème République: Positions du Parti Socialiste S.F.I.O., du Parti Républicain Radical et Radical Socialiste, du M.R.P. et du Centre National des Indépendants devant certains Problèmes posés par cette évolution de 1946 à 1958.* Paris: typed study presented to the *Institut d'Etudes Politiques de l'Université de Paris* prepared under the direction of M. Panouillot, 1960.) The positions of the SFIO and the MRP so influenced Senghor's thought that the conclusions made by Saint-Victor can be applied to the study of Senghor's thought.

An interesting historical study of French Africa has been published by a member of the French Communist Party specializing in African history. This helps to place Senghor's early life in the context of the evolution of French colonialism in Africa. (Suret-Canale, Jean *Afrique Noire: l'Ere Coloniale 1900–1945*. Paris: Editions Sociales 1964.)

A number of unpublished studies on Senegalese politics are available at the *Faculté de Droit* of the University of Paris. These *mémoires* are the work of Senegalese students. Those by Diahité, Bakary Traoré, and Gandolfi, are particularly relevant.

VI. Books and articles in French which contribute background information on Senghor's socio-economic thought

Again there is nothing in French to compare with the Friedland and Rosberg *African Socialism* published for the Hoover Institution by the Stanford University Press. One should refer to the bibliography of that volume for many of the relevant studies in French which went into it.

Georges Balandier's works helped me greatly. But his remarks have not yet been published *in extenso*. Some of his ideas are contained in a brief summary of a lecture he gave in Tunis. (Balandier, Georges 'De la négritude au socialisme'. *Jeune Afrique.* 111, 3–9 décembre 1962, 28–29.)

The historical background of African Socialism is found in a highly useful, if too violently anti-Communist, pamphlet. The various opinions of Marx on the *mir* can be found here. (Milon, René *Marxisme, Communisme et Socialisme Africain.* Paris 1962.) The texts by Marx which Senghor used in 1948 are essential. (Rubel, Maximilien 'Un inédit de Karl Marx – le travail aliéné'. *La Revue Socialiste* 8, février 1947, 154–68; and 'Karl Marx et le socialisme populiste Russe'. *La Revue Socialiste* 11, mai 1947, 544–59.) A facsimile of Marx's letter to Véra Zassulich, very difficult to find elsewhere, is in the latter study. (An English translation and interesting commentary appear in Wilson, Edmund *To the Finland Station: A Study in the Writing and Acting of History.* New York: Doubleday, 1940, 348–9.)

The *Plan du Sénégal*, an enormous study undertaken by the group of economists related to *Economie et Humanisme* provides an inventory of Senegalese resources and confidential suggestions for a better utilization of the riches of the country. It is possible to consult the study at the Compagnie d'Etudes Industrielles et d'Aménagement du Territoire (CINAM), rue Rougement in Paris. For an understanding of the practical objectives of Senegalese socialism it is essential to study the *Plan.* I was particularly interested by the sections dealing with the problem of Muslim religious groups and their rôle in the economy,

A short study covering the basic philosophy behind the Plan was published by another organization dealing with Senegalese economic questions. (IRFED-Institut de Recherche et de Formation en Vue du Développement Harmonisé. *Le Sénégal en Marche: le Plan de Développement.* Malines, Belgium. Creations de Presse: Les Cahiers Africains no. 5, 1961.)

But the December 1962 crisis seems to shed much more light on the functioning of the Plan than the studies which appeared in order to explain it. It is absolutely essential to read the article inspired by the planners who left Senegal after the fall of Mamadou Dia and written by Paul Thibaud, a Catholic journalist. The political mechanisms of post-independence Senegal as well as the difficulties of applying Socialism to this country are made clear. (Thibaud, Paul 'Document: Mamadou Dia, L. S. Senghor, et le Socialisme Africain'. *Esprit* 320, septembre 1963, 332–48.) The response of the Senegalese government does not seem to invalidate many of the facts reported by Thibaud. (Diouf, Khar N'Dofène and Thiam, Habib 'Lettre ouverte à Jean-Marie Domenach, Directeur de la Revue *Esprit*'. *l'Unité Africaine* 82, 30 janvier 1964, 13–14.) President Senghor feels that this particular judgement of mine is erroneous. See above, Appendixes, Senghor's letter of 5 December 1964.

The point of view of the Senegalese financial interests is expressed in an interesting and revealing article. ('Sénégal: retour de la confiance'. *Le Moniteur Africain du Commerce et de l'Industrie: l'Hebdomadaire de l'expansion et de l'unité économique ouest-africaine* 64, 22 décembre 1962, 1. For the political viewpoint on the crisis *Le Monde*'s former correspondent for French-speaking Africa should be consulted. (Decraene, Philippe 'Réflexions sur les récents événements au Sénégal'. *Comptes Rendus Mensuels des séances de l'Académie des Sciences d'Outre-mer*. Tome XXIII: Séances du 1 et 15 février 1963.) This article should be compared with a prediction of the actual crisis. (Meisler, Stanley 'Two views of Sénégal: as seen by Stanley Meisler'. *Africa Report* 7 (8), August 1962, 17–19.)

The opinion of the Senegalese opposition parties and of orthodox Marxists is always interesting to consult. (MacLorin, Will 'La bourgeoisie Sénégalaise dans les conditions du néo-colonialisme'. *La Nouvelle Revue Internationale: Problèmes de la Paix et du Socialisme*, octobre 1962, 31–42. XXX, 'Sénégal: le Programme du parti africain de l'indépendance' *France Nouvelle: Hebdomadaire Central du P.C.F.* 880, 29 août–4 septembre 1962, 18–19. Diop, Majemout 'La politique de L. S. Senghor et ses conséquences'. *France Nouvelle* 935, 18–24 septembre 1963, 22–23.)

Other studies which influenced my opinion to a lesser degree are: Calvez, Jean-Yves 'Socialismes Africains'. *Revue de l'Action Populaire* 159, juin 1962, 657–72. Father Calvez is a Jesuit specializing in Marxist thought. Another Jesuit, this time of African extraction, wrote specifically on Senghor's socialism, but the article is confusing. (Kachama-Nkoy, S. 'De Karl Marx à Pierre Teilhard de Chardin dans la pensée de L. S. Senghor et de Mamadou Dia'. *Civilisations* 12 (1–2), 1963.) Another article which is not very helpful, despite its promising title, was written by an African observer. (Kanouté, Pierre 'Socialisme africain: expression de l'humanisme africain'. *Afrique Nouvelle* 799, 30 novembre–6 décembre 1962, 8–9.)

Two works by Mamadou Dia are helpful for an understanding of the major options of the Senegalese planners before 1963. Despite the fact that Dia is no longer in charge, his thought helps clarify certain activities which are presently continued under Senghor's government. (Dia, Mamadou *Réflexions sur l'Economie de l'Afrique Noire*. Paris: Présence Africaine 1961. Dia, Mamadou *Nations Africaines et Solidarité Mondiale*. Paris: PUF 1960.) An English translation of the latter published by Praeger is available. The pragmatism of the Senegalese 'Road' is evident throughout the pages written by Mamadou Dia. Dia's economic background is also revealed. Senghor's writing seems to lack the familiarity with economics that was Dia's, although recently he has become much more involved with figures and statistics than in the period preceding 1963.

The most recent analysis of Senghor's socialism from the philosophical point of view was made by the same Dakar professor who analysed *négritude* in such detail. The analysis is very penetrating because, in showing the various elements of Senghor's socialism, the author attempts to define the various dilemmas in which Senghor became involved: insufficiency of Marxism, by-passing of Marxism, traditional African social organization and its contributions, equality and inequality, monolithic social organization or dualistic social organization, personal life or community life, African Socialism as a philosophy and a social practice, African Socialism as a specific and as a universal socialism, etc. (Thomas, L.V. 'Le Socialisme de Léopold Sédar Senghor et l'âme africaine'. *Afrique Documents* 75, 4ème Cahier 1964, 167–93. Now published in his two-volume study, *Le Socialisme et l'Afrique*. Paris: Le Livre Africain 1966.)

Other studies which give background are: Decraene, Philippe 'Le Sénégal en mue'. *Preuves* 170, avril 1965, 43–54. République Française, Ministère de la Coopération. *Economie et Plan de Développement: République du Sénégal*. Paris: Direction des Affaires Economiques et Financières, Sous-Direction des Etudes Générales et de la Documentation, mai 1964. (Available at Ministère de la Coopération, 20, rue Monsieur, Paris, 7ème.)

A pioneer study on social classes in Africa was made by a communist author. It clearly invites a more impartial study. The author attempts to refute a basic tenet of Senghor's socialism. (Barbe, Raymond *Les Classes Sociales en Afrique Noire*. Paris: *Economie et Politique: Revue Marxiste d'Economie*. mars 1964.)

Several of the professors of the *Ecole Pratique des Hautes Etudes* have contributed studies to a scholarly journal's issue devoted to social class in Africa. (*Cahiers Internationaux de Sociologie* 38, janv.–juin 1965. See especially the articles by Balandier and Mercier, pp. 131–42, 143–54.)

A Frenchman, presently teaching in Montreal, has published a brilliant article extracted from his doctoral dissertation on African socialism. (Charles, Bernard 'Le socialisme Africain – Mythes et Realities'. *Revue Française de Science Politique* VI (5), octobre 1965.)

Index

Abraham, Willi, 243
Achille, L. Th., 41, 104, 227
African
  civilization, contribution of, 40–41
  heritage of Senghor, 6–7, 10, 15, 25
Africanists, 60–70
Alcandre, Sylvère, 240
Alduy, Paul, 158, 247
Alexandre, Pierre, 241
American Negro culture, 53–9, 84, 93, 117
Amorin (of Togo), 113
anti-Americanism, 31, 180
Apithy, S.M., 113, 145, 146, 260
Apollinaire, G., 40, 46
Aquinas, St Thomas, 12, 50, 190, 259
Aragon, Louis, 46
Aristotle, 12, 190
Aron, Robert, 31, 103, 239
art, Negro, 33, 34, 40–1, 63–4, 101–2
assimilation
  active and passive, 89–95, 117
  'assimilate, don't be assimilated', 24, 80, 88, 89–90, 116–17
  cultural, 18–19
  French policy of, 36–7, 39
  political, 143–4
Association of West African Students, 80–1, 94
asynchronie, 3, 4, 192
Augustine, St, 99, 135
Aujoulat, Louis, 219, 263
Aurobindo, Shri, 103
Azikiwe, Nnamdi, 35

Badiou, Alain, 235, 244
Baillache, Me., 270
Baker, Josephine, 33
Balandier, Georges, 119, 196, 214, 220, 221, 228–9, 236, 250, 252, 254, 255, 258

Baldwin, James, 282
Balthazar, 103
Bancal, Jean, 252
Barma, Kotye, 12, 99, 219
Barrès, Maurice, 7, 10, 25, 26–7, 28, 29, 30, 33, 47, 50, 54, 72, 95, 96, 143–4, 150, 158, 161, 180, 181, 182, 187, 192, 217, 218, 222–4, 239, 245, 259, 264, 267
Barthes, René, 119
Bastide, Roger, 134, 244
Baudelaire, Charles, 16, 75, 93
Baye-Salzmann, P., 40–1, 51, 226, 229
Bayet, Albert, 15
Béchard, Paul, 159
BDS, 167, 188, 200
Béhanzin, Louis, 113, 146
Benoît, James, 14, 220
Bergson, H., 45, 47, 48, 50, 51, 104, 122, 125, 130, 192, 222, 259, 267, 280
Bernanos, Georges, 30
Bernstein, Eduard, 192
Beti, Mongo, 284
Beuve-Méry, Hubert, 265, 266
Béville, Albert, 113
Biarnes, Pierre, 254, 256
bibliography, 286–8
black legacy to the West, 99–108
blackness, 37–8, 120–1
'Black Orpheus', 24, 73, 119–24, 193
Blanchet, André, 251
Blas, Ruy, 10
Blum, Léon, 74, 272
Bonaparte, Napoléon, 10
Borella, François, 246
Bouqui (Uncle), 62
bourgeois
  anti-, 31, 47, 61, 180
  conflict between peasant and, 8
Bourlon, Abel, 250
Braithwaite, William S., 275
Braque, Georges, 101